WALK THROUGH THE BOOK OF GENESIS

WALK THROUGH THE BOOK OF GENESIS

A Verse-By-Verse Exposition

IAN TOPPIN

RESOURCE *Publications* · Eugene, Oregon

WALK THROUGH THE BOOK OF GENESIS
A Verse-By-Verse Exposition

Copyright © 2022 Ian Toppin. All rights reserved. Except for brief quotations in critical publications or reviews, no part of this book may be reproduced in any manner without prior written permission from the publisher. Write: Permissions, Wipf and Stock Publishers, 199 W. 8th Ave., Suite 3, Eugene, OR 97401.

Resource Publications
An Imprint of Wipf and Stock Publishers
199 W. 8th Ave., Suite 3
Eugene, OR 97401

www.wipfandstock.com

PAPERBACK ISBN: 978-1-6667-5562-6
HARDCOVER ISBN: 978-1-6667-5563-3
EBOOK ISBN: 978-1-6667-5564-0

11/17/22

All scripture quotations, unless otherwise indicated, are taken from the Holy Bible, New International Version. Copyright © 1973, 1978, 1984, by International Bible Society. All rights reserved.

While I appreciate the love and support of family and friends who encouraged me in this endeavor, this book was written to strengthen the faith of believers, and to refute those who doubt the existence of God, and His involvement as Creator and Sustainer of everything. The Book of Genesis is often used by believers and unbelievers alike, to support their cases for accepting or rejecting the existence of God. It has become an adversarial battleground between those who believe in the Bible and those who believe in science as the only source and final arbiter of truth. I dedicate this book to those who are interested in examining the facts about how, from the very beginning, God made all things perfect for mankind, and when they messed it up, He embarked on a plan to redeem them and make it perfect once again. This does not infer the need for an adversarial relationship with science. On the contrary, unbiased science affirms God's wisdom and superior intelligence by the way creation is ordered, and it helps reveal creation's beauty, which is an undeniable tribute to God's handiwork. The scientific fact is, creation could not have happened by itself, it had to have an original source outside of itself. The Book of Genesis reveals that Source. This book is dedicated to those interested in learning more about that Source, and His plan for the future of everything He created, particularly those He created in His image through Jesus Christ. This book traces God's plan to redeem mankind by establishing a covenant people, starting with the patriarchs, the nation of Israel, and finally the Church.

Contents

Preface | ix
Introduction | xi
Genesis Chapter One | 1
Genesis Chapter Two | 16
Genesis Chapter Three | 26
Genesis Chapter Four | 39
Genesis Chapter Five | 48
Genesis Chapter Six | 52
Genesis Chapter Seven | 58
Genesis Chapter Eight | 63
Genesis Chapter Nine | 68
Genesis Chapter Ten | 75
Genesis Chapter Eleven | 79
Genesis Chapter Twelve | 85
Genesis Chapter Thirteen | 91
Genesis Chapter Fourteen | 96
Genesis Chapter Fifteen | 102
Genesis Chapter Sixteen | 109
Genesis Chapter Seventeen | 118
Genesis Chapter Eighteen | 125
Genesis Chapter Nineteen | 133
Genesis Chapter Twenty | 144
Genesis Chapter Twenty-One | 150
Genesis Chapter Twenty-Two | 158
Genesis Chapter Twenty-Three | 164
Genesis Chapter Twenty-Four | 168
Genesis Chapter Twenty-Five | 177

Genesis Chapter Twenty-Six | 185
Genesis Chapter Twenty-Seven | 192
Genesis Chapter Twenty-Eight | 202
Genesis Chapter Twenty-Nine | 207
Genesis Chapter Thirty | 215
Genesis Chapter Thirty-One | 223
Genesis Chapter Thirty-Two | 233
Genesis Chapter Thirty-Three | 239
Genesis Chapter Thirty-Four | 244
Genesis Chapter Thirty-Five | 251
Genesis Chapter Thirty-Six | 258
Genesis Chapter Thirty-Seven | 261
Genesis Chapter Thirty-Eight | 270
Genesis Chapter Thirty-Nine | 276
Genesis Chapter Forty | 282
Genesis Chapter Forty-One | 286
Genesis Chapter Forty-Two | 295
Genesis Chapter Forty-Three | 303
Genesis Chapter Forty-Four | 311
Genesis Chapter Forty-Five | 317
Genesis Chapter Forty-Six | 324
Genesis Chapter Forty-Seven | 329
Genesis Chapter Forty-Eight | 336
Genesis Chapter Forty-Nine | 341
Genesis Chapter Fifty | 347
Bibliography | 353
Subject Index | 355
Scripture Index | 369

PREFACE

The intended audience for this book is individuals who consider the Book of Genesis to be a viable source for proving or disproving the existence of God and His involvement in creation. This book is also intended to highlight the hope God gives through His redemptive plan for humankind, as demonstrated through His interactions with Adam and Eve, and their descendants, particularly the Nation of Israel.

Scientists have made several discoveries, which appear to be in conflict with what is written in the Book of Genesis. For example, there appear to be conflicts between biblical and scientific views about the age of the earth and rest of the universe. This has implications for the apparent biblical view that the earth was created and literally populated in six days. This book is intended to discuss and offer explanations to some of these apparent conflicts.

This book will discuss events surrounding the fall of Adam and Eve, and its impact upon all their descendants. Following their fall, they were expelled from the Garden of Eden, sin and death was introduced to the human realm, and the need for a Savior became necessary to reconcile humankind to a Holy God. Humankind chose to believe the lie Satan told Adam and Eve, that the knowledge of good and evil would cause them to become like God, but such knowledge actually caused them to become more like Satan.

The condition of humankind is hopeless without a Savior. Hence, God immediately embarked on a plan of redemption. His plan commenced with His involvement in the lives of individuals such as Seth, Enoch, Noah, Shem, Abraham, Isaac, and Jacob. It continued with His involvement with the Nation of Israel, and particularly with Joseph, who was used to preserve the nation, and Judah, who became a forefather of Jesus Christ in the flesh. This book contends that Jesus is the Savior and Redeemer humankind needs, and He is the only way back to a right relationship with God.

INTRODUCTION

The book of Genesis is the first book of the Bible, and first of five books or Pentateuch (Genesis, Exodus, Leviticus, Numbers, and Deuteronomy) attributed to Moses as their primary author. The traditional view held by Jews and Christians alike, that Moses was the primary author of these books is supported by passages in the books themselves, such as: Exod 17:14; 24:4; 34:27; Lev 1:1; 4:1; 6:1, 8, 19, 24; 7:22, 28. In the New Testament, Jesus and the apostles also affirmed Moses as author of the Pentateuch. Notice Mark 1:44; 7:10; 10:3-4; Luke 5:14; 16:29, 31; John 5:45-46; 7:22-23; Acts 3:22; Rom 10:5, 19; 1 Cor 9:9; 2 Cor 3:15.

Though there is a preponderance of evidence to support Moses as primary author of the Pentateuch, there are also reasons to conclude that Scribes made editorial changes and additions to the original manuscript. Two key reasons for this conclusion may be found in the fact that Num 12:3 asserts that Moses was the humblest man on the face of the earth. Certainly, if he wrote that statement himself, he would not have been the humblest man on the face of the earth, rather, the opposite would be true. Additionally, Deut 34:1-8 discuss circumstances surrounding Moses' death, and how the Children of Israel mourned for him. He could not have written these details himself. It is more likely they were written later by Scribes who translated the original manuscript.

Scholars who delve into criticisms of the Mosaic text, may fall into any of the following four categories: Yahweh (J), Elohim (E), Deuteronomy (D), or Priestly (P). In simplified terms, these critics examine the names used for God and attempt to determine authenticity of the text and its likely author. It is important to note that none of this scrutiny has been successful in diminishing the Bible's core message, nor its power to lead unbelievers to faith. As 2 Pet 1:21, and 2 Tim 3:16 teaches, Holy Spirit is really the Bible's author; hence, believers can be confident in its authenticity.

GENESIS CHAPTER ONE

THE FOUNDATION OF FAITH

Hebrews Chapter Eleven is often called the "Hall of Fame of Faith." If this is true, Genesis Chapter One, should be called the "Foundation of Faith." Notice verse 1 says, "In the beginning God (Elohim—plural) created the heavens and the earth." This is the point where faith must begin. If the reader doubts these words, reading the remainder of the Bible may prove to be a futile exercise, and may call the reader's motives into question. It should also be noted that the word "beginning" does not refer to the beginning of God, but to the beginning of everything He created—the heavens and the earth.

Faith is required to believe that whenever the beginning was, God is before it. He caused the beginning, and it was He who created it. An exhaustive description is not given about how God created the heavens and the earth, it simply says, He did it! Faith is required to believe God has the power to speak and it be done! And, that all of the necessary ingredients for creation were brought into being and coalesced at the power of His word. Therefore, step-by-step procedures are not necessary. What is clear from the first verse of the Bible is that the heavens and the earth did not always exist, nor did they emerge from nothing or nowhere on their own. Rather, they were brought into existence (created) by God. Faith is required to accept this. However, faith in alternate philosophical perspectives is also required to reject it, since there is no reasonable scientific proof, which contradicts what the Bible says.

Erickson proposes that it may well be that what God did originally was merely to create matter from nothing, and then in His subsequent creative activity, He fashioned everything from the atoms He had created. The various species created at that later time would be just as much God's doing as was the origin of matter.[1]

THE BIG BANG THEORY

Does the Big Bang theory conflict with the Biblical assertion that God created the heavens and the earth? The answer is no! In fact, cosmological evidence, still exists to indicate that the birth of the universe was initiated by a cataclysmic explosion! This is a discussion which is beyond the intended scope of this book but suffice it to say that the Big Bang was such a violent explosion, that to this day it is still the main reason why the universe is expanding, rather than contracting. The question is, who created the matter which banged? The naturalist response is, no one, it happened on its own. The Biblical response is, God caused it. The reader must decide which of these perspectives makes more sense.

The logical reason for believing God caused the Big Bang is simple. The universe is made up of matter, such as atoms and related compounds. There is no matter in the entire universe, which has ever demonstrated an ability to independently transform from non-existence to existence, much less cause itself to explode in a manner, which was evident in the Big Bang. Hence, those who claim that the universe came into existence from nothing, or brought itself into existence, can never provide scientific evidence to support that claim. Therefore, such a position is merely philosophical, rather than scientific, because it can never be duplicated or subjected to scientific method. In other words, creation of the universe is not a humanly observable phenomenon, nor can it be duplicated in a laboratory. Therefore, faith is required for any beliefs held about it.

Geisler and Turek noted that the less evidence you have for a position, the more faith you need to believe it.[2] It takes more faith to believe the philosophical claim that the universe brought itself into existence, than it does to believe the theological claim that God brought it into existence. One must either believe that God created everything from nothing (ex nihilo), or that nothing created everything from nothing. Obviously, the latter choice makes no sense!

Tillman pointed out that the universe cannot be younger than the objects contained inside of it. Therefore, by determining the age of the oldest stars, and by measuring how fast the universe is expanding, scientists were able to estimate the age of the universe. They estimate that the universe

1. Erickson, *Christian Theology*, 399.
2. Geisler and Turek, *I Don't Have Enough Faith*, 26.

came into existence approximately 13.8 billion years ago.[3] If this estimation is correct, from a scientific perspective, it means that prior to 13.8 billion years ago, nothing in the natural universe existed.

More importantly, the claim that the universe is eternal and always existed, is dismissed by the mere fact that science itself attributes an age to it. It cannot have existed eternally, and at the same time be approximately 13.8 billion years old. However, while nothing physical existed prior to that time, from a theological perspective someone spiritual did, God, and God alone existed. This is precisely what Genesis 1:1 conveys. Whenever the beginning was, God was already there, and it was He who created the heavens (universe) and the earth.

WHO CREATED GOD?

Consider for a moment, the silliest of questions, which is sometimes asked by skeptics who desire to remove God from the creation narrative. The question they ask is, if God created everything, who created God? This is a ridiculous question! However, suppose one were to explore the nonsensical idea that God was created, wouldn't it be true that whatever, or whoever created God is greater than God, and is therefore God? So, it obviously results in the very thing the skeptic would be trying to avoid in the first place! It takes them right back to God!

The fact is, God does not need a creator, because only created things need a creator. God was not created, so He does not need a creator. Therefore, the divine glory of God will indeed be a sight to behold! It is the only thing humans will ever lay eyes on, which did not come from anything else. God is totally self-efficacious! He does not need anything or anyone to exist! He has life within Himself and gives life to everything that lives.

The writer of the book of Hebrews explains why faith is required to believe Genesis 1:1. Hebrews 11:3, reveals that by faith we understand that the worlds have been formed at God's command, so that what is seen was not made from what is visible. In other words, the visible world did not evolve from the visible world, instead it was created by the invisible God! But, if the Biblical evidence is not enough, logical reasoning should suffice. There is undeniable, intelligent orderliness in what is observable about the universe. It would be extreme to assume that such orderliness resulted by chance, or by means that are not themselves intelligent and orderly. In

---

3. Tillman, *How Old is the Universe?* Https://www.space.com/24054-how-old-is-unverse.html.

other words, chaos in nature only produces further chaos, it does not consistently produce intelligent order.

ELOHIM AND MONOTHEISM

Skeptics are not alone in their struggle with what is written in Genesis 1:1. Some within monotheistic faiths also take issue with portions of this verse. For example, the fact that the Hebrew word used in this verse to describe God is "Elohim," is an issue. In discussing the meaning of the word "Elohim," Ryrie pointed out that this term means strong, indicating a deity of great power.[4] It is a plural rendering, which suggests that from the very beginning of Judeo-Christian Scripture, the idea of multiple persons in the Godhead was at least hinted. The problem is, at surface level, this idea appears to contradict monotheism, but deeper observation will show that it really does not.

In everyday life there are many examples of objects and substances, which are one, yet comprised of multiple attributes. Fire is such an example. It produces heat, light, and smoke, but it is one entity. Another example is water. It is made of three bonded atoms—two hydrogen atoms (H_2), and one oxygen atom (O) to form water (H_2O). The fact that these examples exist in the physical realm, should make it easier to conceptualize how it could also be possible in the spiritual realm, and how the one divine essence known as God, can consist of distinct persons.

The word "Trinity" is commonly used by Christians to refer to the concept of three distinct persons in the Godhead. This word is not found in Scripture, but the idea it conveys definitely is. Admittedly, belief in the Trinity also requires faith, but the plural description of God, Elohim, as presented in Genesis 1:1, is unavoidable. What is this saying? It is saying from a Christian perspective that God, the Trinity, created the universe. And, since He (God) created the universe, He is greater than the universe, or anything in it. It also means He must exist in a different realm, which is separate from the universe He created "In the beginning."

Also notice, God created the universe, the universe did not create Him! And, though it is possible to explain how things in the universe, such as fire and water, consists of multiple components, and yet are one, it is impossible to explain with certainty how God is one divine essence, and yet three distinct persons. Faithless people usually do not care whether or not God is a Trinity, this is more of a concern for some who claim to be among the faithful.

4. Ryrie, *Basic Theology*, 51.

It should also be mentioned here that there are discussions among Biblical scholars who delve into the area of textual criticisms, about whether the commonly accepted claim that Moses wrote most of the Book of Genesis is actually true. The reason these scholars question this claim, is because the Hebrew word "Elohim" is only used in the Book of Genesis, but not in other Old Testament Books attributed to Moses. Instead, in most cases "Yaweh" (YHVH), and "Jehovah" are more commonly used. These critics contend that if Moses wrote Genesis, he would have been consistent in his use of words to refer to God.

The most likely explanation for the apparent discrepancy is, in Genesis 1:1, the intent was to show that the entire Godhead was involved in the act of creating the heavens and the earth, whereas, in most other areas of Scripture, emphasis may have been on one member of the Godhead, so there was no reason to imply tri-unity, when there was only unity. Additionally, Jesus Himself affirmed Moses (Exod 17:14; 24:4, 7; 34:27; Deut 31:9; Matt 19:8; Mark 12:26; John 5:46–47; John 7:19; Acts 3:22) as the author of the Pentateuch—first five books of the Bible.

SEPARATION (GAP) THEORY

Before moving on from Genesis 1:1, it may be worthwhile to briefly insert the discussion of Separation, or gap theory. This theory proposes that there is a gap in earth's history between the first and second verses of Genesis chapter one. In other words, events mentioned in those two verses could have been separated by billions of years. The reason some adhere to this position is because, as mentioned above, verse 1 asserts that God created the heavens and the earth, but verse 2, does not seem to present details of an earth that was being brought into existence. Rather, it seems to present a chaotic earth, already existing, but needing to be fixed up.

Erickson explains that gap theory holds that there was an original, quite complete creation of the earth perhaps billions of years ago. Some sort of catastrophe occurred, so that the creation became empty and unformed. God then re-created the earth a few thousand years ago...[5] Notice verse 2, says, the earth was formless (tohuw—to lie in waste) and empty (void), darkness (choshek—obscurity) was over the surface of the deep, and the Spirit of God was hovering (rachaph—grow soft, relax) over the waters. Observe that there was already an earth, and there was water on it. But it says, the earth was formless, and empty. No details were presented here about how the earth or water were created. It does not describe how

5. Erickson, *Christian Theology, Second Edition*, 406.

water came to be on the earth or any other planet, or how the earth became formless and void. No information is given about how or when water came into existence.

Separation, or gap theory is not an accepted belief in many Christians circles. MacArthur stated that the order of creation itself rules out the possibility that the days of Genesis 1, were really long ages.[6] Yet, some Christians regard gap theory as reasonable. The latter argue that though Genesis makes it clear God created the heavens and the earth, it does not say when He created either. They agree with scientific evidence, which seems to indicate that something traumatic happened to the earth between the time when God initially created it (v 1), and where it says it was formless and void (v 2).

The idea that a gap in time may have occurred does not seem far-fetched. In fact, it may have been during that gap, when creatures, such as prehistoric man (Neanderthal), and dinosaurs existed; However, the second verse in the Book of Genesis, begins the story of when God renewed the earth to make it livable for modern humans, as it is today. Psalms 104:30, may support those who hold to this position. It infers that when God sent forth His Spirit, they were created, and He RENEWED the face of the ground (earth).

One thing is clear, dinosaurs existed at some point in earth's history. Those who adhere to gap theory find it inconceivable such imposing beasts could have co-existed with humans, and yet the Bible makes no mention of them, such as it does with relatively less significant beasts, such as lions and bears. The thought is, the Bible does not mention dinosaurs because they were extinct and irrelevant by the time it was written. They perished during the gap period between Genesis verses one and two.

To be clear, Christians who adhere to gap theory have no problem with Genesis 1:1, which states that God created the heavens and the earth, but they view verse 2, as a renewal of the earth following some dreadful event and period in time, which resulted in the earth becoming un-inhabitable, formless, and void. If this is true, it raises questions about the actual age of the earth. The most popular view held by Christians is that the earth is only approximately 6000 years old. MacArthur asserts that the Bible will not support a date for the creation of man earlier than 10,000 B.C.[7]

On the other hand, Tillman contends that by dating earth's crust, as well as rocks on its neighboring planets such as the moon and other meteorites,

---

6. MacArthur, *The Battle for the Beginning*, 63.
7. MacArthur, *The Battle for the Beginning*, 63.

scientist calculate the earth is 4.54 billion years old.[8] Several methods, such as fossil records, carbon dating, and radioactive mineral decay rates, have been used to calculate earth's age, but scientists believe the latter method is most accurate. For example, Braterman regarded the controversy as having been resolved by the adoption of the radiometric timescale, which incorporated advances in spectrometry, sampling, and laser heating.[9] The resulting knowledge has led to the current understanding that the earth is 4.5 billion years old.

Archer noted that in the Gulf of Mexico, sediment is deposited at a rate of a few inches a year; Yet, successive layers of deposit as thick as 28,000 feet have been found, indicating the passage of well over 100,000 years in time.[10]

TURN ON THE LIGHT

Verse 3, states that God said, ""Let there be light," and there was light." Where did the light come from? Skipping ahead in this chapter, it shows in verses 14–19, that on the fourth day, the sun and moon were commissioned to govern the day and the night, so where did this early light, prior to the sun and moon's commissioning come from? An exhaustive response at this point would pre-empt the discussion ahead dealing with events on day four, but what is warranted here is to point out that in this verse, God said, "Let there be light," singular. On day four, He said, "Let there be lights," plural. This single light probably came from no other celestial source, except the sun, and may indicate that the moon and other celestial objects currently visible in earth's galaxy may not have been created yet.

As fascinating as it may be to speculate about where the light God referred to came from, suffice it to say that when God said, "Let there be light," there was light! The light immediately obeyed God and penetrated the darkness. In that moment, time began. God made it so that day and night would become measurements of times and seasons. Unbelievers, who discount God's involvement in creation have no other reference for how time began and can be measured, other than that, which is presented in the Book of Genesis. The world would be a much better place if humans would endeavor to obey God in the same way the light, He commanded obeyed Him.

---

8. Tillman, *How Old is the Earth?* https://www.spave.com/24854-how-old-is-earth.html.

9. Braterman, *How Science Figured Out the Age of Earth*, https://www.scientificamerican.com/article/how-science-figured-out-the-age-of-the-earth/.

10. Archer, *A Survey of Old Testament Introduction*, 182.

DAY ONE

Verses 4-5—God saw that the light was good, and He separated the light from the darkness. God called the light "day" and the darkness He called "night." And there was evening, and there was morning—the first day.

The only way light can be separated from darkness is by turning on the light. Therefore, when God caused light to shine on earth, it would have continued to shine unceasingly on one portion of the earth, had He not set limits on where it would shine at various times. In other words, He caused earth to rotate on its axis, so that the light would be turned on and off in different places at different times. Note that God did not need light in order to see, but He knew the creatures He would create to live all over the earth, would need it. And, that they would also need darkness in order to rest, so He separated light from darkness, by causing it to shine in different places at different times.

Notice, it says God saw that the light was good, but it does not say that about the darkness. In fact, it appears that because God saw the light was good, He separated it from darkness. Darkness was neither commended for being good, nor condemned for being bad. Darkness is necessary, but it is simply prohibited (separated) from co-existing simultaneously with light, and vice versa. Sadly, many do not see things the way God did. He commended light as being good. Many today, commend darkness as being good. John 3:19 says that men love darkness because their deeds are evil.

Obviously, there is much symbolism in this verse where God separated light from darkness. It illustrates the reality that He ordained them both to have periods of dominance. Light dominates the day and typifies His eternal glory, while darkness dominates the night and typifies eternal condemnation. Yet, God is in control of both the day and the night, and one day He will bring both to an end, when time (day and night) will be swallowed up by eternity.

DAY TWO—WHAT IS A FIRMAMENT?

Verse 6 shows that God said, "Let there be a vault (raqia—expanse or extended surface) between the waters to separate water from water." There is no mention here of how, or when water came into existence, only that it needed to be separated. This is another reason why gap theory adherents believe creation week to be a renewal of earth, rather than the initial creation of it. It appears that before the vault (firmament, expanse) was created, earth had become a blob of water, like a water balloon. If this was the case, the light God made to shine on day one, would not have had much effect, because earth was nothing but a deep watery planet.

Notice, God not only commanded there be an expanse to separate water from water, but He also made (created) the expanse. Verses 7–8 says, "So God made the vault (firmament) and separated the water under the vault from the water above it. And it was so. God called the vault "Sky." Wright describes what God did on day two as the most significant geological event to ever occur in the history of earth's existence.[11] And there was evening, and there was morning—the second day." So, the firmament or expanse, which God created, was formed by separating oceans, which covered the entire earth below, from clouds that were densely filled with water in the heavens above. He created empty space between the two. The fact that God created empty space is literally mind-boggling! And yet, the entire universe is filled with it!

The work God did on day two, made the light he commanded to shine on day one more effectual. Though thick clouds of water filled the entire sky (firmament above), which hovered over the oceans covering earth's surface below, there was now a space between them, which needed to be illuminated. Incidentally, this imagery explains why some Christians believe there was a canopy of water-filled clouds above the earth prior to the flood, which occurred in the days of Noah. This canopy is said to have reduced the impact of the light of the sun, and may have contributed to why people lived much longer during pre-flood days than they did post-flood.

MacArthur asserts that before the flood, it was common for men to live nine hundred years or longer. After that, the human life span decreased notably almost immediately.[12] During the flood, it is believed that God essentially burst the water-filled cloud canopy, which hovered over the earth. This not only caused most living things on land to drown, but it also reduced the lifespan of subsequent generations, by affording them greater exposure to the sun's rays.

DAY THREE

In verses 9–10 God said, "Let the water under the sky be gathered to one place, and let dry ground appear." And it was so. God called the dry ground "land," and the gathered waters he called "seas." And God saw that it was good.

---

11. Wright, *Beginning with Genesis: A Journey from Knowledge to Wisdom*, 9.
12. MacArthur, *The Battle for the Beginning*, 151.

The work God did on days one and two, was concentrated on preparing areas of creation that were above the earth, such as causing light to shine and separating the firmament above from that below. But starting with day three, He turned His attention to preparing earth itself. Therefore, He commanded the sea to roll back and gather in one place, so that there may be dry land. This was by far a more spectacular miracle than what He would perform years later, in rolling back the Red Sea, to allow Israel to escape from captivity in Egypt (Exod 14:21-22).

With dry land available, verses 11–13, states that God said, "Let the land produce vegetation: seed-bearing plants and trees on the land that bear fruit with seed in it, according to their various kinds." And it was so. The land produced vegetation: plants bearing seed according to their kinds and trees bearing fruit with seed in it according to their kinds. And God saw that it was good. And there was evening, and there was morning—the third day.

Notice, the land God made to appear was previously covered by water, so it did not initially have anything growing on it, nor would anything have grown on it, had God not commanded it to be so. In other words, vegetation on the land did not come into existence on its own, but by the command of God. Does this mean that microevolution has not occurred with time? No, it does not mean that. Indeed, vegetation can adapt to its surroundings, and through natural processes, plants do evolve within their species. But, God is the initial cause of everything there is, including plants.

It should also be observed that God commanded plants to bear according to their kind. In other words, He set an order in motion, such that plants do not bear fruit of other plants that are different from their kind. As such, no reasonable person should approach an apple tree, expecting it to produce oranges. The reason this does not occur is not arbitrary, it is so because God designed it that way. From simple to complex, both the heavens and the earth are filled with evidence of God's handiwork, and His intelligent design.

DAY FOUR

Verses 14-19 reveal that God said, "Let there be lights (plural) in the vault of the sky to separate the day from the night, and let them serve as signs to mark sacred times, and days and years, and let them be lights in the vault of the sky to give light on the earth." And it was so. God made two great lights, the greater light to govern the day and the lesser light to govern the night. He also made the stars. God set them in the vault of the sky to give light on the earth, to govern the day and the night, and to separate light from darkness. And God saw that it was good. And there was evening, and there was morning the fourth day.

As noted above about verse 3, on day one, God had already commanded that there be light (singular). The source of that light was most likely the sun. This would mean that the sun was already in existence before earth, moon, and many stars visible in the Milky Way Galaxy. Therefore, verse 16, where it says God made two great lights, the greater (sun) to govern the day, and the lesser (moon) to govern the night, is not a commentary on when they were created, but rather, on what their functions were.

In other words, no conflict necessarily exists with what science asserts. They contend that the sun came into existence approximately 4.6 billion years ago, while the moon came into existence slightly before earth but both within close timeframe of each other, approximately 4.5 billion years ago. The point is, science itself affirms that the sun and moon came into existence approximately about the same time as earth, which was about the 4-billion-year timeframe.

The lights (plural) God commanded to shine during day four, did not only refer to the sun and moon (greater and lesser lights), but to stars as well. Because God caused it to be so, the firmament above the earth became a brilliant cacophony of lights, as it is to this day. Therefore, the Apostle James referred to God as "the Father of heavenly lights" (James 1:17), and king David proclaimed that the heavens declare the glory of God and the skies proclaim the work of His hands (Ps 19:1).

A particularly important function of the lights God placed in the firmament above, was not only to give light to the earth below, but to also serve as signs to mark sacred times, days, and years. This is why Solomon said there is a time for everything, and a season for every activity under heaven (Eccl 3:1). Thus, unlike no other, humans were created as time-conscious creatures, with an ever-present awareness of the temporal nature of life. But, an ability to mark sacred times would become highly important once God started dealing with the Nation of Israel.

DAY FIVE

Verses 20–23—And God said, "Let the water teem with living creatures, and let birds fly above the earth across the vault of the sky." So, God created the great creatures of the sea and every living thing with which the water teems and that moves about in it, according to their kinds, and every winged bird according to its kind. And God saw that it was good. God blessed them and said, "Be fruitful and increase in number and fill the water in the seas, and let the birds increase on the earth." And there was evening, and there was morning—the fifth day.

As mentioned earlier, no information is given about when God created water. However, day five describes how He populated it. Apparently, there was water, but nothing inhabited it until God commanded the water to teem with living creatures. It says, He created the great creatures of the sea and every living thing with which the water teems and that moves about in it, according to their kinds. This means that fish and other sea creatures did not come into existence through evolution. Instead, they were created according to their kinds. In other words, fish and the great creatures of the sea, do not give birth to any species other than their kind. Everything was ordained to function within the specific order of its own kind.

Birds were also created and commissioned to fly across the sky. They too were instructed to increase in number and fill the earth, according to their kind. Again, there is unmistakable order and intelligence in creation. Most notably, fish and birds existed before modern humans did, and there was no inherent desire or planning on their part to reproduce, other than they were blessed and ordained by God to do so.

Following His work on day five, it says God did something He had not done on any other day to this point in His creation activities. He blessed the birds, fish, and great creatures of the sea, which He created. Why did He bless them and not the firmament, or the seas He rolled back, or the vegetation he caused to grow? Any response here would be speculative, but a reasonable answer might relate to the responsibility He assigned them. They were instructed to be fruitful, and increase in number, and fill the water and the earth.

Neither the water nor the earth had anything inherent within themselves to cause them to populate themselves. This task could only be accomplished with God's blessing and approval for the creatures He placed in them to do so. New birth cannot occur unless God authorizes it. He, rather than the water, or earth, or even the doctor, or scientist, is the giver and sustainer of life.

DAY SIX

In verses 24–25 God said, "Let the land produce living creatures according to their kinds: the livestock, the creatures that move along the ground, and the wild animals, each according to its kind." And it was so. God made the wild animals according to their kinds, the livestock according to their kinds. And God saw that it was good. Notice that God created vegetation (day three) before He created the wild animals, who would need it for food. Once again, divine intelligence is undeniable.

An important notice from these verses is that God commanded the land (ground) to produce living creatures, such as livestock, creatures that move along the ground, and wild animals. In other words, their flesh was made from the same source as that of humans, the ground. And again, God instituted order in reproduction of all His creatures. Meaning, they reproduce according to no other kind, except their own. This was a perpetual barrier God placed on every species in nature.

CREATION OF MANKIND

Verses 26–27 indicate, then God said, "Let us make mankind in our image, in our likeness, so that they may rule over the fish in the sea and the birds in the sky, over the livestock and all the wild animals, and over all the creatures that move along the ground." So, God created mankind in His own image, in the image of God He created them; male and female He created them.

Again, God said, "Let us make man in our image, in our likeness. . ." "God," was again described using the plural term "Elohim." But, how could mankind (male and female) be made in the image or likeness of God? The rationale God gave for creating mankind in His image, was so they may rule over the living things He had created. The list included: fish, birds, livestock, wild animals, and creatures that move along the ground.

God had also created lights in the heavens, and a firmament between heaven and earth (an atmosphere). He also created wind and water, but He did not expressly state that these things were placed under man's rulership. In other words, man does not rule the skies, nor the heavens, though because of modern technologies, he may think he does. This is why natural phenomena, such as earthquakes, tornadoes, and hurricanes are vivid reminders of who is really in control of the land, sea, and skies.

There was a notable difference between mankind and everything else God had created. That difference was, mankind were the only creatures made in the image and likeness of God, and they were the only ones endowed with responsibility to rule. Therefore, the image of God, which was given by God to mankind, was one of rulership, and authority, rather than one of resemblance. The Bible makes it clear, God is not a man (Num 23:19; Hos 11:9). However, humans were made in His image, and to that end, have been endowed with some measure of authority over, and responsibility for, the environment they inhabit.

Having said that, it should also be pointed out that though every human has been made in God's image as it relates to authority over things on earth, not every human has been conformed to His likeness. What this means is, humans have all been endowed with authority to rule, but not all humans rule like God would have them to. Humans do not act in the way God would act unless He enables them to do so. Hence, humans are inclined to act in their own self-interest, and they possess a proclivity to abuse the authority God gave them.

Verses 28-31—God blessed them and said to them, "Be fruitful and increase in number; fill the earth and subdue it. Rule over the fish in the sea and the birds in the sky and over every living creature that moves on the ground. Then God said, "I give you every seed-bearing plant on the face of the whole earth and every tree that has fruit with seed in it. They will be yours for food. And to all the beasts of the earth and all the birds in the sky and all the creatures that move along the ground—everything that has the breath of life in it—I give every green plant for food." And it was so. God saw all that He had made, and it was very good. And there was evening, and there was morning—the sixth day.

God blessed humans, just as He had blessed fish and birds when He created them and commissioned them to be fruitful and multiply. He gave this same command to humans, and it also came with a blessing, because it cannot be accomplished apart from God's blessing and approval. Yes, children are a blessing from God. A notable difference was, fish and birds were blessed, but they were not given authority to rule over anything.

Additionally, God commissioned humans to not only rule over fish and birds, livestock, wild animals, and creepers, but also over plants and trees (vegetation). This means, man is steward of the earth. He is to care for it, rather than exploit and destroy it. To do such, is to dishonor God and His creation. Man's disregard for God's command causes nature to respond in ways, which are detrimental to humans themselves. Notice, God gave Adam dominion over everything, except other humans.

God's stamp of approval was bestowed upon all His creation. He said it was very good! Therefore, the question begs to be asked, why are bad things evident in creation today? Clearly, mankind has not maintained it as he was supposed to. In fact, rather than maintaining it, humans have exploited creation for their own benefit. Consequently, extinction of many life forms, pollution, and global warming are persistent environmental concerns. Nature is under such stress that sometimes it responds violently in retaliation for the harsh treatment it endures at the hands of mankind. However, Rom 8:19-22, reveals that help is on the way, as creation eagerly awaits the Children of God to be revealed, because for too long it has been subjected to frustration, not by its own will, but by the will of the one who subjected it. . . the whole creation is groaning as in pains of childbirth to this very day. These verses make clear that God expects those who love Him, His children, to also love His creation and take good care of it. Especially, since He described it as very good!

GENESIS CHAPTER TWO

The previous chapter surveyed God's activities in bringing all things into existence within a timeframe described as six days. This chapter provides a summary, and in some cases, further details of what was described in chapter one, particularly as it pertains to creation of mankind.

DAY SEVEN

Verse 3, states that the heavens and the earth were completed in all their vast array. And, by the seventh day God had finished the work He had been doing; so, on the seventh day He rested from all His work. Then God blessed the seventh day and made it holy, because on it He rested from all the work of creating that He had done. Notice, on this seventh day, there is no mention of evening and morning. It was as if the rest God took continues to this very day.

WHAT DOES IT MEAN, "GOD RESTED"?

This passage presents a few important questions that are worth considering further: 1. Why did God rest on the seventh day, was He tired? The answer is a resounding no! God does not get tired! God Himself is the source of strength. Indeed, strength gets it strength from God! So, why did He rest? Because His creation work as it relates to earth, was finished! God did not rest until then! He did not leave unfinished work in deference to creating a Sabbath, or carving out time for rest.

The Hebrew word "rest" (shebii) should not be viewed as God needing a nap. Instead, a more appropriate context is God, having completed all His creation work, and having nothing left to create on planet earth, ceased creating anything further. His creation work, where planet earth was concerned, was done! This "rest," therefore, had nothing to do with God's need for recuperation. Indeed, God's creative hand is still observable in the vast realms of His universe. The heavens (space) were created in the beginning, but the work of populating it with stars and galaxies continues. This is why evidence of the birth of new planets, is still observable today. Rest, in Genesis 2:3, refers to God reaching a satisfactory conclusion where creation on earth was concerned.

    2. Because God rested on day seven, some conclude that the seventh-day Sabbath was established from creation as a day of worship. Truth is, God rested but He did not, in this passage, command humans to do the same. Nor does it say, in this passage, that any acts of worship occurred. God simply ceased from doing anything further with respect to creation on earth. Whether or not He rested from creating things in other parts of the universe is questionable. On a Jewish Sabbath, Jesus said that His Father is always working, and He too is working (John 5:17). So, the rest referred to in Genesis 2:3, cannot be all-encompassing, and there was no command given, in this passage, for man to rest as God had rested on day seven.

    3. Why did God bless and make day seven rather than any other day holy? The passage itself provides the answer. It says, God blessed and made day seven holy (set apart) because He rested on that day. Note, He did not rest because the day was already holy, instead the opposite is true. The day was made holy because He rested in it. He controlled what He did on that day! The day did not control what He did! And, once again, notice there was no evening and morning on day seven on which God rested. This implies that His rest never ended. In fact, Hebrews 4:1-7, make this very clear. Verse 6 specifically indicates that God's rest can still be entered into by those to whom it is preached, and who are obedient in belief. So, the day was made holy because of what God did, He rested in it.

    4. Can humans make a day holy (set apart) by refraining from work, and resting on that day? Yes, humans can set apart a day when they refrain from doing anything further, and simply rest. In this case, rest should imply recuperation, and hopefully worship. Rest honors what God did, and worship is a necessary discipline for maintaining a healthy relationship with Him. But note, from a spiritual perspective, since day seven on which God rested never ended, it obviously continued across the other days of the week. Therefore, no single day is better than the other. Any day of the week can be set apart for rest and worship.

WHAT DID "DAY" MEAN?

It might be useful here to focus on how the apparent discrepancy between a seven-day creation week may be reconciled with scientific evidence, which indicates that the earth is billions of years old. Those who attempt to resolve this apparent discrepancy question what is meant in Genesis chapters one and two, by the Hebrew word "Yom" (Day). There are at least three common perspectives in response to this question. Firstly, many Christians believe "day" (Yom) refers to a literal 24-hour period, but this belief disregards scientific evidence, and presents difficulty when other parts of the creation narrative are considered, especially as it relates to the sixth day, when mankind (male and female) was created, as discussed below. Also, the seventh day, which apparently never ended, as a literal 24-hour day does.

Secondly, others assert that "day" (Yom) refers to a relational day. In other words, this position postulates that it took six days for God to reveal visions to Moses, about how creation occurred. In this view, the narrative in Genesis does not necessarily have anything to do with how long it took to complete creation, but rather about the timeframe in which God revealed it in visions. Therefore, according to this view, each day's creation events, represents a new vision, which continued in sequence for six days, in which case, Moses had six visions. On the seventh day, there were no further visions.

This view is not supported by any internal or external Biblical evidence. Archer points out that there is nothing in the text or elsewhere to suggest that details of a dream were being communicated when Moses wrote the Genesis account.[1] Instead, it reads like a straightforward history. Archer also mentioned that the volume of details given in the two opening chapters of the Book of Genesis, should not have required six days of visions. Furthermore, everything communicated in the text relates to things that can be observed. None of the details about creation appear to be fantasy.[2] This perspective can be considered far-fetched.

Archer presented a third view, which postulates that "day" (Yom) refers to a geologic age. According to this view, the word "day," represents stages or cycles during which, God performed His creation activities. Each age (day) could extend for billions of years. Genesis 2:4, seems to be evidence of this. The same word, "day" (Yom) is used to describe all six days, rather than just one day.[3]

---

1. Archer, *A Survey of Old Testament Introduction*, 182.
2. Archer, *A Survey of Old Testament Introduction*, 182.
3. Archer, *A Survey of Old Testament Introduction*, 182.

More importantly, verses 11–13, state that on day three God said, "Let the land produce vegetation: seed-bearing plants and trees on the land that bear fruit with seed in it, according to their various kinds." Yet, verse 8 indicates that on day six when the man was created he was placed in a garden, which the Lord God had planted in the east, in Eden. If "Yom" represented a literal day, it would mean that the plants and trees God placed in His garden were fully grown within three days, so that the man could begin tending them on day six when he was created. While this is not impossible for God, it is highly unlikely since He commanded the land to produce the vegetation. In other words, He decreed things to grow by natural, rather than supernatural means.

Moreover, in Genesis 1:26–31, it says that on day six, God created man in His own image, male and female He created them. In other words, it infers that Adam and Eve were created on the same day. Yet, Genesis 2:7, indicates that God created the man before He created his wife. After creating the man, God placed him in the garden He had planted in Eden. He paraded all the animals He had created before the man and had the man give each one a name. In the process of naming each animal God observed the man and concluded that he was lonely and needed a suitable helper. It was at that point that God created the woman.

It most likely took more than one day (the sixth day), and probably more than one week for all the events described above to have occurred. It seems to imply that the sixth day, when male and female were created, was not a literal 24-hour period of time, but may have been a cycle (evening and morning) when God turned His attention to creating mankind.

Further proof that "Yom" could not refer to a literal day, is found in the fact that day seven on which God rested, never ended. No evening or morning was mentioned in reference to that day. In essence, the seventh day continues today. Notice also that once God rested, it doesn't say He returned to work the following week! Therefore, where creation on planet earth is concerned, God is still at rest. There is nothing left for Him to do! All the stages of creation on earth are complete!

Thus, the most reasonable conclusion, which does not violate the integrity of Scripture, is rather than referring to a literal day, or to visions, "Yom" can indeed refer to a geologic age, or cycles (denoted as evening and morning) within which creation activities occurred. This can also occur over billions of years.

FURTHER DETAILS ABOUT CREATION

Verses 4–5 state, "This is the account of the heavens and the earth when they were created, when the Lord God made the earth and the heavens. Now no shrub had yet appeared on the earth and there was no one to work the ground." This scene is similar to what scientist observe on some planets today. There is no life, no growth, and certainly no one living there! However, verse 6, provides one notable difference. It says that streams came up from the earth and watered the whole surface of the ground. This means that when God rolled back the waters, which covered the earth, and gathered them in one place, which He called seas, the residual effect was, rivers and streams were left. These sources watered the earth from below before rain ever watered it from above.

Verse 7 provides further details about what God did when He created man. It says, the Lord God (Jehovah Elohim) formed a man from the dust of the ground and breathed into his nostrils the breath of life, and the man became a living soul (nephesh—soul, self, person, mind, desire, emotion, passion). A new description for God was provided in this passage—Jehovah Elohim, or Lord God. Once again, this reference indicates involvement of an additional person in the Godhead participating in the creation process.

This passage also indicates that God became more intimate with the man He created than with anything else in His creation. He literally gave the man a kiss of life! He breathed into his nostrils the breath of life. It is important to notice that God formed the man from the same dust of the ground, from which He had formed the livestock and wild animals. They too were formed from the ground, and they too received life, but it does not appear that life was given to them in the same intimate manner in which man's life was given to him. Additionally, the man did not become a man until God breathed into his nostrils the breath of life. In other words, being formed from the dust to look like a man did not make him a man. No more than a statue can look like a man, but is not a man, because it has no breath of life in it.

It was the breath of life, which God breathed into man's nostrils that made all the difference! For this reason, prehistoric man (Neandertal), may look like a man, but unless scientist can prove that he received the same breath of life that modern man received from God, then he was not a man in the same sense that modern man is. There was something about that breath, which gave man the spirit he has, a spirit that enables him to be the high-functioning creature he is. And allows him to operate beyond the limits of mere instinct. Most importantly, that breath enables mankind to have a relationship with the One who breathed it into him, namely his Creator, God.

Verse 8 indicates that the Lord God had planted a garden in the east, in Eden (Pleasure); and there He put the man He had formed. Interestingly, the man was not formed in Eden, nor was he formed from the dust of Eden. There is no indication of the exact location where the man was formed. Wherever that place was, God took the man from there, and brought him to Eden. Therefore, Eden may be viewed as the man's intended home, rather than his indigenous home.

Verse 9 shows that the Lord God made all kinds of trees grow out of the ground—trees that were pleasing to the eye and good for food. In the middle of the garden were the tree of life and the tree of the knowledge of good and evil.

There are at least three things about any tree, which makes it pleasing to the eye: the color of its leaves, the color and size of its fruits, and its stature. Trees in Eden most likely had all these characteristics. However, speculatively, the tree of the knowledge of good and evil may have surpassed them all. In fact, it may have been more impressive and appealing to the eye than the tree of life. Nevertheless, they both represented choice, and were a test of man's obedience to the Word of God. Observe, they were both in the middle of the garden, which meant the man saw them often. But the tree of the knowledge of good and evil was really a tree of death, depending on the choice the man and woman would make. The record shows, eating from that tree resulted in perpetual death and decay.

Verses 10–14, show a river watering the garden flowed from Eden, and from there it separated into four headwaters. The name of the first headwater was Pishon (Increase); it wound through the entire land of Havilah (Circle—Probably Northwestern Yemen—Asia Minor) where there was gold. The name of the second river was Gihon (bursting forth—Spring near Jerusalem where Solomon was anointed); it wound through the entire land of Cush. The name of the third river was Tigris (rapid); it ran along the east side of Ashur (Assyria—Modern-day Iraq). The fourth river was the Euphrates (fruitfulness—rose in the Armenian mountains and flowed southward to the Persian Gulf). These rivers represented the plushness, beauty, and sheer fertility of the land. And note, even though rivers were flowing, there was still no mention of rain.

LIFE IN PARADISE

Verses 15–17 say that the Lord God (Jehovah Elohim) took the man and put him in the Garden of Eden to work it and take care of it. And the Lord God commanded the man, "You are free to eat from any tree in the garden;

but you must not eat from the tree of the knowledge of good and evil, for WHEN (in the day) you eat from it you will certainly (surely) die." It should be noted here that if the Sabbath was established from creation as a day of worship as some suggest, this would have been a perfect point at which God should have informed the man of such. Instead, He gave the man one command, "do not eat from the tree of the knowledge of good and evil. . ."

Please notice, the word used for "day" was again the Hebrew word "Yom" as it is in chapter one. Yet when Adam and Eve ate the forbidden fruit, they did not die that day. Instead, Adam lived many more centuries (Gen 5:5), giving further proof to the idea that "Yom" can imply a cycle or season, rather than a 24-hour timeframe.

It is also important to note that based on the sequence of the narrative, the man received this command from God before the woman had been created. Therefore, it is reasonable to conclude that there was a period of obedience by the man. The length of that period is uncertain but observe that the command began by expressing the freedom the man had to eat from any tree in the garden, except one. There could have been hundreds of trees from which he could eat, including the tree of life, but the prohibited one was the most tempting.

A reasonable question is, why would God want the man (and his descendants) to avoid the tree of the knowledge of good and evil? The answer is clear. For sure, God wanted the man to have the knowledge of good. Everything He created, including the man was good; He said so! Hence, knowledge of good was easy for the man to attain, because it came from God and was evident in all of creation. However, the knowledge of good and evil, was a juxtaposition, which the man would have to seek on his own.

While knowledge of good was evident everywhere in the man's world, knowledge of evil was not. Such knowledge could only enter his world if he pursued an alternate source to attain it. There was no good reason to pursue the knowledge of evil, and God wanted man to avoid it, because He had already seen what such knowledge had done in the angelic realm. Angels were already familiar with the knowledge of evil. They had seen it in Satan and in one-third of their ranks who joined him and lost their place in heaven for rebelling against God.

God's preference was for the knowledge of evil to stay outside the human realm, but He ordained things in such a way that attaining the knowledge of evil could only occur at the choosing of those who would occupy the human realm. Because of His love, He gave the man a choice, rather than force His preference on him. The man's knowledge of good and evil would place him and his descendants in a perpetual struggle to choose between the two and would cause the human realm to become as rebellious as some in the angelic realm were.

It should be noted here that when Adam was created, he was immortal; He could not die. The only thing that could change his condition was sin. The day he disobeyed God, and ate from the tree of the knowledge of good and evil, would be the day his condition would change from immortal to mortal. That would be the day when death would begin to rule over him, and all his descendants after him.

Despite God's admonition for the man to refrain from eating of the tree of the knowledge of good and evil, He hinted His knowledge of the choice the man would make. He predicted what would happen WHEN, rather than IF, the man disobeyed His command and took of the tree. God said when he took of that tree, he may not IMMEDIATELY die, but he would SURELY die. In other words, from that day forward, the man would become the walking dead! He would no longer be immortal but would become a mortal man.

Verse 18 indicates that The Lord God said, "It is not good for the man to be alone. I will make a helper (ézer) suitable for him." Note that God did not consult with the man about his condition of loneliness, nor did He ask for the man's opinion about what the solution to his condition of loneliness should be. Instead, God independently drew His own conclusion about the man's loneliness and the solution for fixing it. If God had asked, the man would not have known what the solution to his loneliness should be, because he had never seen a woman, nor did he know such a creature could even exist!

God alone decided what a suitable helper for a man should be. As such, He decided that another man, an animal, a bird, or fish, would not have been suitable helpers. In God's view, the only suitable helper for a man, was a woman. Has God's view on this change? Many religious people argue that it has not changed, still others, some religious, argue that it has. Hence, same-sex marriage is now a common, legal occurrence, rendering God's view questionable by proponents of such unions.

If the helper the man needed was someone to assist him with his work in the garden, it would have been wise for God to create another man, or to use one of the animals He had already created. But the man's loneliness was not about his work, it was about his desire to enjoy pleasure in his home of pleasure. It was a love and sexual intimacy connection God was making!

Verses 19-20 say that the Lord God had formed out of the ground all the wild animals and all the birds in the sky. He brought them to the man to see what he would name them; and whatever the man called each living creature, that was its name. So, the man gave names to all the livestock, the birds in the sky and all the wild animals. But for the man no suitable helper was found.

God allowed the man to exercise authority over the wild animals and birds by naming them. Remembering their names was a demonstration of the man's brilliance and extraordinary memory capacity. This also informs today's reader that the man was given a language. Notice, God did not outrank the man by changing any of the names he had assigned to anything. Instead, whatever the man called each living creature, that was its name. But it appeared that during the process of naming those creatures, was when the man's loneliness seemed more pronounced. After naming everything, he found nothing to name that was a suitable helper for himself. This was rather sad. The man had everything, except someone compatible with whom to share it. There are many men (and women) in a similar predicament of loneliness today.

Verses 21–22 say that the Lord God caused the man to fall into a deep sleep; and while he was sleeping, He took one of the man's ribs (tsela—rib, side-chambers or cells, plank) and then closed up the place with flesh. Then the Lord God made a woman from the rib he had taken out of the man, and He brought her to the man. This procedure is easier to comprehend in contemporary times than it was in historical times. God essentially performed a cloning procedure on the man in order to create the woman.

Cloning is a hot topic in medical and scientific circles today, and such procedures have been successfully done on animals. However, God was way ahead of modern science in this regard. Notice, once God created the woman, He simply brought her to the man, but He did not force the man to choose her. The man could have regarded her as an unsuitable helper, but he did not. Therefore, the woman was chosen above all else, and received by the man as his only suitable helper, and as someone with whom he could share everything.

Verses 23–24 indicate that the man said, "This is now bone (étsem—body, limbs, members) of my bones and flesh (basar—kindred, blood relations) of my flesh; she shall be called 'woman,' for she was taken out of man." That is why a man leaves his father and mother and is united to his wife, and they become one flesh.

It is not clear how the man knew what God had done in order to create the woman, but his pronouncement that she was bone of his bone, and flesh of his flesh, suggest that he was well aware of what God had done. And notice that the man gave her a categorical name, just as he had given categorical names to all the other creatures God had brought before him. This time, he named a creature that he found to be a suitable helper for himself. He called her woman because she was taken out of man.

She was the solution to his problem of loneliness. This is why a man leaves his father and mother and is united with his wife, and they become one flesh. She is supposed to squelch his problem of loneliness! And there is no other bond that is described as 'one flesh' except the bond that is formed when a man and a woman are united in marriage. God somehow views the two as one! There is no Biblical evidence to suggest that God extends this view to other types of unions.

Generally speaking, there comes a point in a man and woman's life when their father or mother are incapable of resolving their problem of loneliness. This is usually a sure sign that they need companionship, which may lead to marriage. But there is a significant problem when those who are already married begin to feel lonely again. If this situation is left unattended, unfaithfulness, divorce, or thoughts thereof will remain a reality.

Notice, God in His wisdom created the man first, because males possess an X and Y chromosome, while females possess two X chromosomes. Therefore, the sex of an offspring is determined by the male chromosome rather than that of the female. If God had created the female first, and took the male out of her, He would have defied the natural order He intended to set in motion as it related to reproduction, since females do not possess a Y chromosome. This is also further evidence for the presence of intelligence in creation, for which evolutionist can give no reasonable account.

Verse 25 says that the man and his wife were both naked (àrown—bare), and they felt no shame. Nakedness in marriage is one of the ultimate forms of personal disclosure. In other words, the man and woman were bare, or totally exposed before each other, and they felt no humiliation. They had nothing to hide! What an ecstatic place to be in marriage, and in life! They were totally free! There was nothing to hinder their relationship with each other, and more importantly there was nothing to hinder their relationship with God. Such a pure, unadulterated state of affairs would never again exist. To this point, they had the best home and marriage in human history.

GENESIS CHAPTER THREE

As mentioned in the previous chapter, God had planted a garden, and in the middle of it He placed two trees: the tree of life and the tree of the knowledge of good and evil. He commanded the man not to eat from the latter tree, but knowing what the man would do, He predicted that the day he ate of it, he would surely die. This chapter examines the choice the man made to follow his wife in listening to the serpent, and ignoring the instructions God gave them. It was a choice which led to the fall of mankind and the need for a Savior who would restore the relationship between mankind and God.

TROUBLE IN PARADISE

Verse 1 says the serpent (nachash—enchanter, diviner, deceiver) was craftier than any of the wild animals the Lord God had made. He said to the woman, "Did God really say, 'You must not eat from ANY tree in the garden'?" The serpent was obviously one of the creatures the man had previously named, which means the man, at that time, had authority over him. But as it says, this serpent was craftier than all the other wild animals because it was possessed by Satan himself. Thus, this serpent, unlike any other in history, was able to speak! It also had knowledge of good and evil and was willing to use that knowledge to deceive the woman, so that through her and her husband, that knowledge would enter the human realm, just as it had already entered the angelic realm.

Notice the serpent's line of questioning: "Did God really say. . .?" This line of questioning became common among skeptics from that time forward. Its purpose was to promote doubts about the truth of God's Word. It was also quite possible that since God did not speak directly to the woman, the serpent seized the opportunity to create doubt by suggesting: Did God really say that, or did you hear it from your husband? In today's vernacular, this line of inquiry would translate to something like this: "How do you know what the Bible (God's Word) says is true, since it was written by men?"

The fact is, the Bible's true author is Holy Spirit. Second Timothy 3:16, says all Scripture is God-breathed. Additionally, Second Peter 1:21 makes it clear that prophecy never had its origin in human will, but even though prophets were human, they spoke from God as they were carried along by Holy Spirit.

Notice the remainder of the serpent's questioning, and how the truth was subtly twisted: "Did God really say, 'You must not eat from ANY tree in the garden'?" God did not say that! God told the man he was free to eat from every tree in the garden, except one! The man was given far more freedoms than restrictions. Obviously, if God had said they could not eat from ANY tree in the garden, their diet would have been severely restricted, or they would have starved to death! God did not say they could not eat from ANY tree, but again, the serpent's intent was to sow doubt, and to cause them to become suspicious about God and His word.

The woman responded correctly by asserting in verse 2, "We may eat from the trees in the garden, but God did say, 'You must not eat fruit from the tree that is in the middle of the garden, and you must not touch it, or you will die.'"

The woman inserted a comment that was not recorded in the original command (Gen 2:16-17). She inserted that God said, "you must not touch it." Maybe her husband gave her that instruction to make sure she stayed far away from the tree! Whatever the case, her insertion amplified the need for them to have nothing to do with the tree! Consequently, the woman's interpretation was closer to truth than the serpent's. She was like so many today; she knew and could quote the Word of God, but she did not know what it meant. She certainly did not know what it meant to die. Her world was perfect; she had never seen anything, or anyone die.

Notice the serpent no longer pursued his initial line of questioning about whether the woman heard God's command correctly. He saw that she was strong in that area, so he turned his attention to obscuring what she heard, and he blatantly refuted God's Word. In verse 4 he said to the woman, "You will not certainly (surely) die." In other words, "look at me! I have the knowledge of good and evil and I am not dead! God is not telling you the truth!" He literally called God a liar in the man's (Adam's) hearing, and the man said nothing! The real question here was, whose word would they trust? It was indeed a significant dilemma between choosing good over evil.

The serpent promoted the woman's right to self-determination. Notice he added in verse 5, "For God (Elohim) knows that when you eat from it your eyes will be opened, and you will be like God, knowing good and evil."

Observe that throughout this passage God was referred to as Lord God (Jehovah Elohim) but the serpent, Satan, only referred to Him as Elohim. This was because by that time, he could not deny Him as God, but had rejected Him as his Lord.

The serpent continued by suggesting that by obeying God's Word, their eyes, and by extension their minds, were still closed. This is the exact claim many today make against those who have the audacity to believe the Word of God; They are considered closed-minded. The serpent suggested that the only way for them to rid themselves of the scourge of ignorance was to try something new, explore life, and pursue knowledge of good and evil on their own, since they could not depend on God to give it to them.

To be sure, the man and woman's eyes were indeed closed to the knowledge of evil, but there was nothing wrong with that! Some things are simply not worth knowing, especially if the only way to know them, is by way of evil experiences. The serpent pressed the issue by asserting he was there to set them free! Obviously, he and God had the knowledge of good and evil, but God did not want them to have it, because God did not want them to be like Him. In essence, the serpent emphasized their right to self-determination, by promoting the idea that God was holding back on them, because He would somehow be threatened by their acquisition of knowledge. So, he was there to show them how to be like God! Nothing was further from the truth!

TREE OF THE KNOWLEDGE OF GOOD AND EVIL

The tree of the knowledge of good and evil, represented choice. Since humans were created with an ability to make choices, there had to be something from which they could choose. Conversely, the tree of the knowledge of good and evil represented the love of God, because as God, He had the power to force humans to love Him, even if to do so by making it instinctual. But that would not be real love since both parties would not have agreed to it. True love involves a conscious choice by all parties to love each other.

Therefore, God, in His love for mankind, allows mankind to freely choose to love Him in return. Forced, or coerced love is not love. God wants to be loved out of reverence, submission, and obedience. The tree of the knowledge of good and evil would prove whether the man in particular, would choose to love and obey God, who loved him, and proved it by breathing life into him, and by making everything in his world perfect for him. Or, whether he would choose to acquire information and experiences apart from God. That choice has also been bequeathed to descendants of the first man and woman, and just as God did everything to enable them to love Him, He does the same for their descendants.

INNOCENCE LOSS

Verse 6 indicates that when the woman saw (ra'ah—to look at, learn about, look upon, find out) that the fruit was good for food and pleasing to the eye, and also desirable for gaining wisdom (sakal—prudent, wisely understand, prosper), she took some and ate it. She also gave some to her husband, who was with her, and he ate it.

The woman took control of the situation, based on the information she received from the serpent, but the man refused to take it back, based on the information he received from God. They chose a serpent who had done nothing for them, over God who had done everything for them. This remains the saddest commentary in the entire history of humanity because it represents the birth of the fallen nature of mankind.

This is an ideal point at which to put any criticisms of the first man and woman into context. In other words, every human descendent of theirs should exercise caution in blaming them, as though another purely human individual might have done better than they did. The fact is, they were the best humanity had to offer, because they had no heritage of sin. Yet, with no heritage of sin, they failed because they allowed temptation to linger long enough to promote unbelief and disobedience.

Their failure made it impossible for any of their imperfect descendants, who inherited a heritage of sin from them, to do better than they did. Therefore, one of their descendants, yet one who did not inherit a heritage of sin from them, was needed to come and undo what they did, in order to redeem their descendants from the sure penalty of sin and eternal death. His name is Jesus.

Notice how the woman determined that the fruit was good for food; she saw it, and she liked what she saw! It was pleasing to her eyes! She had seen it before, but now she saw it differently in light of the information she received from the serpent. The fruit looked better now than before, and she lusted for it. The apostle John described this as, lust of the eye (1 John 2:16). This led to what he also described as, pride of life. Notice, the woman saw that the fruit was desirable for gaining wisdom. In other words, she wanted to be wiser than she already was, especially, since the serpent informed her that this fruit could help her to become like God. She thought, why settle for being a mere human when she could be like God?

Finally, her lust of the eye and pride of life, led to lust of the flesh; she took some and ate it. She had to have it! Not only did she have to have it, but she also gave some to her husband, who was with her, and he ate it. Most likely, her husband was with her the entire time during which she conversed with the serpent, and he said absolutely nothing! He withheld the authority he had over the serpent, and in obeying him and eating the fruit, he completely lost authority over him.

It was not the woman to whom God had given the command not to eat of the tree, it was the man; therefore, since he was with the woman, and joined her in deliberate disobedience to God, he was just as guilty. Thus, Paul wrote in Second Timothy 2:14, that Adam was not the one deceived; it was the woman who was deceived and became a sinner. No doubt, the man also became a sinner, but not because he was deceived. He became a sinner by his own will. As a result, he was incapable of saving his wife from her sin, because he was complicit with her in it; hence, they both needed a Savior.

Verse 7 shows that the eyes of both of them were opened, and they realized they were naked; so, they sewed fig leaves together and made coverings (chagowr—loin coverings) for themselves. With their newly acquired knowledge of good and evil, rather than becoming like God, as the serpent promised, nakedness, which is the ultimate form of personal disclosure between a husband and wife, was the first thing they recognized and tried to hide. They viewed their nakedness as evil. This was a direct threat to the human family! It made no sense for nakedness to be viewed as something evil when they were the only two humans alive to see each other! To be sure, nakedness should be a source of shame between grown people who are strangers to each other, but marriage should remove any shame associated with nakedness.

Did Adam and Eve's sin cause them to become bad people? Not necessarily, relatively speaking. Did it cause them to become sinners? Absolutely! Hence, those who believe being a good person can merit a place in God's kingdom, should learn a lesson from Adam and Eve, who were good people, but the moment they sinned one time, they realized they needed to be covered in the presence of a Holy God. How much more so are their descendants in need of a covering. They sewed fig leaves together to make coverings to hide their nakedness. These were the humble beginnings of today's multi-billion-dollar clothing industry! Enormous amounts of money are spent each year on clothing in order to avoid the shame of nakedness. On the other hand, there are those, particularly in the entertainment industry, who sell nakedness, or something close to it, to promote their personal brand. Nakedness in its purest form, should symbolize innocence, this is why babies and toddlers are not concerned about it. But their innocence is replaced by shame the moment they are old enough to realize they are naked. This is what happened to the man and woman; They lost their innocence.

BROKEN FELLOWSHIP

Not only did they lose their innocence, they also lost the close fellowship they had with God. Verse 8 says the man and his wife heard the sound of the Lord God as He was walking in the garden in the cool of the day, and they hid from the Lord God among the trees of the garden. The language in this verse is referred to as, anthropomorphic language, or earth-talk. This is where God is referenced in human terms for the purpose of human understanding. The fact is, while God can choose to travel by foot, that would not be the most efficient way to traverse a vast universe and beyond! The idea in this passage was to depict God in human terms, and to illustrate His steadiness. There was no problem with Him! He was taking a walk and enjoying His creation as though nothing had occurred, and as if, He was totally unaware of the sin the man and his wife had committed.

It is of paramount importance to observe who were the ones in hiding. It was certainly not God! The passage says while God was taking a walk, the man and his wife only heard the sound of His footsteps! They had not seen Him, yet they hid themselves among the trees of the garden! The man used to have sweet fellowship with God as he talked to Him face to face, now he and his wife hid from God! This behavior is reflective of the condition of many today, who are in hiding from God. Some have not seen or experienced Him but have heard about His moral standards, and they are afraid to deal with Him because His standards conflict with theirs.

Some are hiding because of sin. They are ashamed of what they have done and do not believe God can and will forgive them. They know they need His forgiveness but at the moment may still be caught up in the ways of this world, so they find it easier to hide than to ask for forgiveness. Sadly, hiding has become a major part of human nature, but it is also a source of human bondage. Freedom from sin cannot occur while continuing to hide it, or to be hidden in it.

Hiding was the result of the man and his wife's quest for knowledge of good and evil, and they would not have come out of hiding, had God not called them out. Verse 9 says the Lord God called to the man, "Where are you?" Once again, this was earth-talk. God did not ask this question because He lacked knowledge of the man's geographic location. This question was way deeper than that! It was a spiritual and relational question.

God called to the man because it was the man to whom He gave the command not to eat of the tree. So, He called to him rather than to his wife. In fact, to this point, there was no evidence that God had any direct conversations with her. It should also be stated that if God had not called to the man, it was unlikely the man would have called to God. Fellowship would have remained broken if God had not made the first move. This move was perpetual, as God is still calling to every man and woman, and asking the question, "where are you my son, where are you my daughter?" To be sure, He knows where they are, but this question is intended to provoke introspection.

ASSESSING THE DAMAGE OF SIN

The man's answer to God's question was very revealing about his new sinful condition. He never directly answered the question, "where are you?" Instead, verse 10 says he answered, "I heard you in the garden, and I was afraid because I was naked; so, I hid." Obviously, the art of hiding requires concealing the place where one is located. So, the man never said, "Here I am, behind this tree!" Instead, the man gave an excuse for his hidden condition.

The excuse he gave was fear due to his condition of nakedness. Something changed for the man, because his condition of nakedness was not new, but his perspective on it was. He now viewed it as something to be ashamed of, and worth hiding from God, who created him and had seen him naked all his life! His fellowship with God was indeed broken.

As soon as the man and his wife sinned, a new emotion entered the human realm. It was called "fear." Fear is an emotion humans experience when they are startled by circumstances beyond their control, or when they are concerned about the adverse actions of something or someone, who is in or out of control. Interestingly, the man did not express fear of being in the presence of God, or of what God might do to him in response to the sin he had committed. Instead, he was afraid of being in the presence of God as a naked sinner. As sinners, the man and his wife knew they were going to die, and they fully deserved and expected to do so immediately. Their situation was a fearful prospect for all of humanity!

Verses 11–12 state that God asked, "Who told you that you were naked? Have you eaten from the tree that I commanded you not to eat from?" The man said, "The woman you put here with me—she gave me some fruit from the tree, and I ate it." The man set precedence for how many guilty men after him respond when they get caught; he refused to give a direct answer. He never answered the question, "who told you that you were naked?" The fact was, no one told him he was naked! It was the first thing he discovered on his own once he disobeyed God.

The next question God asked was, "have you eaten from the tree that I commanded you not to eat from?" The short answer was yes! Instead, the man who was supposed to be in charge, tried to find scapegoats by blaming God and his wife. He said, "The woman YOU put here with me, she gave me some fruit from the tree, and I ate it." He implicated God in his actions by insinuating that some of the blame was His, because He was responsible for putting the woman there with him! And, indeed it was God who decided that she was a suitable helper for him, but he also chose her himself! Therefore, from the man's perspective, God was also complicit in his sin.

He implicated his wife by placing on her the blame for his access to the fruit. She gave it to him, and all he did was eat it. In other words, as far as he was concerned, his role was the least significant. The man's response was far from a true confession. Hence, since God could not get a direct answer from the man, He turned to his wife, and for the very first time in Biblical record, God spoke directly to the woman. It was as if God spoke to the woman because He could not get a direct answer from the man.

Verse 13 shows that the Lord God said to the woman, "What is this you have done?" The woman said, "The serpent deceived me, and I ate." Based on what Paul wrote in First Timothy 2:13, the woman's response was closer to a true confession than her husband's. She gave a more accurate reason for why she sinned. Indeed, the serpent deceived her, but her husband, who was not deceived, allowed him to do it. Her husband withheld his authority over the serpent because he shared the same curiosity she did, about the tree of the knowledge of good and evil. He joined her in the quest for knowledge of evil and the desire to become like God by taking control into his own hands for his life and destiny.

RESULTS OF SIN

God did not question the serpent, He simply cursed him. In verses 14–15 it says, "So the Lord God said to the serpent, because you have done this, "Cursed are you above all livestock and all wild animals! You will crawl on your belly and you will eat dust all the days of your life. And I will put enmity between you and the woman, and between your offspring and hers; He will crush your head, and you will strike His heel."

Herein God revealed a plan, which was only previously known to members of the Godhead; It was a redemption plan. Satan had no prior knowledge of this plan because heretofore it was not necessary. The fact that Satan not only led angels in rebellion against God, but had now also led humanity in the same, provided evidence of his irreversible, unrepentant state, and the justified sentence of condemnation God passed upon him.

Meanwhile, the friendship the woman thought she had developed with the serpent was dismissed with the pronouncement that he would strike the heel of her descendants, while they would crush his head. A state of war was declared between the serpent and the woman's descendants. His head was wounded in Jesus' victory on the cross, which was a comprehensive act of redemption for mankind. But the final crushing blow is yet to come, when the real serpent, Satan, will be bound and cast into the lake of fire for all eternity.

Verse 16, "To the woman He said, 'I will make your pains (sorrows) in childbearing very severe; with painful labor you will give birth to children. Your desire will be for your husband, and he will rule over you.'" Note that God did not curse the woman, instead He prescribed pain in childbearing. Pain was introduced to humanity because of sin. Thus, the woman, and all women after her, were sentenced to experiencing pain in childbearing, before experiencing the joy of delivery.

Her position in the marriage relationship also changed. Previously, the man and woman were equals, there was no hierarchy; she was his helper. After they sinned, God informed the woman that her husband would rule over her. This arrangement works best when husbands love their wives, and wives submit to their husbands as Paul stated (Eph 5:22–25). Unfortunately, from that time forward, tensions around leadership and authority have destroyed many marriages.

In verses 17–19, God said to Adam (Red, First Man), "Because you listened to your wife and ate fruit from the tree about which I commanded you, 'You must not eat from it,' Cursed is the ground (adamah—ground, land) because of you; through painful toil you will eat food from it all the days of your life. It will produce thorns and thistles for you, and you will eat plants of the field. By the sweat of your brow you eat your food until you return to the ground, since from it you were taken; for dust you are and to dust you will return."

This was the first place where the man was referred to by the name Adam. Interestingly, his name meant red, rather than black, white, brown, or even yellow. It also meant "first man," which suggests all others (black, white, brown, and yellow) descended from him. They are all his children. The fact that Adam named everything else demonstrated his authority over everything, but God named him as a reminder of whose authority he was supposed to be under.

God did not curse Adam, but the sentence against him touched on three important areas of his life and the lives of his descendants. Firstly, the ground was cursed because of him, such that rather than being productive and fruitful in its entirety, a vast majority of it would be barren, bearing thorns and thistles. Secondly, the ground would cease to be productive on its own. Now, it would need to be cultivated by the sweat of the man's brow, before it would cooperate in producing food for his stomach. Thirdly, this would be the man's lot until he returned to the dust from whence he was taken. In other words, despite what the serpent said, God reiterated that he would surely die.

The hierarchy established by God as a result of Adam and his wife's sin was once again intimated by the fact that verse 20 shows, Adam named his wife Eve (Chavvah—life, living) because she would become the mother of all living. Naming her established his position of authority over her. God could have immediately killed them both, but the fact that names were given to them, and their futures were predicted, gave hope, and highlighted God's amazing grace.

TEMPORARY COVERING FOR SIN

God further demonstrated His love in verse 21, where it says, "The Lord God made garments of skin for Adam and his wife and clothed them." He could have, and would have been in the right, to allow them to remain afraid and naked. Instead, He replaced the fig leaves they sewed with garments of skin. This meant, for the first time in the new creation, something (an animal) died to cover the shame and nakedness of humans.

It was also very possible that Adam and Eve witnessed for the first time, what it meant to die. An animal's life was possibly taken so that God could make garments of skin to cover their nakedness. If this was the case, nothing is said about what happened to the flesh of the animal, since Adam and Eve were vegetarians. As a matter of conjecture, the animal's flesh may have been sacrificed as an atonement for their sin.

Verse 22 shows that the Lord God said, "The man has now become like one of us, knowing good and evil. He must not be allowed to reach out his hand and take also from the tree of life and eat, and live forever." Indeed, God knows good because good is what He is, but He does not know evil experientially. He knows it because He had seen it in Satan and his demons who followed him. Hence, when God said the man had now become like one of us, He was not only referring to the Godhead, but also to the angelic realm, which also had the knowledge of good and evil.

Once Adam and Eve gained knowledge of good and evil, their nature became more like Satan's than it did like God's. And indeed, this was Satan's plan all along! His entire agenda was to cause them and their descendants to become familiar with evil and to join his ranks, the ranks of the fallen.

FATE OF FALLEN MAN

In addition to the tree of the knowledge of good and evil, the tree of life was also in the Garden of Eden. Adam and Eve had access to that tree before they sinned. That tree was the choice they could have made if they choose to only know good, rather than good and evil. God did humanity a favor by removing access to the garden, so that Adam and Eve could not access the tree of life while in a fallen condition. What a colossal tragedy it would have been, and a victory for Satan, if God allowed humanity to live forever under the power and penalty of sin! In such a scenario, God would have had to destroy all of humanity along with Satan. Thankfully, God in His grace closed off access to the tree of life, until a later time and so that some of humanity can be saved.

Fortunately, Adam and Eve's sin occurred in time rather than eternity, and once they sinned, God expelled them from the garden so that they had time to repent without taking from the tree of life in their sinful condition. He literally protected them and their descendants from an eternally sinful state. By banishing them from the garden, God saved them from easy access to eternity while in their sinful condition. He knew if they entered eternity that way, their condition would be irreversible.

Unfortunately, rather than believing in God's redemptive plan through Jesus Christ, many of Adam and Eve's descendants choose to depart time, by way of death, and enter eternity in a sinful state. Their condition can only be reversed, if decisions made in time, can be reversed in eternity. God has not given any evidence of this; consequently, it would be silly for humans to take such a chance.

Verse 23 says, "So the Lord God banished him from the Garden of Eden to work the ground from which he had been taken. After He drove the man out, He placed on the east side of the Garden of Eden cherubim and a flaming (lahat—angelic flame) sword (cherub—sword, knife) flashing back and forth to guard the way to the tree of life." The man was sent back to his original home, to the place where the dust from which he was created came from.

Whereas Adam once enjoyed a friendly relationship with God, once he was expelled from the garden, he was treated like an enemy. A sword was drawn against him to make sure he did not unlawfully attempt to re-enter the garden from which he had been evicted. Moreover, the way to the tree of life was sealed off. Adam and his wife Eve, had no further access to it, and every descendant after them would have no other choice, but to look to an offspring who would crush the serpent's head and regain access. From that time on, they would be filled with wonder about who that offspring would be. He would be the only hope for humanity, and the only one who could reconcile the relationship between God and man, and reopen the way back to the tree of life. Humanity needed a Savior, and thankfully God provided one. His name is Jesus. Through Him the way to the tree of life has been reopened.

FATE OF FALLEN ANGELS

When God created angels and humans, He gave them the ability to choose, rather than be governed by instinct. Satan and his demonic cohort were banished from heaven because of the rebellious choice they made (Isa 14:12–15). Similarly, Adam and Eve were banished from Paradise because of the sinful choice they made; They were denied access to the tree of life. However, while access to the tree of life has been restored to Adam and Eve's descendants, such access has not been granted to Satan and his evil cohort. The reason they will not be redeemed is because their rebellious choice against God occurred in eternity, rather than in time. In essence, they accessed (took of) the tree of life (eternity) when they were created, after which they proceeded to sin against God. Adam and Eve sinned against God before they were allowed to take of the tree of life.

Miriam Webster's Online Dictionary defines eternity as: everlasting, forever-ness, infinity, or perpetuity.[1] Therefore, eternity may be viewed as an everlasting or infinite state. Hence, when Satan and his demons sinned, their condition became irreversible because they did so in eternity, which is an irreversible state. The state of eternal existence also applies to God. Hence, He is eternally perfect and good (Luke 18:19), and Scripture teaches that God does not change (Mal 3:6; Heb 13:8).

Additionally, angels do not have a heritage of sin as humans do because of Adam and Eve's sin. In other words, they do not possess an inherited sin nature from someone who gave birth to them. Instead, each angel was individually created by God, and bears personal responsibility for their actions. When one third of them chose to disobey God, they did so by their own corrupt will. Consequently, they were banished from heaven, being

---

1. Webster, *Synonyms for Eternity*, https://www.merriam-webster.com/dictionary/eternity?src=search-dict-box2021.

also reserved for eternal punishment in hell (Rev 12:4). This is an irreversible judgment because they were created in eternity and sinned in eternity.

Thankfully, the judgment against mankind can be less severe because of God's grace toward them, and because He created them in time and their sin occurred in time. Hence, He has given them a Savior, who bore the penalty for their sin, and time to repent of them.

GENESIS CHAPTER FOUR

The previous chapter ended on a dubious note, with Adam and Eve being evicted from their perfect home and finding themselves in a rather hopeless situation. However, by the grace of God, they were not immediately terminated, but were allowed to have offspring, and a future on earth, albeit their future would take a different turn. The evil they chose to know, would impact their descendants for the remainder of humanity's existence on earth. From that point forward, the Bible provided insight into the impact their decision had on their descendants. This chapter will examine the power of sin upon their son Cain, which led him to murder his brother Abel.

THE FIRST FAMILY

Verse 1 says that Adam made love to his wife Eve, and she became pregnant and gave birth to Cain (Possession). At Cain's birth, Eve said, "With the help of the Lord (Jehovah) I have brought forth a man."

This meant that despite the circumstances, routines of life continued for Adam and Eve. They made love, Eve became pregnant, and gave birth to a son, whom they named Cain (Possession). She probably thought the son she brought forth would be the one God told them about, who would crush the serpent's head, and restore a right relationship between them and God. Unfortunately, this was not that man, but throughout history the coming of that man remained a mystery until He was brought forth and reveal.

Verse 2 indicates that later she gave birth to his brother Abel (Breath). Some believe these brothers may have been twins, but that is conjecture. Very few details were provided about Cain and Abel's childhood. As boys, they probably played together while growing up. Insight was given about their occupations as they grew up. Abel kept flocks, and Cain worked the soil. This meant one was a shepherd, and the other a farmer.

Abel's occupation was interesting, since to that point, there was no evidence that anyone ate meat. Adam and Eve, and most likely their sons, were still vegetarians. Conceivably, Abel's farm animals were used in worship and as sacrifices to God. In any case, the world was literally Cain's and Abel's. They could go wherever they wanted to go and be whatever they wanted to be. Unfortunately, that level of freedom did not prevent Cain from becoming jealous of his brother Abel.

JEALOUSY OVER A BROTHER'S OFFERINGS

Verse 3 says that in the course of time, Cain brought some fruits of the soil as an offering to the Lord. The Bible does not explain what prompted this action on Cain's part, but notice when he brought his offering: In the course of time! In other words, Cain's offering appeared to be an after-thought, rather than a forethought. More importantly, being a farmer, if he brought his offering 'in the course of time,' it could have been that his gift was no longer fresh. Some of his fruits of the soil could have been rotten.

On the contrary, verse 4 says, Abel also brought an offering. Again, there is no indication of what prompted this action by Abel. Notice, they were fat portions from some of the firstborn of his flock. His offering was certainly not an afterthought, nor was it given grudgingly. There was a clear difference in the quality of the gift, and attitude of giving, displayed by the two brothers. The Lord recognized this difference, as verse 5 says, the Lord looked with favor on Abel and his offering, but on Cain and his offering He did not look with favor. So, Cain was very angry, and his face was downcast.

Not only were there differences in their gifts, and in their attitudes toward giving, but Hebrews 11:5, shows there were also clear differences of faith between the two brothers. More importantly, if Adam their father served as priest, accepting their gifts on God's behalf, he would have communicated God's favor to Abel, and His displeasure to Cain. And, without faith, Cain would have seen this as parental favoritism toward Abel, and rejection toward him. Some assert that the problem with Cain's gift was, he brought fruits to God, and God has never ordained fruits to be used as an atonement for sin. They claim, he should have done like his brother and brought an animal sacrifice.

This assertion would be true, if it was clear that the reason the brothers brought offerings to the Lord, was for an atonement of their sins. But the Bible does not say the offerings were for atoning sin, nor does it say the Lord even asked them to bring Him offerings. They could simply have been free-will offerings. In any case, Cain's anger was unwarranted. All he had to do, was bring a better offering! Additionally, since the Lord was the one who looked with favor on Abel but not on Cain, his problem should have been with the Lord, not with Abel! In other words, Abel did nothing egregious to provoke his anger.

LESSONS IN ANGER MANAGEMENT

Verse 6 shows how the Lord sought to counsel Cain off the cliff on which he found himself. God said to him, "Why are you angry? Why is your face downcast?" The first lesson in dealing with anger is to figure out why it is present in the first place. If there is no clear reason for anger, and yet it is present, it may result in irrational behavior, which could be misdirected toward those who are innocent. This was what Cain did in targeting his innocent brother Abel. Cain's anger was so pronounced and irrational, that it affected his appearance. It was visibly observable in his countenance. This meant his anger had grown to bitterness, and while it is possible to be angry and not sin (Eph 4:26), when anger wells up into bitterness, sin usually follows.

In verse 7, the Lord continued by asking "If you do right, will you not be accepted? But if you do not do what is right, sin is crouching at your door; it desires to have you, but you must rule over it." The second lesson in dealing with anger should be self-examination. It is important to make sure we are doing what is right, before becoming angry, and charging others with doing what is wrong. If Cain would have done this, the tragedy, which unfolded at his hands, could have been avoided, and he would have indeed been accepted.

The third lesson in dealing with anger is to pause and consider the results of our actions. What would the likely outcome be if we act out in anger, and do not do what is right? The Lord provided the answer for such a scenario. He said, "sin is crouching at your door; and it desires to have you." Sin is always the result of anger that has welled up to the point where it is visible (bitterness). Most importantly, sin desires to have the sinner, more than the sinner desires to have sin. It literally crouches at our door, but the choice about allowing it into the house, is ours.

The fourth lesson in dealing with anger, is to master the sin it can produce. Anger, which can result in sin, is a powerful emotion; therefore, it must be confronted and mastered, otherwise it will master all who possess it. Jails and prisons are crowded with individuals who would not be there, had they taken a moment to practice these lessons, especially to master anger, which results in sin. How can this type of anger be mastered? Time, rather than impulsiveness, can assist in mastering it. Separating from the situation can be a useful strategy for mastering it. Above all, talking to God about it is the most powerful antidote. It takes a commitment to keep forgetting, or letting go of whatever it was that promoted feelings of anger. Anger is a powerful human emotion, but it can and must be mastered, and kept from festering.

TRAGEDY IN THE FAMILY

Cain did not learn any of the anger management lessons he could have from the questions the Lord asked him. His anger was way too deep; it had welled up into bitterness, which usually relieves itself in sin. Verse 8 shows that Cain said to his brother Abel, "Let's go out to the field." While they were in the field, Cain attacked his brother Abel and killed him. Cain's premeditation of his crime was highlighted by the fact that he did not kill his brother at his house, he killed him in the field. In other words, like his father Adam, he thought he could hide his crime, but rather than hiding behind trees and fig leaves, he tried to hide behind the overgrowth of the field.

If the death of animals did not make the point for Adam and Eve about what death looks like, Cain's crime should have. Their son Abel died at the hands of his brother, simply because he was a man of faith, who delighted himself in giving cheerful offerings to the Lord. What a tragedy this was! The very first human death in history, was that of a man of faith, who delighted himself in giving the Lord the best offering he could afford.

CAIN'S RESPONSE AND ATTITUDE TOWARD HIS CRIME

Verse 9 says, "Then the Lord said to Cain, "Where is your brother Abel?" "I don't know," he replied. "Am I my brother's keeper?" It is not known how much time passed before the Lord asked Cain about the whereabouts of his brother, but it is quite revealing that He asked Cain and no one else. He did not ask Adam or Eve, "Where is your son Abel?" The Lord asked Cain because He knew he was the main suspect, and sole perpetrator! As the older son he certainly bore responsibility for his younger brother. He was supposed to be his mentor and friend, not his enemy and murderer!

Notice, he blatantly lied to the Lord. He responded, "I don't know, am I my brother's keeper?" His answer suggested that he had no remorse whatsoever for his actions. He was as callous as could be, in the face of his precedent-setting deed. He gave his parents and every human after them a vivid image of what the knowledge of evil looked like, the results it produces, and what it meant for a human to die.

Cain's response also showed his lack of reverence for the Lord. No wonder he gave Him a stingy offering! He did not understand that the Lord's questions were opportunities for him to confess and repent. Cain could not understand this because First John 3:12, says he was of the evil one. In other words, he was an agent of Satan! This is a profound claim, because it sheds light on the game Cain was playing when he brought an offering to God. He knew he did not belong to God, nor did he harbor any love for God. Yet, he wanted to appear Godly by bringing Him an offering. This above all else, clarified the difference between him and Abel, and why Abel and his offering were looked on with favor, while Cain and his offering were not.

As a farmer, and Adam's firstborn son, the responsibility to be the creation's keeper, should have passed to Cain, but since he rejected his role as his brother's keeper, he subsequently disqualified himself as keeper of the entire creation. Albeit, despite what he said, he was indeed supposed to be his brother's keeper.

CAIN'S TRIAL

Verses 10-11 show that the Lord said, "What have you done? Listen! Your brother's blood cries out to me from the ground. Now you are under a curse and driven from the ground, which opened its mouth to receive your brother's blood from your hand."

The Lord asked Cain, the same question He had asked his mother before him (Gen 3:13), "What have you done?" This was Cain's opportunity to confess, but the spirit of remorse was not in him. The Lord then told Cain to do something he had not done to that point. He told him to listen! Cain thought that by killing his brother, he could cause the Lord to accept him and his unacceptable offering, but the Lord did not accept him, because he belonged to Satan, and He did not accept his offering, because it was given from a stingy heart.

Abel belonged to the Lord, and his offering was given from a heart of worship; therefore, when he was unjustly murdered, his blood cried out to God, to whom he belonged. But Cain's voice refused to cry out in confession and remorse! In fact, Cain never confessed to killing his brother, and no other human had seen him do it; Yet, at the cry of Abel's blood, the Lord pronounced a sentence on him. In other words, the cry of Abel's blood was the only witness at Cain's trial!

CAIN'S SENTENCE

God pronounced a sentence in verse 12. He told Cain, "When you work the ground, it will no longer yield its crops for you. You will be a restless wanderer on the earth." What this meant was, Cain, in his rebellion may have attempted to continue to be a farmer, but since the ground would no longer cooperate by yielding crops for him, he would have to change his profession. This was not an easy thing to do, since at that time, farming was an essential survival skill. This was a major blow to Cain! It also showed that the ground was more gracious to Abel, by receiving his body and his blood, than it was to Cain, by refusing to continue to provide his livelihood.

Without a viable profession, no doubt Cain became a restless wanderer. In other words, he went into perpetual hiding, while simultaneously trying to earn a living. Notice, Cain said in verses 13-14, "My punishment is more than I can bear. Today you are driving me from the land, and I will be hidden from your presence; I will be a restless wanderer on the earth, and whoever finds me will kill me." Clearly, Cain's wandering resulted in him having to hide for fear of his life, but his response to his sentence contained a few exaggerations.

Firstly, he claimed his punishment was more than he could bear, yet he seemed to forget that he killed his brother; a crime deserving death. Secondly, he claimed he was being driven from the land. Technically, he may have been driven from the land in terms of his occupation as a farmer, but by God's grace, he was not buried in the land as a corpse; He could go on to take up a different occupation. Thirdly, he claimed that as a wanderer, whoever found him would kill him.

It should be noted that when Cain killed his brother Abel, there was no written or verbal law to prevent him from doing so. Such a law was not given until after the flood (Gen 9:5-6). However, there was a moral law, by which Cain knew what he did was wrong and deserved to be punished by death. Realizing he deserved to be put to death, Cain could not trust anyone, which probably made him a more dangerous man. He would view others as threats to his life and worthy to be killed before they killed him.

Cain seemed to view his punishment as unjustified, which again, highlighted his lack of remorse. Moreover, he accelerated the degradation of society, where killings, and wars, would become unceasing human tragedies. His concern about being hated, and becoming an object of revenge, became the concern of every murderer after him. Civil societies hate murder, and all of them have stringent laws against it. Some actually still have the audacity to put murderers to death.

The Lord said to Cain in verses 15–16, "Not so; anyone who kills Cain will suffer vengeance seven times over. Then the Lord put a mark on Cain so that no one who found him would kill him. So, Cain went out from the Lord's presence and lived in the land of Nod (Shaking), east of Eden." While Cain may have become a hated man, God lovingly ministered to his humanity. His concern about being killed by others who might find him, suggested that he was worried that when Adam and Eve had other children, they might eventually seek revenge against him.

Some have speculated about what the mark God placed on Cain was, but no one can be sure, and it is uncertain how Cain eventually died. What is clear is, the Lord did not chase Cain from His presence; instead, he went out from the Lord's presence on his own. A life lived in hiding, and away from the presence of the Lord, must have been absolute torment! Furthermore, there is no evidence once Cain went out from the Lord's presence that he ever returned, which meant Adam and Eve basically lost both of their sons.

CAIN'S CITY

Verse 17 says Cain made love to his wife, and she became pregnant and gave birth to Enoch (Dedicated). Cain was then building a city, and he named it after his son Enoch. Some also speculate about where Cain found a wife, since there were few people alive, and most of those mentioned in the Bible were men. Frankly, some of the speculations are ridiculous and not worth repeating here since they amount to sodomy, and some are even patently racist.

However, the answer to where Cain found a wife is found in Genesis 5:4, where it shows that Adam had other sons and daughters. Cain was born within the first century of Adam's life. Since Adam and Eve birthed other sons and daughters, who in turn also gave birth to sons and daughters, Cain had choices of women he could marry. New births were occurring at a faster rate than deaths, and people at that time lived hundreds of years. This is a more reasonable explanation for how Cain found a wife than the nonsense some have postulated on this topic.

Cain was removed from the land, which caused his career as a farmer to cease. Evidently, he found a new career as a builder. He built a city, but rather than naming it after himself, he named it after his son Enoch. This was understandable since he viewed himself as a fugitive. Based on what the Bible says about Cain, it appears unlikely he will inherit a heavenly city, so he built one for himself here on earth. He invented urban living in defiance to God's command.

When God created mankind, He instructed them (Gen 1:28) to increase, multiply, and fill the entire earth. By building a city, Cain demonstrated his objection to that command. His city was an attempt to find strength in numbers and human power, rather than in God. Most importantly, by building a city Cain was the first human to set up a system whereby he, and others he approved, would gain dominion over other humans, which God did not ordain in the instructions He gave Adam.

CAIN'S OFFSPRING

Verses 18-24 provide a record of some of Cain's descendants. Notable diversions from the norm can be observed in what is said about them. For example, the first instance of polygamy in the Bible is recorded in verse 19, where it says, Lamech married two women. Their names were also recorded for posterity, Adah, and Zillah. This was a blatant violation of the original law, which said two would become one flesh. Lamech introduced three to the marriage relationship.

In any case, God blessed Lamech's marriages with gifted children. Adah gave birth to Jabal, who was the father of those who lived in tents and raised livestock. His brother, Jubal, became the father of all who played stringed instruments and pipes. Zillah on the other hand, also had a son. He was a gifted metal worker. His name was Tubal-Cain, and he forged all kinds of tools out of bronze and iron.

Lamech was the seventh generation from Cain, but Cain's murderous spirit was alive and well in him. Verses 23-24, show that Lamech boasted to his wives, saying, "I have killed a man for wounding me, a young man for injuring me. If Cain is avenged seven times, then Lamech seventy times seven." In other words, Lamech was saying, "You mess with me, and you die!" He possessed a vengeful, warrior spirit! It is notable that of all of Cain's descendants, Lamech was the one highlighted, because he epitomized the perpetual depravity of Cain's descendants.

Cain was definitely not the Redeemer, nor were any of his descendants, as they seemed to get worse with every generation. Therefore, verse 25 says that Adam made love to his wife again, and she gave birth to a son and named him Seth (Compensation) saying, "God has granted me another child in place of Abel, since Cain killed him."

Not only did God give Adam and Eve a son in Seth, but He also gave them a grandson through Seth, his name was Enosh (Man). Interestingly, it was after Seth and his son Enosh came on the scene that the Bible declares that people began to call on the name of the Lord. It is highly likely they had something to do with that! Seth and his son Enosh may have started a revival! Especially, since Cain was gone! They provided hope for Adam and Eve, and it would be through Seth that the Redeemer would eventually come.

All of Adam and Eve's descendants, including those through Cain, were destroyed in the great flood, but one called Noah, from Seth's line survived to make sure the Redeemer, whom God promised Adam and Eve, would come to fruition.

GENESIS CHAPTER FIVE

The previous chapter highlighted progressive degradation of human society within a short timeframe after Adam and Eve were created and started a family. Cain killed his brother Abel for no good reason. But the chapter ended with a glimmer of hope in the arrival of Seth and his son Enosh. It was at that time when people began to call on the name of the Lord. This chapter furthers that theme, as it is a reminder that God's plan cannot be destroyed by Satan's schemes, nor by human action.

In this chapter, the genealogy of Adam's son Seth, will be examined. An account is provided of his descendants through the first millennium-and-a-half (1656 years). The human ancestry of Jesus Christ flowed through Seth's line; consequently, it excluded Cain's descendants, and those of all Adam and Eve's other children.

COVENANT CONTINUED THROUGH SETH AND HIS DESCENDANTS

Verse 1 says, this is the account of Adam's family line, when God created mankind, and made them in His likeness. As noted above, Adam and Eve had other sons and daughters, but Seth's line received Biblical focus because it was the one through which Christ came. However, this verse reiterated the fact that God created mankind, he was not his own creator, and therefore cannot be his own master.

Verse 2 is a reminder that God created male and female and blessed them. He also gave them the name "Mankind" when He created them. God was the one who decided what gender they would be (male and female). He created them that way! He also decided that Eve was a suitable helper for Adam because her gender complemented his.

Verse 3 says that when Adam lived 130 years, he had a son in his own likeness, in his own image; and he named him Seth (Compensation). This means the murder of Abel occurred within 130 years of human existence. Also worth noting, Adam was made in the image and likeness of God (Gen 1:27), but when he began to have offspring, they were born in his sinful image and likeness, rather than the holy image and likeness of God. Seth was born in Adam's sinful likeness and image, but somehow, it appeared that he developed a relationship with God. Therefore, Seth looked like Adam, and was endowed with the rights and responsibilities that were bestowed upon Adam, but unlike Adam, Seth was obedient to God.

Seth, rather than Cain, continued Adam's legacy. He was Adam's third-born son, but he became like his first-born son. When Cain murdered his brother, and ultimately went out from the Lord's presence, his status as an heir in the family changed. Seth took Cain's place as heir, and inheritor of the covenant lineage of the Messiah and Redeemer.

Verses 4-5 indicate that after Seth was born, Adam lived 800 years and had other sons and daughters. Altogether, Adam lived a total of 930 years, and then he died. He lived almost a full millennium, a long time to deal with the struggles of life. Ultimately, the pronouncements God made came true. Adam lived a long life, earned his living by the sweat of his brow, but eventually the sentence of death was carried out against him.

Verses 6-8 states that when Seth had lived 105 years, he became the father of Enosh (Man). After he became the father of Enosh, Seth lived 807 years and had other sons and daughters. Seth lived a total of 912 years, and then he died. Very few people seem to wonder about where Seth found a wife, as much as they do about where Cain found one. He most likely also married a family member.

Verses 9-20, outline the genealogical record of Seth through his descendants Enosh (Man), Kenan (Possession), Mahalalel (Praise of God), Jared (Descent), and Enoch (Dedicated). The names of Seth's sons seemed to suggest he created a legacy of worship in his family. No wonder, men began to call on the name of the Lord, once he came on the scene. His line was the opposite of Cain's line. First John 3:12 reveals that Cain belonged to the evil one, which meant he was an idolater and most likely taught his idolatry to his descendants.

Seth had five sons, but Messiah's genealogy was reckoned through his fifth son Enoch. As shown above, it appears as if his were worshippers of the true God, but the fact that only Enoch's descendant Noah and his family survived the flood, shows that the majority of Seth's descendants eventually became as depraved as the rest of the world in which they lived.

ENOCH'S WALK WITH GOD

Verses 21-24 state "When Enoch had lived 65 years, he became father of Methuselah (man of the dart, or he dies). After he became father of Methuselah, Enoch walked faithfully with God 300 years and had other sons and daughters. Altogether, Enoch lived a total of 365 years. Enoch walked faithfully with God; then he was no more, because God took him away."

The fact that Enoch walked faithfully with God, was repeated twice in these verses. He walked with God, rather than contrary to God; therefore, his religion was authentic. He walked with God, rather than men, which placed him at odds with men. He was a priest who preached the Word of God, and who spoke on behalf of God. Jude verse 14, says he prophesied about the coming of the Lord. He was taken away by God, which meant he did not live like other men, nor did he die like other men. Enoch was different in every way!

Enoch's faith-walk began when he turned 65 years old, and after he became father of Methuselah. It was at that point that he began to walk with God. Prior to that, he apparently walked like, and with men, but at age 65 something seemed to change. It is unclear what that change was, but his prophesy mentioned in Jude verse 14, may provide a hint. It says, Enoch prophesied, "See, the Lord is coming with thousands upon thousands of His holy angels, to judge everyone, and to convict all of them of all the ungodly acts they have spoken against Him."

Enoch was way ahead of his time. He acquired a heavenly perspective, which placed him at odds with the society in which he lived. He began to obey God and speak on His behalf. By contrast, his society increased in disobedience and spoke against God. All of this forced Enoch to find a friend in God, since he could no longer find one in men. So, he walked with God until he was taken at the relatively young age of 365 years.

Except for Adam, who died 57 years earlier, all of Enoch's predecessors were still alive when God took him away. His exit without death should have served as an example of the benefits of righteous living. He was the only one on whom the sentence of death was not executed, but it seemed to do little to change the trajectory of the society in which he lived. Thankfully, his children, particularly his son Methuselah, were beneficiaries of a fatherly example of righteous living.

METHUSELAH AND HIS OFFSPRING

Verses 25–27 say when Methuselah (Death) had lived 187 years, he became the father of Lamech (Powerful). After he became the father of Lamech, Methuselah lived 782 years and had other sons and daughters. Altogether, Methuselah lived 969 years, and then he died. He died the same year as the great flood. It is quite likely he died in the flood, but not everyone agrees with this assertion. The point is, he lived longer than any other human in history, yet, his name meant, and his end was, "death." His father did not experience death, but the sentence of death, which God pronounced on humanity was carried out on him.

Verse 28 indicates that when Lamech had lived 182 years, he had a son. He named him Noah (Rest) and said, "He will comfort us in the labor and painful toil of our hands caused by the ground the Lord has cursed." After Noah was born, Lamech lived 595 years, and had other sons and daughters. Altogether, Lamech lived a total of 777 years, and then he died.

Lamech spoke as one who was tired of the struggle to earn a living from a cursed ground. For almost 777 years, he was condemned to earning a living by the sweat of his brow. As a result, he hoped for relief through the birth of his Son, Noah; but humanity's true relief would not come for many generations in the future, through his descendant Jesus Christ. Notably, Lamech preceded his father Methuselah in death. He died five years before (1651) the flood in which all humans, except Noah and his family perished.

Verse 32 states that after Noah was 500 years old, he became the father of Shem (Name), Ham (Hot), and Japheth (Opened). These three sons would become the new patriarchs of all living. Genesis 10:21 indicates that Japheth was actually the eldest son, but since Shem was the son through whom the covenant would continue, his name was mentioned first.

Through Noah, God moved to cleanse the earth of ungodliness. Some of what Enoch prophesied came true. God indeed judged everyone, and convicted all of them, except Noah and his immediate family, of all the ungodly acts they had done and spoken against Him. A new start would be initiated through Noah. He would indeed, as his name suggested, usher in a time of rest upon the earth.

GENESIS CHAPTER SIX

Chapter five provided the beginning of the genealogy of Christ, starting with Adam and his son Seth. Enoch was highlighted as a main character, because he stood out in contrast to other men of his time. For at least 300 years, he walked with God, rather than with men, and was commended for doing so. Ultimately, he was taken away by God, having escaped the sentence of death, which is the end of every human's journey on earth. He became father of Methuselah, the record-holder of longevity in the flesh. Methuselah was Noah's grandfather. Noah was a servant of God. This chapter summarizes some of the wicked activities mankind were doing, which led to God informing Noah of His plan to destroy the earth.

"SONS OF GOD" AND "DAUGHTERS OF MEN"

Verses 1-2 declare that when humans began to increase on earth, and daughters were born to them, the sons of God saw that the daughters of men were beautiful, and they married any of them they chose. Humans increased on earth because God blessed them and admonished them to increase and fill the whole earth (Gen 1:28). However, as humans increased in numbers, they also increased in wickedness.

There have been numerous speculations about who the sons of God were. Some have even suggested this statement referred to angels who married daughters of men and had offspring by them. Those who subscribe to this position, or claim that spiritual beings can have sex with humans, use the conception of the virgin Mary for support, but there are significant problems with the suggestion that angels can produced offspring with humans. In fact, this idea is heresy!

Firstly, the birth of Christ was not the result of a sexual encounter between Mary and an angelic being, nor was it the result of a sexual encounter between her and God. Sex is a human activity, which may result in conception. However, the birth of Christ was not an event which brought Him into existence, rather it was an event which revealed His existence. In other words, He always existed! Therefore, Mary's miraculous conception, occurred apart from a sexual encounter. Secondly, Jesus made it clear (Mark 12:25) that angels do not marry. They do not engage in sexual activities, and they do not reproduce.

Therefore, sons of God, most likely referred to Seth's descendants, who at some point, were worshippers of the true God. As such, his descendants needed to choose wives who were also worshippers of the true God; Instead, they became as depraved as others around them and began to marry any of the daughters of men they chose. Their decision to marry such women further corrupted their worship and lead them away from God.

Notice also, what influenced their decision to marry the daughters of men; the women were beautiful! Their decision was based on lust, rather than religion, and the idea that they married any of them they chose, implied they most likely became polygamists. They joined Cain's descendants in complicating God's command, which said two (and no more) would become one flesh. Therefore, the majority of Seth's descendants died in the flood in the same manner the bulk of humanity did.

Verse 3 reveals God's pronouncement that His Spirit would not contend with humans forever, because they are mortal; their days will be one hundred and twenty years. This verse provided further evidence that the sons of God were not angels. They were called humans, and were those with whom God's Spirit contended, or who were supposed to be led by His Spirit. He threatened to remove His Spirit from contending with them, because of His displeasure with their marriages. Furthermore, if they were angels, He would not have restricted their days to one hundred and twenty years.

Verse 4 indicates that Nephilim were on the earth in those days, when the sons of God went to the daughters of men and had children with them. This verse says nothing about whom Nephilim descended from, it simply says they were on earth at that time. It is possible Seth's descendants married some of them and had children by them. They were the heroes of old, men of renown. Nephilim were giants, and a physically imposing group of people. Their size and strength obviously intimidated their neighbors.

Marriages between sons of God (Seth's descendants) and daughters of Nephilim would have produced children with physical characteristics of Nephilim. They were terrifying individuals, such that they became heroes and men of renown. In those days, heroes and men of renown gained such reputations from victories in violent conquests. Their names, rather than God's name, became renown among the people of that time. It was also quite likely that offspring of the sons of God and daughters of men behaved as if they were gods themselves.

GOD'S DISPLEASURE WITH MANKIND'S SIN

Verses 5-6 signaled the extent to which humanity had degenerated. It states that the Lord saw how great the wickedness of humanity had become, and that every inclination of their thoughts was only evil all the time. The Lord regretted that He had made human beings, and His heart was deeply troubled.

God not only saw the wickedness that was being done, He also saw the wickedness men constantly thought about doing! Not only were their actions corrupt, but their thoughts were also continuously corrupt. This assertion illuminated the fact that their corrupt actions were premeditated, deliberate, and unrepentant.

The passage used anthropomorphic language, or "earth-talk" in stating that the Lord regretted He had made humans, and His heart was deeply troubled. The Lord is omniscient and does not harbor regret, but God's position on their sin was stated in human terms to show how displeased He was with their conduct. It also said His heart was troubled, but God's heart cannot be troubled in the same sense that human hearts are. This imagery was presented to provide human understanding of God's absolute displeasure with the thoughts and deeds of His prized creation. God was pictured in a similar manner as disappointed parents would be over the behavior of persistently rebellious children.

GOD'S PLAN TO JUDGE MANKIND'S SIN

As a result of the degenerate state of human affairs, verse 7 declares, the Lord said, "I will wipe from the face of the earth creatures that move along the ground, for I regret that I have made them." God solidified His decision concerning man's fate after: 1. it was clear they spurned the contention of His Spirit. 2. He saw the wickedness they were doing, and 3. He saw the wickedness they thought about doing all the time. God did not only resolve to destroy mankind, but He also determined to destroy all creatures that move along the ground. Those creatures that were made and placed in the care of mankind, would be destroyed along with mankind.

In the face of impending devastation to be visited upon mankind, verse 8 says, "But Noah found favor in the eyes of the Lord." As a descendant of Seth's, Noah was also a son of God, who had not done as other sons of God had done. Like his great grandfather Enoch, he walked with God, and found favor in His eyes. In fact, verse 9 makes this very clear. It says Noah was a righteous man, blameless among the people of his time, and walked faithfully with God. Noah was like water in the midst of a vast desert. He excelled in righteousness, while all others excelled in wickedness.

Verse 10 states that Noah had three sons: Shem, Ham, and Japheth. Again, Genesis 10:21 points out that Japheth was most likely the eldest of the three sons; however, Shem's name appears first, because somehow, he became heir of the covenant. It was through his line that Messiah would come. Ham was actually the youngest son (Gen 9:24).

Verses 11–12 reiterate progressively worsening conditions on the earth. It repeated that the earth was corrupt in God's sight and was full of violence. God saw how corrupt the earth had become, because all the people on the earth had corrupted their ways. God's grievances against the earth were striking. The earth was corrupt in His sight! It's worship and societal dealings were corrupt. It was violent. Violence was a threat to human life and wellbeing. It was a dangerous world, and one in which it was impossible for the righteous, though few, to survive. God was compelled to do something about such a world.

God saw for Himself, how corrupt the earth had become. No one had to tell Him what was going on! He was an eyewitness to the corruption! The evidence was therefore undeniable, as the Judge Himself was a witness to the crime-scene! Notice, it said, "All the people on the earth had corrupted their ways." There were almost no exceptions to what God saw! Interestingly, it says, they corrupted their own ways, which meant they did so willingly.

GOD'S PLAN REVEALED TO NOAH

While it became impossible for God to communicate with such a corrupt world, He resolved to disclose His plans to Noah, who was the only one with whom He could still converse on friendly terms. Verse 13 shows that God said to Noah, "I am going to put an end to all people, for the earth is filled with violence because of them. I am surely going to destroy both them and the earth."

God's repetition of His plan to destroy the earth confirmed His resoluteness to do what He said. As such, God's decision was fixed! As a just God, He most likely informed Noah of His plans so that Noah could warn the people. Therefore, Second Peter 2:5, refers to Noah as a preacher of righteousness. This was the righteousness he probably preached: Turn from your wicked ways or face the wrath of God!

Notice God did not initially tell Noah exactly how He would destroy all people and the earth, but His subsequent instructions made it clear how He planned to do it. In verses 14–16, God instructed Noah to make himself an ark of cypress wood, He gave him the precise design, materials to use, and dimensions by which to build it. Finally, in verse 17, God informed Noah that He would indeed bring floodwaters on the earth to destroy all life under the heavens, every creature that has breath of life in it. Again, He repeated that everything on earth would perish.

GOD'S PLAN TO SAVE AND PRESERVE NOAH AND HIS FAMILY

When God told Noah He would destroy all people, then instructed him to build an ark, He basically hinted that He would destroy all people, except him. Hence, God involved Noah in the process of his own salvation. He instructed him to build an ark, which was his shelter from the storm. The ark Noah was instructed to build was not an easy, nor was it a short-term assignment. It was a massive, painstaking undertaking! It was a test of Noah's faith, and a testimony to the world as they watched him build it. Working out salvation can be similar in this evil world today.

At this point, it is worth revisiting the discussion from chapter one (day two), where it was mentioned that prior to the flood, and close to 1656 years after creation, it still had not rained. If this was true, Noah's contemporaries probably thought he was crazy! Why prepare for something that had never happened in history? His preaching made no sense to them!

God provided further details about His plan in verse 18, where He told Noah, "I will establish My covenant with you, and you will enter the ark, you and your sons, and your wife, and your sons' wives with you." This was another clear example of the irreversible nature of God's plan. While all others were progressively wicked, Noah was progressively righteous, and he became inheritor of the covenant. God also made provisions for his descendants to ensure the covenant would continue long after Noah.

God made provisions for continuation of His covenant with mankind, but He also made provisions for continuation of His covenant with creation. As such, He instructed Noah to bring into the ark, two of all living creatures, male and female, to keep them alive. Two of every kind of bird, of every kind of animal, and every kind of creature that moves along the ground. Notice He told Noah, "these creatures will come to you to be kept alive." Noah did not have to go hunting for them, they came to him by divine volition.

In other words, those creatures did what Noah's wicked contemporaries refused to do. They also participated in the process of their own salvation.

God was able to convince animals of their need for salvation but could not do the same with the majority of mankind. It also illustrated the nature of animals at that time. Their nature had not become as violent as that of mankind. They came to Noah to seek refuge in the ark, but wicked and corrupt mankind would not come. In essence, the nature of those creatures was by far more tamed than that of mankind.

Finally, God told Noah to take every kind of food that is to be eaten and store it away as food for him and for the creatures he brought into the ark with him. All those preparations took time, they represented Noah's diligence and focused obedience to God. The chapter ended in verse 22, with the words, "Noah did everything just as God commanded him." In other words, he did not present any alternate plans of his own, nor did he negotiate with God in any way. He simply did as God told him to do. Remarkably, not a single utterance from Noah was recorded in this chapter. Noah's example was one to be emulated by sons and daughters of God in any and every generation, he simply obeyed.

GENESIS CHAPTER SEVEN

In the previous chapter, God made known His absolute displeasure with mankind. Sons of God married any of the daughters of men they felt like and had children with them. Human society had become irreversibly violent and corrupt. Despite those conditions, Noah walked with God and found favor in His eyes. Therefore, God informed Noah of His plan to destroy the earth. He instructed him to build an ark to save himself, his family, and all the creatures He would cause to come to him to be preserved beyond the flood.

With that framework, this chapter examines details of the flood, and how Noah and those with him in the ark, made it through that colossal event in the history of earth and its inhabitants. Verses 1–3, show where the Lord instructed Noah to, "Go into the ark, you and your whole family, because I have found you righteous in this generation." Some translations (NKJV) state that God told Noah to "Come into the ark." This is an important difference because it indicates that God was there before He invited Noah in. He also told him to take seven pairs of every kind of clean animal, male and female, and one pair of every kind of unclean animal, male and female. Also, seven pairs of every kind of bird, male and female, to keep their various kinds alive throughout the earth.

The reason God told Noah to do all this, was given in verse 4, where the time was set. He told Noah "Seven days from now, I will send rain on the earth for forty nights, and I will wipe from the face of the earth every living creature I have made."

SIGNIFICANCE OF THE ARK

Some believe it took Noah 120 years to build the ark. One reason for this estimation is because God said man's lifespan would be 120 years (Gen 6:3). In other words, this pronouncement was made 120 years before the flood, when God told Noah to begin building the ark, and when He knew all mankind who were not in the ark would die.

The fact that God told Noah to go (or come) into the ark, indicated that he was not living in it prematurely, despite knowing its purpose. Noah trusted God to inform him when the time came to take shelter in the ark. The ark represented salvation. It was a place of safety. Observe the tremendous tribute God paid to Noah. He told him to go into the ark, because He found him righteous in his generation. Those who were not found righteous were left to be destroyed outside the ark. This pictured the final judgment to come, when the righteous will be saved, while the wicked will be judged.

Interestingly, God not only used the ark to save humans, but He also used it to save other living creatures from the devastation of the flood. In so doing, He preserved mankind for Himself, but He preserved the other creatures for mankind. Therefore, there were differences in numbers between clean and unclean creatures that were sheltered in the ark. Clean animals, which are usually found in large herds and flocks, were used for sacrificing to God, and became a means for supplementing man's diet. Whereas, unclean animals roam in smaller packs, and are used to maintain balance in nature. Therefore, God saved them in the ark, so that order could be restored once He had completely destroyed all wicked, violent, and corrupt people who lived on the earth at that time.

SEVEN DAYS BEFORE THE FLOOD

Note, God finally gave Noah an exact timeframe of when storms would begin, and how long they would last. They would begin in seven days, and last forty nights. There was no reason to believe that since Noah's contemporaries did not heed his warnings over 120 years, they would heed them in seven days, especially if, as some believe, they lived under threat of rain that had never fallen to that point in history. It took God seven days, whether literal or not, to complete His creation, and seven days to give final contemplation of how He would destroy it.

Verse 5 says Noah did all that the Lord commanded him. He was completely obedient to God! Albeit this was a sad mission for Noah. Shortly after seven days, every physical aspect of his past would be wiped out. By the time he emerged from the ark, all his relatives, friends, and possessions would be erased! Noah might have been heartbroken by the magnitude of loss he was about to experience, but his despair did not cause him to disobey God. He agreed with God that the judgement He was about to pass in seven days was justified. As a result, Noah did, not just some, but all that the Lord commanded him. God said go into the ark, so he went into the ark without a single objection and waited for the floods to begin in seven days.

THE FLOOD

Verses 6–10 declare that Noah was six hundred years old when floodwaters came on the earth. Noah and his sons, his wife, and his son's wives entered the ark. Pairs of clean and unclean animals, of birds, and of all creatures that move along the ground, male and female, came to him and entered the ark, as God had commanded him. After seven days floodwaters came on the earth.

A survey of Noah's family indicates that neither he nor his sons had become polygamists, as some in their society were (Gen 4:13; 6:2). Each of them had one wife. Presumably, neither were their wives selected from among the daughters of men. Rather, their wives were selected from among daughters of the sons of God. It was from this small remnant of humans and other creatures, that all living today somehow descended.

Verses 11–12, states that in the six hundredth year of Noah's life, on the seventeenth day of the second month, on that day, all the springs of the great deep burst forth, and the floodgates of the heavens were opened. Rain fell on the earth forty days and forty nights. The 600th year of Noah's life was 1656 years after creation. This date can be easily calculated from the genealogies of the patriarchs (Gen 5).

The seventeenth day of the second month, is a date scholars are yet to decipher. However, whenever that date was, the springs of the great deep burst forth. Recall that when God caused land to appear on earth, He did so by causing the waters, which covered it, to gather in one place, which He called seas (Gen 1:9–10). During the flood, those waters were allowed to exceed their boundaries and cause a tsunami from below, while from above, the floodgates of heaven were opened. Waters, which were gathered in thick clouds above (Gen 1:7), which had never fallen, finally gushed forth in a massive deluge. Earth and its inhabitants did not stand a chance, unless they had appropriate shelter. Conceivably, the only creatures outside the ark, which could likely survive such a torrent, were fish and creatures of the sea. Everything on dry land perished.

Verses 13–15 rehearsed the list of humans and creatures that entered into the ark with Noah, but verse 16, makes a sobering statement. It says, "…then the Lord shut him in." God, rather than Noah, or any other inhabitant of the ark, closed the door. In that moment that chapter in earth's history ended. It was also a moment when mercy ended for anyone on the outside of the door God closed. It was a time of judgment, and this judgment belonged to God, rather than Noah.

The ark pictured the plan of God concerning man's salvation. Those who are outside of Christ are outside the ark, and this is the time to get in. Just as it was impossible for Noah to fall out of the ark once he entered it and once God shut him in, it is impossible for those who enter a sincere relationship with Christ to fall out of the security of His salvation. God shuts them in, just as He did with Noah and his family; Their salvation is sealed. No one who is saved by the power of Holy Spirit can lose their salvation.

When God shut the door to the ark, no one else could enter. All opportunities for others to enter the ark ceased. God's action also insulated Noah from the sufferings of those on the outside. Genesis 5:30, showed that after Noah was born, his father Lamech had other sons and daughters. This meant, Noah had brothers, sisters, nieces, and nephews, among many other family members who died in the flood. He certainly knew many of those who died, but he was protected from hearing their cries and witnessing their demise. Most importantly, he had done all he could to warn them, and there was nothing else he could do.

Verses 17–20 indicates that for forty days, floodwaters kept coming on the earth, and as waters increased the ark was lifted high above the earth. Waters increased greatly on earth, and the ark floated on the surface of the water. All the high mountains under the entire heavens were covered to a depth of more than fifteen cubits (23 feet) of water. There was nowhere to run for safety. In fact, with such volumes of water, mountains became treacherous terrain, and those who fled to them found them no safer than valleys.

Verses 21–23 declare that every living thing that moved on land perished, birds, livestock, wild animals, all the creatures that swarm over the earth, and all mankind. Everything on dry land that had the breath of life in its nostrils died. Every living thing on the face of the earth was wiped out; people and animals, creatures that moved along the ground, and the birds were wiped from the earth. Only Noah and those with him in the ark survived.

These verses emphasized the utter destruction caused by the flood. Every living thing that moved on land perished. One may ask, why were the birds and animals destroyed, what did they do? The likely answer is, God created those creatures for mankind, so when God destroyed mankind, He also destroyed everything over which He gave mankind dominion. It should be noted also that in destroying mankind, children may also have perished. Such are difficult realities of God's justice, but one thing is for sure: God's judgments are always right. It should also be noted that before the flood, mankind was already submerged in a flood of wickedness, violence, and corruption, and God warned them to no avail.

People today seem more comfortable focusing on God's love and mercy than they do on His anger and justice. Indeed, God is abundantly loving and merciful, but the flood in Noah's day was an example of what His anger and justice look like. God is not easily provoked to anger the way humans are, but when He is, His wrath can easily overwhelm anything or anyone that is an affront to Him. It is the type of anger described by the Greek words "orge," or "thumos," which depict a strong emotional displeasure for sin, often leading to revenge or punishment.

God's wrath as displayed during the flood, illustrated what could happen when His strong displeasure towards sin reaches its limit. It should also serve as a warning to all since that time, of what it will be like in that day of reckoning, which has been prophesied to come at the end of the age. It is going to be a dreadful event for all who are found dressed in their own righteousness.

Verse 24 concludes the chapter by stating that waters flooded the earth for a hundred and fifty days. It should be noted here that there is much discussion about dates given for when the flood began, and 150 days before waters receded. Scholars find it difficult to nail down the precise months in question, and there is uncertainty about which calendar was in use at that time.

In any case, nothing outside the ark survived, but for those on the inside, there was probably a mixture of worship and wonder. Worship because Noah was a man of God, who no doubt, thanked God for saving him and his family. Wonder because 150 days was a considerable amount of time to ponder the devastation to be witnessed on the outside. Nevertheless, when it started God told them when to go into the ark; it was He who shut them in. Hence, when it was finished, it was He who opened the door and told them when to come out. God was in total control of their salvation, just as He is for all those who are saved.

The New Testament states that as it was in the days of Noah, so shall it be at the second coming of Christ (Matt 24:37; Luke 17:26). Obviously, the days of Noah were characterized by colossal wickedness, corruption, and Godlessness. Men married whomever they chose, and rather than worshipping God, they nominated heroes from among themselves. It is becoming increasingly clearer what the days of Noah were like, as much of what was done in those days, seem to be occurring today. While it is impossible to predict when Christ will return, signs of His coming are progressively clearer. Meanwhile, the message of salvation is being preached, but sadly, to the majority, it seems to be of no avail. The flood in Noah's time should be instructive for today, yet some do not even believe it occurred, much less use it as a reason to repent. Hopefully, God will send a massive revival, before He exercises His justice once again.

GENESIS CHAPTER EIGHT

The previous chapter showed God's tender mercies toward Noah, his family, and all the creatures, which found shelter in the ark. Noah was instructed when to enter the ark and given details about how long the flood would last. Once Noah and those with him entered the ark, God closed the door behind them. Floodwaters came from below and above, overwhelming any drainage systems that may have existed. Floodwaters pooled to a height of fifteen cubic (23 feet) above the highest mountain. It did not recede until 150 days later. Everything outside the ark was completely destroyed. This chapter summarizes events, which occurred after the flood, when Noah and his family resumed life on earth as the new patriarchs of all generations to come. It was a new start.

Verses 1–5 declare that God remembered Noah and all the wild animals and livestock with him in the ark, and He sent a wind over the earth, and the waters receded. The springs of the deep and the floodgates of the heavens had been closed, and the rain had stopped falling from the sky. The water receded steadily from the earth. At the end of 150 days the water had gone down, and on the 17th day of the seventh month the ark came to rest on the mountains of Ararat. The waters continued to recede until the 10th month, and on the first day of the tenth month the tops of the mountains became visible.

DID NOAH WONDER IF GOD FORGOT HIM?

God's meticulous nature was highlighted in the fact that He did not lock Noah and those with him in the ark and forget about them; Instead, it says He remembered them. Once again, this was anthropomorphic language, as it is it impossible for God to forget, except that He wills Himself to do so. However, when it said that God remembered Noah, He also remembered all of Noah's descendants who were yet unborn. In other words, He remembered everyone alive today and in the future!

Interestingly, when God told Noah He would flood the earth, He also told him the floodwaters would keep coming for 40 nights, but there is no evidence He told him how long it would be before the floodwaters receded. Therefore, the extended period of time after the 40 days of flooding, could have caused Noah to begin to wonder if he had been forgotten by God. Hence, the assertion that God remembered Noah, was a reminder of His commitment to His covenant. It was a reminder that He is merciful even in wrath.

To that end, God sent a wind over the earth, and the waters receded. He not only controlled the waters, which caused the flood, but He also controlled the wind, which chased the flood. The wind He sent most likely accelerated the floodwaters' exit from land, and hastened their return to the seas, rivers, springs, and other confines of their boundaries. Thankfully, the earth was cleansed as floodwaters receded, but sadly, the receding waters most likely took with them the dead bodies of all who perished.

Noah entered the ark on the seventeenth day of the second month, but it was not until 150 days (the seventh month) later, before the waters began to recede, and not until the 10th month that the tops of the mountains became visible. This meant, the valleys were still covered with water. More importantly, it meant Noah was already in the ark for eight months! No wonder, he may have wondered if God had forgotten him.

Verses 6-7 indicate that after 40 days Noah opened a window he had made in the ark and sent out a raven, and it kept flying back and forth until the water had dried up from the earth. Notice that Noah sent the raven out around the time God had told him the flood should end, but since God did not seem to tell him how long it would take for the waters to recede, Noah had no idea how long he would have to stay in the ark. Forty days proved to be way too soon! Hence, the raven kept flying back, and may have continued to do so for at least four more months.

Verses 8-12 show where Noah sent out a dove to see if the water had receded, but the dove could not find anywhere to perch because there was water over all the surface of the earth; so, it returned to Noah in the ark. Noah took the dove back into the ark and waited seven more days before sending it out again. When the dove returned in the evening, in its beak was a freshly plucked olive leaf. Then Noah knew the water had receded from the earth. He waited seven more days and sent the dove out again, but this time it did not return to him.

Noah was a faithful man, but he was a man! Therefore, verses 8-12, revealed his eagerness to exit the ark. Those verses also suggested that he had no idea when, or how he would get out of the ark, and may have indeed wondered if God had forgotten him! Notice that in going from a raven to a dove, he seemed to change birds to see if the news he was receiving would get better, but initially it did not. Those were days of silence from God. Yet, the news Noah so much longed for, would not come from birds, but from God, in His own time. Finally, Noah received good news by the dove not returning; nevertheless, he still needed to wait to hear from God, because it was God who called him into the ark, and shut the door behind him, and it would be God who would open the door and call him out.

Verses 13-14 indicate that by the first day of the first month of Noah's 601st year, the water had dried up from the earth. Noah then removed the covering from the ark and saw that the surface of the ground was dry. By the 27th day of the second month the earth was completely dry. Notice the 27th day of the second month, meant Noah had been in the ark for one year and 10 days! This was longer than he expected! In fact, he spent his 601st birthday in the ark!

Interestingly, even though Noah was able to remove the covering from the ark, looked outside, and saw that the surface of the ground was dry, he did not prematurely attempt to leave on his own. Instead, he waited for God to call him out! This was a testament to his obedience and trust in God! If he had any doubts about whether God had forgotten him, his doubts did not cause him to take matters into his own hands.

WORSHIP DESPITE SORROW

Verses 15-17 states that God said to Noah, "Come out of the ark, you and your wife, your sons and their wives. Bring out every kind of living creature that is with you, the birds, the animals, and all the creatures that move along the ground, so they can multiply on the earth and be fruitful and increase in number."

No doubt, in calling Noah and those with him out of the ark, God most likely did so after opening the door He closed when they entered. It was a rollcall, as though God was affirming His commitment to their safety and reminding them that He had not forgotten them. He called out all of those who went in, and they were all there! Kept safely through the most dreadful disaster in human history! Everyone and everything else were destroyed, but they were securely kept by God! Interestingly, God called out Noah and his family, but he told them to bring out the creatures with them, once again affirming their authority over other creatures.

Also noteworthy, was the reason God told Noah to bring out the creatures: "so they can multiply on the earth and be fruitful and increase in number." When those creatures were initially created, God blessed them saying be fruitful, and increase in number and fill the earth (Gen 1:23). As a result, there was no need to bless them again. Instead, they were simply released to go forth and do what they were created and perpetually blessed to do.

God called Noah out of the ark, and his obedience was again demonstrated in Genesis 8:18-20, where it states that Noah came out of the ark, together with his sons and his wife and his sons' wives. All the animals and all the creatures that move along the ground and all the birds, everything that moves on land, came out of the ark, one kind after another. God called them out, so they came out!

Shortly after coming out of the ark, verse 20 says, "Then Noah built an altar to the Lord and, taking some of all the clean animals and clean birds, he sacrificed burnt offerings on it. The Lord smelled the pleasing aroma and said in His heart: Never again will I curse the ground because of humans, even though every inclination of the human heart is evil from childhood. And never again will I destroy all living creatures, as I have done."

This scene depicted one of the very first things Noah did when he came out of the ark, he built an altar and sacrificed burnt offerings to God. There is no indication that God told Noah to do this. It is also the first reference to a burnt sacrifice being made to God. Somehow, Noah knew this was the right thing to do, and that it would be acceptable to God. Again 'earth talk' was used to describe God's response to the burnt sacrifice. The passage indicates that the Lord smelled the pleasing aroma and said in His heart. . . God was described in finite terms, having the sense of smell, and a heart.

Also, the words spoken by God indicated that if the sin of man caused Him to grieve that He created him, having to destroy man grieved God just as much or more; He is never willing that any should perish. It is important to note from this passage that, after the flood God lifted the curse (Gen 3:17) He had pronounced on the ground because of Adam's sin. Therefore, after the flood even the ground was cleansed from its past pollution by wicked men.

God said He would never again curse the ground because of mankind. Nor would He ever again destroy all living creatures. These words indicate God's preference for mercy over justice. However, His justice is always righteous, and in this case, proved that for a short while at least, in the absence of wicked, violent, and corrupt men, the world was indeed a better place. But such men will only be totally absent when Satan the instigator of them is absent. Therefore, this renewal would only last a short while. Since Satan was still present, it would only be a matter of time before Noah's world would return to its previous state of wickedness, such as would later be seen in Nimrod and the Tower of Babel, and in Sodom and Gomorrah.

Verse 22 concludes the chapter with a promise from God. He said, "As long as the earth endures, seedtime and harvest, cold and heat, summer and winter, will never cease." The promise God made is contingent upon the earth enduring. As long as it endures, regular seasons will endure, which also means, time will endure. When earth no longer endures, time will end, and eternity will begin.

GENESIS CHAPTER NINE

Chapter eight described the duration of the flood, and the possibility that as months passed, Noah may have wondered if God had forgotten him. However, God's care and provision for Noah and his family was demonstrated in that He spoke to Noah again and called him out of the ark, proving He had not forgotten him, nor any of those with him. They all exited the ark safely. On exiting the ark, the first thing Noah did was build an alter and offered a burnt sacrifice to God. Noah and those with him were given a new start, this chapter will examine what they did with it.

A COMMAND TO RULE

Verse 1 says God blessed Noah and his sons, commanding them to be fruitful and increase in number and fill the earth. This command was mostly for Noah's sons as there is no indication that Noah, being over 601 years old, had any additional children of his own. But, once again, whenever reproduction was mentioned, it was accompanied by a blessing.

In blessing them, God also told Noah and his sons that the fear of them would fall on all the beasts of the earth, on all the birds of the sky, on every creature that moves along the ground, and on all the fish in the sea. God most likely told them this because they were severely outnumbered. This pronouncement was meant to embolden them to move about without fear of attack by any wild animal. They had nothing to fear from any of the creatures over which they were given authority.

A NEW DIET

Observe verse 3, that God told Noah and his sons, everything that lived and moved would be food for them. Just as He gave them green plants, He gave them everything. This verse indicated that the idea of eating meat came from God. He was the one who changed their diet from plant-based to animal-based. Obviously, the previous chapter (v 20) showed that Noah and his family already knew the difference between clean and unclean animals. Therefore, presumably, the animals they were authorized to eat were clean ones. However, this distinction was not spelled out until later in God's dealings with the Nation of Israel, where He specified what He considered clean for them.

Verse 4 shows that in allowing Noah and his family to eat meat, God gave them an important stipulation. He told them not to eat any meat, which had blood in it. The reason for this would be clarified later (Lev 17:11), where it states that the life of a creature is in its blood, and blood was to be used for making atonement at the altar for their lives. This passage also clarified that Noah, and his family ate clean animals, since clean animals were chosen for the burnt offering, which he offered on exiting the ark. The blood of clean animals would also have been used as an atonement. So, God permitted Noah and his family to eat meat of clean animals, but they were not to eat blood.

A NEW LAW CONCERNING MURDER

In verse 5, God continued by telling Noah and his sons He would demand an accounting for their lifeblood. In other words, they were prohibited from taking their own lives by committing suicide. But, not only were they accountable for their own lifeblood, but He also held them accountable for the lifeblood of every animal. Finally, He demanded an accounting for the lifeblood of other human beings. In other words, no one was allowed to callously take their own life, an animal's life, or the life of another human being, which certainly included the life of the unborn. Again, unlike Cain, they were expected to be their brother's keeper and stewards of God's creation. Once more, God did not give Noah and his sons dominion over other humans.

Verse 6 says, "Whoever sheds human blood, by humans their blood should be shed, because in the image of God has mankind been made." This command was the law of God as it related to capital punishment. It was given to Noah and his sons, and by extension, to all who descended from them. This law concerning sanctity of life was given to humanity, Jew and Gentile alike, and in it, God affirmed capital punishment in murder cases. Some today describe capital punishment as inhumane, but the question must be asked to those who take such a position, are they more righteous than God? Was it inhumane of Him to demand that whoever shed human blood, should have their blood shed by another human in authority?

COVENANT OF A RAINBOW

Verses 7-9, God again commanded Noah's sons to be fruitful and multiply in number on the earth. Then He established His covenant with Noah and his sons with him and with their descendants. It is highly important to understand what that covenant was, otherwise, God could be mistakenly held to keeping a promise He never made. Verses below will clarify what that covenant was, but suffice it to say, the covenant God made was witnessed by Noah and his three sons Japheth, Shem, and Ham, which spoke to the immutability of what God promised.

Verse 10 shows that God also made His covenant with every living creature that was with Noah in the ark. So, what was that covenant? Verse 11 reveals that God covenanted to never again destroy all life by the waters of a flood, and never again will there be a flood to destroy the earth. That was the covenant God made! The flood in Noah's day was the flood of all floods! God's covenant must have been a source of relief to Noah and his sons. It removed any need for them to be repeatedly traumatized at the sight of a dark cloud, or by the sound of thunder!

Notice, God not only made the covenant, but He also gave a sign, which was to serve as a reminder of what He said. Verses 12-16 state that God said, "This is the sign of the covenant I am making between Me and you and every living creature with you, a covenant for all generations to come: I have set My rainbow in the clouds, and it will be the sign of the covenant between Me and the earth. Whenever I bring clouds over the earth and the rainbow appears in the clouds, I will remember my covenant between Me and you and all living creatures of every kind. . ."

Interestingly, today the rainbow has become a symbol of many things, which have nothing to do with its original purpose. Yet, God referred to it as His rainbow! Those who claim the rainbow as their symbol can only draw one on paper, but they cannot draw one across the sky. The rainbow is referred to today as a symbol of diversity because of its multiple colors, but that was not its original purpose. Its original intent was to serve as a perpetual reminder to mankind that their sins deserve to be punished by drowning in a torrent of floodwaters; However, God remembers His promise to never again use that form of punishment as universal retribution for sin. In fact, the darker the cloud, the brighter His rainbow.

Remarkably, God did not ask Noah nor his sons to swear to anything. Really, His covenant was with Himself, and with every new generation of Noah's descendants, because none of the original generation, who were present when the covenant was made, would be able to attest to the longevity of it beyond their lifetime. Therefore, verse 17 revealed God said to Noah, His rainbow would be a sign of the covenant He established between Himself and all life on the earth. His covenant is between Him and the living, rather than the dead. There will never be another flood like the one Noah and his immediate family witnessed.

Though mankind may have forgotten what happened in the days of Noah, thankfully God has not forgotten. The rainbow still reminds Him of the promise He made over 4000 years ago. Every new generation has been able to attest to the fact that since then, there has not been another flood, which has destroyed the entire earth and all life on it, except a few survivors. Though many have forgotten the original purpose of the rainbow, thank God for remaining faithful to His promise!

NOAH'S SONS

Verse 18 indicates that the sons of Noah who came out of the ark were Shem, Ham, and Japheth. By order of birth, the names should be stated as Japheth, Shem, and Ham. However, Shem's name will always be mentioned first because he became father of the covenant line. Interestingly verse 18, continued by stating that Ham was the father of Canaan, but nothing was said about Japheth's offspring. In essence, it appears Japheth's descendants, for the most part, went into Biblical obscurity, while there seemed to be perpetual conflict between Shem's and Ham's descendants.

Verse 19 reiterated that Shem, Ham, and Japheth were the three sons of Noah, from whom came the people who were scattered over the whole earth. In other words, all people before the flood, including Noah and his family, were counted as descendants of Adam and Eve, but all people after the flood would be counted as descendants of Noah's. Hence, the genealogy of all the various races of people existing today is tied to Noah's three sons. This was indeed a fresh and exhilarating start for Noah and his family.

A FRESH START

When Adam and Eve were created, before they sinned, they were the best humanity had to offer. They were perfect, having no heritage of sin, and therefore could not die, because the wages of sin is death (Rom 6:23). Once they sinned, the penalty of death entered the human realm. Nonetheless, to keep other humans, particularly religious folks, from being too critical of Adam and Eve, and from assuming they would have done better than they did, God provided Noah and his family a fresh start. It was a demonstration that no other imperfect human could do better than Adam and Eve did. And, once sin entered mankind's camp, it became like a fire they are incapable of extinguishing on their own.

Hence, if it were possible for humans to save themselves, and to do better than Adam and Eve did, Noah and his sons had the perfect opportunity to do so. They had the benefit of retrospect. They were able to interact with people who knew Adam and Eve personally, and who were able to communicate their story to them, and what happened to cause their expulsion from the Garden of Eden. They witnessed how depraved all of Adam and Eve's descendants had become, and God's displeasure with their sins. They observed God's wrath against mankind's sins, and most importantly, they were the only humans to experience His salvation from death in the flood.

Noah and his family were a bridge between the old world (pre-flood), and the new world (post-flood). They were the only humans who were fortunate to cross that chasm. Therefore, if humanity had any hope of saving itself, they were in the best position to get the job done! But unfortunately, even though Noah was a righteous man, he, and his sons, possessed a fallen nature, which they inherited from Adam and Eve, and that nature accompanied them beyond the flood. So, it would not be long before their world would become as sinful as the world was before the flood. They were incapable of redeeming mankind, much less restoring the utopia Adam and Eve briefly enjoyed.

Noah, like Cain, was a man of the soil, so he planted a vineyard (v 20). "When he drank some of its wine, he became drunk and laid uncovered inside his tent." It is not clear what the occasion might have been, which caused Noah's three sons to be at his tent at the same time. Conceivably, being grown married men, who were commissioned to increase and multiple, they most likely had their own tents. Therefore, it is possible the reason they were all there, was because they were invited by their father to celebrate with him after a bountiful wine harvest.

The Biblical record does not reveal whether Noah had ever been drunk before or after this occasion, but this event reveals that even those who are the most perfect (Gen 6:9) of people can make mistakes at times. It should also be stated here that because Noah was drunk on this occasion, does not mean he should be classified as a drunkard, or as someone who habitually got drunk. Nonetheless, his drunkenness was a sin, which disrupted the dynamics of his role as a father, and as a righteous man. While the serpent enticed Adam and Eve to eat, he enticed Noah to drink, and because Adam and Eve ate, their nakedness was revealed. Noah's nakedness was also revealed because he drank too much wine.

SIN CONTINUED THROUGH NOAH'S SON

Verse 22 says, "Ham the father of Canaan, saw his father's nakedness and told his two brothers outside. But Shem and Japheth took a garment and laid it across their shoulders; then they walked in backward and covered their father's nakedness. Their faces were turned the other way so that they would not see their father's nakedness (v 23)."

After Noah's sin of drunkenness, which revealed his nakedness, God was not the one to directly clothe him as He had done with Adam and Eve, but He left that job to Noah's sons. Ham seemed amused by the condition of his father and showed a lack of respect for him. If he was not interested in covering his father's nakedness, why didn't he call Noah's wife to do it? Why as a father himself did Ham see his father's nakedness as a funny spectacle? The answer is, he was likely influenced by Satan, who from the beginning of time, led humanity to view nakedness as either a condition of which to be ashamed, or one to be used seductively beyond the confines of marriage and monogamy.

CURSE OF HAM'S SON CANAAN

Verse 24 indicates that when Noah awoke from his wine and found out what his youngest son had done to him. . . Some suggest that what Ham did to his father was something of a sexual nature, but the Biblical record does not reveal that. What it does say is that Noah said (v 25), "Cursed be Canaan! The lowest of slaves will he be to his brothers." He also said, "Blessed be the Lord, the God of Shem! May Canaan be the slave of Shem. May God extend the territory of Japheth; may Japheth live in the tents of Shem, and may Canaan be his slave."

Again, the Biblical record does not spell out how Noah found out what Ham did to him. It seems obvious that someone may have told him, since he was drunk and asleep. In any case, what Ham did, angered Noah so much that he pronounced a harsh curse on Ham's son Canaan, not on Ham. Why did he curse Canaan and not Ham, when Canaan apparently had nothing to do with his father's sin? Speculatively, Noah may have cursed Canaan rather than Ham, because God had already blessed Ham, hence, Noah could not curse him. If he could have cursed him, the depth of his anger would have led him to do so. However, since as a son, Ham chose to disrespect his father, his son Canaan would likewise disrespect him and his legacy, by bearing the lowest form of human disrespect, which is slavery.

It should be noted here that Ham had four sons (Gen 10:6), but Noah only cursed one, Canaan, who may have been the eldest, and known to Noah at that time; However, Canaan's name is always listed last among the sons of Ham. The fulfillment of the curse against him occurred when the children of Israel entered the Land of Canaan. All descendants of Canaan who were not killed were enslaved, but this incident was never meant to be a justification for modern slavery.

A RIFT IN NOAH'S FAMILY

Of all that Noah experienced through the flood, the only words attributed to him in the Biblical record, were curses on his grandson Canaan, and blessings on his sons Shem and Japheth. Once again, verses 25–27 say, "Cursed be Canaan! The lowest of slaves will he be to his brothers. Praise be to the Lord, the God of Shem! May Canaan be the slave of Shem. May God extend Japheth's territory; may Japheth live in the tents of Shem, and may Canaan be the slave of Japheth." Apparently, Noah said nothing of or to Ham, but what a tragic burden Canaan would have to bear, all because of his father's wickedness.

The rift, which developed in Noah's family showed that a cleansed earth, a new covenant, and a fresh start, was not enough to reverse the path, which led to the destruction of mankind in the first place. Imaginably, the relationship between Noah and his son Ham was never again the same. Nor was it ever again the same among Noah's three sons. The potential for sibling rivalry between the brothers probably increased. Rather than becoming a united family and one with brothers who felt equal, they became a fragmented family with one brother being told his offspring would be a slave to the others. This meant that throughout the generations, Noah's sons would always be fighting each other, because slavery occurs and is sustained through violence, and war.

Verses 28-29 reveal that after the flood, Noah lived 350 years, to an age of 950 years, and then the sentence of death, which all humans face, was carried out on him. The flood occurred during the year 1656, which reveals that if Noah died 350 years later, he lived into the second millennium, and died around 2006 years after creation. It also exposes the fact that by the time he died the trajectory of his family was not heading in a positive direction. Not even a fresh start and the benefit of hindsight, were enough for Noah and his sons to reverse the tragedy, which occurred during the fall of mankind in the Garden of Eden. If they could not save mankind, time would prove it was increasingly unlikely that anyone on earth could. A Savior would have to come from heaven.

GENESIS CHAPTER TEN

The previous chapter discussed Noah and his family's safe exit from the ark, and God's command, particularly to Shem, Ham, and Japheth to be fruitful and multiply. He also gave them instructions concerning their diet, civic behavior toward each other, and toward the rest of creation. Sadly, things took a negative turn because Noah drank too much wine, and laid naked in his tent. His son Ham somehow disrespected him, which resulted in Noah pronouncing a curse of slavery on Ham's son Canaan. Chapter 10 provides a record of the early descendants of Noah's three sons, who became forefathers of all humanity after them. Through them God replenished populations of the earth.

Verse 1 commences with the claim that it is an account of the descendants of Shem, Ham, and Japheth, Noah's sons, who themselves had sons after the flood. Obviously, they had daughters too, otherwise reproduction would have ceased. However, as a patriarchal society the record only listed the sons' names. Verse 1 also confirmed that Noah's sons started reproducing after the flood, as they were commanded to do. All of Adam and Eve's other descendants who were alive before the flood, died in it. Certainly, none of Cain's descendants lived beyond the flood. A new chapter began in the history of humanity.

JAPHETH'S DESCENDANTS

Verses 2-4 provide a record of the descendants of Noah's eldest son Japheth. Their names were, Gomer, Magog, Madai, Javan, Tubal, Meshek, and Tiras. Interestingly, it is these descendants, who are prophesied (Ezek 38:6; Rev 20:8) to wage war against Christ at His second coming. Japheth had seven sons, but only his descendants through Gomer and Javan were provided in this account. Gomer's sons were, Ashkenaz, Riphath, and Togarmah. Javan's sons were, Elishah, Tarshish, the Kittites, and the Rodanites. Verse 5 says that by these, the islands of the Gentiles were spread out in their lands, according to their languages, families, and nations.

HAM'S DESCENDANTS

A more exhaustive record was provided for the descendants of Ham. Verse 6 indicates that Ham had four sons, Cush, Egypt (Mizraim), Put (Phut), and Canaan. Canaan was most likely the eldest son, but his name is mentioned last because he was also the cursed son (Gen 9:25).

Verse 7 lists five of Cush' six sons. Their names were, Seba, Havilah, Sabtah, Raamah, and Sabteka. The sons of Raamah were Sheba and Dedan. Descendants of Sheba and Dedan became traders (Ezek 27:20, 38:13). Verse 8 shows the name of Cush' sixth son was Nimrod. He was listed separately because he distinguished himself from his brothers and other men of his time. It says he began to be a mighty one in the earth. He was a mighty hunter before the Lord: wherefore, it was said, "Even as Nimrod the mighty hunter before the Lord."

Nimrod's fame was reminiscent of pre-flood heroes who had gone before him (Gen 6:4), but who were destroyed in the flood. His prowess and skill at hunting animals caused him to be revered by men, which inadvertently resulted in him hunting them as well. They were willing to follow him because they believed he, rather than the Lord could protect them. Notice verse 10 says Nimrod built a kingdom, in which he created cities, the first of which were Babel (Babylon), Erech (Uruk), Accad (Akkad), and Calneh (Kalneh) in the land of Shinar.

Verse 11 declares that from Shinar, Nimrod moved on to Asshur (Assyria), where he built Nineveh, Rehoboth, Calah, and Resen. So, whereas God had given a command to be fruitful, and multiply, and replenish the earth (Gen 1:9), Nimrod's ambitious plan was to congregate in cities, thereby finding strength in numbers. It was a defiant plan to cause people to rely on him, and on each other, rather than on God. Once again, by building cities Nimrod continued in Cain's footsteps by perpetuating a system whereby humans would have dominion over each other, which God did not ordain in the beginning.

Verses 13-14 point out that Egypt (Mizraim) was the father of Ludim (Ludites), Anamim (Anamites), Lehabim (Lehabites), Naphtuhim (Naphtuhites), Pathrusim (Pathrusites), Casluhim (Kasluhites—from whom the Philistines came), and Caphtorim (Caphtorites). Interestingly, many nations and peoples have lost their identities and locations over the centuries, but the identity and location of Egypt remained much the same over time. This is further evidence that not all of Ham's descendants were cursed.

Verses 15–19, highlight Canaan's descendants. It says he was the father of Sidon his firstborn, Heth (Hittites), Jebusite, Amorite, Girgasite (Girgashites), Hivite, Arkite, Sinite, Arvadite, Zemarite, and Hamathite. Later the Canaanite clans scattered and the borders of Canaan reached from Sidon toward Gerar as far as Gaza, and then toward Sodom, Gomorrah, Admah and Zeboyim, as far as Lasha. The names of these descendants of Canaan's were those who were either killed or enslaved by the Nation of Israel, when they entered the Land of Canaan. Verse 20 concluded with the assertion, "These were the sons of Ham by their clans and languages, territories, and nations."

Canaan was cursed by his grandfather Noah, who designated him to be a slave of his brothers; yet, he was blessed by God to have offspring, and to inherit a coveted territory, which would later be known as the Promised Land. What this meant was, Canaan was under a curse, but for a while, his land was better than Japheth's or Shem's land. This proves that those who are blessed may not always appear to be, or to have the best, while those who are cursed can appear to prosper above all others. However, the prosperity of those who are cursed always eventually collapses. Hence, they should not be envied or emulated when they appear to be doing well, because such prosperity is always temporary.

SHEM'S DESCENDANTS

Verse 21 provides an interesting note. It says Shem was father of all the sons of Eber. However, Eber was Shem's grandson, so why was this note provided before listing his sons? This note was probably provided because Abraham was a descendant of Eber. It also provided context for the direction in which the Biblical record would pivot once Abraham came on the scene. He and his descendants would become its main characters, while all others would only be mentioned as they came into contact with Abraham, or his descendants. In that sense, Eber was an important figure.

Verse 22 shows that Shem had five sons, Elam, Ashur, Arphaxad, Lud, and Aram. Nonetheless, a record of descendants was provided for only two of Shem's five sons: Aram and Arphaxad. Aram would become important as his descendants often interacted with Arphaxad's descendants (Israel). For example, Aram is where Isaac and Jacob (Arphaxad's descendants) went to find wives. Descendants of Aram would also have multiple interactions with the Nation of Israel throughout their history. Therefore, a genealogy of

Aram's offspring was most likely to provide a framework of who they were. Verse 23 says, the sons of Aram were Uz, Hul, Gether, and Meshek (Mash).

Verse 24 points out that Arphaxad was father of Shelah, and Shelah was father of Eber. Two sons were born to Eber, one was Peleg (Division), because in his time the earth was divided. This division may be a reference to what occurred at the Tower of Babel, when God divided the earth by languages (Gen 11:1-9). This may have occurred about the time when Peleg was born. Chapter 11 will provide a more exhaustive record of Peleg's descendants since he was father of the covenant people.

Meanwhile, verses 26-30 indicate that Peleg's brother's Joktan, was father of Almodad, Sheleph, Hazarmaveth, Jerah, Hadoram, Uzal, Diklah, Obal, Abimael, Sheba, Ophir, Havilah, and Jobab. The area where they lived stretched from Mesha toward Sephar, in the eastern mountainous area. Verse 31 concluded by affirming that these were the sons of Shem, after their families, languages, territories, and nations. Additionally, verse 32 established these genealogical records as the clans of Noah's sons, according to their lines of descent, within their nations. From these the nations spread out over the earth after the flood.

GENESIS CHAPTER ELEVEN

The previous chapter provided records of the descendants of Noah's three sons, Shem, Ham, and Japheth. It showed that Nimrod was a prominent descendant of Ham's. He set out to establish his fame by building great cities. This chapter will examine the impact of his efforts to establish cities. It will scrutinize events from the Tower of Babel, which was located in his most famous city, Babylon, and which led to God dividing mankind based on their languages. A more exhaustive account of the descendants of Shem's son Arphaxad will also be provided, leading up to Abraham, who became one of the most renown figures in all three monotheistic faiths: Judaism, Christianity, and Islam.

TOWER OF BABEL (BABYLON)

Genesis 10:10 revealed that Babel (Babylon) was the first city Nimrod built in the land of Shinar (Babylonia). This chapter will provide insight into what occurred in the cities he built, and the purpose for which he built them. Verse 1 states that the whole world had one language and common speech. A common language meant they understood what each other said, which fostered cooperation among them. A common speech meant they understood how things were said, whether spoken or unspoken, and were united in a shared purpose.

Verse 2 notes that as people moved east, or from the east, they found a plain in Shinar (Babylonia) and settled there. This was an act of rebellion against God's command to replenish the earth. Notice, they settled in the plain as a sign that they were not going any further. They respected Nimrod's efforts to congregate in the plain, more than they did God's command to populate the earth!

Verse 3 reveals that they said to each other, "Come, let's make bricks and bake them thoroughly." The area where they chose to settle was void of stone, hence, they decided to bake bricks. This took time and effort, but what was for sure, tents, which were common dwelling places at that time, were not an option. They intended to establish permanent, rather than temporary dwellings. This was a sign they had no plans to ever leave Babylon!

Verse 4 discloses that they decided to build a city, with a tower that reaches to the heavens, so they may make a name for themselves, because they feared being scattered over the face of the whole earth. Having one language and speech and living in a city with a tower that reached the heavens, was a recipe to return to greater wickedness than their predecessors before the flood.

In fact, the reason for the high tower may not only have been for worship, but also for protection against another flood. In which case, they would have been demonstrating mistrust towards God, and doubts about His promise to never again destroy the entire earth by flood. It may be that in their minds, a high tower would have offered a certain measure of security. If this was the way they were thinking, it might have been wiser to build the tower on a mountain rather than in a plain. However, rational thinking is often absent in the presence of rebellion.

Another important observation was their concern about making a name for themselves. They believed that being scattered would cause them to go into obscurity, while being together, and building a city with an imposing tower would enhance their fame. They wanted to become heroes like Nimrod, rather than remaining nameless like those who died in the flood. Yet not a single name of those who attempted to build that tower remained in the historical record beyond their lifetime. The real purpose for the tower of Babylon was to serve as a symbol of pride for a generation eager to make a name for themselves, and an object for man-made worship in defiance of the true God. It was an early humanistic symbol, but God ensured that it did not last.

GOD'S RESPONSE TO THE TOWER OF BABEL

Verse 5 uses anthropomorphic language by asserting that the Lord came down to see the city and the tower they were building. It depicted God as an eyewitness to what they were doing. He came down to see it for Himself! Interestingly, God could have stopped the project during its planning phase, but He apparently allowed them to make progress before He intervened.

Verse 6 discloses the Lord's response to what He saw. It does not reveal whom He spoke to when He came down, but He expressed concern that if as one people, speaking the same language, they began to build a city and a tower to reach heaven, nothing they planned to do would be impossible for them.

It should be noted that God was not afraid of their oneness in language and speech, but it was obvious He was concerned about how quickly after the flood, their oneness resulted in rebellion. If left uncheck, there would indeed be no limit to their wickedness. Satan's power would have been strengthened if the people were allowed to remain as one, and future generations would have been progressively, and immeasurably perverse. Something needed to be done to slow their pace of degeneration.

Verse 7 reveals God's judgement against them. Again, anthropomorphic language was used to illustrate that God did not act from heaven, but decided to come down and confuse their language, so they could not understand each other. God was in their midst, and they did not know it! Thankfully, His judgement was not proportionate to their sin. He could have and would have been right to kill all of them! Instead, He decided to only confuse their language. Suddenly, they were unable to understand each other, which halted their ability to work together.

Their attempt to establish humanism as an alternative to true religion, failed, because God personally intervened. Some today might have separated them by race, but God separated them by language, because it was their language rather than their race, which united them in revolt.

Verse 8 reiterates that the Lord scattered them from there over all the earth, and they stopped building the city. He made it difficult for men with divided tongues to work together with united hearts and hands. He forced them into the very situation they were afraid of, being scattered. Moving forward, anyone who joined them wherever they were scattered, would have to learn a new language. God's command to be fruitful and increase in number and fill the earth, was back on track!

Verse 9 echoes this by asserting that Babel earned its name, because it was there that the Lord confused the language of the whole world, and from there the Lord scattered them over the face of the whole earth. Once scattered, they never came together in this way again. God's purpose is always accomplished with, or without, men's willing cooperation.

SHEM'S DESCENDANTS THROUGH ARPHAXAD

As mentioned earlier, Shem had five sons (Gen 9:22); however, the Bible only provides accounts of the descendants of two of his sons. Aram's descendants were listed in the previous chapter (Gen 9:23-29), because they interacted with Abraham and his descendants. This chapter provides an account of

Shem's other son Arphaxad. From this point on, focus of the Biblical record became centered primarily on his descendants, as they became the covenant people of God. Other peoples are only mentioned as they came into contact with his descendants.

Verses 10–11 assert that this is the account of Shem's family line. Two years after the flood, Shem was 100 years old, when he became father of Arphaxad, he lived 500 years and had other sons and daughters. However, verses 12–32 provide an account of Arphaxad only because he was a forefather of Abraham.

ABRAM'S HISTORY

Verse 26 provides a record of Abraham's immediate family. It indicates that when Terah was seventy-five years old, he became the father of Abram, Nahor, and Haran. And Haran became the father of Lot. Notice Haran's age when he became Lot's father was not provided because his mention was for a different purpose. It was for the purpose noted in verse 28, where it says that Haran died before his father Terah in his native land of Ur of the Chaldees. Therefore, Lot was listed along with Terah's other sons because he became Terah's responsibility once his father Haran died. In other words, Lot was Abram's nephew, but they were like brothers. In fact, he would play a more significant role in Abram's life than his actual remaining brother Nahor would.

It is noteworthy that Ur of the Chaldees was mentioned as Abram's family's native land. It is unclear how his brother Haran died at such an early age. This was unusual in those days, but it highlighted Abram's early experience with tragedy. It may have also contributed to his family's predisposal to exiting that place. Ur was an idolatrous land. In fact, it was stated (Josh 24:2) that Abram's family served other gods in that land. This was an important mention because Abraham would become known as "father of the faithful" (Rom 4:11), but his early history was anything but faithful. More importantly, his early experiences with paganism would play a significant role in his life as he began to interact with the true God. A beautiful picture of spiritual growth on Abram's part, and patience on God's part would emerge.

Youngman stated that Ur was the center of worship of the moon god, Sin.[1] The moon god's temple was placed high on an enormous mount called a ziggurat, which was ascended by hundreds of stone stairs. People gathered in the temple, called the "House of the Great Light," where human sacrifice, usually of the first-born male, was practiced. A ghastly ritual

---

1. Youngman, *The Lands and Peoples of the Living Bible*, 13.

was also performed on some occasions when a reigning king died and was buried. Human sacrifice on a large scale would occur. He went to his rest surrounded by his soldiers, courtiers, women, and attendants, all victims of a wholesale slaughter. This was the world from which God called Abraham.

Verse 29 mentions that Abram and his brother Nahor took wives. The name of Abram's wife was Sarai, and the name of Nahor's wife was Milcah, the daughter of Haran, who was the father of Milcah, and Iscah. This meant that Nahor's wife was his and Abraham's niece and Lot's sister.

As for Abram's wife Sarai, once again, his father Terah was not only an idolater, but he may have been a polygamist as well. Abram revealed this in Genesis 20:12, where he referred to Sarai (Sarah) as his father's daughter from a different wife. Hence, Abram was predisposed to the idea of polygamy when Sarai presented it to him as an option to start a family of his own through Hagar. He was also predisposed to human sacrifice, when God tested him to sacrifice his son Isaac. These were common practices in Ur of the Chaldees and may have been practiced in Abram's extended family.

Verse 30 initiates a recurring theme in reference to Sarai. It says, she was barren, and had no children. Verse 31 mentions that Terah took his son Abram and Lot the son of Haran, and Sarai his daughter-in-law and they left Ur of the Chaldees, to go to the land of Canaan. Youngman suggests that because Terah was a moon-worshipper, when Hammurabi conquered Ur and set up sun-worship, claiming the sun-god gave him his laws, Terah refused to change, and immigrated to Haran, where the moon god ziggurat was still worshipped in a temple called, "House of Joys."[2]

Whatever the case, the Bible says they came to Haran, and dwelt there. It meant they were headed to Canaan, but they only made it half the way as they stopped in Haran and settled there. This verse indicates that Terah was the reason they left Ur, but while he may have had his own reasons for doing so, Chapter 12 provides greater insight into the real reason why Abram left. It shows he was prompted by God to do so.

Verse 32 ends this chapter by indicating that Terah lived 205 years and died in Haran. Speculations abound about why God did not allow Terah to make it to Canaan, but those conjectures cannot be substantiated. At 205 years, he was an old man for his time and his age may have hindered him from completing the journey. However, the idea that God did not allow him to make it to Canaan because he was an idolater, does not hold merit, because there were already idolaters living in Canaan, and that remained the case for hundreds of years later. The departure of Terah's family from Ur, was the beginning of a unique faith-walk for Abram. Therefore, while his father

2. Youngman, *The Lands and Peoples of the Living Bible*, 19.

only made half the journey, he would eventually make it the entire way. Hopefully, this is encouraging to those who are first-generation believers; God is still faithful to His people, and He does enable them to complete every journey on which he places them.

GENESIS CHAPTER TWELVE

The previous chapter started with rebellion of those who were determined to make a name for themselves, by establishing a city and building a tower, intending it to reach heaven. God Himself came down and thwarted their plans by confusing their language. As such, they were scattered to various parts of the earth. The chapter also provided a history of Shem's descendants all the way to Abram. It described Abram's immediate family and their move from Ur of the Chaldees to Haran, where his father Terah died. This chapter will continue from there to examine Abram's journey into Canaan and events surrounding his temporary stay in Egypt.

ABRAM'S FIRST CALL

Verse 1 says the Lord had told Abram to leave his country, his people, and his father's household and go to the land He would show him. This seems to contradict verse 31 of the previous chapter, where it said Terah took his family and left Ur, which made it seem as though the idea to leave Ur came from Terah. As mentioned earlier, Terah may have had his own reasons for leaving Ur, which may indeed have been a result of the new king, Hammurabi, who changed their worship from the moon god to the sun god. However, the True God instructed Abraham to leave Ur, and his departure may have coincided with that of his father Terah, so they left together.

Another reasonable explanation could be, Abram shared the command God had given him with his family and they all, except for Nahor and his family, decided to leave Ur and head to Canaan. The only problem was, God intended for Abram to leave his people, and only take his wife and everything they owned, which was probably very little. His father Terah, and his nephew Lot were among his people. Therefore, they were not supposed to be on the journey with him, unless of course, his father, being advanced in years, and his nephew having become his father's responsibility, had by then become part of Abram's household.

In any case, the command was clear. Abram needed to get out of his native land and go to a land God would show him. In verse 2, God made four promises to Abram. He told him: 1. I will make you a great nation; 2. I will bless you; 3. I will make your name great; and 4. you will be a blessing. God's promises to Abram continued in verse 3, where He repeated His intent to bless him, but He also added that He would curse those who cursed Abram, and in him all families of the earth would be blessed. These were lofty promises, which Abram may have shared with his family, and which made them all more eager to get out of Ur of the Chaldees.

ABRAM'S SECOND CALL

While the family was living in Haran, verse 4 says Abram left, as the Lord had told him, and Lot went with him. Under normal circumstances, Lot would have been one of Abram's people, whom he was supposed to leave, but once again, Abram may have inherited responsibility for him due to the death of Lot's father Haran, and his grandfather Terah, who had assumed responsibility for him. With both of them deceased, Abram became his closest relative.

Ultimately, Lot did what most people would have done if they learned that God had promised to give their uncle an entire country, and to bless him in the way He promised to bless Abram. While this was a walk of faith for Abram, it may have begun as a walk of fortune for Lot. He went with Abram to see how things would unfold.

Verse 4 continued by saying Abram was seventy-five years old when he left Haran to go to Canaan. Verse 5 says he also took Sarai his wife (who would have been 65 years old), Lot his brother's son, and all their possessions they had accumulated, and the servants they had gotten while in Haran. They set out for the land of Canaan, and safely made it there. Interestingly, verse 6 says Abram passed through the land until he reached Shechem, to the oak of Moreh. And the Canaanites were in the land, yet none of them seemed to view Abram as a threat, or otherwise sought to bother him.

In verse 7, it shows that the Lord appeared to Abram and told him, to his offspring (not him), He would give that land. So, Abram built an altar there to the Lord, who had appeared to him. And all of this time, Lot was with him, hearing of these promises and waiting to see how they would unfold.

Verse 8 shows that Abram departed from the area near Shechem and journeyed to the mountain on the east in Bethel, and pitched a tent, having Bethel to the west, and Ai to the east. There he also built an altar to the Lord, and for the first time, Scripture indicated that Abram, a former pagan (Josh 24:2), called on the name of the Lord. After building an alter and calling on the name of the Lord, verse 9 indicates that he journeyed even further to the south.

Verse 10 says there was a famine in the land, and Abram went down to Egypt, to live there for a while because the famine was severe. It seemed, in times of famine Egypt was the place to go to find relief. Many years later that would also be the reason the children of Israel would go to Egypt, but it would take them four hundred years before they would be able to leave.

It is paramount to observe what happened to Abram shortly after reaching the land God told him to go to and promised would be an inheritance for his offspring; a severe famine occurred! The question begs to be asked, was this simply a natural disaster, or was it a test of faith for Abram? If it was a test of faith for Abram alone, why did the entire land and its people have to suffer? This leads to the conclusion that it may have been both, a natural disaster, which also served as a test of faith for Abram. Famines were common occurrences in that region, but it was also an early test of Abram's faith. It also demonstrated that obedience to God does not mean life will be trouble-free.

ABRAM'S JOURNEY TO EGYPT

Verses 11-12 show that Abram concocted a scheme by which he would attempt to preserve his life. It says as he was about to enter Egypt, he told his wife Sarai, that he knew what a beautiful woman she was. Therefore, when the Egyptians saw her, they would decide to kill him, but let her live, to get her for themselves.

Abram's reasoning may have been informed by what he knew about the people of his time, but it was not informed by his faith in what God said to him. Based on the promises God made, the Egyptians were incapable of killing him; especially since the promises were yet to be fulfilled. Additionally, Abram seemed willing to sacrifice his wife to save his own life. On the brighter side, Sarai was over 65 years old at that time. So, to be considered so beautiful as to cause other men to want to murder her husband to get her, was a tribute to how God preserved her for His purpose. It meant at her age she was still more beautiful than the younger women of Egypt.

The fact that Scripture exposed Abram's reasoning in this situation, is a tribute to its authenticity. Abram remains one of the most revered characters in the Bible, and yet this passage points out that he was not perfect. When the Bible is compared with other religious books, this level of honesty about such highly respected individuals sets it apart from those books.

Verse 13 says Abram told his wife to say she was his sister (Gen 20:12), so that he would be treated well for her sake and his life would be spared because of her. He placed the burden for his safety on his wife, rather than on God, whose name he called upon at Bethel. He also exposed both his wife and the Egyptians to the possibility of sin. Most importantly, he assumed that by killing him to get his wife the Egyptians placed higher value on adultery than they did on murder.

Abram's plot provided a few peripheral insights. It showed the value people in his time, including pagans, placed on marriage. A woman was only available if her husband was deceased. So, he thought the Egyptians would kill him to get his wife. It showed that at that point in Abram's journey, his faith was still in its infancy, even though God had spoken to him, and he had reached a point where he built an altar and called on the name of the Lord. Another insight is, before Abram arrived in Egypt, he reasoned what the Egyptians would do, and what his fate would be once they saw his wife, yet he decided to go to Egypt anyway. His calculations were good reasons for him not to go there.

Finally, a very important insight was the fact that Lot was with him the entire time. And, if he had become like a father to Lot, certainly Sarai had become like a mother to him. Therefore, to observe Abram's willingness to sacrifice her to save his own life, must have been unsettling for Lot. It was certainly not a good example.

ABRAM'S DECEPTION

Verses 14-15 show that when Abram arrived in Egypt, the Egyptians saw that Sarai was a very beautiful woman, and when Pharaoh's officials saw her, they praised her to Pharaoh, and she was taken into his palace. Immediately, Abram's concern became reality! The first and only thing the Egyptians seemed to notice about Sarai, was her beauty. She was obviously stunning, even at her age, but they cared less if there were other character deficiencies worth knowing about her. They were only captivated by her beauty!

Also worth noticing, as beautiful as Sarai was, none of the officials wanted her for themselves. Instead, they praised her to Pharaoh! They obviously had the same fear Abram did. If they had beautiful wives, their lives might have been in danger as well!

Verse 16 says Pharaoh treated Abram well for Sarai's sake, and Abram acquired sheep and cattle, male and female donkeys, male and female servants, and camels. In other words, at that point, Pharaoh, rather than God, blessed Abram and made him rich, while Sarai was in danger of sexual violation. The gifts Pharaoh gave to Abram, assuming Sarai to be his sister and not his wife, were payments for her. Pharaoh was buying Abram's favor, and Abram was selling it. If God did not intervene quickly, something bad would have happened!

It would be a massive oversight to ignore that servants were among the gifts Pharaoh gave Abram. Undoubtedly, Hagar, was one of those servants. She would eventually become Sarai's rival. But, had she been as beautiful as Sarai, she would have been among the women in Pharaoh's palace, rather than among his gifts of servants. In giving Hagar as a gift to Abram, in an ironic twist, he caused Abram more trouble than he could have imagined. He created a rift in Abram's family that Abram was incapable of reconciling, and which exists to this very day.

GOD'S INTERVENTION

Verse 17 says the Lord inflicted serious diseases on Pharaoh and his household because of Abram's wife Sarai. Not only did Pharaoh suffer with serious diseases, but his household also suffered. All of this, yet he had no idea what his offense was. His suffering, and that of his household was due to Abram's plot! It is not clear how Pharaoh and his household discovered that their diseases were because of Sarai, except that she may have been the only person in the household who did not suffer with the diseases the Lord inflicted.

In those days, people were highly superstitious. If they became ill, they associated it with something the gods were punishing them for. Hence, Sarai would have stood out, if she appeared to be the only one who was not being punished. In any case, had God not set about to rescue Sarai from Pharaoh, Abram appeared to have no desire to do so, and Lot observed this.

Verses 18–19 represent the climax of Abram's ill-conceived plan. Pharaoh summoned him, which no doubt must have been terrifying. Then Pharaoh asked him a series of questions: "What have you done to me?" "Why didn't you tell me she was your wife?" "Why did you say, 'She is my sister,' so that I took her to be my wife?" Pharaoh told him, "Here is your wife. Take her and go!" This was the point at which if Pharaoh was capable of killing Abram, he would have done so, and his actions would have been justified. But God not only rescued Sarai, He also rescued Abram from the hand of Pharaoh.

ABRAM'S EXPULSION FROM EGYPT

Once again, it is not clear how Pharaoh discovered Abram's scheme, but once he did, unlike Abram, he moved quickly to rectify his mistake. He conducted himself more honorably than Abram did, and certainly more honorably than Abram gave him credit for. Pharaoh said he took Sarai to be his wife, but there is no evidence to suggest she became his wife, especially since he gave her back to Abram, telling him to take his wife and go. It is doubtful he would have been able to return her had he sexually taken Sarai to be his wife.

Verse 20 says Pharaoh gave orders about Abram to his men, and they sent him on his way, with his wife and everything he had. In other words, even though Abram deceived Pharaoh, he allowed him to leave with all the gifts he had given him, and with his wife. Pharaoh had every right to take back his gifts, but he didn't. He willingly allowed Abram to plunder him, so that he could get the diseases lifted from his household.

This episode in Abram's life should never be forgotten in any discussion about how he acquired his material blessings. Indeed, God blessed him, but Pharaoh did as well. Abram learned from this incident, which may be the reason in his future dealings he was very careful about accepting gifts from other leaders who offered them to him. He did not want them to be able to take credit for making him rich.

GENESIS CHAPTER THIRTEEN

The previous chapter provided details about Abram's travels to Egypt to avoid a severe famine in Canaan. It also summarized Abram's plot to preserve his life by deceiving Pharaoh into believing Sarai was his sister, rather than his wife. Once his plot was discovered, Pharaoh expelled him from Egypt with a bounty of livestock, goods and servants. As a result, Abram left Egypt much richer than when he entered. This chapter will examine a sharp dispute, which developed between Abram and Lot. Possible underlying causes for this dispute will be examined, as it was an event from which they never fully recovered, and which caused them to permanently separate from each other.

Verse 1 begins with the statement, "So Abram went up from Egypt to the Negev, with his wife and everything he had, and Lot went with him." The fact that Lot went with Abram to Egypt, and made it out alive presents two possibilities: 1. He was not married, or 2. If he was married, his wife was not as beautiful as Sarai, which sheltered him from the concern Abram had about losing his life because of her beauty. This verse also reiterated whose wife Sarai really was. She was indeed Abram's, rather than Pharaoh's wife, and what God had joined together, not even Abram was able to put asunder.

Verse 2 echoed how Abram gained the riches he had at that point. It says he had become very wealthy in livestock and in silver and gold. Pharaoh paid him off well! But was the famine in Canaan over by the time Pharaoh expelled him from Egypt? More than likely, it was not. This meant, the places to which Abram traveled after leaving Egypt, were places to which he could have gone instead of going to Egypt.

ABRAM RETRACED HIS STEPS

After leaving Egypt, Abram went to the Negev, which was desert territory. This was not the most ideal place to go in good times, much less during a severe famine. Therefore, verses 3-4 indicate that from the Negev Abram went from place to place until he came to Bethel, to the place between Bethel and Ai where his tent had been earlier and where he had first built an altar. There Abram called on the name of the Lord (Gen 12:8).

In the previous chapter, Abram left the vicinity of Bethel to go to an area surrounding the Negev Now, on his way back, he left the Negev to go back to the vicinity of Bethel. Apparently, this was what Abram should have done in the first place when he decided to go to Egypt. The word "Beth-El," literally means House of God. The House of God is always a great place to find nourishment and refuge during physical and spiritual famines.

Interestingly, verse 5 says Lot, who was moving about with Abram, also had flocks and herds and tents. Hence, some of the blessings Abram received, spilled over to Lot. This meant Lot was now capable of being on his own. Verse 6 says the land could not support them while they stayed together, because their possessions were so great that they were not able to stay together.

Normally, this situation would be a good problem for family and friends to have. However, something apparently occurred to fracture the relationship between Abram and Lot, such that they acted more like foes than like family, and more like enemies than like friends. No doubt, his experiences in Egypt, and possible diminished respect for Abram after observing his treatment of his wife Sarai, could have been a contributing factor to their adversarial relationship. In any case, it was like having grown, well-paid working adults, living at home with their parents. There comes a time when they need to move out on their own. That time had come for Lot.

QUARRELING BETWEEN LOT AND ABRAM

Verse 7 indicates that quarreling arose between Abram's herders and Lot's. The Canaanites and Perizzites were also living in the land at that time, which meant they were possibly aware of the rift between Abram and Lot, who were foreigners among them. Interestingly, they were together from the time they left their native land, Ur of the Chaldees. They were together while the family lived in Haran; together during the moved to Canaan, and the trip to Egypt and back to Canaan. In essence, they were together while they were poor, but could not stay together when they became rich. This is reflective of many families today, which have been destroyed by the success they were willing to sacrifice so much to achieve.

Once again, the fact that the Canaanites and Perizzites were mentioned as being in the land, indicates they did not view Abram's and Lot's presence as a threat to them. In fact, once quarreling arose between them, Abram would begin to have a better relationship with the inhabitants of the land than he did with his nephew Lot.

To resolve the contention, verses 8–9 indicate that Abram told Lot, "Let's not have any quarreling between you and me, or between your herders and mine, for we are close relatives. Is not the whole land before you? Let's part company. If you go to the left, I'll go to the right; if you go to the right, I'll go to the left."

These verses provided further details to suggest that quarreling was not only occurring between the herdsmen, but also between Abram and Lot. Previously, Lot seemed contented to be a silent beneficiary of Abram's blessings, but that changed. He finally began to view his uncle as his rival. Riches affected his level of respect for his uncle, but again, the conduct he observed from Abram while in Egypt could have also played a role.

Regardless, Abram's statement seemed to indicate that quarreling was unnecessary. More importantly, this was a quarrel Lot could not win, because God had not, to that point, made any promises to him. In fact, he was blessed because of Abram. Nevertheless, this was obviously not a quarrel which could be resolved by staying together and trying to work it out. This quarrel could only be resolved by parting ways. Indeed, some disputes can only be resolved through distance rather than discourse. Sadly, once they parted ways, there is no evidence that Abram and Lot ever again enjoyed a cordial relationship with each other. The fact is, God can enable reconciliation between Himself and anyone, but sometimes humans are incapable of reconciling with each other.

ABRAM AND LOT SEPARATE

Verse 10 provides a few important insights. It says Lot looked around and saw the whole plain of the Jordan toward Zoar, and that it was well watered, like the garden of the Lord (Eden), and like the land of Egypt. This meant, rather than going to Egypt, Zoar was an area to which Abram could have gone to escape the severe famine. As for Lot, the fact that he decided to choose first, rather than allowing his uncle to do so, was evidence of his character. Little did he know, this was his choice of a lifetime. This choice not only impacted where he would live, but how he would live. This would result in his downfall.

It is not clear if Lot had ever seen the garden of the Lord (Eden), since God restricted access to it, but being from Ur (located in modern-day Iraq) he may have known where it was located. He obviously heard about it and knew how perfect it was. As such, he compared the plain of Jordan to it, which meant the plain of Jordan was more beautiful, at that time, than the area where he was standing, and where Abraham lived. Lot also seemed to have been impressed by what he saw in Egypt, and he aspired to live in a place like it. It also infers that he may not have wanted to leave Egypt and could have harbored a grudge against Abram for getting him expelled from there. His plight was to find a place, which offered everything he had seen in Egypt.

From a distance, Lot looked around and saw the whole plain of the Jordan toward Zoar. There is no evidence he had ever previously set foot in that area, nor did he know anything about the people who lived there. Yet, verse 11 says, he chose for himself the whole plain of the Jordan and set out toward the east. So, he and Abram parted company. This was not a pleasant break-up, yet it was necessary for the sake of peace, and to avoid bloodshed between close relatives. This divorce was due to God-ordained irreconcilable differences.

Verse 12 points out that Abram stayed in the land of Canaan, while Lot lived among the cities of the plain and pitched his tents near Sodom. Lot made a fateful decision, and it would cost him dearly. Little did he know, he left the Land of Promise to go to a land of promiscuity.

Hence, verse 13 points out that the people of Sodom were wicked and sinning greatly against the Lord. It is doubtful Lot knew much about the people who lived in Sodom before he went there to live. This was a big decision, but for Lot, it was an uninformed decision, which basically set his life on a downward trajectory. His riches could not be sustained in such a wicked environment. He would either join the crowd and spend his wealth on wickedness or have to protect them from being stolen by wicked people.

After Lot looked up and chose for himself the place where he would live, verse 14 presents a contrast. It says the Lord said to Abram "Look around from where you are, to the north and south, to the east and west. All the land that you see I will give you and your offspring forever. I will make your offspring like the dust of the earth, so that if anyone could count the dust, then your offspring could be counted. Go, walk through the length and breadth of the land, for I am giving it to you." It was as though God waited until Lot left, before He revealed to Abram the blessings He had in store for him.

Abram did not choose for himself a place to live, God chose for him. More importantly, while Lot chose a place to live based on his sight, God showed Abram where he would live, and revealed the blessings He had in store for him, which he would receive by faith. The land God showed Abram was not as impressive at that time, as the Plain of Jordan, otherwise

Lot would have chosen it. Additionally, Abram was over 75 years old and Sarai ten years younger, when God made these promises about countless offspring, yet at his mature age, Abram had no children. Nevertheless, God told him his offspring would become as numerous as dust on the earth, which meant the land he showed him would only be their starting point, they would eventually become too numerous to fit in that land and some would be scattered to the ends of the earth.

Once God made promises to Abram, verse 18 says Abram went to live near the great trees of Mamre at Hebron, where he pitched his tents. He also built an altar to the Lord there. Abram settled down once Lot left, and once God showed him the extent of his inheritance. Abram lived as a stranger and foreigner in the land God promised him. But he was not a stranger to God, nor was God a stranger to him. Wherever he settled, he built an altar. This meant worship began to play a significant role in his life. Believers today can also worship in confidence because Jesus said He was going to prepare a place for them that where He is, there they may also be (John 14:2). In other words, they also have an eternal Promised Land.

GENESIS CHAPTER FOURTEEN

The previous chapter examined Abram's return to Canaan after being expelled from Egypt. He returned with far more possessions than he had when he left. But Lot was still with him, and he also had acquired many possessions. Therefore, they could not stay together because quarrelling arose between them. Abram settled the dispute by allowing Lot to choose another location in which to live; Lot chose Sodom. After he departed to go to his new residence in Sodom, God appeared to Abram and showed him the extent of the inheritance He would give his descendants. So, Abram settled in an area near the great trees of Mamre in Hebron. While Abram was settled, this chapter will survey the unsettling results of Lot's decision, and Abram's campaign to rescue him from those who invaded Sodom and took him captive.

WAR BETWEEN NATION-STATES

Verses 1-4 explain that during the time when Amraphel was king of Shinar (Babylon), Arioch king of Ellasar, Kedorlaomer king of Elam and Tidal king of Goyim, these kings went to war against Bera king of Sodom, Birsha king of Gomorrah, Shinab king of Admah, Shemeber king of Zeboyim, and the king of Bela (that is Zoar). All these latter kings joined forces in the Valley of Siddim (that is, the Dead Sea Valley). For twelve years they had been subject to Kedorlaomer, but in the thirteenth year they rebelled.

This is the first Biblical record of war between nation-states, and it occurred because one group of nations, which were subjects of another group, became tired of their subservient position and decided to rebel. Interestingly, the conquering kings were from areas close to Ur of the Chaldees, where Abram and Lot were originally from. Those kings travelled a long way to make war and to subjugate other nations to their rule. Notice, the only king's name, which was omitted from the list, was the name of the king of Bela (Zoar). This could be because Zoar was such a small territory that a king of that area would have been afforded little significance. In any case, what it highlighted was, the area where Lot chose to live was occupied, subservient, and as previously mentioned, wicked territory.

Verses 5–7 indicate that in the fourteenth year, Kedorlaomer and the kings allied with him went out and defeated the Rephaites in Ashteroth Karnaim, the Zuzites in Ham, the Emites in Shaveh Kiriathaim and the Horites in the hill country of Seir, as far as El Paran near the desert. Then they turned back and went to En Mishpat (that is, Kadesh), and they conquered the whole territory of the Amalekites, as well as the Amorites who were living in Hazezon Tamar.

These verses basically indicate that on their way to fight a war in the Valley of Siddim (that is, the Dead Sea Valley), and to put down a rebellion, those conquering kings wiped out every nation through which they passed. This was indeed a formidable force! There is no record of how many lives were lost along the way, but indeed the subjected nations had much to fear, and may have received news before-hand about the fierceness of the force, and impending calamity they were facing.

Verses 8–9 state that the king of Sodom, the king of Gomorrah, the king of Admah, the king of Zeboyim and the king of Bela (that is, Zoar) marched out and drew up their battle lines in the Valley of Siddim against Kedorlaomer king of Elam, Tidal king of Goyim, Amraphel king of Shinar and Arioch king of Ellasar—four kings against five, but the four outmatched the five in power and skill of war. The four had travelled a long way to put down the rebellion and were determined to do so.

Verse 10 reveals that the Valley of Siddim was full of tar pits, and when the kings of Sodom and Gomorrah fled, some of the men fell into them while the rest fled to the hills. Observe that the battle was fought on their territory, but that did not appear to be an advantage for them. They were obviously unskilled in war-planning, otherwise the tar pits could have been used as traps into which the invaders would fall, and the hills could have provided offensive superiority. Instead, they fell into their own tar pits, and fled to the hills in fear. Notice also, the king of Sodom and king of Gomorrah fled, but there is no mention of what happened to the other three kings, whether they were capture or killed. However, when kings fled, it was a sure sign of weakness and expectation of defeat.

LOT TAKEN PRISONER OF WAR

Verse 11 points out that the four kings seized all the goods of Sodom and Gomorrah and all their food; then they went away. Seizure of all the goods and food, served as repayment for the tribute they had stopped paying, and it was the victor's spoil. But it was also a sign of a demoralizing defeat! Seizure of all the goods and food meant those who were left behind had nothing to eat. They were left destitute and would have to struggle to survive to put the pieces of their lives, and their cities, together again.

Of greater significance, verse 12 noted that they also carried off Abram's nephew Lot and his possessions, since he was living in Sodom. In other words, to evade capture, Lot's leader, the king of Sodom fled, but Lot himself was not so fortunate. He was captured along with all his possessions. Therefore, he shared in the calamities of those among whom he chose to live. It was impossible for him, as it would be for anyone else, to become embedded in such a wicked environment, without being impacted by it, and sharing in its punishment.

Notice verse 12 also provided a reminder of the family relations between Abram and Lot. It was a reminder that Lot was in the wrong place. It was similar to the name of the son of a righteous man, being associated with sinful behavior. Not only did they carry off Lot, they also carried off his possessions, which were the source of his contention with his uncle. In fact, Lot gained his possessions because of Abram, and some of them may have been taken from Abram. But the invaders carried off Lot, everything he held dear, and all he built his life upon.

ABRAM RESCUES LOT

Verse 13 reveals that a man who had escaped came and reported to Abram the Hebrew that Lot had been captured. Abram was living near the great trees of Mamre the Amorite, a brother of Eshkol and Aner, all of whom were allied with Abram. These three brothers (Mamre, Eshkol, and Aner) were Abram's friends, but at face-value, their forces were no match for the invaders. Yet, they align themselves with Abram, as a matter of trust, and to avert the likelihood of themselves becoming victims and subjects of the invaders. It is also important to note that there was no one else who could help Lot. This was a mission of mercy to save Lot from a tragic end.

Verse 14 shows that when Abram heard his relative had been taken captive, he called out the 318 trained men born in his household and went in pursuit as far as Dan. These 318 trained men were born in Abram's household but may not have been living in his household at the time, which meant it may have taken some effort to get them all assembled and ready for the mission.

Additionally, this was the only war the Bible records Abram being involved in, so it is not clear why he kept trained men in his household. The most reasonable explanation might be, these men were trained to protect his possessions, and to respond to those who would make war against him to take what he had. Their skills would be tested against a force, which had devastated every other force it came up against.

Verses 15-16 indicate that during the night, Abram divided his men to attack them and he routed them, pursuing them as far as Hobah, north of Damascus. He recovered all the goods and brought back his relative Lot and his possessions, together with the women and other people.

Abram demonstrated that he was not a stranger to the strategies of war. He divided his men to attack the enemy from multiple directions, and to make his few men seem like many. He also attacked at nighttime when the invading army was tired and asleep. He routed them, pursuing them along the same path they had taken when they flattened those nations on their way to the Valley of Siddim. Most importantly, he recovered everything and everyone they had taken. This meant, the invading force returned home empty. The campaign they thought was successful became a sudden failure, because they took Abram's nephew Lot, which drew Abram (and his God) into the fight.

ABRAM'S VICTORY

Without a doubt, Abram's fame grew from this victory. He defeated a force that no other had been able to defeat. Verse 17 says, after Abram returned from defeating Kedorlaomer and the kings allied with him, the king of Sodom came out to meet him in the Valley of Shaveh (that is, the King's Valley). Notice that while the people were taken captive this king was in hiding. But now, he came out of hiding to meet Abram. He most likely had never met or heard of Abram before, so the honor was his to meet such a great man, who had proven to be much braver than he was. He came out to meet Abram in the King's Valley, which was synonymous with treating Abram as though he were a king. But suddenly, the story of their meeting was interrupted by another meeting Abram had, which was by far more important.

It is important to mention that, in addition to Mamre, Eshkol, Aner, and all the trained men, Abram had another friend in the fight; that friend was God. Therefore, verses 18-20 state that Melchizedek king of Salem (Heb

7:1-10) brought out bread and wine. He was priest of God Most High, and he blessed Abram, saying, "Blessed be Abram by God Most High, Creator of heaven and earth. And praise be to God Most High who delivered your enemies into your hand." Then Abram gave him a tenth of everything.

The assumption that this is where tithing began may not be accurate. Abram's intent was not to institute a law of tithing, instead, he did what was commonly done in his day. He gave a tenth, because that was regarded as the king's portion. Hence, to the extent that Abram regarded Melchizedek as a Great King, he gave Him the King's portion; Additionally, Melchizedek was Priest of God Most High. He was not afraid to remind Abram of how he gained the victory against such a formidable force. He reminded Abram that God delivered them into his hand.

Following his meeting with Melchizedek, the story of Abram's meeting with the king of Sodom resumed. Verse 21 says the king of Sodom said to Abram, "Give me the people and keep the goods for yourself." Why did he want the people more than the goods? The most reasonable possibility was because his kingdom could not survive without people. Goods could be recovered more quickly if there were people to acquire them. In essence, he knew that a kingdom without people was not a kingdom. Abram had become possessor of Sodom and its people, but it was a kingdom he did not want. And, to the extent that Lot was a citizen of that kingdom, Abram at that point owned Lot.

This was an opportunity for Abram and Lot to reconcile. Lot could have moved back to Canaan where Abram was, if he was so inclined. But he was so bent on remaining in Sodom, that not even a war in which he was taken captive, was enough to dissuade his intentions. Instead, he was among the people Abram returned to the king of Sodom, because he preferred to live under the king of Sodom's rule, than to live at peace near his uncle Abram.

Verses 22-24 reveal how Abram responded to the king of Sodom's request to keep the goods and give him the people. It also provides insight into additional details about his meeting with Melchizedek. Abram responded to the Sodomite king by telling him that with raised hand, he had sworn an oath to the Lord, God Most High, Creator of heaven and earth, that he would accept nothing belonging to the king of Sodom, not even a thread or the strap of a sandal, so that he will never be able to say, 'I made Abram rich.' As such, he accepted nothing, except what his men had eaten and the share that belonged to the men who went with him—Aner, Eshkol and Mamre.

Abram's response maybe an indication of why the story was interrupted after verse 17, when Melchizedek came onto the scene. It may have been during his meeting with Melchizedek when Abram swore to the Lord, God

Most High that he would not accept anything from the king of Sodom. It also demonstrated that he had learned his lesson after taking possessions from Pharaoh, who had indeed made him rich and may have boasted about it.

Abram took an oath with raised hand, similar to what a witness in court does, and he swore not to take anything for himself from the king of Sodom; Yet he took a tenth, which he gave to God. Additionally, while he did not take anything for himself, he did not impose that restriction on his friends Mamre, Eshkol, and Aner. They received a share commensurate with repayment for their trouble. No doubt, the 318 trained men with him most likely received their share as well, but Abram took nothing for himself. For him this fight was a mission of mercy, rather than a mission for riches. This event was a sign of significant growth in Abram's relationship with God. His humility was well-displayed, in giving glory to God Most High for his victory in battle. His example is instructive for those facing obstacles today and having to fight unavoidable battles of life. The key is to remember, in all things, to God be the glory.

GENESIS CHAPTER FIFTEEN

The previous chapter summarized events, which led to the capture of Abram's nephew Lot, and Abram's military campaign to rescue him. It also reviewed Abram's meeting with Bera, king of Sodom, as well as his meeting with Melchizedek, King of Salem. Bera's request was for Abram to keep the goods but return the people who were taken captive. Melchizedek's request was for Abram to remember the only reason he won the battle, was because God Most High, had given the enemy into his hands.

Following this meeting, Abram honored Melchizedek by giving him a tenth of the spoils of victory. He also returned to the king of Sodom all the people and goods, except that which was given as payment to those who went with him into battle. This chapter will examine Abram's concern about being childless, and God's response and demonstration by way of a solemn ceremony, to reaffirm to Abram that his state of childlessness would not be permanent. He reaffirmed His commitment to bless Abram and to give him a great reward.

ABRAM'S VISION AND CONCERN ABOUT CHILDLESSNESS

Verses 1-3, show that after Abram returned home from his victory to rescue Lot, the word of the Lord came to him in a vision saying, "Do not be afraid, I am your shield (Sovereign), your very great reward (or your reward will be great)." Notice Abram's response, "Sovereign Lord, what can you give me since I remain childless and the one who will inherit my estate is Eliezer of Damascus? You have given me no children; so, a servant in my household will be my heir."

It was interesting that after such a great victory in battle, God began His discourse with Abram by telling him "Do not be afraid." It is not clear what fears Abram was experiencing, but his response to God might provide some insight. Abram immediately responded to God with fear about his estate and about being childless. It was Abram's way of asking God, "how can you say you are my Sovereign and great reward, and yet allow me to be childless?" At his advanced age, childlessness may have become Abram's greatest fear; especially since it was now clear, even after a daring rescue, Lot was not coming back. Hence, Abram thought his servant Eliezer would become his heir.

Abram had the same fear, some today who are desperate to have children have. Advancing age became a catalyst for panic, as the biological clock kept ticking for his wife. But during those years of childlessness, God had a plan for Abram, just as He does for all others whom He allows to remain childless. His plan for Abram was growth of his faith, and development of a closer walk with Him. Abram's faith could not be in his children, since at that time he had none; his faith had to be in God, who was the only one who could grant his greatest need. Most importantly, with God being his Shield and Great Reward, Abram could not have been any safer, or any better supplied. He had all he needed, except patience to wait until it unfolded. He wanted a child, immediately!

The details of Abram's complaint should not be overlooked. He did not complain about God, but he certainly complained to God. He asked God, what can you give me, since you have given me no children? In other words, Abram was saying I don't want anything else, all I want is a child! The fact that he repeatedly used the words "give(n) me," suggest he may have been witnessing God giving children to others, but not to him! In that moment, he was so focused on what he wanted, and what he did not have, that he had forgotten the words God had spoken immediately after Lot left him (Gen 13:16), "I will make your offspring like the dust of the earth. . ."

God had indeed promised Abram offspring, but he did not tell him when, or how he would get them. Thus, Abram and his wife Sarai speculated about the process, and even tried to manipulate it. They were so desperate, they would likely have tried in-vitriol fertilization (IVF), if it were available at that time.

GOD'S RESPONSE TO ABRAM'S CONCERN

Notice, verses 4–5, God responded to Abram's complaint, by reassuring him that Eliezer would not be his heir, but a son from his own flesh and blood would be his heir. Then He took Abram outside and told him to look up at the sky and count the stars—if indeed he could count them. Then He said to him, "So shall your offspring be." This was the first time God had informed Abram that his offspring would be his own flesh and blood. This confirmed for him that his offspring would not be through adoption, or any other means of conscription. But, once again, God's reassurance to Abram, involved an important omission, which would play a significant role later on. It excluded any mention of his offspring also being flesh and blood of his wife Sarai.

Therefore, verse 6 says Abram believed the Lord, and He credited it to him as righteousness (Heb 11:4). Abram was indeed a great man, but those who would worship him, need to recognize that his belief in what God said was credited to him as righteousness, rather than debited from him. In other words, he had no righteousness of his own from which his belief could be debited. Therefore, God credited his belief as righteousness. God changed his unbelief (unrighteousness) into belief (righteousness) by reassuring him that his offspring would be his own flesh and blood. This encounter helped Abram grow in his faith-walk.

Notice the reminder God gave Abram in verse 7. He told him, "I am the Lord (Jehovah), who brought you out of Ur of the Chaldeans to give you this land to take possession of it." In other words, God reminded Abram that he did not make it to where he was on his own. God could have left him in Ur of the Chaldees, where he would have languished in paganism like all those who still lived there. In that moment, when Abram had triumphed over his enemies, when his fame was at its peak, and when he thought it a good time to focus on and complain about what he did not have, God reminded him of how he got all he had. God reminded him that He brought him from Ur of the Chaldees, where he had nothing, to give him the land where he was living, so that he could take possession of it.

ABRAM'S CONCERN ABOUT POSSESSION OF CANAAN

In verse 8, Abram responded by saying to God, "Sovereign Lord, how can I know that I will gain possession of it?" Since it was already stated that Abram believed God, this was most likely a question to support his belief, rather than one from a position of unbelief. In other words, Abram was asking God for clarity about how he might be able to possess the land. He probably saw it as such a massive and impossible task, one he could not see with his own eyes. Indeed, this land could not be taken by Abram, nor his descendants; it had to be given to them by God.

Verse 9 shows how God proceeded to explain this impossible task to Abram. He told him to bring a heifer, a goat, and a ram, each three years old, along with a dove and a young pigeon. Without a doubt, this request took time on Abram's part, especially catching the dove and young pigeon. However, verse 10 says Abram brought all of them to God! He was instructed by God to cut them in two and arrange the halves opposite each other, except for the birds, which he did not cut in half.

Verse 11 indicates that birds of prey came down and lighted on the carcasses, but Abram drove them away. In responding to Abram's question, God decided to give him a sign in these sacrifices, as well as a sign in the supernatural. Birds of prey tried to ruin Abram's sacrifices, but to prevent that, he had to keep watch, remain vigilant, and drive them away, otherwise they would not voluntarily leave until his sacrifices were ruined. In other words, Abram had to work before he received an answer from God. Many people seek answers from God while remaining idle, refraining from doing the work necessary, which God requires to get answers from Him. There are always "birds of prey" trying to ruin the sacrifices of the people of God, but like Abram, they must not allow it!

On the other hand, God's people must realize there is only so much they can do. God must be trusted to keep watch beyond our ability to do so. Parents sometimes believe it to be their job to control every aspect of their children's lives, but they must never cease to commit their children to God, especially as their ability to control them expires. Employees sometimes become territorial about work, but there comes a time when territories are overtaken by others and God must be trusted as Provider. The point is, every human life will end someday, but even then, the plan of God continues, He is able to bring every concern to fruition according to His will.

GOD PROMISED THE LAND TO ABRAM'S DESCENDANTS

Verses 12–16 indicate that it was not until the sun was setting, when Abram fell into a deep sleep, and a thick and dreadful darkness came over him, then the Lord responded to him. In other words, Abram did not get a response until circumstances seemed ominous. God answered and said, "Know for certain that for four hundred years your descendants will be strangers in a country not their own, and they will be enslaved and mistreated there. But I will punish the nation they serve as slaves, and afterward they will come out with great possessions. You, however, will go to your ancestors in peace and be buried at a good old age. In the fourth generation your descendants will come back here, for the sin of the Amorites has not yet reached its full measure."

Abram asked for details about how he would possess the land, but it is reasonable to wonder if the details he received were what he hoped for. He was informed that he would not possess the land in his lifetime, instead, his descendants would possess it in years to come. Notice also, before Abram fell asleep, he was busy guarding the sacrifices so that birds of prey would not ruin them. But, once the windows of his soul were locked in a deep sleep, so that he could not be disturbed during the vision, he could no longer watch over the sacrifices; God had to do that.

This imagery was meant to reveal to Abram that even though he would not possess the land in his lifetime, when he died, the task of securing his possession was no longer his; that task belonged to God. The signs Abram received about his possession of the land were not for his time, instead, they were unmistakable evidence of the Sovereignty of God; Only He could bring them about. It would take over four hundred years to unfold, when Abram would have been dead for many years, but God, who is Sovereign would forever be alive!

Another important mention was, God informed Abram that his death would occur in his old age. This should have assured him that he still had time for the offspring God promised him to be born. God also informed him that in death he would go to be with his ancestors. In other words, people he knew would be waiting for him there. This was interesting because many of Abram's relatives were idolaters, and people who worshipped other gods in Ur of the Chaldees (Josh 24:2). Yet, knowing death would be a reunion with his ancestors must have been a comforting, rather than a frightful thought.

Finally, God informed Abram that He would wait until the sin of the Amorites reached its full measure. This was evidence of God's patience, mercy, and slowness to anger. He could have given Abram possession of the land in his lifetime, but He waited four hundred years to give it to his descendants, and to give the Amorites an opportunity to reverse their sinful trajectory, if it were possible for them to do so. But, because the reversal of sin is impossible, apart from the sinner responding to the grace God gives, it was impossible for the Amorites to reverse their condition, despite four hundred years of grace. The land would indeed become the inheritance of Abram's descendants.

At this point it would be reasonable to ask, on what basis was the sin of the Amorites measured, since insofar as is known from the Bible, God did not directly give them any laws to abide by? This question may be answered based on what was shown in Genesis 9:6–17, where God gave moral and environmental laws to Noah and his sons. These laws applied to all humanity after them. Hence, the ancient world had a moral conscience about sins such as murder, adultery, stealing, etc. Therefore, God did not judge the Amorites based on their relationship to Him, since they did not know Him. Instead, He judged them based on how they treated each other, and how they took care of the natural environment He gave them.

God showed Abram that for four hundred years, his descendants would be enslaved in a country not their own. Yet, He did not ordain that they should inherit that country (Egypt) where they would be enslaved; rather, He promised them the land of Canaan. The fact that Abram's descendants would inherit Canaan after coming out of slavery, showed God was not giving it to them because they were better than the Amorites. The reason He gave it to them, was not due to any merit on their part, it was because He promised Abram to do so. He did it out of His own good will and pleasure. It was a demonstration of His Sovereignty and ability to watch over His covenant beyond the lifetime of its human beneficiaries. In other words, after Abram's death, God chase away every bird of prey, which would attempt to steal or destroy Abram's sacrifice.

GOD RATIFIED HIS PROMISE

Verses 17–21 show that when the sun set and darkness had fallen, a smoking firepot with a blazing torch appeared and passed between the pieces of meat Abram had prepared. It says on that day, the Lord made a covenant with Abram and said, "To your descendants I give this land, from the Wadi of Egypt to the great river, the Euphrates—the land of the Kenites, Kenizzites, Kadmonites, Hittites, Perizzites, Rephaites, Amorites, Canaanites, Girgashites and Jebusites."

This was an anthropomorphic proceeding, in which, when God passed between the pieces of meat, He was literally taking an oath which said, "May I be cut into pieces like these pieces of meat, if what I say does not come to pass." This was a solemn, irreversible oath to which God bound Himself. Even though He is Sovereign, He condescended in this interaction with Abram, to reveal to him over four hundred years in advance, what the sinful condition of the Canaanites would be like, and what His response to it would be. But before his descendants could take possession of the land, God also showed Abram their sinful condition as well, and their punishment of slavery in Egypt for four hundred years. After that period of time, Abram would inherit the land through his descendants.

God elevated His interactions with Abram, by demonstrating His sovereignty in keeping His covenant. He also revealed further details about His plans for Abram's descendants by promising he would have offspring, who would be his own flesh and blood, and His plan to give them possession of the land of Canaan. Hence, the original promise that through Abram's seed, all peoples of the earth would be blessed, began to make more sense, but the process by which Abram would have seed, remained a mystery. There was still no revelation about Sarai giving birth to his seed.

GENESIS CHAPTER SIXTEEN

The previous chapter examined Abram's complaint to God about being childless, and God's reassurance that his childlessness would not be indefinite. God not only promised Abram children, but He also promised to give him the land of Canaan as an inheritance to his descendants. God confirmed His promise in a solemn ceremony, in which He showed Abram future events, which would lead to his descendants coming out of slavery, and into possession of the land. This chapter will examine how Abram and his wife Sarai attempted to change their state of childlessness, by developing a plan, which was different from the one God intended.

SARAI'S PLAN TO START A FAMILY

Rather than devising her own plan, it would have been better if Sarai had talked to God as Abram had done, to discover His plan for her as it related to childbearing. However, because she was approximately seventy-four years old at the time, she may have given up and thought it futile to even pray about a thing like that. So, she came up with her own alternate plan.

Verse 1 says that Sarai, Abram's wife had borne him no children. But she had an Egyptian maidservant named Hagar. It is likely that Hagar was among the servants Pharaoh gave Abram as a payoff, to hasten his departure from Egypt after Abram brought trouble on the Egyptian kingdom, by deceiving Pharaoh into believing Sarai was only his sister. He did not tell him she was also his wife (chapter 12). So, when Sarai brought Hagar into the picture, she inadvertently allowed Pharaoh to get revenge on Abram, by causing strife among his descendants from that time forward to this very day.

In verse 2, Sarai stated that the Lord had kept her from having children; therefore, she admonished Abram to go sleep with her servant, and perhaps she could build a family through her. Abram agreed to what Sarai said.

IMPACT OF FAMILY AND CULTURE UPON ABRAM AND SARAI'S PLAN

Abram and Sarai developed their own plan to have a child. While Sarai has borne the brunt of criticism for this plan, few people pause to wonder why it seemed so easy for them to devise and then follow through with it. While no one can be certain, there are a few possibilities worth considering. For example, in the previous chapter, when Abram complained to God about being childless, and about having to assign Eliezer as his heir, God assured him that Eliezer would not be his heir, because he would have offspring, who would be his own flesh and blood. Once Abram heard this, he believed it, and his belief was credited to him as righteousness.

However, Abram did not ask, nor did God reveal whether Sarai his wife, would be the child's mother. And, at Sarai's age (approximately 74 years old), it was humanly reasonable to assume she would not be the mother. Thus, in their thinking, this would leave one other alternative, someone other than Sarai would be the mother. And, as noted before, Sarai did not discuss with God His will for her, as it related to childbearing. As far as she was concerned, such a discussion was unnecessary at her age.

Additionally, it was not unusual in Abram's time and culture for men to enhance their legacy by having children with other women. Indeed, this was the case in Abram's and Sarai's immediate family. For example, Sarai was not only Abram's wife, she was also his sister by a different mother (Gen 20:12). So, for them to conceive of the idea that the child God promised Abram would come by a different woman, due to Sarai's age, was only perpetuating what was common in their own family and culture.

Besides, God had spoken to Abram and confirmed for him that he would not remain childless, but there is no record of any such conversations between Him and Sarai, until the time came for her to conceive. These facts provide clues as to why Abram and Sarai made the decision to assist God in His plan to give them offspring.

Sarai thought she could build a family through Hagar. In other words, since God did not build a family through her, she would build herself one through someone else. Either way, in their minds, Abram was going to receive the offspring God told him about. As strange as it may seem, she may have hatched her idea because of her love for her husband and her desire to see him have children by any means necessary. As such, she selected Hagar because she was a servant and had no say in the matter, despite her feelings about the plan. Sarai decided to use Hagar as a surrogate.

Once again, before judging Sarai too harshly, it is important to remember that her idea of giving her husband to another woman, was no different from his idea of giving her to another man, which he did in Genesis 12:10–20, in giving her to Pharaoh. Therefore, if he could give her up to save his life, she may have thought she could give him up to build her family. Whatever the reason, this was a problematic plan from the very start, because Sarai was exercising more faith in Hagar than she was in God.

POSSIBLE REASONS WHY SARAI CHOSE HAGAR

Hagar was a servant, but the fact that she was Sarai's first and only choice of women to sleep with her husband, suggest that Hagar was a trusted servant. No doubt, the two women were on good terms with each other at that time and may even have been friends. Surely, they were not yet enemies. In a contemporary setting one can imagine them being such good friends they may have even gone shopping together! Whatever the case, there had to be a reason why, of all the servants Sarai had, she chose Hagar. Obviously, she did not pick the first slave girl she could find.

Certainly, Sarai chose Hagar because she was young and still in her child-bearing years. She was probably also a beautiful woman. Undoubtedly, Sarai would not choose an ugly woman to bear her offspring! She wanted good-looking, healthy offspring, so she probably chose what she thought was the best she had.

TWO COVENANTS

Sarai and Hagar represented two covenants. Sarai represented the New Covenant, while Hagar represented the Old Covenant. Paul explained this by saying:

> Tell me, you who want to be under the law, are you not aware of what the law says? For it is written that Abraham had two sons, one by the slave woman and the other by the free woman. His son by the slave woman was born in the ordinary way; but his son by the free woman was born as the result of a promise. These things may be taken figuratively, for the women represent two covenants. One covenant is from Mount Sinai, and bears children who are to be slaves: This is Hagar. Now Hagar stands for Mount Sinai in Arabia and corresponds to the present city of Jerusalem, because she is in slavery with her children. But the Jerusalem that is above is free and she is our mother.[1] (Gal 4:21–26, NIV)

---

1. Barker et al., *The NIV Study Bible*, Galations 4:21–26.

CONSUMMATION OF SARAI'S PLAN

Verse 3 says that after Abram had been in Canaan 10 years, Sarai his wife took her Egyptian maidservant and gave her to him to be his wife. Therefore, Sarai, who according to Paul, represented the new covenant, brought Hagar, who represented the old covenant, and gave her to Abram, who represented faith, and they all got married, or joined together on that day. This was indeed a convoluted spectacle!

Verse 4 indicates that Abram slept with Hagar, and she conceived. This passage does not reveal how many times he slept with her, but when a couple are intentionally trying to conceive, they usually sleep with each other more than once. Therefore, it is possible Abram slept with Hagar on multiple occasions. Where was Sarai when this was happening? What was she doing while Abram was doing what he was doing? What thoughts did she think? People from contemporary western cultures may wrestle with these questions, but once again, based on the family and cultural background from which Abram and Sarai came, this situation may have seemed quite normal.

In any case, since Abram and Sarai had been trying to have a child for a long time, she obviously understood the process, so what would she be thinking knowing what her husband was doing with the other woman, or what the other woman may have been doing to him? How could she sleep? Pondering such questions should highlight the level of desperation Abram and Sarai had for a child, especially since God had only revealed Abram's half of the story about how they would have one. At this point in the story, He had not revealed how Sarai would be involved.

Continuing in verse 4, it says when Hagar knew she was pregnant, she began to despise her mistress. This implies she probably liked her mistress before she conceived, but from that moment on, the woman who represented the old covenant was no longer willing to submit as a slave to the woman who represented the new covenant. Figuratively speaking, the two covenants began to compete, and this was where the problem between the old and new covenants, as represented by these two women, began. The relationship between them changed.

It is worth pausing to point out that as long as the old covenant, represented by Hagar, was in submission to the new covenant, represented by Sarai, things were fine. But that changed once Hagar conceived. Sarai would soon learn how big her mistake was! And Abram would soon have his wings clipped! No more late-night walks, hopping from tent to tent! Soon he would learn how difficult it would be to negotiate peace between the two covenants. He would eventually have to choose. Indeed, as Jesus said (Matt 6:24; Luke 16:13), no one can serve two masters.

Sarai found out that when she shared her husband with Hagar, they became equals in Hagar's mind. Imagine Hagar showing off her pregnancy and saying to Sarai: He is my man too, and everybody knows it! This was the last thing on Sarai's mind when she came up with the idea of sharing her husband. She did not conceive of the possibility that a slave like Hagar would try to take her man! She would come to see that waiting on God was not so bad after all.

STRIFE BETWEEN SARAI AND HAGAR

Verse 5 reveals that Sarai confronted Abram and accused him of being responsible for the wrong she was suffering from Hagar. And Abram probably thought: what did I do? I simply obeyed what you told me! But there was a reason Sarai said this. Notice that when hostility broke out between the two women, Abram remained silent. He said nothing! And he apparently did nothing to stop it! Therefore, Sarai said: it is your fault! She said, "I put my servant into your arms, and now that she knows she is pregnant, she despises me. May the Lord judge between you and me."

Scripture does not reveal how Sarai found out Hagar was pregnant, or how she found out Hagar despised her. But it is likely that either Hagar or another one of her servants informed her. And even after complaining to Abram, he did nothing! It seemed as if Abram had gotten accustomed to living with two wives (two covenants). Figuratively speaking, he was trying to live with the new covenant and the old at the same time. It cannot be done! Sarai called on the Lord to judge between her and Abram. She could not call on Abram to judge the situation himself, because she knew his judgement had become tainted.

The first response from Abram about the hostility is found in verse 6, notice the kind of response it was. Abram told Sarai, "Your servant is in your hands, do with her whatever you think best." In other words, it is up to you! If you want something done, do it yourself! It should be noted here that this was the same Abram, who had proven at other times to be a very skillful negotiator. Yet, he could not stop the war in his own house; He could not reconcile the two covenants.

Examples of Abram's negotiating skills can be seen in Genesis 13, beginning in verse 5, when there was quarrelling between Lot's herdsmen and his herdsmen. It shows how skillful he was in being able to settle that dispute. He said, "Let's not have any quarrelling between you and me, or between your herdsmen and mine, for we are brothers, is not the whole land before you? Let's part company. If you go to the left, I'll go to the right; if you go to the right, I'll go to the left." And quickly, Lot's heart was changed, and the dispute was settled. Why could he not use this same skillfulness in negotiating the trouble between his two wives in his own house? Why could he not bring the woman who represented the old covenant and the woman who represented the new covenant together?

Again, in Genesis 18:23-33, it shows where Abram used his negotiating skills to bargain with spiritual beings concerning the fate of Sodom and Gomorrah. Once more, in Genesis 21:22-34, Abram, whose name by then was changed to Abraham, was able to negotiate a treaty to settle a dispute with the servants of Abimelech concerning a well. All these things he did successfully, but the one thing he was not able to do was restore peace in his own house. He could not bring those two women who represented the old and the new covenants back together. Jesus Christ is the only one who can reconcile them, and who, through the cross, has negotiated peace between the two covenants (Eph 2:14-16).

HAGAR FLEES SARAI'S MISTREATMENT

Continuing in verse 6, it shows that Sarai mistreated Hagar, so she fled from her. Abram and Sarai's marriage seemed to be on shaky ground, until Abraham said, "Your servant is in your hands, do with her what you think best." It was then that Sarai knew where Abram stood, and what her status was with him. But even then, he made no efforts to resolve the situation himself, which gave Hagar the right to believe she had a shot at being his number one. Abram seemed tossed between two opinions. He had gotten accustomed to having two wives! While the women feuded with each other, he did nothing to stop it!

Finally, Abram said to Sarai, if you want something done, do it yourself, and she did. She mistreated Hagar, so Hagar fled from her, taking nothing on her journey. Her plight would have been difficult under any circumstances, but it was especially harsh for her as a pregnant woman. Hagar's decision to flee, put her life and that of her unborn child in mortal danger. For her to be willing to take such risks, provides insight into the severity of mistreatment she endured at the hands of Sarai. More importantly, it underscored the level of apathy on Abram's part for doing nothing to help her or the unborn child she was carrying, which he (and Sarai) so desperately wanted.

GOD INTERVENED ON HAGAR'S BEHALF

While Abram did nothing to assist Hagar and her unborn child, God intervened to assist her. Verses 7–8 show that after Hagar fled, apparently taking nothing with her on her journey, the angel of the Lord found her near a spring in the desert. It was the spring (or fountain) that is beside the road to Shur. And he asked her two questions worth pondering in today's times as well. The first question was, "Hagar, servant of Sarai, where have you come from?" Since this angel knew Hagar's name and whose servant she was, certainly he also knew where she came from. The angel was actually asking Hagar, an Egyptian, whom Paul said represented the old covenant, what is your history? What is your past? What road have you traveled to get to this point?

The second question he asked her was: And where are you going? What is your future? How will your journey end? What awesome questions these were! Where have you come from, and where are you going? Hopefully, those who are in an unstable place in life today, who feel like giving up and running away from it all, will ponder these questions as well. Hopefully, they can muster better answers than those Hagar gave. Firstly, she never told the angel where she came from, and secondly her generic answer suggested she did not know where she was going.

The truth was, after Hagar discovered she was pregnant, she began to despise her mistress Sarai, and started competing for the position as Abram's number one wife. This caused Sarai to mistreat her in order to re-establish her dominance and remind Hagar of her status as a slave. She wanted to force Hagar back into submission. But the emotional and physical pain, caused Hagar to run away, taking nothing with her on the journey. Evidently, the plan Abram and Sarai concocted to use Hagar as a surrogate to bear their offspring, was different from the plan Hagar had for herself. She did not want to only be a surrogate, she also wanted to be equal as a wife.

Thankfully, verse 9 says, the angel of the Lord told her, "Go back to your mistress and submit to her." In other words, do not make a mockery of her, thinking you are better than her, because you were able to conceive. You, who represented the old covenant, must give in, and submit to her, who represented the new covenant. She is number one! And unless the old covenant submits to the new, there will never be peace between the two! This was tough advice for Hagar. It meant she would have to surrender her hopes and dreams. Most importantly, it meant she would have to exist in an environment in which she was no longer welcomed. Her eventual departure was inevitable, but this was not the right time. While Sarai was ready for her to leave, Abram was not. Hagar and her unborn child were still in his heart. They had become his family, rather than Sarai's.

God demonstrated His mercy to Hagar in verse 10, and He spoke tenderly to her, by way of an angel, to demonstrate His compassion toward her situation. He informed her that He would increase her descendants so much that they would be too many to count. Notice, despite Sarai's plan, God referred to Hagar's descendants as hers, rather than Sarai's. In fact, God did not even refer to Hagar's descendants as Abram's, because He never intended Abram's descendants to be reckoned through Hagar. This meant that from God's perspective, Abram and Sarai were never supposed to build a family through Hagar. The angel also said to her:

> You are now pregnant. You will have a son. You will name him Ishmael (God hears). That is because the Lord has heard about your suffering. He will be like a wild donkey. He will use his power against everyone. And everyone will be against him. He will not be friendly toward any of his relatives.[2] (Gen 16:11-12, NIRV)

Some translations (NIV) indicate that Ishmael was prophesied to be a wild donkey of a man, which meant he would not be easily led. As a wild donkey, he would have a wealth of potential to be industrious, but his wildness would prevent his potential from being realized. His sin would be, his hand being against everyone, but his punishment would be, everyone's hand being against him. This also meant Ishmael would not trust others, nor could he be trusted by others. More importantly, he would live in perpetual hostility. The jealousy and despised feelings his mother Hagar felt toward Sarai, would be borne out in him and his feelings toward Sarai's descendants. This was quite a prophecy!

Verse 13 shows that Hagar spoke back to God. It says she gave this name to the Lord who spoke to her, saying, "You are the God who sees me. I have now seen (or seen the back of) the One who sees me." The angel said God hears, but Hagar said He not only hears, but He also sees. Verse 14 explained, that is why the well where Hagar was found was called Beer Lahai Roi (well of the Living One who sees me). Undoubtedly, this encounter with God, who hears and sees, changed the rest of Hagar's life.

BIRTH OF ISHMAEL

Verse 15 declares that Hagar bore Abram a son, and Abram, named him Ishmael. Abram was eighty-six years old when Hagar bore him Ishmael (God hears). Again, Ishmael never became Sarai's son. In other words, her plan did not work! In fact, the day Ishmael was born, must have been a sad day

---

2. Barker et al., *The NIV Study Bible*, Genesis 16:11–12.

for her. However, the question to be asked is, once Ishmael was born, did the relationship between Abram and Hagar cease?

It is unclear what the nature of Abram's and Hagar's relationship was once she gave birth to Ishmael, but what is clear is that while Abram gave Sarai license to mistreat Hagar, there is no evidence he mistreated her himself. What will also become clear from later chapters, is that Abram became satisfied with having Ishmael as a son, such that he appeared hesitant when God again told him he would have another son, through whom his offspring would be reckoned. Nevertheless, by reading further, it will become more evident that God's plan always eventually prevails.

GENESIS CHAPTER SEVENTEEN

The previous chapter examined Abram and Sarai's botched plan to use their slave Hagar, as a surrogate, through whom they thought they could build a family. Hagar did indeed conceive and bore Abram a son, whose named was Ishmael, but their plan did not work. It caused more strife in Abram's household than it did to fix their problem of childlessness. This chapter will inspect God's appearance to Abram once again, and His restatement of the covenant. In chapter fifteen, God gave Abram a sign of His intent to keep the covenant. In this chapter God would in turn require a sign of circumcision from Abram, all males in his household, and all his male descendants, as a mark of their intent and obligation to keep the covenant.

GOD APPEARED TO ABRAM AGAIN

Verses 1–2 indicate that when Abram was ninety-nine years old, the Lord appeared to him and said, "I am God Almighty (El-Shaddai); walk before me faithfully and be blameless. Then I will make a covenant between Me and you and will greatly increase your numbers."

At the time of this visit, Abram, being a ninety-nine-year-old man, had given up on having more children. By then Ishmael was thirteen years old. God identified Himself as El-Shaddai, rather than Jehovah. In describing Himself as El-Shaddai, God implied to Abram that there is nothing He cannot do! Nothing is impossible for Him. He is God Almighty! Abram needed to hear this, because at ninety-nine years old, and with Sarai being eighty-nine, the birth of a child between them could only be brought about by One who is Almighty.

Notice, this was a conditional covenant. In other words, it was effective as long as Abram walked faithfully and blamelessly before God. If Abram did this, then God said He would make a covenant between them and would greatly increase his numbers. Therefore, Abram's role in the covenant was to walk faithfully and blamelessly before God. This would also become the role of his descendants, who would become inheritors of the covenant.

The fact that Sarai blamed Abram for her predicament with Hagar, suggested that Abram was not a blameless (perfect) man by nature. Evidence in previous chapters, showing Abram's decision to go to Egypt, and to preserve his life there, by giving his wife to Pharaoh, was further proof that Abram was not a blameless man. Yet, God required him to walk faithfully and blamelessly before Him. It obviously meant that those things, which were done when his name was Abram, were to be behind him. He had to focus on the future when God would give him a new name, Abraham, and expect more from him in the way of faithfulness and blamelessness.

GOD'S ROLE IN THE COVENANT

Notice Abram's response to God. He fell facedown, and God said to him:

> As for me, this is my covenant with you: You will be the father of many nations. No longer will you be called Abram (Exalted Father); your name will be Abraham (Father of many), for I have made you a father of many nations. I will make you very fruitful; I will make nations of you, and kings will come from you. I will establish my covenant as an everlasting covenant between me and you and your descendants after you. The whole land of Canaan, where you now reside as a foreigner, I will give as an everlasting possession to you and your descendants after you; and I will be their God.[1] (Gen 17:3-8, NIV)

God initiated the Covenant by describing what He would do, before telling Abram what He expected him to do. God also established the terms of the covenant. Despite Abram's late start, he would have more offspring than anyone else known to man. His descendants in the flesh would include un-countable offspring, and kings, by way of Ishmael, Isaac, and his second wife Keturah. But his offspring in the spirit would include every believer in God, as he would become "Father of the Faithful" (Gal 3:29; Rom 4:13).

God concluded His role in the covenant by reiterating that He would give the land of Canaan to Abram, whom He renamed Abraham, and to his descendants. He also stated that He would be their God. This was an important statement in light of the fact that the Canaanites worshipped other gods. God made it clear He would be Abraham's descendants' God. They were not to be idolaters. This was an important factor in the covenant.

---

1. Barker et al., *The NIV Study Bible*, Genesis 17:3–8.

ABRAHAM AND HIS DESCENDANTS' ROLE IN THE COVENANT

After God stated His role in the covenant, verses 9–14, describe what Abraham and his descendants' role was to be. God said to Abraham:

> As for you, you must keep my covenant, you and your descendants after you for the generations to come. This is my covenant with you and your descendants after you, the covenant you are to keep: Every male among you shall be circumcised. You are to undergo circumcision, and it will be the sign of the covenant between me and you. For the generations to come every male among you who is eight days old must be circumcised, including those born in your household or bought with money from a foreigner—those who are not your offspring. Whether born in your household or bought with your money, they must be circumcised. My covenant in your flesh is to be an everlasting covenant. Any uncircumcised male, who has not been circumcised in the flesh, will be cut off from his people; he has broken my covenant.[2] (NIV)

The covenant God made with Abraham was not only to give the land of Canaan to him and his descendants, but it was also a covenant of circumcision (Acts 7:8). The significance of circumcision was to serve as a sign that Abraham and his descendants were covenant people (Rom 4:11–13). It identified and set them apart from other nations with whom God had not made any covenants. As circumcised people, their responsibility was to keep the whole law (Gal 5:3). They were supposed to do whatever God commanded.

Notice also that the covenant of circumcision was not only for Abraham and his descendants, but verse 12 says, it was also for any stranger in his household, who was not his direct descendant. This included gentiles and demonstrated that God's covenant plans from the beginning were not meant to be exclusive. However, strangers were to become like Abraham and his descendants, rather than vice versa. Abraham and his descendants were not to become or behave like strangers to God.

Some denominations, use passages such as Colossians 2:8–15, to argue that under the New Covenant, circumcision has been replaced by baptism as the sign of who God's covenant people are. This position is problematic since a person can be baptized and not have a covenant relationship with God. Nonetheless, Romans 8:9 makes it clear that the identifying sign of

---

2. Barker et al., *The NIV Study Bible*, Genesis 17:9–14.

who God's covenant people are today, is the indwelling of His Holy Spirit in those who are saved. It says if a person does not have the Spirit of Christ, that person does not belong to Him, even though they may be baptized.

The fact is, both circumcision and baptism are ceremonial proceedings, which are performed by men. However, dispensing His Spirit to a believer, is an act only God can perform. He knows all to whom He has given His Spirit. Moreover, Romans 8:16 says, His Spirit bears witness with our spirit that we are His children. In other words, He knows His children, because He has given them His Spirit. And, they know Him, because His Holy Spirit bears witness with their human spirit, that they are His children. What a beautiful picture this is of how divine heritage works!

GOD'S PLAN FOR SARAI

God told Abraham he would have offspring who would be his own flesh and blood, but this would be the very first time He made any such promise concerning Sarai. Notice verses 15–16, God said to Abraham, "As for Sarai your wife, you are no longer to call her Sarai (my princess); her name will be Sarah (princess). I will bless her and will surely give you a son by her. I will bless her so that she will be the mother of nations; kings and peoples will come from her." It is also important to observe that God did not speak directly to Sarai, instead, He spoke to her husband Abraham. At Sarai's age, this was certainly a promise for which God needed to prove Himself to be El-Shaddai. Indeed, only the Almighty could do this!

Recall, Genesis 15:4, God told Abraham he would have offspring who would be of his own flesh and blood. Abraham believed God, and it said his belief of what God said, was credited to him as righteousness. In other words, as old as he was, he was able to conceive of the possibility of having offspring, because he was a man, and the biological clock for men can continue to work in their old age. But he had greater difficulty wrapping his mind around the possibility of Sarah, being an old woman, becoming pregnant at her age.

Notice his reaction when he was told his wife Sarah would give birth. Verses 17–18 show that Abraham fell facedown; he laughed and said to himself, "Will a son be born to a man a hundred years old? Will Sarah bear a child at the age of ninety?" Observe that Abraham kept his thoughts to himself! He did not share them openly at the time. So, the reason his thoughts are known today, is because he probably shared them later. In any case, it does not say he doubted what he was told. He simply thought it was funny, and indeed it was!

Abraham's additional comment sheds light on his frame of mind and desires for Ishmael. While he kept his thoughts to himself about Sarah becoming pregnant, notice what he openly said to God: "If only Ishmael (or Ishmael only) might live under your blessing!" Abraham was basically telling God he was contented with his son Ishmael only, and at his and Sarah's ages, did not need to have another son. His request was for Ishmael only and no other son, to inherit all the blessings God had foretold; In which case, Hagar would have indeed triumphed over Sarah! Thankfully, she was not present to hear this conversation, otherwise her fury against Abraham may have been unquenchable.

God listened to Abraham's request concerning Ishmael, but in verse 19, He reiterated His plan for Sarah. He again informed Abraham that his wife Sarah would bear him a son, and he should call him Isaac (Laughter). God restated His intent to establish His covenant with Isaac as an everlasting covenant for his descendants after him. In other words, God made it clear to Abraham that His plan for the posterity of His covenant, was through Isaac, rather than Ishmael. And God was not interested in entertaining any alternative ideas from Abraham about how His plan should be executed.

Albeit, in verses 20–21, God graciously indicated that He had not forgotten Ishmael. He said, as for Ishmael, He heard Abraham's petition concerning him; therefore, He promised to bless him, to make him fruitful, and greatly increase his numbers. God said, Ishmael would be the father of twelve rulers, and He would make him into a great nation. However, His covenant, He would establish with Isaac, whom Sarah would bear to Abraham by that very time the following year. When God had finished speaking with Abraham, He went up from him. In other words, the conversation was over! God did not need to hear anything else from Abraham, or to say anything else to him. Abraham's role at that point was to walk faithfully and blamelessly, remain intimate with his wife Sarah, and not be an obstacle against God's plan coming to fruition. Most importantly, he needed to go home and share the good news with his wife Sarah, but evidently he did not.

ABRAHAM CIRCUMCISED HIS HOUSEHOLD

Following his encounter with God, Verse 23 shows Abraham's first efforts to walk faithfully and blamelessly. It also provides insight into why he gained the title, "Father of the Faithful." It says on that very day when God spoke to him, without delay, Abraham took his son Ishmael, and all those born in his household or bought with his money, every male in his household, and circumcised them, as God told him. In other words, Abraham immediately obeyed God! He did not ask God any questions as to why He required such a gruesome procedure on the most private organ on a man's body. Instead, Abraham immediately set out to uphold his end of the covenant, and he circumcised all the males, as a sign that his was a covenant-keeping household.

Most importantly, since Abraham was circumcised on the very day when God spoke to him, it demonstrated that he made sure he took care of his end of the covenant before working on having the son God promised him by Sarah. Circumcision delayed sexual intimacy with Sarah, until healing took place. This was why God told him it would take a complete year before his son Isaac would be born. Apparently, three months were allotted for healing from circumcision, and for conception to occur. Nine months were allotted for pregnancy and birth of the child. To fit within the one-year timeframe God gave, Abraham had to start working immediately, and he did.

Verses 24–27 point out that Abraham was ninety-nine years old when he was circumcised, and his son Ishmael was thirteen. Abraham and his son Ishmael were both circumcised on the same day. And every male in Abraham's household, including those born in his household or bought from a foreigner, was circumcised with him.

Notice, Abraham circumcised Ishmael, even though he was told the covenant would not be perpetuated through him. As long as he was a male in Abraham's household, he had to be circumcised. This must have been a painful, but intimate exercise for Abraham and his son, and for all the males in his household. All of them had to either be circumcised or cut off (excommunicated) from the household. By submitting themselves to circumcision, they demonstrated loyalty to Abraham, and by extension to God, but it is possible that some men gave up membership in Abraham's household to avoid undergoing the gruesome practice of circumcision.

Once circumcised, Abraham's household demonstrated trust in God, because circumcision made them vulnerable to attack. They had to rely on God to maintain peace during that period of time. The day when Abraham circumcised all the males in his household, he literally caused all manly activities in his society to be halted until their wounds were healed. There was no sexual intimacy, no hunting or fishing, no working or playing. During that period, every manly activity stopped! This was a significant act of obedience to God.

Unfortunately, female circumcision is practice in some cultures even today. This was never commanded or intended by God and is essentially mutilation of the female reproductive organ. In fact, the Christian faith teaches that men are no longer required to practice circumcision. Paul says that circumcision is nothing (1 Cor 7:19). He also wrote in Romans 2:28–29, that what counts is not circumcision of the flesh as an outward sign to other people, but circumcision of the heart as an inward sign of praise to God.

Therefore, what God required Abraham and His descendants to do, by circumcising themselves, as a sign that they were His covenant-keeping people, has been replaced by a new circumcision, which takes place in the heart, through the indwelling of God's Spirit. Holy Spirit circumcises the hearts of believers. However, whether circumcised inwardly or outwardly, God requires the same from His covenant people that He did from Abraham, and that is, for them to walk faithfully and blamelessly before Him.

GENESIS CHAPTER EIGHTEEN

The previous chapter delved into details of God's appearance to Abram after identifying Himself as El-Shaddai. He changed Abram's name to Abraham and instructed him to walk faithfully and blamelessly before Him. God also provided new details about His plan to give him a child. He informed Abraham that His covenant would not be perpetuated through Ishmael, but through a son He would give him and his wife Sarai, whose name He changed to Sarah. Finally, God commanded Abraham to circumcise himself and every male in his household as a sign of the covenant. Abraham immediately did everything God instructed, but he neglected to take care of one important detail, which will be revealed in this chapter.

This chapter will also review Abraham's encounter with three visitors. His ability to convince them to stay with him and enjoy a meal will be recognized. However, their willingness to spend time with Abraham was not only to enjoy a meal, but to also ensure that the detail Abraham neglected to take care of was addressed. Additionally, the visitors would inform Abraham about their plan to destroy Sodom and Gomorrah, where Lot lived. Abraham pleaded for a reversal of the plan, but his pleading was unsuccessful. The visitors made their way to Sodom and Gomorrah to do as they said they would.

ABRAHAM ENCOUNTERS THREE VISITORS

Verses 1-2 indicate that the Lord appeared to Abraham near the great trees of Mamre while he was sitting at the entrance to his tent in the heat of the day. It says Abraham looked up and saw three men standing nearby. When he saw them, he hurried from the entrance of his tent to meet them and bowed low to the ground.

The scene in these verses indicate that Abraham was sitting at the entrance to his tent. This meant he had reached a reasonable point in his healing after being circumcised, as seen in the previous chapter. His position at the entrance to his tent, allowed him to be aware of what was going on inside, as well as outside his tent. It was also a location where he could relax in the shade, while cooling off in whatever fresh air was available.

From Abraham's vantage point, he should have been able to see anyone approaching his tent from way in the distance, but in this case, he did not. What was most interesting was, by the time Abraham looked up, the three visitors were already standing nearby! In other words, Abraham never saw them coming! He only seemed to notice their presence when they were already up close! They seemed to appear out of nowhere!

Notice his approach to them. He bowed low to the ground. His approach was like a dog approaching its master, not knowing its master's current mood. Abraham seemed to know right away that after such a sudden appearance, his visitors were not ordinary men. In fact, he may have recognized some of them from previous meetings. So, he approached them in a submissive, worshipful, and non-threatening manner. Observe also, at his age, and despite his recent circumcision, he hurried to meet them. Abraham still had a swiftness about himself, even though he was approaching 100 years old!

Verses 3–5 show Abraham's spirit of hospitality. He said to them, "If I have found favor in your eyes, my lord, do not pass your servant by. Let a little water be brought, and then you may all wash your feet and rest under this tree. Let me get you something to eat, so you can be refreshed and then go on your way—now that you have come to your servant." "Very well," they answered, "do as you say."

Notice, Abraham did not immediately ask their names, or what their business was. He simply asked their permission to serve them. His accommodations were not elaborate, but they were enough, as they flowed from a heart of generosity. As such, his offer was accepted by the visitors, and it set up the perfect opportunity for them to take care of an issue, which Abraham needed to, but had not.

Verses 6–8 say Abraham hurried into the tent to Sarah, rather than Hagar. He said to her "Quick! get three seahs (approximately 36 pounds or 16 kilograms) of the finest flour and knead it and bake some bread!" Then he ran to the herd and selected a choice, tender calf and gave it to a servant, who hurried to prepare it. He then brought some curds and milk and the calf that had been prepared and set these before them. Abraham prepared the best meal he could afford, and while they ate, he stood near them under a tree.

Abraham prepared a feast for his visitors! The amount of fine flour he used indicate that quite a few cakes were made! Plus, he slaughtered and prepared an entire calf and placed it before them! This was a large meal, which took time to prepare! Notice, after preparing the meal and placing it before them, Abraham did not consider himself worthy to eat with them, though they were at his house. Instead, he stood near them under a tree, much like a waiter in a restaurant, who remained ready and watchful for any other requests his guests might have.

What a tremendous image of service and humility! Once again, though Abraham may have recognized at least one of his visitors from previous encounters, he did not inquire about who they were, or the purpose for their visit, but he interacted as if he was familiar with them.

SARAH OVERHEARS GOD'S PLAN

Verse 9 says they asked Abraham, "Where is your wife Sarah?" Notice what they did not ask him. They did not ask; do you have a wife? And what is her name? Instead, the question basically affirmed that they already knew he had a wife, and they knew her name. As such, they certainly knew where she was! In any case, Abraham courteously responded by telling them she was there in the tent. This meant Sarah was out of sight, but not out of hearing. She was eavesdropping, and that was exactly what the visitors wanted her to do!

Knowing full well that Sarah was in the tent behind Abraham listening to what was being said, verses 10-12 reveal that one of the visitors said, "I will surely return to you about this time next year, and Sarah your wife will have a son." When Sarah heard this, she laughed to herself as she thought, "After I am worn out and my lord is old, will I now have this pleasure?"

Sarah's inward thoughts seemed to question God about why He waited so late to bless her with a child. However, she was not as worn out as she thought, and the reason God waited so late, was to show that only He (El-Shaddai) could do what would be done in her life. Hence, one of the visitors prophesied in her hearing, and prophecy, when fulfilled, is a witness against unbelief.

Notice verse 13, where it identified one of the visitors. It says the Lord asked Abraham, why did Sarah laugh and say, "will I really have a child, now that I am old?" This event was a theophany, where the pre-incarnate Christ was one of the visitors who appeared to Abraham. When Abraham was asked why did Sarah laugh? He may not have known she laughed, as it says she did so to herself! She was in the tent, where he could not see her, and most likely did not hear her laugh. But the Lord heard her laughter and her inward thoughts. The fact that He called out her inward thoughts, helped to convince Sarah of the seriousness of what was said, and the authority of the One who said it. But the Lord did not question Sarah, He questioned Abraham.

It is quite possible that the Lord questioned Abraham about why Sarah laughed, because this was not the first time Abraham heard about the plan for Sarah to give birth to a son. The previous chapter (17) showed where God appeared to Abraham and told him this, but evidently, Abraham was so hopeful Ishmael would receive the blessing, that he never told Sarah about the son they were supposed to have together.

Therefore, Sarah laughed because the prophesy she overheard was news to her, but it should not have been. Consequently, the visitors wanted Sarah to eavesdrop, so she could hear what they were saying. Her response was no different from Abraham's. When he was told, he also laughed, but his laughter was not questioned; hers was questioned because had Abraham shared the news with her, as he was supposed to do, she would have taken it more seriously when she heard it from the Lord. In fact, if Abraham had told her, the Lord might not have found it necessary to deliberately say it, knowing she was listening; by then it would no longer be a joke!

Thus, in verse 14 the prophecy was repeated, and the question was asked, "is anything too hard for the Lord?" Then, the Lord promised to return at the appointed time the following year when Sarah would have a son. The prophecy was repeated because it was as good as done! Obstacles in Sarah's mind, such as hers and her husband's ages, were not obstacles for the Lord; He is El-Shaddai (God Almighty)!

Verse 15 says, Sarah was afraid, so she lied and said, "I did not laugh." But He said, "Yes, you did laugh." Sarah was most likely afraid because she was inside the tent eavesdropping, and yet the Lord knew exactly what she was doing and thinking. This frightened her and caused her to realize she was not dealing with ordinary men. Notice that while the Lord exposed Sarah's actions and thoughts in Abraham's presence, He did not expose in her presence Abraham's failure to tell her about the prophecy. Instead, He basically took care of Abraham's failure by telling her Himself.

In any case, Sarah spoke up and joined the conversation from inside the tent! She answered a question that was not posed to her, but to her husband! She proved she was eavesdropping! And it was a good thing she was, otherwise, only God knows how much more time would have passed before Abraham would have told her what God had told him.

Interestingly, the Lord pointed out that Sarah laughed, but He did not scold her for it. Sarah lied in fear, but she was obviously not a habitual liar, no more than someone, who may on a rear occasion have gotten drunk, should be considered a drunkard. The Lord proved to Abraham and Sarah that He knew what was going on inside and outside the tent. And He proved His authority to predict with certainty what would happen in their lives a year ahead and beyond.

Abraham's three visitors were not only there to visit him and inform Sarah about her upcoming pregnancy and delivery, they were also on another mission to the cities of Sodom and Gomorrah. They could have eliminated the visit to Abraham's tent and travelled directly to those cities, but if they had done so, the news they delivered to Sarah would have been delayed, since Abraham neglected to inform her. With that task completed, they turned their attention to the other task on their agenda, which was to address the sinful and dangerous condition in the cities of Sodom and Gomorrah.

GOD'S PLAN TO DESTROY SODOM AND GOMORRAH

Verse 16 shows that when the visitors got up to leave, they looked down toward Sodom, and Abraham walked along with them to see them on their way. This was a very friendly gesture on Abraham's part. It also allowed him the opportunity to have private time with them, away from his wife's hearing. Most importantly, it demonstrated that Abraham had no fear of his visitors. He mingled with them in a respectful, but friendly manner.

Verses 17–19 echoed a friendly atmosphere, as it shows that the Lord said, "Shall I hide from Abraham what I am about to do? Abraham will surely become a great and powerful nation, and all nations on earth will be blessed through him. For I have chosen him, so that he will direct his children and his household after him to keep the way of the Lord by doing what is right and just, so that the Lord will bring about for Abraham what he has promised him."

Henry points out that according to Jewish tradition God told Abraham what he was going to do in the Land of Canaan, because he had bequeathed the land to Abraham and did not want to do anything in it without telling him.[1] However, the Biblical passage itself communicates a few reasons why the Lord thought it best to inform Abraham about His mission.

Firstly, He said Abraham will surely become a great and powerful nation. The implication was, when Abraham becomes that great and powerful nation, he would do well to know what behaviors would sustain his greatness, and those which would result in his downfall, such as would be the fate of Sodom and Gomorrah. Secondly, He said all nations on earth will be

---

1. Henry, *Matthew Henry Commentary on the Whole Bible, Complete and Unabridged*, 46.

blessed through Abraham, which was a messianic prophecy, assuring that the Messiah would descend from Abraham's line. Hence, sharing the news with Abraham was like sharing with family.

Thirdly the Lord said, He has chosen Abraham, so that he will direct his children and household to keep the way of the Lord by doing what is right and just. In other words, Abraham would direct his children in the way of righteousness and justice. As declared later in Proverbs 14:34, righteousness exalts a nation, but sin is a reproach (condemnation) to any people. Therefore, God revealed His plan to Abraham to show contrasting results of righteous conduct, versus sinful and unrighteousness conduct.

Verse 21 shows where the Lord said, "The outcry against Sodom and Gomorrah is so great and their sin so grievous that I will go down and see if what they have done is as bad as the outcry that has reached me says. If not, I will know." God used anthropomorphic language (earth talk) to describe His response concerning Sodom and Gomorrah. God, who knew what Sarah was doing and thinking behind the closed curtain of her tent, said He would go down and see what was going on in Sodom and Gomorrah. Once again, this was earth talk. God did not need to come down to see what was going on. He knew what was going on because He is omniscient! He knows everything!

Again, it would be reasonable to ask, on what basis was the sin of Sodom and Gomorrah measured, since insofar as is known from the Bible, God did not directly give them any laws? As mentioned before regarding what was said in Genesis 15:16 about the sin of the Amorites, this question may be answered based on what was shown in Genesis 9:6–17, where God gave moral laws to Noah and his sons. These laws applied to all humanity after them. Hence, the ancient world had a moral conscience about how they were to treat each other. Therefore, God's judgment against Sodom and Gomorrah was not based on their relationship to Him since they did not know Him. Instead, it was based on their debased treatment of others.

What was most egregious about the sin of Sodom and Gomorrah, was the fact that these were the same nations Abraham risked his life to save a few years previously. All the people of those cities, and their possessions were captured, and had it not been for Abraham, there was no hope for them! Abraham literally saved them! Yet, following that salvation experience, their sinful condition multiplied. They squandered a second chance!

Verse 22 states that the men who visited Abraham turned away and went toward Sodom, but Abraham remained standing before the Lord. So, all along he was conversing with three individuals, now he was left with one, and that one was described as the Lord. Again, this was a theophany, and a beautiful picture of friendship between God and Abraham. This was a one-on-one conversation between the Lord and His friend Abraham. The reason details are known today about this encounter is because Abraham subsequently shared those details.

ABRAHAM PLEADS FOR SODOM AND GOMORRAH

With the other two visitors departed and on their way to Sodom and Gomorrah, verses 23-25 reveal that Abraham approached (drew near—in a heart-to-heart manner) Him and said: "Will you sweep away the righteous with the wicked? What if there are fifty righteous people in the city? Will you really sweep it away and not spare the place for the sake of the fifty righteous people in it? Far be it from you to do such a thing—to kill the righteous with the wicked, treating the righteous and the wicked alike. Far be it from you! Will not the Judge of all the earth do right?"

Abraham did not condone the behavior of the people of Sodom and Gomorrah, yet he tried to intervene on their behalf on a humanitarian basis. In fact, his appeals to God in this instance, are regarded as his first Biblically recorded prayers. Albeit his negotiations proved he did not have all the facts. He began by assuming there might have been fifty righteous people in the city who would have suffered God's wrath. He also leaned on God's mercy by asserting that it would be outside of God's character to destroy the righteous along with the wicked.

Notice, Abraham referred to the visitor he was talking to as the Judge of all the earth, which reaffirmed that this was indeed a theophany. However, he asked a very interesting question, which was: "Will not the Judge of all the earth do right?" His position was, it would be a wrong judgment if the Judge of all the earth destroyed the righteous along with the wicked. He probably used this line of reasoning because of the flood, in which God spared Noah and his family, while all the wicked perished. Abraham highly regarded God's reputation as a protector of the righteous. He did not want to see that reputation tarnished.

Notice verse 26, where the Lord said, "If I find fifty righteous people in the city of Sodom, I will spare the whole place for their sake." In other words, based on Abraham's reasoning, God had the right to destroy the city since there were less than fifty righteous people there. But, having lost that round of negotiations, verses 27-28 say, Abraham spoke up again and said: "Now that I have been so bold as to speak to the Lord, though I am nothing but dust and ashes, what if the number of the righteous is five less than fifty? Will you destroy the whole city for lack of five people?" God reassured

Abraham, who recognized his unworthy state, that if He found forty-five righteous people in the city, He would not destroy it.

Verses 29–32 record Abraham's persistent negotiations on behalf of Sodom and Gomorrah, until he reached the number ten. He said, "May the Lord not be angry but let me speak just once more. What if only ten can be found there?" The Lord answered, "For the sake of ten, I will not destroy it." This reply confirmed the wretched state of those cities and God's right to destroy them. It also amplified Abraham's concern for his nephew Lot and his family.

Verse 33 indicates that when the Lord had finished speaking with Abraham, He left, and Abraham returned home. The fact that Sodom and Gomorrah were ultimately destroyed suggests there were less than ten righteous people there. In fact, it became more expedient for God to remove the few people to whom He attributed righteousness, than to spare the city in which there were hundreds of unrighteous people. The fate of Sodom and Gomorrah, and particularly Lot and his family, was once again a troubling spectacle for Abraham, but on this occasion, he had no means by which to rescue them from divine retribution. Their only hope was the grace of God.

GENESIS CHAPTER NINETEEN

Chapter Eighteen described Abraham's encounter with three visitors who came to his tent. They agreed to his request to prepare a meal for them. At some point the visitors inquired about Sarah, who was sitting inside the tent. One of the visitors, who was identified as the Lord, revealed that in a year's time, Sarah would give birth to a son. Abraham was supposed to inform Sarah about this, but he apparently had not, which was one reason the visitors repeated it at his tent. The other reason they came to Abraham's tent was to inform him about their plan to destroy the cities of Sodom and Gomorrah. Despite Abraham's pleas against the plan, their fate was settled. This chapter will delve into events surrounding their destruction.

LOT WELCOMED TWO VISITORS TO SODOM

Verse 1 indicates that two angels arrived at Sodom in the evening, and Lot was sitting in the gateway of the city. When he saw them, he got up to meet them and bowed down with his face to the ground. By sitting in the gateway of the city, Lot saw everything that came and went from the city. In other words, he witnessed much of its sinful behaviors. The city gate was also the place where business was conducted, so Lot was positioned to observe much of the corruption that went on and how people treated each other.

No wonder Second Peter 2:7 declares that Lot was a righteous man, who was distressed by the depraved conduct of lawlessness he witnessed. It also says that by living among them, day after day his righteous soul was tormented by the lawless deeds he saw and heard. Quite frankly, if the Bible did not describe Lot as a righteous man, it would be challenging to find a single righteous choice he made, or act he performed in the entire book! Having grown up with Abraham, he had a great foundation, but his life reflected a downward spiral from the day he chose for himself where he would live.

Lot said in verse 2, "My lords, please turn aside to your servant's house. You can wash your feet and spend the night and then go on your way early in the morning." They answered, "No, we will spend the night in the square." Lot presented the same offer of hospitality that Abraham did, but while Abraham's offer was accepted without objection, his offer was not. However, Lot must be commended for being persistent in his offer to be hospitable. For his part, the visitors would not spend the night in the square. Lot seemed to recognize they were not like others he had seen enter and leave through the city gate. He knew they were worthy of an invitation to his house. Others in the city did not have this awareness.

The visitors initially refused Lot's offer of hospitality, but verse 3 says he insisted so strongly that they did go with him and entered his house. He prepared a meal for them, baking bread without yeast (unleavened), and they ate. There were obvious differences between Abraham's situation and Lot's. Abraham lived in a tent, Lot lived in a house. The meal Abraham prepared was more elaborate as Lot's riches seemed to have dwindled from what they were when he left Abraham. At that time, he had servants, cattle and herds, which required him to have land. Now he lived in the city, and no longer seemed to have much. Apparently, either he moved into the city, or the city grew to engulf him. The fact that he prepared unleavened bread (bread without yeast), symbolized his humble position, and he no longer seemed to have servants. Hence, it appears he prepared the meal himself.

MEN OF SODOM'S DEPRAVED REQUEST

Verses 4-5 highlight the degenerate condition of Sodom. It says that before they had gone to bed, all the men from every part of the city of Sodom—both young and old—surrounded the house. They called to Lot, "Where are the men who came to you tonight? Bring them out to us so that we can have sex with them."

Their demand was clear. The men of the city wanted to have sex with Lot's visitors, angels who revealed themselves in the form of men. This was a homosexual request, but admittedly, it was more than that. It was also a request to commit gang-rape. Notice the men of the city were both young and old. This meant the future of the city would be no better than its past or present. Its sinful condition would only go from bad to worse.

A few determinations must be made before deciding if what the men of Sodom requested Lot to do was sinful. Was it their request to have a homosexual relationship with the men that was sinful? Or was it their request to gang-rape the men that was sinful? A contemporary view has emerged, which subscribes to the position that there was nothing wrong or sinful, if all the men of Sodom wanted was to have a consensual homosexual relationship with the visitors. This view postulates that the real problem or sin, was the men of Sodom's desire to gang-rape the visitors.

While it is true that gang-rape is sin, the Bible also unequivocally opposes homosexuality as well. To this day, the events which occurred in the city of Sodom is where the word "sodomy," came from. In most societies this word is still used to show contempt for what occurred in Lot's day.

LOT'S PROPOSAL TO THE MEN OF SODOM

Verse 6 shows that Lot went outside to meet with the men of Sodom, and he shut the door behind him. In other words, Lot tried to protect the reputation of his city by not allowing his visitors to hear what the men outside were saying. It did not seem to occur to him that a closed door could not prevent his visitors from seeing or hearing what was occurring on the other side. It is also conceivable that Lot may have closed the door behind him, because he did not want the visitors to hear the proposal he would make in his attempt to negotiate with the depraved men outside his house.

Lot tried to negotiate with them in verses 7-8, where he said, "No, my friends. Don't do this wicked thing. I have two daughters who have never slept with a man. Let me bring them out to you, and you can do what you like with them. But don't do anything to these men, for they have come under the protection of my roof."

Lot tried to reason with unreasonable men, even referring to them as friends, though they were anything but friendly. Notice, he also referred to what they wanted to do as a "wicked thing." Again, was this a reference to their desire to have a consensual homosexual relationship with the visitors? Or was a "wicked thing" in reference to their desire to gang-rape the visitors? It was clear Lot's characterization was in reference to their desire to have a homosexual relationship with the visitors. This conclusion can be drawn, because rather than agreeing to their desire to gang-rape his male visitors, he proposed that they gang-rape his virgin daughters instead! His proposal was also egregious, but it showed that homosexuality, rather than gang-rape, was the "wicked thing" he was concerned about.

As a citizen of Sodom, Lot appealed to the custom of his day, by reminding the men that his visitors had come under the protection of his roof. However, he would soon realize it was his roof that had come under the protection of his visitors. The men of Sodom had become so inflamed by their passions, that were it not for his visitors, his roof would have no protection whatsoever! Interestingly, he reasoned that the visitors should be left alone because they had come under the protection of his roof, but he was willing to give up his virgin daughters who lived under his roof! He removed any protection they had! However, the men of Sodom who came to his door, were not interested in a sexual relationship with women, they wanted men, consensual or not.

MEN OF SODOM RESPOND TO LOT'S PROPOSAL

Verse 9 shows that the men of Sodom responded by telling Lot to "Get out of the way!" Then they referred to Lot as someone who came to Sodom as a foreigner, who now wanted to play the judge. Moreover, they threatened to treat him worse than they would treat his visitors. Then they kept bringing pressure on Lot and moved forward to break down his door.

The accusation that Lot was one who came to Sodom as a foreigner, was probably made by the older men who knew his history. It also punctuated the horrible mistake he made when he chose that place as his home. Observe also that they accused him of trying to play the judge. In other words, he was accused of being judgmental, which is still an indictment made against religious people, who happen to have an adverse opinion about homosexuality.

The men of Sodom promised that if Lot did not get out of their way, they would treat him, rather than his virgin daughters, whom he offered to them, worse than they treated his visitors. In other words, his turn would be next! This was a dire situation for Lot! Once again, the Apostle Peter referred to Lot as a righteous man, which meant Sodom had become too dangerous of a place for the righteous to live. God was compelled to act in such a situation! What the men of Sodom wanted to do to Lot and his visitors, suggested other visitors to the city may have suffered the same assault. Hence, this may have been where the outcry against the city came from, which God said He heard about and had come down to see. The moral laws God gave to mankind (Gen 9:1–17) were under assault in Sodom and Gomorrah.

Verses 10–11 describe an ominous decline in the situation. It says the men inside reached out and pulled Lot back into the house and shut the door. Then they struck the men who were at the door of the house, young and old, with blindness, so that they could not find the door. Lot's attempt to negotiate with those men made the situation worse. They were no longer willing to wait for him to bring out the visitors, they were trying to break down his door to go in and get them! After being struck with blindness, they could not find the door, which implies that even then, they were still trying to find it. Hence, not even blindness defused their passions.

SODOM'S FATE SEALED

Lot's visitors took control of the situation. Notice verses 12–13, the two men asked Lot, "Do you have anyone else here, sons-in-law, sons, or daughters, or anyone else in the city who belongs to you? Get them out of here because we are going to destroy this place. The outcry to the Lord against its people is so great that He has sent us to destroy it."

The visitors finally revealed their purpose to Lot. God had come down to see if the outcry was as great as He heard it was, and indeed it was great! The fact that they wanted to have sex with angels, amplified how depraved they had become! Hence, as a righteous man, Lot was given an opportunity to save himself and others. God has given this same opportunity to the righteous today, who are also living in a dangerous and depraved world. He also gives this offer to sinners who are willing to repent and join the righteous in their journey to safety.

Verse 14 makes a startling declaration. Firstly, it showed that the number of people whom Lot considered to be close were very few. Secondly, the few he considered to be close, did not take his offer of salvation seriously. It says Lot went out and spoke to his sons-in-law, who were pledged to marry (or were married to) his daughters. He told them to hurry and get out of the place, because the Lord was about to destroy the city! But his sons-in-law thought he was joking.

The question begs to be asked, why at such a critical time did Lot's sons-in-law think he was joking? Was it because he was a habitual joker? Or was it because he communicated the message in a joking manner, which lacked the sound of urgency? It cannot be known with certainty why Lot's sons-in-law thought he was joking, but it is conceivable that they thought he was joking because they were just as depraved as the other men of Sodom. The message of salvation is always a joke to those who do not believe it, and who are caught up in the evil ways of this world. They were like many today, who believe the message about the Lord's return, and His final judgment is a joke.

Additionally, verses 15–16 seem to communicate the possibility that Lot himself was not responding to the situation with urgency. It says as dawn approached, the angels urged Lot, saying, "Hurry! Take your wife and your two daughters who are here, or you will be swept away when the city is punished." When he hesitated, the men had to grasp his hand, and the hands of his wife and of his two daughters, and lead them safely out of the city, because the Lord was merciful to them.

As decadent as the place was, Lot did not want to leave it. His hesitation may also explain why his sons-in-law thought he was joking. He could not convince them of the urgency to leave, because he did not appear to have it himself! It was clear, not only did Lot live in Sodom, but Sodom also lived in him! Thankfully, the Lord was merciful to him and his immediate household. Again, Lot's circle was rather small, but his influence upon them also seemed minimal.

LOT AND HIS FAMILY'S ESCAPE FROM SODOM

Verse 17 indicates that as soon as Lot and his family were brought out, one of the visitors gave them four instructions: 1. Flee for your lives! 2. Don't look back! 3. Don't stop anywhere in the plain! 4) Flee to the mountains or you will be swept away! As the story progresses, it is worth checking to see how many of those instructions were followed.

Notice Lot's reply in verses 18–20. He responded, "No, my lords, (or No, Lord) please! Your servant has found favor in your eyes, and you have shown great kindness to me in sparing my life. But I can't flee to the mountains; this disaster will overtake me, and I'll die. Look, here is a town near enough to run to, and it is small. Let me flee to it, it is very small, isn't it? Then my life will be spared."

In essence, Lot was given instructions about what to do to save his life, but he rejected those instructions in favor of his own plan for how his life should be saved. Again, it is worth keeping an eye on how the story played out to see whose plan ultimately prevailed. Suffice it to say, despite the circumstances and his obvious lack of foresight, Lot once again wanted to choose for himself where he should live, rather than being directed by God in that regard.

Notice the suggestion he gave was to be allowed to flee to a small town nearby. He said if he fled to the mountains, he would die. Now, if death was God's plan for him at that time, why would He rescue him in the first place? Why not let him die with the other people of Sodom? The truth was, Lot did not want to go too far from Sodom because once the disaster past, he was hoping to return there. Sodom had a significant impact on his life. It was the world in, and upon which, he had built his life. As such, the visitors told him to flee to the mountains, or high ground, but Lot preferred to flee to the plain, or low ground.

One of the most puzzling, but glaring observations about this story, is the fact that Lot never requested to take temporary refuge in the area where his uncle Abraham lived. It appears that once they parted company, there is no Biblical evidence they ever communicated again. Albeit Abraham always seemed concerned about his well-being, and Lot may have felt the same. However, they loved each other from a distance, and Lot did not request to go where Abraham was, though it was not very far.

Because Lot insisted he could not flee to the mountains, verses 21–22 indicate that the visitor said to him, "Very well, I will grant this request too; I will not overthrow the town you speak of. But flee there, quickly! Because I cannot do anything until you reach it." That is why the town was called Zoar (small).

Most likely, Zoar would also have been destroyed, but because Lot requested to go there, it was spared for his sake. God in His mercy also delayed destruction until Lot and his family were in a safe place. In other words, He was careful to protect His reputation that He does not destroy the righteous with the wicked.

Verse 23 points out that by the time Lot and his family reached Zoar, the sun had risen over the land. In other words, Lot and his family made their escape during the night. After an eventful night and daring escape, by the time they arrived in Zoar, they would have been tired and needing to sleep. The fact that the sun rose that day, signaled to the Sodomites that it was just another normal day. Little did they know, unparalleled disaster was about to overtake them!

DESTRUCTION OF SODOM AND GOMORRAH

Verses 24–25 declare that the Lord rained down burning sulfur from the heavens on Sodom and Gomorrah. Thus, He overthrew those cities and the entire plain, destroying all those living in the cities, and also the vegetation in the land. God brought about this destruction in such a way as to leave no doubt it was His doing. He rained down burning sulfur from the heavens to destroy those cities and no others. He also destroyed the people of those cities and the vegetation, while other cities were left unharmed. God literally unleashed a strategic assault upon Sodom and Gomorrah, and surrounding cities in the plain.

Notice verse 26 says that Lot's wife looked back and she became a pillar (nĕtsiyb—garrison, officer, or variant) of salt. One of the instructions the angel gave them was, do not look back! This was tough guidance for Lot's wife, who was probably a Sodomite, and who obviously lamented the destruction of her city and all she was leaving behind. More importantly, the fate of Lot's wife served as a perpetual reminder to those God is saving. They must not look back with desire for the past. Lot's wife did not become a pillar of smoldering ashes like her fellow Sodomites, who serve as a reminder of the reward for sin. Instead, she became a pillar of salt, as a reminder of those who look back with a desire to preserve a sinful past.

Jesus referred to the destruction of Sodom, and specifically Lot's wife, in Luke 17:29-33. He predicted that on the coming great day, when He is once again revealed, it will be a normal day, just like it was on the day when Lot left Sodom, when fire and sulfur rained down from heaven and destroyed them all. He specifically admonished believers to remember Lot's wife. Then He said, whoever tries to keep their life will lose it, and whoever loses their life will preserve it. Lot's wife was physically on her way to escaping Sodom, but mentally and emotionally, she never left. As such, her actions serve as a memorial to those who are physically in one place, but mentally and emotionally in another, whether it be marriage, religion, employment, or any other walk of life. It is also a warning against longing for a sinful past, from which God has provided rescue.

ABRAHAM SEES SODOM AND GOMORRAH'S DESTRUCTION FROM AFAR

Verses 26-28 show that early the next morning Abraham got up and returned to the place where he had stood before the Lord. He looked down toward Sodom and Gomorrah, toward all the land of the plain, and he saw dense smoke rising from the land, like smoke from a furnace.

It appeared that once God told Abraham what He was going to do to Sodom and Gomorrah, it stayed on Abraham's mind. When he saw smoke billowing from that direction, he immediately knew what had occurred. He knew there were less than ten righteous people in the city, and he undoubtedly wondered about the welfare of his nephew Lot.

Since the cities were destroyed sometime after the sun came up, Abraham arose early the next morning, when it would have been easier to see the smoke in that direction. He went back to the place where he previously stood before the Lord, and where the Lord told him what He was going to do. Now, he saw what the Lord had done. The fact that Abraham could see the smoke from Sodom and Gomorrah, meant it was not too far from where he lived. Lot could have found temporary refuge with his uncle, just as Abraham had found temporary refuge in Egypt, but that was not to be, because Lot lived in Sodom, and Sodom lived in him.

Verse 29 makes the interesting comment that when God destroyed the cities of the plain, he remembered Abraham, and He brought Lot out of the catastrophe that overthrew the cities where Lot had lived. So, did Lot, whom Second Peter 2:7, referenced as a righteous man, escape the catastrophe because he himself was righteous? Or did he escape, as the apostle Peter said, because God remembered his righteous uncle Abraham? It is clear the latter was true. And notice, it says God brought Lot out of the catastrophe; otherwise, he would never have made it out, because he would never have left on his own.

LOT FLEES TO THE MOUNTAINS

Verse 30 says that Lot and his two daughters left Zoar and settled in the mountains, for he was afraid to stay in Zoar, so he and his two daughters lived in a cave. It was shown above that when the angel told Lot to flee to the mountains, he said he could not, because if he did, he would die! Now Lot and his daughters were exactly where they were told to go in the first place, the mountains!

The question must be asked, why did Lot and his daughters become afraid to stay in the small town of Zoar, which he insisted to flee to in the first place? Most likely, they became afraid because being the only survivors out of Sodom, they would have garnered attention from the residents of Zoar. During the timeframe in which they lived, it was believed disaster was brought about by the gods in response to human misdeeds. Since Lot and his daughters were the only survivors, the residents of Zoar may have blamed them for what happened in Sodom, and would have wondered if they, and their city, were next. Lot and his daughters were certainly not welcomed in Zoar!

It is worth pausing at this point to consider the state of affairs in Lot's life. When he and Abraham parted company (Gen 13:10), he was a rich man, with servants, cattle, and herds. He looked around and saw the whole plain of the Jordan toward Zoar, that it was well watered, like the garden of the Lord (Eden), and like the land of Egypt, and he chose that area for himself as a place to live. It appeared to be a beautiful place! He thought it was the best place, certainly a better place than where his uncle lived.

Now, here it was, most of the plain he saw back then, which was well watered, like the garden of God, and like Egypt, had become a plain of smoldering ashes. He had to flee for his life, and found himself alone, destitute, and living in a cave. This was quite a turn of events, all because he left the promised land, to go to a promiscuous land. His choices in life took him on a downward spiral from the start; yet this righteous man tried to the bitter end to cling to that depraved world.

INCEST IN LOT'S FAMILY

The following verses attest to the veracity of the Bible, and why it is a book, which is different from any other religious book. It does not sugar-coat its characters and make them out to be perfect individuals when they were not. These verses will describe some of the most unfortunate events imaginable in any family, but especially in the family of a righteous man.

Verses 31–32 indicate that one day, Lot's older daughter said to the younger, "Our father is old, and there is no man around here to give us children, as is the custom all over the earth. Let's get our father to drink wine and then sleep with him and preserve our family line through our father." Lot's daughter was correct in her assertion that men all over the earth had sexual relations with women, in order to produce children. However, she was unspeakably incorrect in assuming, who those men were, did not matter. Those men were not fathers of the women with whom they produced children. The idea she proposed was taboo, even during the times in which she lived!

Cases of incest involving parents and children, are usually initiated by the parents. But, in this case, it was Lot's daughters who initiated this horrific act. Their warped thinking was clearly influenced by their upbringing in Sodom! They were no longer living in Sodom, but Sodom still lived in them! If God did not intend to preserve their family, why would He deliver them from the catastrophe He brought on their city? Besides, having lived in Zoar for a short while they would have seen men who were still alive there and in other cities, with whom they could have built families. However, they became overwhelmed by their miss-guided passions and took matters into their own hands.

It is not clear if Lot was an alcoholic while he lived in Sodom, but he appeared to become one while living in the mountains. The toll of losing his wife and everything he owned and held dear, could have drove him to drink. However, it was clear, his daughters had no doubt, once they got him to start drinking a skin of wine, he would not stop until it was empty and until he was unconsciously drunk, to the point where he would be oblivious. That level of unawareness, especially about a sexual encounter, is highly unusual for any man!

Verse 33 points out that on that very night they got their father to drink wine, and the older daughter went in and slept with him. He was not aware of it when she lay down or when she got up. Lot was unconsciously inebriated! He did not know what happened to him! But both of his daughters knew; yet neither of them took action to correct their behavior. While the serpent in the garden of God caused Adam to fall by what he ate, he caused Noah, and now Lot to fall by what they drank! To that end, Lot bore some responsibility for what happened to him. As the man in charge, he was not supposed to be drunk.

Lot's daughters proved they had no shame or remorse for what they did to their father the first night. Notice, verses 34–36 reveal the very next day, the older daughter said to the younger, "Last night I slept with my father. Let's get him to drink wine again tonight, and you go in and sleep with him so we can preserve our family line through our father." So, they got their father to drink wine that night as well, and the younger daughter went in and slept with him. Again, he was not aware of when she lay down or when she got up. Both of Lot's daughters became pregnant by their father.

Since Lot was described as a righteous man, his daughters' actions and his own alcoholism, must have been tormenting memories for the remainder of his life. He became biological father and grandfather to his daughter's children. His legacy was not only that of a righteous man who escaped tragedy in Sodom, in which all other men perished, but also that of a sinful man, who was known to have sex with, and children by his daughters. What would Abraham have thought when he heard about this?

Verse 37 reveals that Lot's older daughter had a son, and she named him Moab, which sounds like the Hebrew for "from father." It says he is the father of the Moabites of today. Verse 38 also states that his younger daughter had a son, and she named him Ben-Ammi (Bene-Ammon), which means "son of my father's people"; he is the father of the Ammonites of today. Because of this, it is doubtful these women ever got married. No man, not even in those days, would marry a woman who initiated an incestual relationship with her father.

Apart from brief references, there is no further information in the Bible about Lot. It is not clear how, when, or where he died; If his end came in the mountains or back in the plains, in or near Sodom, the place he truly loved. It would have been informative to know how Lot's daughters explained their actions to him, and how he was able to reconcile the new reality in his family.

With all that happened in Lot's life, an obvious take-away is the fact that he was still regarded as a righteous man. This speaks to the fact that because of the grace of God, there is always hope, no matter the level of family or life dysfunction people may experience.

GENESIS CHAPTER TWENTY

The previous chapter reviewed the destruction of Sodom and Gomorrah and events surrounding its day of reckoning. Lot and his two daughters were delivered from that devastation but ended up living in a cave in the mountains. Sadly, the daughters devised a plan to extend their families through incestuous relationships with their father.

Chapter twenty is another, which proves why the Bible is such an exceptional book. Again, it does not conceal the faults of its most celebrated characters. This time, some of Abraham's shortcomings will once again be brought into focus. A summary will be given of how he deceived Abimelech with the same old lie that Sarah was his sister, while withholding the fact that she was also his wife. It was a reminder that Abraham still had more growing to do where his faith-walk was concerned.

ABRAHAM DECEIVES ABIMELECH

Verses 1-2 show that Abraham moved on from the area near Mamre into the region of the Negev, and lived between Kadesh and Shur. For a while he stayed in Gerar, and there he said of his wife Sarah, "She is my sister." Then Abimelech king of Gerar, sent for Sarah and took her.

It is not clear why Abraham moved on from Mamre where he lived in relative peace, to go to Gerar, which was Philistine territory. It could have been he was embarrassed by the incest, which occurred in Lot's family. The Canaanites among whom he lived, knew that Lot was his nephew, as some of them risked their lives in a military campaign to rescue Lot some years earlier. So, Abraham may have thought it best to move to an area where he could escape the stigma associated with being related to Lot. Incest was taboo even in those days.

Abraham's plot to again represent his wife Sarah as his sister, indicated that he needed more growth in his faith. In the previous account (Gen

12:13) when Abraham said Sarah was his sister, he claimed to have done so to save his life from Pharaoh. In this account, he again did it to save his life, but again he also thought the people were more wretched than they turned out to be. In any case, Abraham did what commonly occurs among those who struggle all their lives to overcome certain bad habits. In other words, he relapsed into the same sin he dealt with before, and from which God previously delivered him. But, not only him, verse five indicates that Sarah also colluded in his scheme.

What was most significant this time, was the fact that Sarah was either pregnant or nearing the time to become pregnant. Abraham's idea had the potential to ruin God's plans for his family! Sarah was once again in danger, and this time, her unborn child was as well! Abraham, who was supposed to be overly protective of her, had once again put her in harm's way. Most importantly, every member of Abraham's household who moved with him to Gerar, including Hagar and her son Ishmael, knew Sarah was not only his sister, but also his wife.

It is also worth mentioning that of all the women in Abraham's household, for Abimelech to choose Sarah, an almost ninety-year-old woman, meant she must have been miraculously gorgeous at her age!

GOD WARNED ABIMELECH IN A DREAM

Verse 3 says God came to Abimelech in a dream one night and said to him, "You are as good as dead because of the woman you have taken; she is a married woman." Evidently, Abimelech had taken Sarah to his house but had not yet taken her to his bed. That would have been the next step if God had not intervened. God literally snitched on Abraham to inform Abimelech that Sarah was married! This event shows that God can speak to whomever He chooses. Obviously, Abraham, a righteous man, was not listening to Him at that time, so to get His plan back on track, He spoke directly to Abimelech, a pagan.

Observe that even though the Law of Moses, which condemns adultery, was not yet given, God affirmed to Abimelech that the reason he should not touch Sarah, was because she was married. In other words, God referenced a commonly understood moral law concerning adultery, and Abimelech understood the reference. It was commonly understood that taking another man's wife while he was alive was wrong. However, Abimelech did not know Sarah was Abraham's wife, which is why he took her. He thought she was his sister, as he was told. It took a terrifying dream from God to cause Abimelech to change his course of action. And, the words God spoke to him, should resonate with every other sinner: "You are as good as dead."

ABIMELECH'S RESPONSE TO GOD'S WARNING

Verses 4-5 indicate that Abimelech had not gone near her, so he said, "Lord, will you destroy an innocent nation? Did he not say to me, 'She is my sister,' and didn't she also say, 'He is my brother'? I have done this with a clear conscience and clean hands."

Again, Sarah was complicit in this scheme! The fact that the Lord Himself spoke to her (Gen 18:9:15) and predicted she would give birth within a year's time was not a deterrent. It is not clear why they chose to walk so close to disaster, but it showed that God's plan depended more on Him than it did on them.

Notice, Abimelech appealed to God's justice by saying he acted with "a clear conscience and clean hands." In other words, he was not the guilty one, Abraham and Sarah were! Their consciences were not clear, nor were their hands clean. So, the unanswered question is, why did God threaten to kill Abimelech, rather than kill them?

Verse 6 shows that God said to Abimelech, "Yes, I know you did this with a clear conscience, and so I have kept you from sinning against Me. That is why I did not let you touch her." The only reason Abimelech was not sexually involved with Sarah was because of God. Neither Abraham nor her, seemed to have any concern about the fact that she was married. And, once again, their entire household were aware of what they were doing.

Thankfully, God accepted Abimelech's plea by expressing knowledge of his innocence and stating it as the reason He kept him from even touching Sarah, and from sinning. So, God kept a sinner from sinning, and from the penalty of sin, but He also kept the righteous from suffering its penalty by keeping their sinful plan from coming to fruition.

ABIMELECH RETURNED SARAH TO ABRAHAM

Verse 7 says God told Abimelech to return the man's wife to him, because he is a prophet, and the man would pray for him and he would live. But if he did not return her, he could be sure he and all who belonged to him would die.

Having been warned by God, Abimelech was no longer innocent, nor would his hands remain clean if he persisted in a sexual relationship with Sarah. Also, observe that God told him what Abraham's rightful role was.

This was a role Abraham would rather have hidden at that moment when he was not behaving like a prophet. God said Abraham would pray for Abimelech. Hopefully, he began by praying for himself and for his wife Sarah.

Frankly, Abimelech demonstrated greater character than Abraham and Sarah did. His willingness to allow Abraham to pray for him, after having been deceived by him, and almost costing him his life, was an act of humility. It was also an act of fear, because he wanted to remove the possible sentence of immediate death from his household.

Verses 8–10 declare that early the next morning, Abimelech summoned all his officials, and when he told them all that had happened to him, they were very afraid. Then he called Abraham in and asked him, "What have you done to us? How have I wronged you that you have brought such great guilt upon me and my kingdom? You have done things to me that should never be done." And Abimelech asked Abraham, "What was your reason for doing this?"

Abimelech literally put Abraham on trial to understand why he would do such a thing to him and his kingdom. In other words, what Abraham did, was so unusual that pagans had trouble understanding his actions. In the past, Abraham had proven to be a brave man, who routed armies to save his nephew Lot, but in this case, he proved to be a coward, who surrendered his wife to save his own life. Yet, despite the affect he presented as a coward, those to whom he was speaking were afraid of him, because of what God said about him. The God of heaven put fear in them by placing a death-threat over them, for which they needed Abraham's prayers to have it removed.

Observe that Abimelech asked Abraham, "What was your reason for doing this?" In other words, upon what basis did you think it best to so greatly deceive us? This question should have convicted Abraham and cut to the heart of his actions as one who was supposed to be a prophet. As so often happens, pagans are able to call the righteous into judgment when their actions do not comport with their spiritual profession. In this instance, Abraham's actions were way off-base!

Abraham's response provided further insight into his faith-walk at that point in his spiritual journey. Verses 11–12 point out that Abraham replied, "I said to myself, there is surely no fear of God in this place, and they will kill me because of my wife. Besides, she really is my sister, the daughter of my father though not of my mother; and she became my wife."

Abraham thought there was no fear of God in that place, and even said so to himself. Hence, when he decided to deceive them, he adapted to his environment, and acted as if he had no fear of God himself! In reality, he was wrong! There was a fear of God in the place because God appeared to

Abimelech in a dream and put fear in them to save Sarah from them. In so doing, God showed Abraham He could work in and through whomever He pleases. By that time, Abraham had enough direct interactions with God, along with promises from Him, which were yet to be fulfilled in his lifetime, and which should have informed him that Abimelech could not take his life. Still, in this instance, he walked by sight, rather than by faith.

Abraham continued in verse 13 by saying that when God had him to wander from his father's household, he said to Sarah, "This is how you can show your love to me: Everywhere we go, say of me, He is my brother." Hence, their deceitful plan was not new, it was one they concocted from the day they left home many years before, and they use it wherever they went. Abraham's response suggested he and his wife had been deceitful for so long that their deceit had become a reasonable option everywhere they went. He even invoked God into his plot, by asserting since it was God who made him wander from his father's household, he had to devise a plan by which he and Sarah could survive in the dangerous places to which God caused them to wander.

Verses 14-15 say that Abimelech brought sheep and cattle and male and female slaves and gave them to Abraham, and he returned Sarah his wife to him. And Abimelech said, "My land is before you; live wherever you like."

Just as Pharaoh made Abraham rich (Gen 13:1-2), by paying him off following a similar scheme, Abimelech did the same. However, he also did something Pharaoh did not do, he offered Abraham the opportunity to stay in his country, whereas Pharaoh ordered him to leave (Gen 12:19). Abraham was not deserving of these payoffs, and it is not clear why those who were victims of his deceitful schemes, seemed to bear more of the burden for restitution than he did.

Abimelech said to Sarah in verse 16, he was giving her "brother" a thousand shekels (about 25 pounds, or 12 kilograms) of silver, to cover the offense against her, in the presence of all who was with her. By doing this, he said she was completely vindicated.

Notice Abimelech's sarcastic reference to Abraham as her "brother" rather than her husband. He stuck with what he was told! And even though nothing sexual occurred, the idea of having her, a married woman, in his harem was humiliating enough. Therefore, Abimelech took steps to restore Sarah's dignity in the presence of all who were with them, which included Hagar and her son Ishmael.

After Abimelech took steps to right his inadvertent wrongs, verses 17-18 indicate that Abraham prayed to God, and God healed Abimelech, his wife and his female slaves so they could have children again. The Lord had kept all the women in Abimelech's household from conceiving because of Abraham's wife Sarah.

The Bible does not reveal the words of Abraham's prayer but it must have been awkward, yet powerful, since it not only brought restoration to Abimelech's household, it also forced Abraham to deal with the impact of what he had done. He was forced to pray so that the women in Abimelech's household could have children again, yet his wife Sarah had no children so far. This made it easy for him to deny her as his wife, but God had already told them, their childless situation would soon change. Hence, their scheme was an outright affront to His plan.

Thankfully, God's plan did not depend on Abraham and Sarah; Instead, it was accomplished despite them. It was accomplished because He is sovereign, and able to cause every promise He makes come to pass. However, life is far more peaceful when His human vessels remain on track by following the instructions He has given them.

GENESIS CHAPTER TWENTY-ONE

The previous chapter examined Abraham and Sarah's efforts to derail God's plan, which was for them to have a son within a year's time. Rather than working to promote that plan, Abraham moved his household to Gerar, which was Philistine territory. There, he encountered Abimelech, who took Sarah into his house to be his wife, because Abraham and Sarah deceived him into believing they were only siblings. If God had not intervened to alert Abimelech of the truth, Sarah's integrity would have been more severely compromised. This chapter will review events surrounding the birth of the son God promised them.

BIRTH OF ISAAC THE PROMISED SON

Despite their folly in Gerar, verses 1–3 reveal that the Lord was gracious to Sarah as He had said, and He did for Sarah what He had promised. She became pregnant and bore a son to Abraham in his old age, at the very time God had promised him. Abraham gave the name Isaac (Laughter) to the son Sarah bore him.

Isaac's name, Laughter, was a reminder of what both his parents did when God prophesied to them about him. It also symbolized the joy he brought to their hearts. His birth was similar to that of Christ, because it came about as a result of a promise, and it was miraculous! There were no natural means then, nor do they exist now, by which Sarah, being ninety years old, could give birth to a child. Conversely, his birth was different from the birth of his half-brother Ishmael, because the latter's birth was not the result of a promise, nor was it miraculous. Ishmael's birth resulted from human efforts to work things out their way, rather than patiently waiting for the revelation of God's plan.

Verse 4 indicates that when Isaac was eight days old, Abraham circumcised him, as God commanded him (Gen 17:10–14). Circumcision was a sign of the covenant for Abraham and his descendants, and for those who wanted to be part of his household. It later became a sign of membership in the Israelite community. Any male, citizen or foreigner, who was not circumcised was prohibited from membership. In fact, it was considered an act of defiance against God's command for an Israelite male child to be uncircumcised.

Verse 5 highlighted the fact that Abraham was a hundred years old when his son Isaac was born to him. This meant Isaac did not come about by his doing, but by God's doing. It also meant that from a human perspective, God may at times appear to be slow in fulfilling His promises, but He is more than capable of bringing them to fruition in due time.

Verses 6–7 show Sarah's response to what God did. She said, "God has brought me laughter, and everyone who hears about this will laugh with me." She added, "Who would have said to Abraham that Sarah would nurse children? Yet I have borne him a son in his old age." Everyone would laugh with Sarah, except her enduring enemy Hagar.

These verses indicate that Sarah had gained confidence in the fact that people would no longer laugh at her but would now laugh with her. Notice also that God did not only give her the ability to endure under the pressure of childbirth, but He also gave her vitality, at ninety years old, to be able to nurse the child! She did everything a younger mother would have been able to do. This was truly a miracle!

HAGAR SENT AWAY

Verse 8 indicates that Isaac grew and was weaned, and on the day he was weaned Abraham held a great feast. Weaning occurred between three to five years after birth. It represented a transition in the growth process from milk to meat. After being weaned, milk was no longer the main source of dietary sustenance, as it was simply not enough! So, Abraham held a feast on that day because it probably marked Isaac's graduation from milk to meat, he was finally able to join the feast!

Incidentally, the symbolism between the weaning process for a growing child, and the process for a growing Christian is very similar. One transitions from milk to meat, the other from the elementary to the mature things of the Word of God (Heb 5:12, 6:1).

Verses 9–10 represented a significant change in Abraham's household. These verses point out that Sarah saw that the son whom Hagar the Egyptian had borne to Abraham was mocking, and she said to Abraham, "Get rid of that slave woman and her son, for that woman's son will never share in the inheritance with my son Isaac."

Earlier in this chapter (v 6), Sarah boasted at the birth of Isaac by saying people would no longer laugh at her but would laugh with her. However, Ishmael, who would have been approximately seventeen years old when Isaac was weaned, was mocking him. It is not clear what the nature of this mocking involved, but it could have included insults about the age of his mother. In any case, it was abusive bullying. In fact, Galatians 4:29 referred to what Ishmael did as persecution. It was clear that if Ishmael was allowed to stay in Abraham's household, Isaac's life would have been in danger. It is conceivable Satan might have used him to kill Isaac, to thwart God's plan for the Messiah to come through Isaac's line.

In responding to whatever Ishmael was doing to her son, Sarah's tone suggested she was hot! She was an eyewitness to his mistreatment of her son, and whatever it was, brought her to the conclusion that a casual reprimand would not be enough. She became convinced he could no longer be allowed to stay in the household.

Recall in chapter sixteen, when there were disagreements between Sarah and Hagar, Abraham told Sarah to deal with it as she saw fit, so she mistreated Hagar and caused her to run away. However, in this instance, because of her son's actions, Hagar would not run away, she would be sent away, and there would be no coming back! This time, Abraham would have to deal with it himself, as Sarah's instructions were clear. She told him to get rid of Hagar and her son! This declaration had to come from Sarah, because she was the one who initiated Abraham's relationship with them in the first place (Gen 16:1-2).

Once again, Galatians 4:21-31 describe the symbolism between Sarah, who represented the New Covenant, and Hagar, who represented the Old. The two simply cannot coexist together, and not even Abraham was able to negotiate a peaceful reconciliation between the two. Hagar, who represented the Old Covenant had to be gotten rid of! This is instructive for Christian organizations today, who claim to hold New Covenant beliefs, but adhere to Old Covenant teachings and practices, such as keeping Sabbaths and other "holy" days as a means for salvation. These practices must be gotten rid of in deference to Christ. He is the only one who can and has negotiated harmony between the two covenants (Heb 7:18, 22), and He alone is enough.

Verses 11-12 declare that the matter distressed Abraham greatly because it concerned his son. But God said to him, "Do not be so distressed about the boy and your slave woman. Listen to whatever Sarah tells you, because it is through Isaac that your offspring will be reckoned."

It did not appear to distress Abraham greatly when Sarah suggested he and Hagar should join together (Gen 16:2) to build a family. In fact, it appeared that he readily agreed! However, in this instance where he was confronted with the decision to get rid of Hagar, and his son Ishmael, it greatly distressed him. Notice also that Abraham appeared to make it seem as though his only source of distress was getting rid of his son. But God called out his other source of distress by adding "...and your slave woman." Apparently, Abraham still had feelings for Hagar! He did not want to get rid of her! God had to tell him to do whatever Sarah said!

Scripture does not provide many instances when Sarah said anything, but in those instances when she spoke, it usually had something to do with a child. This time she spoke up to protect her child from the one she thought could have been, but never was hers. God told Abraham to listen to whatever she said, because He was speaking truth through her. If God had not said this to Abraham, he may have done the exact thing he did in chapter 16, which was nothing! He may have left the problem for Sarah to fix herself! In that instance, Sarah dealt harshly with Hagar, who was a woman like her, but this time, something needed to be done about Ishmael, who was a man like Abraham. It was not Sarah's place to deal with him.

In verse 13, God told Abraham He would make Ishmael into a nation also, because he was his offspring. In other words, God assured Abraham that when he sent Ishmael away, he would not die. Rather, he would survive and grow to become a nation. This obviously eased Abraham's mind and gave him assurance that Ishmael's survival did not depend on him, but on God.

Therefore, verse 14 indicates that early the next morning Abraham took some food and a skin of water and gave them to Hagar. He set them on her shoulders and then sent her off with Ishmael. She went on her way and wandered in the Desert of Beersheba. This was obviously a difficult parting for Abraham and his other family. It is very likely many tears were shed between them. However, once Abraham discovered God's will, as spoken through Sarah, and received assurance from God about Ishmael's future, his response was immediate, early the next morning.

This sudden separation gave Hagar and her son no time to prepare for their departure. Hence, they left only with what was given to them by Abraham, rather than what they had an opportunity to take themselves. This was essentially an act of divorce between Abraham and Hagar. What Sarah joined together, she also put asunder.

Interestingly, as grown as Ishmael was at the age of seventeen, still Abraham put the provisions on Hagar's shoulders. It was as though she was responsible for their survival moving forward, and the meager parting supplies, meant they would have to depend on God. Those supplies would not last very long. As such, they wandered in the Desert of Beersheba. Life soon became very difficult for Hagar and her son.

GOD CONFIRMED HIS PROMISE TO HAGAR

Notice verses 15-16 state that when the water in the skin was gone, she put the boy under one of the bushes. Then she went off and sat down a short distance away, because she could not bear to watch the boy die. And, as she sat there, she began to sob.

Hagar began to experience the struggles of being a single parent, living in a world, which was a literal desert. It produced nothing for her. She saw no opportunities for growth, and her circumstances were dire. She was at her wits end and did not know what else she could do to survive. All the food and water Abraham gave her was gone, and there was nothing else to eat in the desert where they were. All Hagar could do was cry.

In that moment, she obviously missed the comforts of Abraham's household but going back there was not an option for her. She was abruptly evicted, and the only solace seemed to be the bushes, which provided shade for her apparently dying son. Hence, whoever planted the bushes, inadvertently blessed her son and contributed to his survival, and to the birth of a nation.

Hagar was not the only one crying, her teenage son was also crying. Notice verses 17-18 reveal that God heard the boy crying, and the angel of God called to Hagar from heaven and said to her, "What is the matter, Hagar? Do not be afraid; God has heard the boy crying as he lies there. Lift the boy up and take him by the hand, for I will make him into a great nation."

Interestingly, these verses reveal that both Hagar and Ishmael cried about their circumstances, but Scripture does not reveal that either of them prayed. Yet, God responded as evidence that He not only hears our prayers, but He also sees our tears. In other words, tears are indeed a language, which God understands. Observe also, He called Hagar by name. This indicated that He knew her, whether or not she knew Him.

God told Hagar to lift (pull) the boy up from where he was lying down, and take (lead) him by the hand, because he was obviously too grown to be carried. God also encouraged Hagar with the very words with which He encouraged Abraham. He told her that Ishmael would become a great nation. In other words, He assured her that as bleak as things looked for them at that moment in the desert, they would not die there. Ishmael still had a future ahead of him, and God's will for his life had to be accomplished.

Having reassured Hagar they would live, verse 19 shows how God immediately moved to prove His intent to take care of them. It says He opened her eyes and she saw a well of water. So, she went and filled the skin with water and gave the boy a drink. Hagar probably could not see the well through the tears in her eyes. Sometimes circumstances of the moment result in tears, which can hinder vision of the bright future just ahead. Whoever dug that well, also played an inadvertent role in Ishmael's survival beyond that day, and in the birth of a nation.

ISHMAEL'S SURVIVAL IN THE DESERT

Verse 20 reiterates that God was with Ishmael, and he grew up. He lived in the desert and became an archer. In other words, Ishmael not only grew up, but he also adapted to his desert surroundings by becoming an archer, which allowed him to be able to survive in that environment, and to provide for himself and for his mother, as sons of single mothers feel obligated to do. It is possible that he may have seen his father Abraham on occasion, but the Bible does not directly say that.

Verse 21 points out that while he was living in the Desert of Paran, his mother got a wife for him from Egypt. Hagar was an Egyptian, who was most likely among the gifts Pharaoh gave to Abraham to get Sarah when he thought she was only his sister (Gen 12:16). So, Hagar got Ishmael a wife from her native country. The selection of a wife was usually a father's role, but the fact that Hagar assumed this role, highlighted the reality of her situation, and Abraham as an absentee father.

SUMMARY OF HAGAR'S LIFE

Once Hagar made sure Ishmael was settled with a wife, he was well on his way to becoming the great nation about which God foretold. Beyond that, scripture does not reveal anything further about what became of Hagar. It is not clear if she remarried, how much longer she lived, or where she died. Her story simply ended.

Hagar became the first single mother and divorcee in Biblical writ. Her words in Scripture are few, and those attributed to her were mostly directed toward God. She was a slave who seemed to accept whatever treatment was dealt to her. Once she became pregnant, she began to despise her mistress Sarah (Gen 16:4–5). It is assumed that the reason she despised her was because she wanted Abraham to herself. While this may be true, it could also be that she despised her, because she knew the plan Sarah devised to build a family through her was not right. Abraham and Sarah made the decision without her input. As a slave, she had no choice but to go along with it.

In other words, Hagar could have despised Sarah because she was forced by her into a situation that resulted in an unwanted pregnancy. Yet, despite all that happened to her, Hagar's story was one in which, if God had not intervened, her life would have ended many years before it did. Thankfully, God was merciful to her.

TREATY AT BEERSHEBA

Recall in chapter 20, Abraham moved from Mamre to the region of the Negev, and for a while he stayed in Gerar, which was Philistine territory. It was there where he deceived Abimelech into believing Sarah was only his sister, and not his wife. Once God intervened to reveal this scheme to Abimelech, he returned Sarah to Abraham along with gifts. He also allowed Abraham to stay in his country, but the following verses reveal tensions associated with that decision.

Verses 22-23 show that Abimelech and Phicol, the commander of his forces said to Abraham, "God is with you in everything you do." As such, Abimelech asked him to swear to him before God that he would not deal falsely with him or with his children or his descendants. Abimelech begged Abraham to show him and his country, where he was residing as a foreigner, the same kindness, which was being shown to him. Those were the terms of the treaty to which Abimelech wanted Abraham to agree.

However, the question begs to be asked, how did Abimelech know God was with Abraham? The answer is, God revealed it earlier when He appeared to him in a dream to inform him that Sarah was not only Abraham's sister, but also his wife. In that dream, God also told him that Abraham was a prophet. So, the fact that God was with Abraham was well established by God Himself! However, Abimelech still had doubts about Abraham's honesty, because even though God said he was a prophet, he had dealt dishonestly with Abimelech before, and almost got him killed! So, Abraham's integrity at that time was understandably questionable.

In essence, the fact that Abimelech, a pagan king, had justified reasons to ask Abraham, a prophet, to deal honestly with him, should have been an embarrassment to Abraham. And this request came after Sarah gave birth to Isaac, which confirmed she was indeed his wife, despite for years he had been lying about her being only his sister. Therefore, the treaty was one to force Abraham to stop lying! Notice verse 24, Abraham agreed to the treaty by swearing he would deal honestly with them.

Following his agreement to deal honestly with them, Abraham complained to Abimelech about a well of water that Abimelech's servants had seized. They literally took Abraham's well from him! This was the kind of action over which wars were waged! But verse 26 shows where Abimelech said he didn't know who did it. He claimed to have no knowledge about the incident prior to Abraham informing him.

Verses 27–29 show that Abraham brought sheep and cattle and gave them to Abimelech, and the two men made a treaty. Abraham set apart seven ewe lambs from the flock, and Abimelech asked him, what was the meaning of the seven ewe lambs he had set apart by themselves. Notice, Abimelech did not ask any questions about the sheep and cattle Abraham gave him, his only inquiry was about the seven ewe lambs. He recognized that they were beyond regular gifts. He saw that they had special significance.

Therefore, in verse 30, Abraham explained the significance of the ewe lambs by asking Abimelech to accept them from his hand as a witness that he dug the well. In other words, Abraham wanted to settle the issue about who the well belonged to. Abimelech obviously accepted the lambs, and the issue was settled on that day. As a result, verse 31 says that place was called Beersheba (Well of Seven, or Well of Oath), because the two men swore an oath there.

ABRAHAM SETTLES IN PHILISTINE TERRITORY

Verses 32–34 indicate that after the treaty had been made at Beersheba, Abimelech and Phicol the commander of his forces returned to the land of the Philistines. But Abraham planted a tamarisk tree in Beersheba, and there he called on the name of the Lord, the Eternal God (Everlasting Power). Then Abraham stayed in the land of the Philistines for a long time. In other words, he was able to enjoy a far more peaceful relationship with the Philistines, than his descendants did.

The birth of a son was the most earnest desire Abraham had. When Ishmael was born, that desire was quenched for him, but not for Sarah. Isaac's birth brought satisfaction to both of them. It was then, they were prepared to get rid of Hagar and her son, to make sure they did not share in the inheritance with Isaac. That was also the time when they were able to gain a clearer picture of God's plan, and what He had been saying to them all along.

With his slave woman and her son gone, Abraham's household became a more peaceful place. Peace with Abimelech and his neighbors added to the enjoyment of his life. Finally, he could see that only an Eternal God, whose power is everlasting, could accomplish all that had occurred in his life. He was reminded that the name of such a God was worthy to be called on and praised.

GENESIS CHAPTER TWENTY-TWO

The previous chapter examined events surrounding the birth of Isaac. It discussed the feast Abraham held when Isaac was weaned, which meant he graduated from milk to solid food. Because of Ishmael's conduct at the feast, both he and his mother Hagar, were expelled from Abraham's household. They lived in the desert, where life was initially a struggle, but God intervened to save them from certain death, and to provide for them. He ensured that Ishmael became the great nation he was foretold to be.

This chapter will examine evidence that Abraham's faith had also graduated from milk to meat. It represents one of the most significant tests of faith imaginable. This chapter will discuss the occasion when God asked Abraham to sacrifice his son Isaac, and Abraham's demonstrated willingness to do so.

To be clear, in this chapter, Abraham would not be tempted by God, but he would certainly be tested by Him. The difference is, temptation is an enticement to do, or to wrongly acquire something attractive. On the other hand, to be tested is to verify by way of performance that the expected quality or reliability is present. It is to ensure that based on prior preparation, performance levels will be achieved or maintained as expected under conditions of pressure. James 1:13, makes it clear that God does not tempt anyone, but this chapter provides evidence that He will certainly test His people.

ABRAHAM REQUIRED TO SACRIFICE ISAAC

In verses 1-2, it says God tested Abraham by saying to him, "Abraham!" "Here I am," he replied. Then God said, "Take your son, your only son, whom you love, Isaac, and go to the region of Moriah. Sacrifice him there as a burnt offering on a mountain I will show you."

Notice God referred to Isaac as Abraham's only son. Obviously, Abraham had another son named Ishmael, but where the covenant was concerned, Isaac was his only son. Sarah made it clear, and God confirmed, that Ishmael would not share in the inheritance with Isaac. Therefore, God identified Isaac by name, as the son He intended Abraham to sacrifice! He also pointed out that this was the son Abraham loved! In other words, this test would not be easy! It would tear at the very core of Abraham's being. This was not the slave woman, Hagar's son, this was the free woman, Sarah's son, whom he loved! Most people could not do to a pet, what Abraham was asked to do to his son!

Also observe that God told Abraham to go to the region of Moriah and sacrifice his son on a mountain He would show him. This meant the journey would be agonizing! Not only because of what he was asked to do, but also by trying to figure out the exact location of the mountain to which he was going.

It should be noted here that child-sacrifice was not an uncommon practice in Abraham's day. This practice occurred in pagan religions of his time, and he may have been familiar with it. Matthews agreed with this position in stating that it seems from the story in this chapter that Abraham was familiar with human sacrifice and was probably not surprised that Yahweh might demand such an offering.[1]

However, this was not just any kind of offering, this was to be a burnt offering, which would have added to the gruesomeness of what Abraham was asked to do. It involved killing his son with a knife, then burning his flesh with fire. Sometimes God still does test the faith of His people by requiring them to make very difficult sacrifices, but this test was extra repugnant! Verse 3 says, early the next morning Abraham got up and loaded his donkey. He took two of his servants with him and his son Isaac. He cut enough wood for the burnt offering, and set out for the place God had told him about.

Once again, this had to be an excruciating journey. More than likely, Abraham never told Sarah about the details of his travels. He seemed to take personal responsibility for preparing for his trip, rather than leaving the preparations to his servants. He most likely did so to make sure he had everything he needed, and to reduce the possibility of being asked too many questions about the nature of his business. Being fully prepared, he set out for the place God told him about, but he would only come to know the exact location, when he was almost there.

---

1. Matthews, *Manners and Customs in the Bible, An Illustrated Guide to Daily Life in Bible Times*, 14.

ABRAHAM ARRIVED NEAR MOUNT MORIAH

Verse 4 says on the third day, Abraham looked up and saw the place in the distance. The fact that his journey took three days is highly instructive. God did not choose a place in the vicinity where Abraham lived, nor did He choose one, which took three hours to get to. Instead, He chose a place, which required a three-day journey! This was a long time for Abraham to contemplate what he was told to do, and to come up with reasons not to do it! It was also early symbolism of the amount of time the ultimate sacrifice, Jesus Christ, who was Abraham's descendant in the flesh, spent in the grave. The similarities were startling!

So much so, that some believe Mount Moriah was the early name of the mount, which was later called Calvary, where Jesus died. Youngman states that Mount Moriah is believed to be one of the mountains of Salem, later called Jerusalem.[2]

Apparently, God did not expressly tell Abraham the place he saw in the distance was the place where the sacrifice was to occur. But somehow once Abraham looked up and saw it, he knew it was. On arriving near the place, verse 5 indicates that he instructed his two servants to stay with the donkey, while he and Isaac go over there and worship, and then return to them.

Abraham thought it best to leave his servants at a distance, to make sure they did not attempt to stop him from doing what God instructed him to do. However, he gave them the confident assurance, that he and the boy would worship and then return to them. This assurance seemed to conflict with the mission he was given by God, which was to sacrifice his son. But Hebrews 11:19, clarifies this apparent discrepancy by indicating, Abraham reasoned that God could even raise the dead. In other words, Abraham rationalized that if he sacrificed his son, God would raise him from the dead, because God had already made promises about Isaac's future.

ISAAC'S INQUIRY ABOUT THE LAMB

Verses 6–8 reveal that Abraham took the wood for the burnt offering and placed it on his son Isaac, while he himself carried the fire and the knife. It discloses that as the two of them went on together, Isaac spoke up and said to his father Abraham, "Father, the fire and wood are here, but where is the lamb for the burnt offering?" Abraham answered, "God himself will provide the lamb for the burnt offering, my son." And the two of them went on together.

---

2. Youngman, *The Lands and Peoples of the Living Bible*, 19.

Isaac carried the wood for his sacrifice, similar to Christ carrying the wooden cross, which was used for His. The procession seemed to arouse Isaac's curiosity, which caused him to speak up! The exchange between him and his father was very intimate. He referred to Abraham as, "My father," and Abraham referred to him as, "My son." This must have made the mission more troubling for Abraham, but he remained focused on the promises God had already made to him. In other words, his faith was built on both substance and evidence.

Isaac saw the wood he was carrying, and fire and knife his father was carrying, and he wondered about the lamb. His inquiry confirmed his familiarity with the necessities for a sacrifice. Hence, he thought, either his father had forgotten the most important necessity, the lamb! Or he began to sense that he might be the lamb! His father responded by telling him, "God himself will provide the lamb for the burnt offering, my son." In other words, "my son, will be the lamb God will provide for the burnt offering!"

ABRAHAM'S FINAL PREPARATIONS TO SACRIFICE ISAAC

Verse 9 discloses that when they reached the place God had told him about, Abraham built an altar there and arranged the wood on it. He bound his son Isaac and laid him on the altar, on top of the wood.

Isaac's role in this sacrifice should not be overlooked, he was a teenager by the time it occurred. He certainly had enough strength to at least attempt to resist his father. Instead, he watched, and may have assisted his father in building the altar on which the wood he carried was placed. Yet, there was still no lamb anywhere in sight! Then, the strongest clue came when his father bound him. If he was not sure who the lamb was, he found out at that point! Yet, he did not seem to fret, fight, nor flee!

Having bound Isaac and placed him on the alter, verse 10 says, then Abraham reached out his hand and took the knife to slay his son. But the angel of the Lord called out to him from heaven, "Abraham! Abraham! Do not lay a hand on the boy. Do not do anything to him. Now I know that you fear God, because you have not withheld from me your son, your only son."

Certainly, God, who is omniscient, did not have to require Abraham to come this close to killing his son, to know that he feared Him. However, Abraham's attempted actions were symbolic of the actions God Himself would take years later, when He would sacrifice His Son, His only begotten Son, whom He also loved. And in that case, there would be no one to call out to stop Him from sacrificing His son Jesus.

GOD PROVIDED A RAM IN THE BUSH

Verses 13-14 reveal that in response to hearing the angel's voice, which was probably quite loud, Abraham looked up, and there in a thicket he saw a ram caught by its horns. He went over and took the ram and sacrificed it as a burnt offering instead of his son. So, Abraham called that place "The Lord Will Provide." Matthews concluded that one point made by this text is that Abraham's God, unlike the gods of the Canaanites found animal sacrifice more acceptable.[3]

It is reasonable to wonder if Abraham's actions might have been different had he seen the ram before attempting to slay his son. This is doubtful, because Abraham was bent on obeying God, who initially told him to sacrifice his son, rather than a ram. His obedience was better than his sacrifice. The real lesson was, a ram became an acceptable substitute for Isaac, but there was no such substitute for Christ. He was the only Lamb who could accomplish the purpose for which His sacrifice was made, which was to take away the sin of the world (John 1:29).

GOD RENEWED HIS PROMISES TO ABRAHAM

Verses 15-18 show where the angel of the Lord called to Abraham from heaven a second time and said, "I swear by myself, that because you have done this, and have not withheld your son, your only son, I will surely bless you, and make your descendants as numerous as the stars in the sky and as the sand on the seashore. Your descendants will take possession of the cities of their enemies, and through your offspring, all nations on earth will be blessed, because you have obeyed me."

Finally, Abraham demonstrated that he had grown up in his faith. This incident demonstrated his unwavering reliance upon the trustworthiness of the promises God had already made to him. God reiterated His promises to Abraham, but this time, He also rewarded Isaac for his submission to his father, by stating the promises in his hearing. In essence, this was the first recorded incident where Isaac may have heard the voice of God. Having concluded his encounter on the mountain with God, verse 19 shows that Abraham and Isaac returned to the servants, and they set off together for Beersheba, and Abraham stayed in Beersheba.

---

3. Youngman, *The Lands and Peoples of the Living Bible*, 19.

NAHOR'S OFFSPRING

Verses 20–24 reveal that sometime later, Abraham was told, Milkah had also become a mother; she had borne sons to his brother Nahor. Uz was the firstborn, Buz was his brother, Kemuel (the father of Aram), Kesed, Hazo, Pildash, Jidlaph, and Bethuel, who became the father of Rebekah. Milkah bore these eight sons to Abraham's brother Nahor. In addition to Milkah, verse 24 reveals that Nahor had a concubine, whose name was Reumah, and she also had sons: Tebah, Gaham, Tahash and Maakah.

These verses made known the fact that God not only blessed Abraham, but He also blessed his relatives, whom Abraham was asked to leave behind in Ur of the Chaldees, in pursuit of a place God would show him. No doubt, the news about his brother's offspring brought comfort to him. Nahor had twelve sons, which was proof that neither he, nor the women in his life experienced similar problems with infertility, which Abraham and Sarah initially experienced. Yet, God promised Abraham to make his descendants as numerous as the stars in the sky, and as the sand on the seashore. In other words, despite his late start, the number of Abraham's offspring would grow to surpass those of Nahor's.

GENESIS CHAPTER TWENTY-THREE

The previous chapter provided details about Abraham being tested by God who asked him to sacrifice his son Isaac as a burnt offering. Abraham demonstrated his willingness to do what God requested, but God intervened by instructing him not to harm his son. Instead, God saved Isaac's life by providing a ram for the sacrifice, as a substitute in his place. Abraham's willingness to sacrifice his son, whom he loved, proved his unwavering obedience to God, and wholehearted trust in the promises He made to him. This chapter will discuss the death of Sarah, and Abraham's purchase of the only property he ever owned on this earth, which he bought to ensure his wife received a proper burial.

SARAH'S DEATH

Verses 1-2 state that Sarah lived to be a hundred and twenty-seven years old. She died at Kiriath Arba (Hebron) in the land of Canaan, and Abraham went to mourn for Sarah and to weep over her.

Sarah's death at 127 years old, meant her husband was 137, and her son Isaac was 37 years old. She lived to see Isaac become a mature adult! The irony of her laughter following the prediction that God would allow her to give birth in her old age, became even more hilarious in the fact that she lived to see him become an established man. She died in Canaan, where she and Abraham dwelt as foreigners, even though God promised their descendants would inherit that land in years to come. In essence, her soul rested in the Promised Land in anticipation of the arrival of her children to take possession of it, in years to come.

The passage points out that Abraham not only went to mourn for Sarah, but he also wept over her. His grief was deeply sincere. Sarah had been with him for the entirety of his sojourn, and they experienced a lot together. Sarah proved her love for him and loyalty to him, by her willingness to endanger her own life to save his. However, the fact that Abraham went to mourn for her, suggest they may have been living in separate places. He may have remained in Beersheba (Gen22:19), while she was in Hebron, where she died.

ABRAHAM PURCHASES A BURIAL SITE

Verses 3-4 show that Abraham arose from beside his dead wife to make funeral arrangements for her burial. Hence, he spoke to the Hittites about acquiring a plot of land for the proper burial of his wife. By then he had lived in the land for many years, yet he admitted to being a foreigner and stranger, who did not even own a plot of land the size of a grave. As such, he beseeched them to sell him some property for a burial site to bury his dead wife.

Abraham's humility was on display in this event. Even though God promised him the entire land of Canaan, he did not approach the Hittites using that as a reason for his request. Instead, he was very modest in what he asked for. He admitted to being a foreigner and stranger among them, who simply needed their help in dealing with a deeply personal matter. This admission from a grief-stricken heart, also suggest that Sarah's death reminded Abraham that this world was not his home.

Verses 5-6 show that the Hittites responded to Abraham by assuring him, as far as they were concerned, he was more than a foreigner or stranger. They described him as a mighty prince among them, and they encouraged him to bury his dead in the choicest of their tombs. In other words, they wanted the tomb of Abraham's dead to reflect the fact that the person in it was related to a mighty prince. They said, "None of us will refuse you his tomb for burying your dead." They owned tombs, Abraham did not. He was a mighty man, but he was not a landowner.

Abraham was encouraged by their willingness to accommodate him. Therefore, verses 7-9 show that he arose and bowed down before them. Then he asked them to advocate on his behalf. He told them, if they were willing to let him bury his dead, he wanted them to intercede with Ephron son of Zohar so he would sell him the cave of Machpelah, which belonged to him and was located at the end of his field. Abraham said he would buy that piece of land for the full price, as a burial site among them.

At 137 years old Abraham was still able to arise and to bow down. In doing so, he expressed his graciousness to the Hittites for their kindness to him. They offered him one of their choicest tombs, as they considered him one of their own. However, Abraham had a different type of tomb in mind.

He preferred a cave to hide, rather than showcase his dead. The location he chose for a burial site, was also close to where he lived in Mamre. In any case, the fact that the cave was at the end of Ephron's property, suggested it may not have been used, and would not have been a major inconvenience if gotten rid of. It also highlighted Abraham's desire to minimize the level to which he would impose on them.

Verse 10 shows that Ephron the Hittite was sitting among his people, and he replied to Abraham in their hearing at the gate of his city. In other words, he heard Abraham's request for himself, which eliminated the need for any of his people to intercede with him on Abraham's behalf. Consequently, he was able to give Abraham an immediate response.

Abraham offered to buy only the cave, but Ephron responded in verse 11, "No, my lord, listen to me; I give you the field, and I give you the cave that is in it. I give it to you in the presence of my people. Bury your dead." Ephron offered to give Abraham, without cost, the cave and the field where it was located. This was a very generous offer! It was a demonstration of the Hittites' peaceful disposition towards Abraham, and the mutually amicable relationship they enjoyed with each other. This relationship would change drastically with subsequent generations.

On hearing Ephron's offer, verses 12-13 show that Abraham again bowed down before the people of the land and he offered Ephron in their hearing, to pay the price of the field. He begged him to accept the price of the field from him, so he could bury his dead there. Abraham insisted on buying the field rather than accepting it at no cost from Ephron.

Finally, verses 14-15 indicate that Ephron answered and told Abraham, the land is worth four hundred shekels of silver, which was nothing between them. He told him to go ahead and bury his dead! But in verse 16, Abraham agreed to his terms and weighed out for him the price he quoted in the hearing of his people, four hundred shekels of silver, according to the weight current among the merchants at that time.

Verses 17-20 declare that Ephron's field in Machpelah near Mamre, both the field and the cave in it, and all the trees within the borders of the field, were deeded to Abraham as his property in the presence of all the Hittites who had come to the gate of the city. So, Abraham buried his wife Sarah in the cave in the field of Machpelah near Mamre (Hebron) in the land of Canaan. The field and the cave in it were deeded to Abraham by the Hittites as a burial site.

Interestingly, Abraham and Sarah lived as foreigners and strangers in all the countries to which they travelled and lived. Yet, the only property they acquired by way of a deed, was a field, which served as a cemetery. Somehow, they understood that this world was not their home, they were simply passing through. Hebrews 11:10 says Abraham looked forward to a city with foundations, whose Builder and Maker is God. This should be an instructive example for all who share Abraham's faith. They should learn to hold on loosely to everything in this world, because there is a burial site at the end of every field of labor.

GENESIS CHAPTER TWENTY-FOUR

In the previous chapter Abraham lost the love of his life, Sarah. She had been with him from the time he left his home in Ur of the Chaldeans. She was faithful to him in all his travels. She obeyed him and even called him her lord (1 Pet 3:6). As an heir to the promise, he buried her in the only piece of land he personally owned on this earth, which he bought from the Hittites. This land was where he was later buried as well. This meant the only land he owned on this earth was a cemetery. Following Sarah's death, finding a wife for Isaac became a major priority for Abraham. This chapter will provide details of his efforts to accomplish that task.

ABRAHAM COMMISSIONED HIS SENIOR SERVANT

Verses 1–4 reveal that Abraham had become very old, and the Lord had blessed him in every way. So, he said to the senior servant in his household, the one in charge of all he had, "Put your hand under my thigh. I want you to swear by the Lord, the God of heaven and the God of earth, that you will not get a wife for my son from the daughters of the Canaanites, among whom I am living, but will go to my country and my own relatives and get a wife for my son Isaac."

By the time Abraham set out to find a wife for his son, Isaac was approaching forty years old. The main reason he had not been married by that time was because he could not marry any of the Canaanite women in the area where he lived. However, following his mother's death, and at his father's advanced age, finding a wife became a priority. So, Abraham assigned that task to the senior, rather than a junior, servant in his household; he was Abraham's Chief-of-Staff. This servant may have been Eliezer of Damascus, whom at one point he thought would become his heir (Gen 15:2). He was a man of character because he oversaw everything Abraham owned, yet he did not envy or harbor any ill-will towards Isaac.

Abraham was very old, which was one reason that prohibited him from traveling back to his native country to assume the task of finding his son a wife. But, more importantly, another reason he was prohibited, was because once he was called out, God did not allow him to go back there.

Abraham knew the qualities the wife for his son should have. His reason for not wanting him to marry a Canaanite woman, was not racially motivated, instead his reason was prophetically motivated. God had already told him the Canaanites were destined for ruin. Therefore, if his covenant line became entangled with them, it would have unnecessarily complicated God's plan. Hence, Abraham made his servant swear he would not get Isaac a Canaanite wife.

Verse 5 indicates that the servant was concerned about what to do if the woman was unwilling to come back to Canaan with him. He asked Abraham, if the woman did not want to come with him to Canaan, should he take Isaac back to the country he came from? But again, Abraham made him swear he would not take his son back there. Abraham told him, "The Lord, the God of heaven, who brought me out of my father's household and my native land and who spoke to me and promised me on oath, saying, 'To your offspring I will give this land', He will send His angel before you so that you can get a wife for my son from there. If the woman is unwilling to come back with you, then you will be released from this oath of mine. Only do not take my son back there."

The servant was obviously concerned about being held responsible for things beyond his control. Abraham reminded him that God was the one who would accomplish the mission on which he was sending him. Obviously, the servant did not want to disappoint his master Abraham, who was sure of the promise God had made, and that he would be successful in finding Isaac a wife. He guaranteed his servant that because of the promise, the angel of God would accompany him on his mission, thus, he could not fail! The woman had to come to the land where Isaac was, but he could not go to the land where she was.

On hearing Abraham's words, verse 9 indicates that the servant put his hand under the thigh of his master and swore an oath to him concerning the matter. Marshall postulates that placing one's hand under the thigh was a euphemistic way to refer to swearing upon the testicles of the master.[1] The testicles were the sign of Abraham's descendants, they literally contained the seed God had promised to bless in Genesis 15, 17, and 22.

---

1. Marshall, *Testimony and Testicles, the Oath of Abraham's Servant*, https://taylor-marshall.com/2008/10/testimony-and-testicles-oath-of.html.

It became customary for Abraham's descendants to swear by placing their hand under the thigh. Jacob would later require Joseph to do the same (Gen 47:29). The thigh may also have been chosen by Abraham and his descendants because it was close to the area of the body God chose for the covenant of circumcision. Hence, an oath taken by placing the hand under the thigh, signified the privacy of the matter, and the witness of a covenant-keeping God.

SERVANT'S REQUEST FOR A SIGN FROM GOD

Having sworn an oath to his master, verses 10–11 say the servant left, taking with him ten of his master's camels loaded with all kinds of good things. He set out for Aram Naharaim (NW Mesopotamia) and made his way to the town of Nahor. He had the camels kneel near the well outside the town; it was toward evening, the time when women went out to draw water.

The amount of goods the servant took, revealed the level of trust between him and his master. There was no concern about the servant taking ten camels, loaded with good things and never returning, or conducting himself in a sinister manner. It also revealed the level of wealth Abraham had. This was a rare occasion when Abraham was compelled to showcase his prosperity to impress others. He had to do so to convince the family, from which his son would receive a wife, that he had the means to take care of her. Most importantly, the servant's preparations, and the things he took on his journey, indicated he had given much forethought to the negotiating strategy he would use.

Having arrived safely at his destination, notice verses 12–14 reveal, then the servant prayed, and said, "Lord, God of my master Abraham, make me successful today, and show kindness to my master Abraham. See, I am standing beside this spring, and the daughters of the town's people are coming out to draw water. May it be that when I say to a young woman, 'Please let down your jar that I may have a drink,' and she says, 'Drink, and I'll water your camels too', let her be the one you have chosen for your servant Isaac. By this I will know that you have shown kindness to my master."

Observe that the servant prayed to the God of his master Abraham, and to no other god, because he knew the God of his master was the true God. By then, he had seen how God blessed his master and worked things out for him. He also proposed that God would give him a clear sign to identify the woman, so there would be no mistake; there was no room for error. He had to be clear about the woman, because she would play a pivotal role in perpetuating the covenant. And, the only way the servant could be absolutely sure, was to rely on revelation from God. His course of action is instructive for those seeking a mate or making any other selective decisions in life. Seeking clear direction from God is always the best course of action.

God's quick response to the servant's prayer is revealed in verses 15–16, where it says before he had finished praying, Rebekah came out with her jar on her shoulder. She was the daughter of Bethuel son of Milkah, who was the wife of Abraham's brother Nahor. She was very beautiful, a virgin; no man had ever slept with her. She went down to the spring, filled her jar and came up again.

The servant saw a beautiful woman, who came out to draw water before he was done praying, but some of the other details given about her were filled in later, such as whose daughter she was, and the status of her virginity. The servant would not have known those things at first glance. Observe that Rebekah was going about her normal, daily business, demonstrating she was an industrious woman. She did not give any indication she was looking for a husband, but a husband was certainly looking for her, and God would cause their paths to cross.

FURTHER CONFIRMATION ABOUT THE WOMAN

Verses 17–21 communicated that the servant hurried to meet this beautiful woman and asked her for a little water from her jar. "Drink, my lord," she said, and quickly lowered the jar from her shoulder to her hands and gave him a drink. After she had given him a drink, she said, "I'll draw water for your camels too, until they have had enough to drink." So, she quickly emptied her jar into the trough, ran back to the well to draw more water, and drew enough for all his camels. Without saying a word, the man watched her closely to learn whether the Lord had made his journey successful.

Rebekah certainly met the requirements for which the servant prayed. She did everything he asked God to cause her to do for him to know she was the right woman for Isaac. In essence, God, rather than the servant found Isaac a wife. Rebekah demonstrated her hospitality and industriousness by giving the servant and his camels water to drink. This task obviously took a while, since a camel can drink up to twenty gallons of water, and the servant had ten camels!

As Rebekah worked, the servant observed her without saying a word. He simply allowed her actions to speak for her. He also allowed God's actions to speak for Him, as he witnessed Abraham's God responding to prayer. This was a beautiful moment, when God confirmed His support for a decision humans needed to make. They sought His input, and He gave it.

Hence, the choice about the woman Isaac would marry, was confirmed in heaven and on earth.

Notice verses 22-25 disclose that when the camels had finished drinking, the man took out a gold nose ring weighing a beka (1/5 ounce, 5.7 grams) and two gold bracelets weighing ten shekels (4 ounces, 115 grams). Then he asked, "Whose daughter are you? Please tell me, is there room in your father's house for us to spend the night?" She answered him, "I am the daughter of Bethuel, the son Milkah bore to Nahor. We have plenty of straw and fodder, as well as room for you to spend the night."

The fact that the servant asked, "whose daughter are you?" confirmed that some of the information in verse 15 was filled in later; the narrative got ahead of itself. However, Rebekah's response revealed that everything the servant asked for in his prayer was confirmed. He found the family to which Abraham sent him, and he found the woman for whom he was searching.

PRAYERS BECAME PRAISE

Notice his response in verses 26-27. It says he bowed down and worshiped the Lord, saying, "Praise be to the Lord, the God of my master Abraham, who has not abandoned his kindness and faithfulness to my master. As for me, the Lord has led me on the journey to the house of my master's relatives."

The servant did not only pray, but he also remembered to thank God for answering his prayer, which spoke volumes about his character. His prayers became praise once they were answered. God demonstrated his sovereignty to this servant by showing His willingness to not only hear Abraham's prayers, but those of a humble servant as well. The evidence in this passage suggest Abraham's God was also his servant's God.

REBEKAH SHARES THE NEWS

Having received such exorbitant gifts from the servant, verse 28 reveals that the young woman (Rebekah) ran and told her mother's household about the things that happened to her. However, verses 29-31 paint a contrast between Rebekah's motives, and those of her brother.

The passage explains that Rebekah had a brother named Laban, and he hurried out to the man at the spring. As soon as he had seen the nose ring, and the bracelets on his sister's arms, and had heard Rebekah tell what the man said to her, he went out to the man and found him standing by the camels near the spring. He said to the man, "Come, you who are blessed by the Lord, why are you standing out here? I have prepared the house and a place for the camels."

Laban's kindness was motivated by the gifts his sister received, and the story he overheard her telling her mother. He knew the gifts could only have come from someone who was prosperous. As such, he referred to the servant as "You who are blessed by the Lord." In other words, he was eager to make room for the servant because he appeared to be rich. Unfortunately, Laban's behavior in being a respecter of the rich, has been a common practice for ages. Therefore, James 2:1-4, warn against such conduct in the Church.

SERVANT REVEALED THE PURPOSE OF HIS MISSION

Verses 32-33 point out that the servant went to the house, and the camels were unloaded. Straw and fodder were brought for the camels, and water for him and his men to wash their feet. Then food was set before him, but he refused to eat until he told them what his mission was. Laban insisted for him to go ahead and tell them.

The fact that Laban (Rebekah's brother) led the conversation was highly unusual, since his father was still alive. This might suggest Laban was either the eldest, or only son, and his father, like Abraham, was advanced in age. Also observe that after an exhausting journey, the servant did not eat before revealing his mission, which was another sign of his character. He valued the concerns of his master over his own concerns. He demonstrated unwavering loyalty to Abraham and his household.

In verses 34-49, the servant provided meticulous details about his journey. He revealed whose servant he was, how God blessed his master, why he was sent, and every detail, including the Lord's guidance along the way, which resulted in him meeting Rebekah at the well. Finally, he concluded his presentation in verse 49, with the words, "Now if you will show kindness and faithfulness to my master, tell me; and if not, tell me, so I may know which way to turn." In other words, their actions would either be kind, or unkind to his master, their relative Abraham, who was depending on them to come through for him by providing a wife for his son Isaac.

RESPONSE TO THE SERVANT'S REQUEST

After the servant provided an entirely transparent account of events, which led to him being in their house, verses 50-51 reveal Laban and Bethuel's response. They said, "This is from the Lord; we can say nothing to you one way or the other. Here is Rebekah; take her and go and let her become the wife of your master's son, as the Lord has directed."

The servant cut to the heart of the matter. He was not distracted by the trappings of their entertainment. Having made his case, if their answer to his master's request was, "No," all of their accommodations would have been superficial. However, Laban and his father Bethuel, trusted the servant, and took his word as truth. They recognized divine providence, and that the servant's mission was from the Lord. That being the case, they concluded there was nothing they could say one way or the other. They surrendered their personal opinions, considering the unmistakable clarity with which God had spoken. Most importantly, if they initially intended to delay the servant to syphon off his wealth, that plan became less attractive, once it was made clear that God was orchestrating events. Instead, they told him, "Here is Rebekah; take her and go. . ."

Notice the servant's response to Laban and Bethuel's declaration. Verses 52–53 indicate that when he heard what they said, he bowed down to the ground before the Lord. Then he brought out gold and silver jewelry and articles of clothing and gave them to Rebekah; he also gave costly gifts to her brother and to her mother. This servant was indeed a praying and a praising man! He worshipped God at every successful stage of his journey.

In providing costly gifts to Rebekah and her family, the servant demonstrated the ability of her prospective husband and family to take care of her. Once again, it was a rare showcase of Abraham's wealth. Laban once more assumed the role normally designated for a father. He, and his mother, received costly gifts, but it does not say his father Bethuel received anything. This may be a result of his advanced age, and Laban, his eldest, or only son, beginning to act on his behalf.

Once the servant received an affirmative answer to his request, verse 54 says, he and the men who were with him ate and drank and spent the night there. When they got up the next morning, he said, "Send me on my way to my master." In other words, they did not eat and drink, or enjoy any other personal satisfaction until they knew the purpose for which their master sent them had been accomplished. These were indeed faithful servants! Notice also, they were eager to return to their master before success turned to failure. They were unwilling to linger in the town of Nahor and in Rebekah's family home, a second longer than was necessary.

In response to the servant's request to be sent on his way back to his master, verse 55 explains that Rebekah's brother and mother asked to let her remain with them for ten days or so. Presumably, this request was to give Rebekah more time to say a proper goodbye. But it could also have been to allow Laban more time to acquire additional gifts from the servant. Their request was not to deny what was clearly an act of God, but to delay it.

The servant refused to be delayed. Verse 56 reveals that he said to them, "Do not detain me now that the Lord has granted success to my journey. Send me on my way so I may go to my master." Again, the servant did not want his success to become failure, by delaying or extending his time in a land to which Abraham and Isaac refused to go. His desire was to spend as little time there as possible.

Having heard the servant's appeal, verses 57–60 show that Laban and his mother decided to let Rebekah decide for herself. They called her and asked, "Will you go with this man?" "I will go," she said. So, Rebekah's parents consented to her marriage after she consented to it. Hence, they sent her on her way, along with her nurse and Abraham's servant and his men. And they blessed Rebekah and said to her, "Our sister, may you increase to thousands upon thousands; may your offspring possess the cities of their enemies." It appears this blessing was pronounced by Laban, whom the Bible will show later (Gen 31:19, 30) was an idolater.

Following the blessing, verse 61 indicates that Rebekah and her attendants got ready and mounted the camels and went back with the man. So, the servant took Rebekah and left. The fact that Rebekah had attendants, indicates she did not have to draw water herself from the well where the servant first encountered her, she had attendants who could do it for her. However, God used her industriousness to accomplish His will.

Her immediate departure from her family was a joyous event because the servant demonstrated that Rebekah was going off to a better life in a Godly family. Yet, it was a sad departure because from the Biblical record, there is no evidence she ever saw her mother, father, brother, or other relatives and friends again. Still, she was ready and willing to go.

MISSION ACCOMPLISHED

Abraham never went back to Haran, nor to Ur of the Chaldeans, where his people lived; nor did he allow his son Isaac to go to those countries. But the fact that he wanted his son to marry a wife from among them was an honor to his people. He certainly did not want to choose a wife for his son from among Lot's incestuous descendants, even though they lived closer. Thus, the best alternative was to choose from back home. As such, neither Rebekah, nor any of her family members inquired about why Abraham or Isaac did not come to them on their own behalf. Instead, they seemed to accept their different paths in life, and were happy to assist in providing a wife who shared a similar racial heritage with Isaac.

ISAAC MEETS HIS BRIDE

Notice verses 62-63 that Isaac had come from Beer Lahai Roi, while he was living in the Negev As he went out to the field one evening to meditate and pray, he looked up, and saw camels approaching. It may be that Rebekah's arrival was exactly what Isaac was praying about, especially in light of his grief following his mother's death. That being the case, her arrival was a welcomed interruption of his prayers, and comfort for his mourning.

Verses 64-65 show that when Rebekah looked up and saw Isaac, she got down from her camel and asked the servant, "Who is that man in the field coming to meet us?" "He is my master," the servant answered. On hearing this she took her veil and covered herself. In other words, Rebekah displayed appropriate modesty by dismounting from her camel, thereby surrendering her elevated position on meeting her husband to be, who was on foot; She came down to his level. And she covered herself as an act of submission to him, who would soon become her head.

Observe, this senior servant had the same respect for Isaac that he had for Abraham. He referred to him as "My master." And Isaac trusted the servant the way his father trusted him, as signified by the fact that the servant, rather than his father was the one who handled the business of finding him a wife and presenting her to him.

Verses 66-67 explain that the servant told Isaac all he had done. Then Isaac brought Rebekah into the tent of his mother Sarah, and he married her. So, she became his wife, and he loved her, and was comforted after his mother's death. In other words, though his mother Sarah died three years prior to his marriage, nothing soothed his grief until he married Rebekah. The old axiom, the way a man loves and treats his mother can inform the way he will love and respect his wife, was true in Isaac's case. The love he had for his mother, was replaced by a different and stronger love for his wife.

It is quite likely that with all the wealth Abraham had, Isaac's marriage was celebrated with more fanfare than is described in this passage. However, fanfare is futile if the main ingredient required for a successful and happy marriage is absent; That ingredient is love. It says Isaac loved his wife Rebekah, but whether she loved him as much would become questionable by the things she did later in their marriage. In any case, Isaac was as complete as a man could be, having found the wife he hoped for and dreamed about.

GENESIS CHAPTER TWENTY-FIVE

In the previous chapter, it was shown that Abraham charged his senior servant with the massively important task of finding a wife from among his relatives for his son Isaac. The servant prayed and praised his way through the entire process. He, with God's help, found Rebekah, who became Isaac's beloved wife. This chapter will close the curtain on Abraham's life and introduce events in the family of Isaac, who became the main character in continuation of the covenant. It will examine the dysfunction which existed in Isaac's household, beginning with Esau's decision to sell his birthright to his brother Jacob for a bowl of lentil stew.

ABRAHAM'S LIFE AFTER SARAH

Verses 1–6 explain that following Sarah's death and Isaac's marriage, Abraham also took another wife, whose name was Keturah. She bore him Zimran, Jokshan, Medan, Midian, Ishbak and Shuah. Jokshan was the father of Sheba and Dedan; the descendants of Dedan were the Ashurites, the Letushites and the Leummites. The sons of Midian were Ephah, Epher, Hanok, Abida and Eldaah. All these were descendants of Keturah. Abraham left everything he owned to Isaac. But while he was still living, he gave gifts to the sons of his concubines and sent them away from his son Isaac to the land of the east.

These verses underscore the fact that Abraham was not able to go to Haran to find his son a wife, but he was able to find himself one. Since he was reticent to travel at that time in his life it is safe to conclude his new bride obviously lived in Canaan. She could also have been a woman who already lived in his household. Interestingly, in his older age, he had more offspring with Keturah than any other woman. By her, he had six sons, which meant, all together Abraham had eight sons. This obviously ensured certainty of the promise God made to him, that he would have innumerable offspring.

By having eight sons, Abraham's estate could have been contested. Therefore, he took care of that issue while he was still alive. He gave gifts to his other sons and sent them away to the east, from his son Isaac. Abraham must have remembered Sarah's words about Hagar and her son Ishmael, when she said the slave woman's son would never share in the inheritance with her son Isaac (Gen 21:10). In this case, neither were Keturah's six sons to share in it. So, Abraham blessed them while he was alive and sent them away, just as he did with Ishmael.

Additionally, Abraham had the right to determine who his heir should be; especially, since God told him his descendants would acquire an inheritance, which was not yet in their possession. He had to be careful not to convolute his legacy, particularly, since he not only had a wife in Keturah, but apparently also had concubines (plural), and all of this in his old age! Hence Abraham sent his other offspring away from Isaac. In other words, he got them out of the land of Canaan, so they would not be among the people his covenant offspring would dispossess in years to come.

Verses 7–8 reveal that Abraham lived a hundred and seventy-five years, then he breathed his last and died at a good old age, an old man and full of years; and he was gathered to his people. Abraham was the first patriarch about whom it was said, "he was gathered to his people." He lived forty-eight years after Sarah's death. His son Isaac was seventy-five years old at that time. His death occurred thirty-five years after Isaac's marriage to Rebekah, and as verse 26 indicates, fifteen years after the birth of his grandsons, Jacob and Esau. God allowed him to see his covenant family well on their way!

WHO WERE ABRAHAM'S PEOPLE IN DEATH?

Again, it says Abraham was gathered to his people. He was not gathered to any other people but his own. The question begs to be asked, who were Abraham's people? It would have been a travesty for God to call Abraham out from among his idolatrous relatives when he lived in Ur of the Chaldeans, only to have him spend eternity with them after he died. As such, the reference to Abraham's people was not necessarily an allusion to his father, mother, or other relatives who preceded him in death. Instead, this statement was a broad reference to the righteous, who preceded Abraham in death; People such as Shem, Enoch, and Noah.

When humans die God does not separate them by race, ethnicity, culture, political affiliation, or any such delineations. Rather, He separates them into two groups, the righteous and the wicked (Matt 25:31–46). From a Christian perspective, righteousness cannot be defined by any amount of good deeds a person does, because the moment they do something bad, and they will, they become unrighteous. Therefore, righteousness is defined by belief, trust, and hope in Jesus Christ and in His sacrifice for sin. Anyone who has this hope is among Abraham's people.

In fact, after Abraham's death, Luke 16:19-31 depict him as one of the people to whom other righteous people are gathered. Therefore, the righteous were, and still are Abraham's people. However, it should be noted that the wicked are also gathered to their people when they die. Beyond death, there is no mixing between the righteous and the wicked (Luke 16:26). This is one of the most interesting realities about eternity. Those who enter eternity in a state of righteousness through Christ will remain infinitely righteous, but those who enter it in a state of unrighteousness will also remain infinitely unrighteous and apart from Christ.

ABRAHAM'S BURIAL

Verses 9-11 explain that Abraham's sons Isaac and Ishmael buried him in the cave of Machpelah near Mamre, in the field of Ephron son of Zohar the Hittite, the field Abraham had bought from the Hittites. There Abraham was buried with his wife Sarah. After his death, God blessed his son Isaac, who then lived near Beer Lahai Roi.

It is not known if any of Keturah's sons, whom Abraham sent away to the east, came back to attend his funeral. However, Ishmael, who at that time was eighty-nine years old, and may still have been living in the desert relatively close by, came back to assist Isaac with their father's burial. Abraham died a wealthy man, with a large household of servants and possessions. Presumably, they mourned for him after his death, but Hebrews 11:10, makes it clear that Abraham lived his life looking forward to a city with foundations, whose Designer and Builder is God.

There are many beautiful cities in this world, but the faithful believe none can compare with that city, which God has designed and built for His people. As such, Abraham did not establish deep roots in this world; rather, he lived in it as a stranger and foreigner. In fact, the only property he is known to have owned in this world was the small plot of land in which his grave was located.

Following the statement about Abraham's burial, the passage made a sharp transition. Immediately after that, it says God blessed his son Isaac. In other words, Abraham died, but God did not. His blessings continued, and His covenant was unrelenting. He was the one who would bring every promise He made to fruition. Therefore, the transition to His involvement in Isaac's life was a demonstration of His intent to do what He told Abraham. It was Isaac's turn to take up the mantel and carry on, and God blessed him to do exactly that.

ABRAHAM'S DESCENDANTS THROUGH ISHMAEL

Verses 12–16 provide a list of Abraham's descendants through the family line of Ishmael, whom Sarah's slave, Hagar the Egyptian, bore to Abraham. These were the names of the sons of Ishmael, listed in the order of their birth: Nebaioth the firstborn of Ishmael, Kedar, Adbeel, Mibsam, Mishma, Dumah, Massa, Hadad, Tema, Jetur, Naphish and Kedemah. These were the sons of Ishmael, and the names of the twelve tribal rulers according to their settlements and camps.

God blessed Ishmael with twelve sons in keeping with the promise He made to Hagar in chapter 16:10. There, He promised to increase her descendants so much that they would be too numerous to count. It also brought God's promise in chapter 17:20 to fruition, where He promised that Ishmael would become father of twelve rulers, from whom a great nation would emerge. His promise to make Ishmael into a great nation was restated in chapter 21:13. So, God was faithful to His promises concerning Ishmael, who indeed became father of twelve sons, whose names ironically bore resemblances to names, which are common in the Middle East to this day.

Verse 17 notes that Ishmael lived a hundred and thirty-seven years. He breathed his last and died, and he was gathered to his people. His descendants settled in the area from Havilah (Saudi Arabia) to Shur (Southern Sinai Peninsula, closer to the Red Sea), near the eastern border of Egypt, as you go toward Ashur (northern Sinai, closer to the Mediterranean Sea leading from Egypt to Canaan). And they lived in hostility toward all the tribes related to them.

When Ishmael died at 137 years old, it does not say he, like his father Abraham, was "full of years." This implied he, like most, wished he had more years on this earth. He was also gathered to his people, but since the Bible speaks very little about Ishmael's faith, it would be presumptive to speculate about whom his people in death were. What is known, is that he was circumcised along with his father, and the foundations of his faith were formed while he lived in Abraham's household. He was circumcised at thirteen years old (Gen17:25), and he was familiar with the God whom his father worshipped; the One who spoke to and rescued he and his mother.

Ismael's mother, Hagar, met the true God in the desert (Gen 21:17–19). She witnessed His deliverance when she was at her wits end. However, the life of hostility, which Ishmael's offspring inherited, undoubtedly came from him. It represented a tension between what he learned in his youth, while with his father Abraham, and what he passed on to his descendants by the way he lived his life as an adult living in the desert. Isaac was 123 years old when Ishmael died. He would live fifty-seven more years, and the mantel of the covenant, and of Abraham's legacy was squarely on his shoulders.

ABRAHAM'S DESCENDANTS THROUGH ISAAC

Verses 19–23 provide insight into how the birth of Isaac's sons occurred. It says Abraham became the father of Isaac, and Isaac was forty years old when he married Rebekah, daughter of Bethuel the Aramean from Paddan Aram and sister of Laban the Aramean. Isaac prayed to the Lord on behalf of his wife, because she was childless. The Lord answered his prayer, and his wife Rebekah became pregnant. The babies jostled each other within her, and she said, "Why is this happening to me?" So, she went to inquire of the Lord. The Lord said to her, "Two nations are in your womb, and two peoples from within you will be separated; one people will be stronger than the other and the older will serve the younger."

When these verses are unpacked, it becomes clear that for twenty years of their marriage, Isaac and Rebekah struggled with infertility issues, just as Abraham and Sarah did. Hence, Isaac prayed for his wife rather than for himself, which suggests she was the infertile partner. As such, Isaac's offspring did not only come about because he was beneficiary of the promise, but also because he was a man of prayer.

During pregnancy, Rebekah became very concerned about the constant jostling between the twins in her womb. This jostling made her sick to her stomach, as well as to her mind. She asked that familiar question so often heard in times of trouble, "why is this happening to me?" Over the years, Rebekah probably observed other women who became pregnant without facing the symptoms she faced. The situation may have caused her to regret her pregnancy, and she needed an explanation as to why she was experiencing such difficulties.

She inquired of the Lord, and He answered her. This is instructive for those who are experiencing unexplained difficulties. God can provide answers if He is asked to do so. Notice, He responded to Rebekah by telling her two nations, rather than two sons, were in her womb. In other words, God sees things beyond the immediate. His interpretation of Rebekah's circumstances stretched beyond her immediate pregnancy and birth of her twin sons. Two nations were jostling in her womb, and their hostilities would continue for generations into the future. Therefore, her sons jostled each other in her womb, as a sign of what they would do once they were born.

History revealed that for a while, the younger of her twins (Jacob), had the upper hand on the older (Esau). Second Chronicles 21:8-10 shows that the Edomites, who were Esau's descendants, served Israel, specifically Judah, for many years, until they revolted. However, Esau's descendants may have been successful in gaining the upper hand during the period when the Ottoman Empire ruled Palestine for approximately 400 years.

Verses 24–26 explain that when the time came for Rebekah to give birth, there were twin boys in her womb. The first to come out was red, and his whole body was like a hairy garment; so, they named him Esau (Red, Hairy). After this, his brother came out, with his hand grasping Esau's heel; so, he was named Jacob (Deceiver). Isaac was sixty years old when Rebekah gave birth to her sons, which meant his father Abraham was still alive at 160 years old, with fifteen more years left to live.

Rebekah gave birth to Esau first. In so doing, Esau became inheritor of the birthright. His appearance, being red and hairy was highly unusual. It seemed to suggest that from birth, Esau had characteristics of a grown man! Jacob on the other hand, grasped Esau's heel, rather than his hand, to show his intent from birth to slow him down, impede his progress, and overtake him. This signified that Jacob would become a competitor, rather than a partner to his brother. God foretold that he would become stronger and would subjugate his brother (v 23).

ISAAC'S DIVIDED HOUSEHOLD

Verses 27–28 indicate that the boys grew up, and Esau became a skillful hunter, a man of the open country, while Jacob was content to stay at home among the tents. Isaac, who had a taste for wild game, loved Esau, but Rebekah loved Jacob. From these verses, insight is given about Esau and Jacob's vocational choices, their lifestyles, and their relationships with their parents.

Esau pursued a gregarious vocation, which endeared him to his father. He was a man's man! He was able to share adventurous hunting stories with his father, as they enjoyed the wild game they both loved to eat. He was his father's favorite son. On the other hand, Jacob stayed at home among the tents, which meant he was probably a local shepherd. Being close to home allowed him to have more time with his mother. He seemed to have more in common with her than with his father, even though he and his father were shepherds. As a mother's boy, he probably learned from her how to cook. The passage made clear he was her favorite son.

Each parent had their favorite, and the fact that it was mentioned in Scripture, suggest they made no efforts to conceal this fact. In other words, each son knew which parent loved him the most. Sadly, there are many households today, in which this type of blatant favoritism exists, but Isaac's household was not a good model to follow. The jostling which was evident between Jacob and Esau before they were born, was perpetuated by the treatment they received from their parents. It got worse as they grew older, and ultimately produced results, which left lasting scars, which took years to heal.

JACOB FRAUDULENTLY ACQUIRED THE BIRTHRIGHT

Verses 29-34 declare that on one occasion when Jacob was cooking some stew, Esau came in from the open country, and he was very hungry. So, he said to Jacob, "Quick, let me have some of that red stew! I'm famished!" (That is also why he was called Edom—Red). Jacob replied, "First, sell me your birthright." Esau said, "Look, I am about to die, what good is the birthright to me?" But Jacob said, "Swear to me first." So, he swore an oath to him, selling his birthright to Jacob. Then Jacob gave Esau some bread and some lentil stew. He ate and drank, and then got up and left. So, Esau despised his birthright.

Esau and Jacob negotiated with collateral they both thought they could afford to lose. Jacob could afford to lose some stew; it did not mean that much to him. Likewise, Esau negotiated with something he thought he could afford to lose, his birthright; it did not mean that much to him, or so he thought. Had he understood the value of his birthright, presumably he would have found something else with which to negotiate. Of course, in that case Jacob would not have negotiated with him, because he knew exactly what he wanted. He wanted nothing else but the birthright, but all Esau wanted was some stew. The outcome was certain to be imbalanced because Esau, being less ambitious, brought more to the table than Jacob had to bring.

To be clear, Esau did not have the right to sell his birthright while his father Isaac was still alive. However, once he swore to do so, the buyer could not truly have the birthright without Isaac's blessing. Acquiring the blessing from Isaac would require ingenuity, because while Esau may not have valued it, Isaac certainly did. He knew the significance of the birthright and its implications for the covenant God had made with Abraham.

Esau claimed he was so hungry he would die without the stew, but this was a gross exaggeration of his situation. In any case, Jacob planned the occasion well, and by refusing to give him anything to eat until he swore to sell him his birthright, he disarmed Esau from changing his mind later. But Jacob may have also foreknown that Esau despised his birthright, and under the right circumstances, could be easily convinced to relieve himself of it. The birthright came with certain restrictions, which the following chapter will show Esau was not prepared to abide by. Therefore, by selling it, he no longer bore the weight of its restrictions, particularly as it related to whom he could marry.

If Esau's decision to sell his birthright was made impulsively, while he was hungry, he would have at least tried to change his mind when his stomach was full, and when he had time to reconsider what he had done. Instead, the passage states that he ate, then he got up and left, without a second thought to what he had just done! Most importantly, his father who loved him and was depending on him to carry on the traditions of the birthright, was never informed by him that he sold it.

Hence, even though Jacob fraudulently obtained the birthright from Esau, he still needed his father Isaac's blessing to legitimize the sale. In essence, it was as if Esau was coerced to sell property he did not fully own, his father still owned it. Hence, Jacob would have to figure out how to also coerce his father to acquire the title to the property. He would soon accomplish this with the help of his mother, who loved him more than Esau.

GENESIS CHAPTER TWENTY-SIX

The previous chapter described the death and burial of Abraham. His offspring through Ismael were identified, as well as those through Isaac, who along with his wife Rebekah, struggled for twenty years to have offspring. When they did, it resulted in a divided household, with each parent showing blatant favoritism to the son they loved. Jacob, who was Rebekah's favorite son, tricked his brother Esau, who was Isaac's favorite son, into selling him his birthright for a bowl of lentil stew.

This chapter will represent a slight diversion in events, as Isaac, like his father Abraham, would have to settle outstanding matters with his close neighbors, the Philistines. This chapter will also provide greater insight into why Esau despised the stipulations of his birthright, and was thus predisposed to selling it.

ISAAC'S ENCOUNTER WITH THE PHILISTINES

Verses 1–6 reveal that there was a famine in the land, besides the previous famine in Abraham's time, and Isaac went to Abimelech king of the Philistines in Gerar. The Lord appeared to Isaac and said, "Do not go down to Egypt; live in the land where I tell you to live. Stay in this land for a while, and I will be with you and will bless you. For to you and your descendants I will give all these lands and will confirm the oath I swore to your father Abraham. I will make your descendants as numerous as the stars in the sky and will give them all these lands, and through your offspring all nations on earth will be blessed, because Abraham obeyed Me and did everything I required of him, keeping My commands, decrees and instructions." So, Isaac stayed in Gerar.

God confirmed to Isaac that He would bless him despite the famine. He did not want him to do as his father did, when he found refuge in Egypt. If the thought of going to Egypt even crossed Isaac's mind, God removed it by making His will clear about what He wanted him to do under the circumstances. He told him, "Stay in this land." In his time, Abraham went to Pharaoh for refuge; here, Isaac went to Abimelech. The fact that he left the Negev (Gen 24:62) and went to Gerar, implied the famine was once again, very severe in Canaan.

This is the first passage in which God reaffirmed the covenant with Isaac, which He had previously made with Abraham, and He did so during a famine, to show Isaac there is no shortage in Him. Hence, He promised Isaac to be with him, to bless him, and to give him and his descendants all the land He promised Abraham. This reaffirmed for Isaac that as severe as the famine was, he would survive, and God's promises would come true. He even used Abraham as an example to remind Isaac that just as He brought Abraham through the famine in his time, He was able to do it again.

Verse 7 reveals that when the men of Gerar asked Isaac about his wife, he said, "She is my sister," because he was afraid to say she was his wife. He thought if he told them the truth, they might kill him on account of Rebekah, because she was beautiful. It should be noted that Isaac's denial of his wife was a familiar family trait. He did the same thing his father before him had done (Gen 12:11-13; 20:5). However, while his father's story was partly true, his was an outright lie! Rebekah was not his sister at all!

Notice also that Abimelech was not the one who asked Isaac about his wife, it was the men of the Gerar who did. Additionally, there is no evidence that Rebekah was aware of the lie he told, like Sarah was aware of Abraham's half-truth. Most importantly, the promises God reaffirmed to Isaac, made his scheme unnecessary. The Philistines could not kill him because God had already prophesied a future, which required him to continue to live a while longer.

Observe verse 8 where it says, when Isaac had been in Gerar a long time, Abimelech king of the Philistines looked down from a window and saw him caressing his wife Rebekah. So, he summoned Isaac and said, "She is really your wife! Why did you say, 'She is my sister'?" Isaac answered him, "Because I thought I might lose my life on account of her." Isaac assumed the same thing about the Philistines that Abraham assumed about them and about the Egyptians; that they placed higher value on adultery than on murder. Therefore, he assumed they would rather kill him, than take his wife while he was yet alive.

Abimelech was aware of what Isaac said concerning Rebekah because his men may have told him. However, he learned the truth for himself after Isaac had been in Gerar for a long time and had probably forgotten the lie he initially told. Rather than eventually coming clean and telling the truth about his marriage to Rebekah, Isaac was contented to have the people of

Gerar continue to believe she was his sister. However, God allowed Abimelech to observe Isaac caressing Rebekah, at which point she had better be his wife and not his sister! If he was found caressing his sister, his life would really have been in danger! Notwithstanding, having been caught lying to the king could also have brought perilous consequences.

Isaac, like his father Abraham, placed greater value on his own life than he did on the life of his wife Rebekah. He and his father Abraham before him were willing to place their wives in harm's way to preserve their own lives. In Isaac's case, his actions made it difficult to make sense of Genesis 24:67, where it said that he loved Rebekah. He certainly did not behave that way in this case, as he was unwilling to lay down his life for her.

Verses 10–11 point out that Abimelech asked him, "What is this you have done to us? One of the men might well have slept with your wife, and you would have brought guilt upon us." So, Abimelech gave orders to all the people that anyone who harmed Isaac, or his wife would surely be put to death. In other words, Abimelech acted more honorably than Isaac did, and was more decent than Isaac expected him to be. Not only did he protect Rebekah, but he also protected Isaac from the Philistine men, who may have felt betrayed and sought revenge against him.

ISAAC PROSPERED IN THE MIDST OF A FAMINE

Verses 12–14 explain that Isaac planted crops in Gerar and the same year reaped a hundredfold, because the Lord blessed him. He became rich, and his wealth continued to grow until he became very wealthy. He had so many flocks and herds and servants that the Philistines envied him.

The strange thing about Isaac's crops was, he reaped a hundredfold the same year in which there was a famine! Crops were not supposed to be that bountiful that year, but the reason for his plentiful crops and increased wealth was because the Lord blessed him. So, as it turned out, the reason the Philistines envied Isaac was not because of his beautiful wife, but because of his bountiful crops. He was a foreigner, living among them during a time of famine, and he was prospering in their land, more than they were. From a human perspective, their envy was understandable.

As a result of their jealousy, verses 15–16 reveal that all the wells Isaac's father's servants had dug during the lifetime of his father, the Philistines stopped up, filling them with earth. Then Abimelech said to Isaac, "Move away from us; you have become too powerful for us."

Isaac had become as wealthy and powerful as Abimelech was, which became a perceived threat. As a result, Abimelech developed a misguided view of the source of Isaac's blessings. He initially thought Isaac's blessings and great wealth came from the wells, rather than from God. His first thought was, Isaac prospered because the wells supplied him with water during the famine. So, the Philistines took the highly aggressive action of stopping up the wells to cut off his water supply, thus, drying up his blessings.

Their actions were instructive even for today's times. There are people today who may not understand the source of the blessings of others, and because of jealousy, they try to stop up their wells. Rather than joining in digging new wells so they too can prosper, they try to stop them up so that no one can prosper. While it is still true that men should praise God from whom all blessings flow, like the Philistines, too often they focus on obstructing others, and harboring envy and jealousy.

Notice Abimelech not only stopped up the wells, but he also expelled Isaac from his country. Having become rich and powerful, Isaac probably had the wherewithal to make war with Abimelech, but instead he departed in peace. In fact, verse 17 says he moved away from there and encamped in the Valley of Gerar, where he settled.

DISPUTES OVER WELLS

Verse 18 points out that Isaac reopened the wells that had been dug in the time of his father Abraham, which the Philistines had stopped up after Abraham died, and he gave them the same names his father had given them. Apparently, these were additional wells found in the valley, rather than the previous ones they stopped up before expelling him from the area close to where Abimelech lived. After Abraham's death, the Philistines seemed to embark on a campaign to remove his legacy from their area. However, because wells were such important resources at that time, their efforts to stop them up were less than prudent.

Notice verses 19-22 say Isaac's servants dug in the valley and discovered a well of fresh water there, but the herders of Gerar quarreled with those of Isaac and said, "The water is ours!" So, he named the well Esek (Dispute), because they disputed with him. Then they dug another well, but they quarreled over that one also; so, he named it Sitnah (Opposition). He moved on from there and dug another well, and no one quarreled over it. He named it Rehoboth (Room), saying, "Now the Lord has given us room and we will flourish in the land."

Isaac's servants opened old wells, which resulted in disputes, they dug new wells, which resulted in opposition. Finally, they found "room!" What this says is the pursuit of peace may at times be difficult, but it should not be abandoned after the first challenge. Instead, even the enemy must eventually respect peaceful persistence. As Matthew 5:9 says, blessed are the peacemakers, because they will be called children of God. Isaac and his household demonstrated the way of peace, by creating room, or space, between themselves and their enemies. Distancing oneself from aggression promotes peace.

GOD REAFFIRMED HIS PROMISE

Verses 23–24 point out that Isaac left the Valley of Gerar and went up to Beersheba, and the Lord appeared to him that night and said, "I am the God of your father Abraham. Do not be afraid, for I am with you; I will bless you and will increase the number of your descendants for the sake of my servant Abraham." Isaac built an altar there and called on the name of the Lord. He also pitched his tent, and his servants dug a well there.

Despite Isaac's hasty disobedience following the previous occasion when God appeared to him, when he proceeded to deceive the Philistines by representing that Rebekah was his sister, rather than his wife, God appeared to him again and reaffirmed His plan to bless him. God initiated the discourse by telling Isaac "Do not be afraid." Isaac seemed to harbor persistent fear for his life. This was the reason he lied to the Philistines about Rebekah and may have been why he continued to dig new wells, rather than make war with them. God gave him a perfect antidote for overcoming fear; He told him, "I am with you." Knowledge of God's presence and advocacy on his behalf was meant to encourage Isaac, because nothing, or no one, can stand against God.

In response to God's promise and His presence, Isaac followed in his father Abraham's footsteps, and for the first time in Scripture, it says he built an altar, and called on the name of the Lord. In other words, he worshipped God. Not only that, he also pitched his tent in that place and dug a well there. It appeared as if Rehoboth (Beersheba) became the perfect place for him!

TREATY AT BEERSHEBA

Verses 26–29 reveal that Abimelech came from Gerar to visit Isaac in Beersheba, with Ahuzzath his personal adviser and Phicol the commander of his forces. Isaac asked them, "Why have you come to me, since you were hostile to me and sent me away?" They answered, "We saw clearly that the Lord was with you; so, we said, 'There ought to be a sworn agreement between us', between us and you. Let us make a treaty with you, that you will do us no harm, just as we did not harm you but always treated you well and sent you away peacefully. And now you are blessed by the Lord."

This royal visit from Abimelech would not have been possible if Isaac had not pursued the way of peace in his disputes with them over the wells. They initially thought the wells were the sources of Isaac's blessings, so they stopped up the wells in hopes of stopping his blessings. However, they finally realized their mistake! They saw clearly that the source of Isaac's blessings was not the wells, it was the Lord, and they could not stop Him! So, they came to make a treaty. They decided to follow the old adage, "if you can't beat them, join them."

Notice there were glaring differences in each person's assessment of how Isaac was treated. Isaac wondered why they came to him, since they were hostile to him, and sent him away. The Philistines said they always treated him well and sent him away peacefully. In fact, Abimelech seemed to suggest the reason he was blessed by the Lord, was because of the benefits he received from them. In other words, he seemed to take credit for setting up Isaac for his blessings from the Lord. Isaac was a peacemaker at all costs, so he did not challenge Abimelech on that point.

Instead, verses 30–31 explain that Isaac made a feast for them, and they ate and drank. Early the next morning they swore an oath to each other, then Isaac sent them on their way, and they went away peacefully. Isaac did not harbor any ill-will toward Abimelech and his people, nor did he demand as a condition of peace, that they reopen all the wells they had stopped up. Instead, he hosted a feast, agreed to the treaty they wanted, and sent them away in peace.

God rewarded Isaac for his handling of the situation. Verses 32–33 disclose that on that very day, after Abimelech departed, Isaac's servants came and told him about the well they had dug. They said, "We've found water!" He called it Shibah (Oath, or Seven), and to this day the name of the town has been Beersheba (Oath, or Well of Seven).

God did not hesitate in reminding Isaac that He, rather than Abimelech, was the source of his blessings. He proved again that He was with him, by helping him find water wherever he went, even in a time of famine. He made this point shortly after Abimelech departed, to indicate that as the real source of blessings, He was still present, and could be trusted to provide. His actions also reiterated to Isaac why he had no reason to fear.

ESAU'S MARRIAGES

Esau's marriages provide insight into why it is said that he hated his birthright (Gen 25:34), and became unfit to be heir of the covenant. One of the stipulations of being heir of the covenant was a prohibition from marrying

Canaanite women, because God had prophesied to Abraham and Isaac and told them, in years to come, He would cause their descendants to destroy and dispossess the Canaanites (Gen 17:8; 26:2–3). Therefore, Esau hated his birthright, because he loved Canaanite women, even though his birthright prohibited him from marrying them. His love for, and marriages to them, had the potential to complicate God's plan if, as heir of the covenant, he had offspring with the very people God intended His covenant people to dispossess.

Abraham understood this issue, which is why he made his servant swear to him that he would not get Isaac a wife from the Canaanites, among whom he lived (Gen 24:4). Abraham's son Ishmael, was free to marry whomever he pleased, because he was not heir to the covenant, but Isaac could not, because he was heir.

Despite the prohibition, verses 34–35 explain that when Esau was forty years old, he married Judith daughter of Beeri the Hittite, and also Basemath daughter of Elon the Hittite. They were a source of grief to Isaac and Rebekah. The probable reason these marriages were a source of grief to them was because from their perspectives, they did not know at that time, Esau had already sold his birthright to Jacob. Having sold the birthright, Esau figured he could marry whomever he pleased, since he was relieved from any of its stipulations, but his marriages were a source of grief to his parents because they were unaware of what he had done.

Esau got married at the same age his father Isaac did, but unlike his father's marriage, his marriages were anything but God-ordained. In fact, Hebrews 12:16 refers to him as sexually immoral and Godless, most likely because he was not supposed to marry Canaanite women. It is doubtful he was called sexually immoral because he married multiple wives, since his brother Jacob also married multiple wives and he was not referred to in that way. Therefore, the reason Esau was regarded as sexually immoral, was most likely because he defied God's command and married Canaanite women.

It appears that Esau did not receive any prior counseling from either of his parents about whom he should or should not marry. Albeit, in his culture, marriage was not entered into without parental consent. The fact that he married, not one, but two women, whom he was prohibited from marrying, suggest he chose to defiantly do things his way. He did not consult his father who loved him, and still believed him to be heir of the covenant.

His parents knew his marriages to Canaanite women were outside the will of God, and few things grieve the heart of God-fearing parents more than knowing their children's actions are outside God's will. In Esau's case, something had to be done to rescue the birthright from his reckless hands. Henceforth, his mother actively sought to do just that.

GENESIS CHAPTER TWENTY-SEVEN

The previous chapter provided details about Isaac's travels to Gerar, and his interactions with the Philistines during a major famine in the entire land of Canaan. God blessed him despite the famine, which provoked envy in the Philistines, and led to them expelling Isaac from their area. He eventually settled in Beersheba, where God continued to bless and prosper him.

The narrative concluded by returning to the life of Esau, who married two Canaanite women. His marriages were a source of grief to Isaac and Rebekah, because as inheritor of the birthright, he was not supposed to marry Canaanite women. However, his father did not know he had already sold his birthright to Jacob. As such, this chapter will describe the colossal mistake Isaac almost made in blessing Esau with the rights of his birth as the older son. Rebekah and Jacob's deceitful scheme saved Isaac from making this mistake.

BATTLE FOR THE BIRTHRIGHT

Verses 1–4 show that when Isaac was old and his eyes were so weak that he could no longer see, he called for Esau his older son and said to him, "My son, I am now an old man and don't know the day of my death. Now then, get your equipment, your quiver and bow, and go out to the open country to hunt some wild game for me. Prepare me the kind of tasty food I like and bring it to me to eat, so that I may give you my blessing before I die."

The words Isaac used to summon Esau were endearing and indicated the love he and Esau shared for each other. He called him "My son." It also suggests that Isaac seemed to come to terms with the grief caused by Esau's marriages to Canaanite women. Therefore, as an old man, who did not know the day of his death, but knew it was nearer than before, Isaac thought he needed to take care of the business of settling his estate. Thus, he thought it was time to pass on the blessing to his older son Esau. In other words, he wanted to put his house in order before he died.

The strength of Isaac and Esau's relationship was also evident by the fact that he instructed Esau to go hunt some wild game and prepare the kind of tasty food he liked to eat. He did not have to tell him what that food was, Esau already knew, because this was probably not the first time Isaac made such a request of him. But this time, his reason for doing so was different. This time, Isaac said it was, "so that I may give you my blessing before I die."

The blessing Isaac had and was going to pass on to Esau, was the blessing of eldership as the older son, and as heir of the covenant of God. If Esau had received that blessing from Isaac, the fact that he had previously agreed to sell his birthright to Jacob would not have mattered, because he sold something he did not yet fully own.

REBEKAH'S DECEPTIVE PLAN

Verses 5–10 explain that Rebekah was listening as Isaac spoke to his son Esau. When Esau left for the open country to hunt game and bring it back, she said to her son Jacob, "I overheard your father say to your brother Esau, 'Bring me some game and prepare me some tasty food to eat, so that I may give you my blessing in the presence of the Lord before I die.' Now, my son, listen carefully and do what I tell you: Go out to the flock and bring me two choice young goats, so I can prepare some tasty food for your father, just the way he likes it. Then take it to your father to eat, so that he may give you his blessing before he dies."

It is not clear if by this time Rebekah knew Jacob had already deceived Esau into agreeing to sell him his birthright, but based on her relationship with Jacob, it is likely he may have shared that information with her. If he did, she would have known the only thing remaining for him to seal the deal, was to receive his father's blessing. This sequence of events provide insight into Rebekah's efforts to wrestle the blessing away from Esau, whom Isaac loved, and give it to Jacob, whom she loved. Her strategy, albeit deceitful, was also an effort to correct the disastrous course on which God's plan seemed to be heading, had Isaac indeed given the covenant blessing to Esau, who married Canaanite women, which he was not supposed to do.

It is not humanly possible to know how God would have otherwise corrected the situation, but it needed to be corrected for the prophecies to occur, which were given to Abraham and Isaac. Esau could not be allowed to continue as heir to the birthright under the circumstances he created for himself. While it is impossible to know how God would have otherwise corrected the situation, what is known is, Rebekah could have tried a more honest approach to correcting it. For example, she could have simply tried talking to her husband, and at least tried to remind him about the stipulations of the covenant, especially since they both shared the same grief about Esau's marriages to Canaanite women. This should have made a conversation about a solution easier.

Isaac also knew what God said about his descendants possessing the land of Canaan in years to come, and this could not occur if his descendants were mixed with the very people they were supposed to dispossess. So, Rebekah could have tried having an honest conversation with her husband, rather than devising a dishonest plan with her son.

The linguistic nuances Rebekah used should not be overlooked. Observe that she repeatedly referred to Esau as Jacob's brother, but not one time did she refer to him as her son. Jacob was her beloved son, but she was beyond disappointed with Esau. She had nothing good to say about him and wanted nothing to do with him! She also repeatedly referred to Isaac as Jacob's father, but never did she refer to him as her husband, which might suggest she had become disenchanted with him over the fact that he still harbored a loving relationship toward Esau, despite his forbidden marriages, and the danger those marriages posed to the future of the covenant.

JACOB'S CONCERN ABOUT REBEKAH'S PLAN

Verses 11-13 reveal that Jacob responded to his mother's idea by reminding her that his brother Esau was a hairy man, while he had smooth skin. He asked her, "What if my father touches me? I would appear to be tricking him and would bring down a curse on myself rather than a blessing." However, his mother told him to let the curse fall on her. She instructed him to just do what she told him to do, and get the items she told him to get, so she could fix the food his father requested.

Once again, it is not clear if Rebekah knew Jacob had already deceived Esau into agreeing to sell him his birthright. If this was the case, she could have informed her husband Isaac about it, to provide additional evidence as to why he should step back from giving Esau his blessing. By selling his birthright, Esau had already showed he disregarded it. However, Rebekah was willing to risk a dangerous scheme, which could have resulted in a curse, rather than a blessing. Neither her, nor her son Jacob, expressed any concern about the deceitfulness of the plan, their only concern was about the consequences of being caught.

Jacob was afraid of bringing a curse on himself, because he would be the one to go in and try to deceive his father, but Rebekah was not afraid of that because she was working behind the scenes. Therefore, her offer to accept the curse was unrealistic, and simply an effort to get Jacob's mind off the danger he faced. More telling was the fact that as they planned, neither Rebekah nor her son Jacob, seemed concerned about how God felt about their actions. Neither of them consulted Him about the situation.

JACOB EXECUTES THE PLAN

Verses 14-17 indicate that Jacob went out and got the items and brought them to his mother, and she prepared the tasty food, just the way his father liked it. Then his mother took the best clothes, which belonged to Esau her older son, which she had in the house, and she put them on her younger son Jacob. She also covered his hands and the smooth part of his neck with goatskins. Then she handed her son Jacob, the tasty food, and the bread she had made.

The fact that Esau's clothes fit Jacob, suggest that even though the brothers were not identical twins, they may have been about the same size. The smell of wild game around the neck of Esau's clothing indicated that after killing wild animals, he hoisted them around his neck to transport them. So, Jacob had to disguise himself, by wearing his older brother's clothing, and by appearing to be his older brother to get his father's blessing. Appearing in his is own image would have brought down a curse on him. This is similar to what Christians believe concerning Christ, who is their Elder Brother. They can only receive the Father's blessing if they appear before Him clothed in the garments of Christ, and in His righteousness alone. His aroma around their necks, is convincing proof they are His.

Verses 18-20 describe what occurred when Jacob went before his father Isaac. It says He went to his father and said, "My father." "Yes, my son," Isaac answered. "Who is it?" Jacob said to his father, "I am Esau your firstborn. I have done as you told me. Please sit up and eat some of my game, so that you may give me your blessing." Isaac asked his son, "How did you find it so quickly, my son?" "The Lord your God gave me success," he replied.

It is unspeakably important to pay attention to the unforgettable words of deceit, which Jacob used to convince his father he was Esau. He said: 1. I am Esau your firstborn; 2. I have done as you told me to do; 3. Sit up and eat some of my game; and 4. The Lord your God gave me success. These were all lies, because he was not Esau, his father did not tell him to do what he was doing, what he presented was not wild game, and the Lord did not give him success in finding it quickly, because he did not go hunting, he went to the goat pen! These lies would follow Jacob for the remainder of his life.

When Rebekah initially presented her plan to Jacob, he responded with skepticism and concern about the possibility of getting caught. However, in executing the plan, he did so flawlessly. He impeccably mastered the art of lying, and it is possible he did so with his mother's help. She not only prepared the food, clothes, and fake hair, but she also prepared Jacob's mind and his answers. As such, he seemed to anticipate every question his father asked, and he had an answer prepared for each one. The capstone to his lies occurred when he invoked the Name of the Lord into his scheme, giving the appearance of having God's help in what he was doing. This lie, more than any other, probably did more to deceive Isaac than anything else Jacob said.

ISAAC'S DOUBTS ABOUT JACOB'S STORY

Isaac was not convinced. Notice verses 21–24. He asked Jacob to come close, so he could touch him, to know whether he was really his son Esau. Jacob went close to his father Isaac, who touched him and said, "The voice is the voice of Jacob, but the hands are the hands of Esau." He did not detect the scheme because Jacob's hands were hairy like those of his brother Esau; so, he proceeded to bless him. "Are you really my son Esau?" he asked. "I am," Jacob replied.

Isaac had to rely on his other senses since his sense of sight no longer worked, but no doubt, this must have been a nerve-wracking experience for Jacob. Isaac listened to him and said the voice is the voice of Jacob, soft and smooth like that of a saint, but by his touch he said the hands are the hands of Esau, rough like the hands of a sinner. If Isaac had stuck with his instinctual knowledge about his sons' voices, he would have uncovered the scheme, because it was easier for Jacob to disguise his hands, than to disguise his voice. But, since Isaac did not know he had already fraudulently acquired Esau's birthright, he had no reason to believe Jacob would try to deceitfully get the blessing too.

In any case, since Isaac was not absolutely sure the person he was blessing was Esau, it might have been wiser to refrain from giving the blessing on that day. However, God allowed it to occur as planned, because it was also His will to remove the birthright from Esau.

ISAAC BLESSED JACOB

Verses 25–29 show that Isaac told Jacob to bring him some of his game to eat, so that he may give him his blessing. Jacob brought it to him, and he ate; and he brought some wine, and he drank. Then his father said to him, "Come here, my son, and kiss me." So, he went to him and kissed him. When Isaac caught the smell of his clothes, he blessed him and said:

> Ah, the smell of my son is like the smell of a field that the Lord has blessed." May God give you heaven's dew and earth's richness, an abundance of grain and new wine. May nations serve you and peoples bow down to you. Be lord over your brothers, and may the sons of your mother bow down to you. May those who curse you be cursed and those who bless you be blessed.[1] (NIV)

In an effort to get one more piece of evidence, Isaac asked Jacob, assuming he was Esau, to come close one final time and kiss him. This also reveals that the relationship between Isaac and his son Esau was very close; he even knew his smell. Notice, Jacob made sure his father not only ate his food, but he also saw to it that he gave him some wine to drink.

Isaac blessed Jacob with four specific things: 1. Heaven's dew and earth's richness, precisely an abundance of grain and new wine (this was prosperity); 2. Service and surrender by other nations (this was power); 3. Leadership (Lordship) over his brothers who would surrender (bow down) to him (this was prominence); And 4. Those who cursed him would be cursed, and those who blessed him would be blessed (this was principle). These blessings (prosperity, power, prominence, and principle) would become pivotal reasons for Israel's success in years to come. However, they would also cause the nation to become arrogant and self-reliant.

ESAU DISCOVERS THE PLAN AGAINST HIM

Verses 30–32 reveal that after Isaac finished pronouncing his blessing, and before Jacob had scarcely left his presence, his brother Esau came in from hunting. He too prepared some tasty food and brought it to his father. Then he said to him, "My father, please sit up and eat some of my game, so that you may give me your blessing." Isaac asked him, "Who are you?" "I am your son," he answered, "your firstborn, Esau."

The fact that Esau returned shortly after Jacob left his father's presence, bears witness to his skills as a hunter. He hunted his game and prepared it

---

1. Barker, et. al. *The NIV Study Bible*, Genesis 27:27–29.

almost as fast as Jacob went to the goat herd and selected a goat for Rebekah to prepare! This was also how close Isaac came to giving the most significant blessing he had to the wrong son. As deceitful as the process was, it would have been a greater tragedy had Esau received the blessing, having totally ignored its most significant stipulation concerning his marriages.

Verses 33–35 show Isaac's response to discovering the person he blessed was not Esau. It says he trembled violently and asked, "Who was it then, that hunted game and brought it to me? I ate it just before you came and I blessed him, and indeed he will be blessed!" When Esau heard his father's words, he burst out with a loud and bitter cry and said to his father, "Bless me, me too, my father!" But Isaac said, "Your brother came deceitfully and took your blessing."

Isaac trembled violently at the thought that he may have been deceived by someone who was not his son at all. However, his fears were relieved as he learned the one he blessed was indeed a son, albeit not the son he intended it to be. In that moment, he may also have been brought to his senses, as he realized Esau's marriages disqualified him from the blessing, and as he remembered God told him the older would serve the younger (Gen 25:23). Esau thoughtlessly sold his birthright to Jacob, but he seemed to want to hold on to the blessings which came with it. However, though Isaac trembled, and Esau appealed with many tears, there was no way to reverse what was done. The birthright and all its associated blessings became Jacob's.

ESAU'S FUTILE APPEALS FOR A BLESSING

Verse 36 indicates that Esau said, "Isn't he rightly named Jacob (Deceiver)? This is the second time he has taken advantage of me: He took my birthright, and now he's taken my blessing!" Then he asked, "Haven't you reserved any blessing for me?"

Esau's statement appeared to be the first time Isaac learned that Jacob had already acquired the birthright. He told his father, this was the second time Jacob had taken advantage of, or supplanted, him. He accused Jacob of taking his birthright, as though he was not complicit in the process, and he accepted no blame for his role in his circumstances. He proved he wanted the blessings, which were benefits of the birthright, but he did not want the responsibilities that went along with it. Hence, he asked, "Haven't you reserved any blessing for me?"

Notice verse 37, Isaac answered Esau and told him, "I have made him lord over you and have made all his relatives his servants, and I have sustained him with grain and new wine. So, what can I possibly do for you, my son?" In other words, Isaac informed Esau that his descendants would serve Jacob's descendants, and that Jacob would be prosperous, with grain and new wine. Having declared the best blessings over Jacob, Esau had to settle for inferior blessings, and under the circumstances, he seemed desperately content with that. He who had the right to all the blessings, ended up having to beg for one.

Verse 38 shows that Esau appealed to his father by asking, "Do you have only one blessing, my father? Bless me too, my father!" Then he wept aloud. No doubt, this was a sad and emotional occasion for Isaac, as he listened helplessly to the appeals and cries of his elder son, whom he loved. Those outside the tent probably heard Esau's weeping and wondered what happened, but Rebekah and Jacob knew the exact cause of his loud wailing.

Verses 39–40 summarize the words Isaac pronounced on Esau, some of which may hardly be considered blessings:

> Your dwelling will be away from the earth's richness, away from the dew of heaven above. You will live by the sword and you will serve your brother. But when you grow restless, you will throw his yoke from off your neck.[2] (NIV)

Esau's dwellings were prophesied to be away from the earth's richness, and away from the dew of heaven, which were the complete opposites of Jacob's blessings. Esau's dwellings appear to be a desert, and it meant the two brothers could not co-exist in the same location. His descendants were also prophesied to live by the sword, or to be violent people. Despite their violence, they would serve their brother, or his descendants, until such time as they grew restless, and were able to free themselves from his yoke (2 Chr 21:8–10).

Hebrews 12:16–17 provide an ideal summary of what happened to Esau. It did so by issuing a warning for believers to make sure none of them are sexually immoral, or godless like Esau, who for a single meal, sold the rights of his inheritance as the oldest son. It says that afterward, he wanted to inherit the blessing, but he was rejected, even though he sought it with tears. He could not change what had been done. This passage described Esau as sexually immoral because of his love for Canaanite women, who may also have led him away from the true God. It underscores reasons why Esau was not qualified to inherit the blessing.

---

2. Barker, et. al. *The NIV Study Bible*, Genesis 27:39–40.

ESAU'S PLAN TO KILL JACOB

Verses 41-45 shed light on Esau's frame of mind following what Jacob did to him. These verses indicate that he held a grudge against Jacob because of the blessing his father had given him. He said to himself, following the death of his father he was going to kill his brother. When Rebekah was told what her older son Esau said, she sent for her younger son Jacob and warned him about what she heard. She also instructed him to flee at once to her brother Laban in Harran, and to stay with him for a while until his brother's fury subsided. She told Jacob that when his brother was no longer angry with him, and had forgotten what he did to him, she would send word for him to come back from Harran. She asked, "Why should I lose both of you in one day?"

Notice the reason Esau hated his brother was not because he took the birthright, but because he took the blessing. His outrage over this was not only kept to himself, but was repeated to others, which allowed Rebekah to hear about it. He planned to kill his brother Jacob. By referring to him as his brother, and yet planning to kill him, represented a major contradiction. A brother should be loved, cared for, and forgiven, not killed. Esau once possessed the birthright because he was the firstborn, but having lost it, his plan was to recapture it by murdering his brother. If Isaac did indeed die as soon as Esau expected, Jacob's life would have been in immediately mortal danger.

Esau's statement about his intent to kill his brother Jacob after his father's death, also revealed how he felt about his mother. He obviously wanted to protect his father from grief but did not seem to care about the grief his mother would have felt. In fact, if by then he found out about her role in the scheme, he probably thought she at least deserved to grieve.

Rebekah instructed Jacob to flee to her brother Laban, who lived in Harran, and to stay there until Esau forgot the offense that was committed against him. However, that offense could never be forgotten, because it had generational implications. Esau's descendants probably remembered it during every moment of servitude to Jacob's descendants. What is not known with certainty is if Esau ever found out the role his mother Rebekah played in deceiving him and the nature of their relationship as a result.

REBEKAH'S DISGUST WITH ESAU'S CANAANITE WIVES

Verse 46 notes that Rebekah complained to Isaac about her disgust with living, because of the Hittite women Esau married. She said if Jacob took a wife from among the women of Canaan, her life would not be worth living. Once

Jacob gained possession of the birthright and blessing, he became prohibited from marrying Canaanite women. If he did as Esau had done and defied that prohibition, all hope would have been lost, especially for Rebekah who worked so hard, albeit deceitfully, to make sure order was restored.

It is not clear if Rebekah informed Isaac about the threat Esau made against Jacob's life, but she used the occasion to raise her discontent about Esau's choice of wives, and her desperate hope that Jacob would never do the same. This conversation should also have reminded Isaac of the stipulations of the covenant, the importance of its heir avoiding entanglement with Canaanites, and how merciful God was in keeping him from making a terrible mistake had he bestowed the birthright blessings on Esau.

From a surface level and contemporary perspective, it may appear as if Rebekah's disgust with Esau's Canaanite wives was racially motivated. If this was the case, it would be more difficult to prove than the prophetic reasons the Bible gives for the inheritor of the covenant blessings to avoid entanglement with the Canaanites. God made it clear, Abraham, and then Isaac's descendants would dispossess the Canaanites and inherit their land in years to come. Rebekah did her best, to make sure the integrity of that promise was upheld. Therefore, God used what appeared to be an evil effort by Jacob and his mother to put His covenant plan back on its correct course.

GENESIS CHAPTER TWENTY-EIGHT

The previous chapter discussed the scheme Rebekah and Jacob devised to prevent Esau from receiving his father's blessing as the firstborn son. Though the scheme itself was vicious, the motive behind it was necessary. It would have been a colossal mistake had Isaac given the birthright blessing to Esau, considering his marriages to two Canaanite women. Offspring from those marriages would have complicated God's intent for Isaac's descendants to dispossess the Canaanites in years to come. Thankfully, Rebekah and Jacob's scheme worked, and Esau lost his birthright and covenant blessings. This chapter will examine Jacob's journey, as he fled to Harran to seek refuge with his uncle Laban, and to escape the fury of his brother Esau, who intended to take revenge by killing him.

JACOB'S BLESSING AND DEPARTURE FOR HARRAN

Verses 1-2 indicate that Isaac called Jacob and blessed him. Then he commanded him: "Do not marry a Canaanite woman. Go at once to Paddan Aram (NW Mesopotamia), to the house of your mother's father Bethuel. Take a wife for yourself there, from among the daughters of Laban, your mother's brother.

It is not clear if Isaac was told one of the reasons Jacob had to leave home was because Esau planned to kill him. If he was told, he did not mention it in his instructions; instead, he attempted to ensure Jacob did not make the same mistake Esau did by marrying Canaanite women. Hence, he gave him some marriage advice. He told him where to go to select a wife (one wife), and the family from which to select her. There is no evidence Esau ever received this kind of advice from either of his parents. He loved Canaanite women and seemed to choose any of them he wanted; Therefore, he was described as sexually immoral (Heb 12:16). Since Jacob had to flee to Harran to save his life, his father instructed him to find a wife while he was there. He did not want him to return to Canaan a single man, and thereby make the same mistake as his brother.

Verses 3–5 reveal that Isaac blessed Jacob by saying: "May God Almighty (El Shaddai) bless you and make you fruitful and increase your numbers until you become a community of peoples. May He give you and your descendants the blessing given to Abraham, so that you may take possession of the land where you now reside as a foreigner, the land God gave to Abraham." Then Isaac sent Jacob on his way, and he went to Paddan Aram, to Laban son of Bethuel the Aramean, the brother of Rebekah, who was the mother of Jacob and Esau.

The significance of Isaac blessing Jacob to become possessor of a land he was about to flee from was to remind him that the place to which he was going was to be a temporary sojourn. Canaan was his home, and he needed to return as soon as possible. Abraham made his servant promise him he would not find Isaac a wife from among the Canaanites (Gen 24: 6, 8). Isaac sent Jacob away with the same instruction. The fact that Jacob had to go to Paddan Aram must have been difficult for Isaac, because once Abraham left there he never returned, nor did he allow him to go there. So, based on what is known from the Biblical record, Isaac had never been to Harran, and it would most likely have been his preference for Jacob to not go there, but he had to go; His life depended on it.

ESAU MARRIES AGAIN

Verses 6–8 present an interesting case, these verses state that Esau learned that Isaac blessed Jacob and sent him to Paddan Aram to take a wife from there, that when he blessed him, he commanded him, "Do not marry a Canaanite woman," and that Jacob had obeyed his father and mother and had gone to Paddan Aram. Apparently, this was when Esau realized how displeasing the Canaanite women were to his father Isaac.

It appears that prior to this event, Esau may have been unaware of the extent of his father's grief over his marriages to Canaanite women. It may be that Isaac was grieved, but he did not share the extent of his grief with his son Esau, whom he loved. Esau learned about the magnitude of his father's grief through the advice he gave his brother, but it does not seem as if he ever received any such advice himself. Thankfully, Esau learned these things after Jacob had already left for Harran, otherwise, it may have exacerbated the situation by intensifying his existing anger towards him.

Notice how Esau attempted to rectify the situation. Verse 9 says, he went to Ishmael and married Mahalath, the sister of Nebaioth and daughter of Ishmael son of Abraham, in addition to the wives he already had. In Esau's quest to find a wife, whom he thought may have been more acceptable to his father, he added an Ishmaelite woman to the two Canaanites he already had. Once again, it does not appear he sought any advice before making his decision. However, Ishmaelite wives would also have been a problem if he was still the birthright holder, because Ishmael and his descendants were not to share in the covenant blessing that was given to Isaac and his descendants.

Notice, in marrying an Ishmaelite wife, Esau was not concerned about pleasing God in his decision, nor was he concerned about pleasing his mother. His only concern was to please his father, who as it appears, said nothing to him about his marriages. The extent of Esau's sexual immorality was demonstrated by the speed with which he took an additional wife for no other reason than to gain favor with his father. It was certainly not because he loved her; He loved Canaanite women. This additional marriage only proved how desperate he was to recapture the blessing if he could.

JACOB'S DREAM AT BETHEL

Verses 10–15 indicate that Jacob left Beersheba and set out for Harran. When he reached a certain point in his journey, he stopped for the night because the sun had set. He took a stone and put it under his head as a pillow and lay down to sleep. While asleep, he had a dream in which he saw a stairway resting on the earth, with its top reaching to heaven, and the angels of God were ascending and descending on it.

Above it (or beside him) stood the Lord, and He said: "I am the Lord, the God of your father Abraham and the God of Isaac. I will give you and your descendants the land on which you are lying. Your descendants will be like the dust of the earth, and you will spread out to the west and to the east, to the north and to the south. All peoples on earth will be blessed through you and your offspring (or will use your name and the name of your offspring in blessings). I am with you and will watch over you wherever you go, and I will bring you back to this land. I will not leave you until I have done what I have promised you."

Notice, Jacob did not stop for the night because he was tired, rather he stopped because the sun had set. The place where he rested was called Bethel. Henry estimates that it was forty 40 miles from Beersheba.[1] This was the place where God appeared to Abraham after he left Harran and first entered the land of Canaan. He promised to give the land to Abraham and his offspring (Gen 12:8). Ironically, the same promise was being made to

---

1. Henry, *Commentary on the Whole Bible Complete and Unabridged*, 63.

Jacob as he was leaving Canaan to find refuge in Harran. It was as though Jacob was reversing the journey Abraham made many years earlier.

After a long hard day of travelling, Jacob used a stone as his pillow and earth as his bed. His life of privilege was suspended during this phase, and he would begin to experience some of the most difficult hardships of his life. The stairway he saw resting on earth and reaching to heaven represented the constant interactions by way of prayer and other divine interfaces between earth and heaven.

He also saw angels going back and forth on the staircase, but angels do not need staircases to traverse between heaven and earth. As spiritual beings they are not restricted by time or space but can be wherever they need to be at the speed of thought. God on the other hand, is already wherever He needs to be, so travel is not necessary for Him. Consequently, the Lord was depicted standing above the staircase because access to heaven can only occur through Him.

Notice the Lord introduced Himself by telling Jacob, "I am the Lord." He also told him, He is the God of Abraham and Isaac, but He did not represent Himself as the God of Jacob, because at that time He may not yet have been Jacob's God. So, Jacob was resting; he was not seeking God, but God was seeking him. He even blessed Jacob with the same blessing he received from his father, but this time, God, who has power to do what He says, informed Jacob He would bring him back to that land. This promise was meant to encourage Jacob that even thought his situation might appear bleak at times; even though he may have a stone as his pillow and the earth as his bed, God was with him.

Verses 16–17 explain that when Jacob awoke from his sleep, he thought, "Surely the Lord is in this place, and I was not aware of it." He was afraid and said, "How awesome is this place! This is none other than the House of God; this is the gate of heaven!"

Bethel seemed to be the last place on earth where Jacob expected the presence of God to be. He awoke absolutely surprised to encounter God in that place! It was interesting that the Lord described Himself as the God of Isaac, yet Jacob did not seem to encounter the Lord while he lived at home with his father Isaac. Instead, it appears as if his first encounter was right there in Bethel.

No doubt, there are times when the presence of God is evident in places where it is least expected, but what happened in Jacob's case? Did Isaac fail to introduce him to the Lord? Could it be that Isaac was so partial to Esau that Jacob never learned about the Lord from him? Was Jacob's unfamiliarity with the Lord the reason why he was so thoughtlessly deceitful? Evidently so, especially since it appears that after this encounter with the

Lord, Jacob seemed to worship the place rather than the person, the Lord, who appeared to him.

JACOB BUILDS A PILLAR AT BETHEL

Verses 18-19 note that early the next morning Jacob took the stone he had placed under his head and set it up as a pillar and poured oil on top of it. He called that place Bethel (House of God), though the city used to be called Luz (Almond Tree).

Observe that Jacob did not set up an altar for worship, instead he set up a pillar for remembrance. He poured oil on the stone in commemoration of the fact that it served as a place where he could lay his head at one of the lowest points in his life. Such times are indeed worth remembering.

Verses 20-22 provide further insight into where Jacob was in his relationship with the Lord at that point in his life. It shows that Jacob made a vow, saying, "If God will be with me and will watch over me on this journey I am taking and will give me food to eat and clothes to wear, so that I return safely to my father's household, then the Lord will be my God, and this stone that I have set up as a pillar will be God's house, and of all that you give me I will give you a tenth."

God had made a sure promise to Jacob by guaranteeing him He would be with him and would bring him back to his father's house. However, being the dealmaker he was, Jacob tried to make a conditional deal with the Lord. He basically told the Lord, if He kept His promise, then He would be his God, just as He is the God of his father Isaac, and Grandfather Abraham. But, if the Lord did not keep His promise, He would not be his God. So, in essence, Jacob challenged the Lord to keep His promise! He also promised to give the Lord a tenth of all he had. Observe, Jacob decided this on his own, God did not command him to do it. However, since a tenth was considered at that time to be the king's portion, Jacob was basically promising that the Lord would not only be his God, but also his King.

The promises Jacob made to the Lord were conditional upon the Lord keeping His promises to him. In other words, Jacob's faith was yet in its infancy during this season of his life. He would only be convinced after seeing the Lord's actions rather than simply hearing His words. There are many believers today who are like Jacob, they put the Lord to the test by doubting His Word, while demanding miracles immediately. Meanwhile, ignoring the many things He has done and is doing in their lives. Thank God for His patience!

GENESIS CHAPTER TWENTY-NINE

The previous chapter showed where Jacob gained sole possession of the birthright and its blessings. This precipitated a time of restlessness in his life. Firstly, he was forced to flee to Harran to escape from Esau, who swore to take revenge by killing him. Meanwhile, to pacify his father's grief over his marriages to Canaanite women, Esau took on an additional wife of Ishmaelite descent. None of this was enough to reverse his situation.

Secondly, while fleeing to Harran, Jacob encountered the Lord in a dream. This encounter would change the rest of his life. In the dream, God reiterated the same promises He made to Abraham and Isaac, as He promised Jacob to bring him back from Harran to the Land of Canaan, which would be his, and his descendants' inheritance. Jacob responded by building an altar and promising God that if He did what He promised, then He would be his God. This chapter will examine his arrival in Harran, his life there, circumstances surrounding his marriages, and his offspring. More importantly, it will show the multitude of things God did to bless and prosper him despite many hardships.

JACOB'S ARRIVAL IN PADDAN ARAM

Verses 1–3 show that Jacob continued his journey and came to the land of the eastern peoples. There he saw a well in the open country, with three flocks of sheep lying near it because the flocks were watered from that well. The stone over the mouth of the well was large. When all the flocks were gathered there, the shepherds would roll the stone away from the well's mouth and water the sheep. Then they would return the stone to its place over the mouth of the well.

God's providential hand guided Jacob to his destination. Notice, the well Jacob saw was in open country, and it was covered by a large stone; This stone served a valuable purpose. It signified that the well was on private property and not for public use, and since it was located in open country without barriers, the stone also protected the sheep, and people, from falling into it and drowning.

Flocks rested by the well because they were watered from it. Symbolically, this is also how it should be with the Church. It should symbolically be like a well, where its flock should be able to rest and be watered. Its shepherds should be trustworthy individuals who are reliable enough to care for them by uncovering the Word of God, as a stone, so they can be watered from the mouth of God.

Verses 4-8 show that Jacob asked the shepherds, "My brothers, where are you from?" "We're from Harran," they replied. Then he asked, "Do you know Laban, Nahor's grandson?" "Yes, we know him," they answered. Jacob asked, "Is he well?" "Yes, he is," they said, "and here comes his daughter Rachel with the sheep." Jacob told them, "Look, the sun is still high; it is not time for the flocks to be gathered. Water the sheep and take them back to pasture." "We can't," they replied, "until all the flocks are gathered, and the stone has been rolled away from the mouth of the well. Then we will water the sheep."

The fact that Jacob was so quickly able to meet people who knew the family he was searching for, and to gain the information he needed about them, was evidence God was with him as He promised to be. As soon as Jacob was told who Rachel was, he immediately pursued a strategy to find private audience with her. He sought to dismiss the shepherds by telling them how to do their jobs as quickly as possible, so they could get out of his way. He did not understand the reason they waited until all the flocks were gathered before removing the stone from the mouth of the well. In other words, he did not understand their communal system, and lack of selfishness in this matter.

JACOB MEETS RACHEL

Verses 9-12 reveal that while Jacob was still talking with the shepherds, Rachel came with her father's sheep, because she was a shepherdess. When he saw her with the sheep, he went over and rolled the stone away from the mouth of the well and watered his uncle's sheep. Then Jacob kissed Rachel and began to weep aloud. He had told Rachel that he was a relative of her father and a son of Rebekah. So, she ran and told her father.

It should be noted that Rachel had servants who worked for her, yet she did not view being a shepherdess to be a condescending occupation. Her occupation also suggest that her father probably did not yet have any sons. Being a shepherdess meant she shared the same occupation as Jacob and had that in common with him. As such, he immediately rolled away the stone before it was time to do so, to keep her from waiting at the well until all the flocks were gathered, and to quickly expedite an end to his long journey.

In rolling the stone away, Jacob also demonstrated his strength, and signaled to Rachel that he was willing to step in and assist her in tending her father's flock. Their encounter was highly emotional for Jacob as he cried aloud and kissed Rachel, but there are no recorded words spoken by her; she simply ran and told her father.

JACOB MEETS LABAN

Verses 11–14 explain that as soon as Laban heard the news about Jacob, his sister's son, he hurried to meet him. He embraced him and kissed him and brought him to his home, and there Jacob told him all these things. Then Laban said to him, "You are my own flesh and blood."

The previous occasion in the Biblical record, when Laban encountered someone from Abraham's household, was when Abraham sent his servant to find a wife for Isaac (Gen 24). The servant arrived with a large display of riches, which demonstrated Abraham's prosperity and ability to provide for the wife his son would marry. So, Laban knew Jacob came from a wealthy family; Yet Jacob did not arrive with the same kind of impressive display of riches that Abraham's servant did, instead, he appeared destitute.

In their conversation about the purpose for his visit, it simply says Jacob told him "All these things," but it is not specific about what that meant, and what he really told him. Both Jacob and Laban excelled in the art of deceit, so it was possible that not everything Jacob told him was true. In any case, Laban accepted Jacob's story by declaring, "You are my own flesh and blood!" In other words, he accepted Jacob as if he were a son, especially since, it does not appear he had any sons at that time.

JACOB'S REQUEST TO MARRY RACHEL

After Jacob had stayed with Laban for a month, verse 15 indicates that Laban said to him, "Just because you are a relative of mine, should you work for me for nothing? Tell me what your wages should be."

It should be noted here that Jacob did not demand a salary from his uncle before he started working for him, nor did he demand one while he was working for him. However, he proved to be skillful at his job and worth keeping, so Laban initiated the conversation about paying him. Nevertheless, Jacob was not only in Harran to escape Esau's wrath, but one of his main goals, as instructed by his father, was to find a wife. He was not to return to Canaan a single man. Having met Rachel and falling in love with her beauty, he wanted to marry her. The fact that they shared the same occupation, allowed them to spend time together, and convinced him he found the woman he was looking for. Hence, rather than negotiating for wages, Jacob decided to negotiate for a wife.

Verses 16-18 point out that Laban had two daughters; the name of the older was Leah, and the name of the younger was Rachel. Leah had weak eyes, but Rachel had a lovely figure and was beautiful. Jacob was in love with Rachel and said, "I'll work for you seven years in return for your younger daughter Rachel."

Notice, Leah was described as the older daughter, who obviously did not have the strength in her eyes that Rachel did. She was not a shepherdess like Rachel, nor was she as gregarious. In fact, Leah's occupation was not even mentioned. Due to her unflattering characteristics, it would have been more difficult for Laban to find her a husband, than it would have been to find one for Rachel. On the other hand, Rachel was described as younger, having a lovely figure, and beautiful. She had the full package, and Jacob absolutely loved her!

As a shepherdess caring for her father's flock, along with Jacob as a new employee, this became an on-the-job attraction. They both worked together, which allowed them to spend time observing, talking, and getting to know each other. Therefore, Jacob offered to work for Rachel, rather than for Leah, because he was more familiar with Rachel. He also offered to work for her, rather than pay her father for her, because he had no worldly possessions with which to pay a dowry. Notwithstanding, he was inheritor of the covenant birthright and blessings. He was also seventy-seven years old at that time, and marriage had become a crucial objective for him; There was no time to waste!

Verses 19-20 indicate that Laban responded to Jacob's request by saying, "It's better that I give her to you than to some other man. Stay here with me." So, Jacob served seven years to get Rachel, but they seemed like only a few days to him because of his love for her.

Seven years were enough time for Jacob to realize what the customs of Harran were concerning marriage, and for Laban to inform him that his request was inappropriate to marry the younger sister before the older. However, it is possible that since Jacob offered to work seven years for Rachel, Laban may have held out to see if his older daughter Leah, might have gotten married within that time. Nevertheless, the fact cannot be ignored that Jacob and Laban were both deceitful men, which removed honesty from their negotiations with each other.

Laban seemed to share his sister Rebekah's preference for his daughters to marry a relative, rather than someone outside the family; So, Jacob unsuspectingly fell into a marriage trap! He and Rachel worked together, and he loved her, which made the seven years seem easier. As shepherds together, they would have seen each other daily, and talked with each other often. Seven years were more than enough time for them to really get to know each other. However, there is no Biblical evidence to suggest Jacob got to know Leah in a similar way. He obviously did not know her as well, because he was not romantically interested in her, nor did he love her.

JACOB MARRIES LEAH AND RACHEL

Verses 21–24 declare that when the seven years were completed, Jacob said to Laban, "Give me my wife. My time is completed, and I want to make love to her." So, Laban brought together all the people of the place and gave a feast. But when evening came, he took his daughter Leah and brought her to Jacob, and Jacob made love to her. And Laban gave his servant Zilpah to his daughter as her attendant.

Jacob described Rachel as his wife, though they were not yet married, because he was espoused to her. Espousal was an exclusive relationship without living together or having a sexual relationship. As such, after waiting and working seven years to get at Rachel, Jacob made his intentions clear, he wanted to make love to her! Yet, he let his guard down and seemed oblivious to the fact that Laban was supremely more deceitful than he was. Therefore, while he was able to easily deceive his honest father Isaac, he was easily deceived by his dishonest father-in-law Laban.

Notice, Laban held a marriage feast in the evening, which meant after the sun was beginning to, or had already gone down. No doubt, there was much wine served at this feast to make sure Jacob's sight and judgment were impaired. Jacob was being repaid for what he did to his father, whose sight was dim, and to whom he served wine along with a meal he pretended was the wild game his father requested. He then presented himself to his father as if he were his brother Esau, and he deceived his father. Laban did a similar thing to him by serving him wine in the evening to make sure he was drunk and could hardly see, and then presented Leah to him, as if she were her sister Rachel.

Verse 25 reveals that when morning came, there was Leah! So, Jacob said to Laban, "What is this you have done to me? I served you for Rachel, didn't I? Why have you deceived me?" The entire night passed, and Jacob made love and was happy with Leah for one night, until morning came. It was then he realized he married the wrong woman, but by then it was too late. He trusted Laban, and married the woman he presented to him, but he never lifted the veil to see who she really was. Hence, when morning came, from his perspective, he married the wrong woman. It appeared as if Laban pulled off the perfect bait-and-switch scheme on Jacob.

There are many marriages today, which are similar. Couples are struggling because they believe they made a mistake and married the wrong person. Darkness has ended, and the light reveals they have not taken appropriate time to lift the veil. As a result, they married someone they really did not know, and they feel trapped. There is no easy solution to this dilemma, which causes many to resort to divorce, rather than working through it. Adding children to the mix also makes the situation more complicated, but this is exactly what Jacob did.

Jacob made love to Leah during the night, and was happy with her, as though she was the one he loved, until morning came and he saw her face and discovered she was not. Morning comes on every relationship. It is at that time when couples finally wake up and must decide how to move forward. Jacob blamed Laban for his predicament, but he also bore some responsibility for it; he did not lift the veil. No doubt, he probably blamed Leah as well, because she knew the truth. She was a co-conspirator in her father's scheme. She could have revealed herself to Jacob during the night, but she did not. Therefore, she, like many women today, made love to a man she knew from the beginning did not love her.

Jacob's past came back to haunt him. He asked Laban, why have you deceived me?" This was the very question his father and brother could have asked him! He was stuck, and it would take the mercies of God to relieve him, and steer him back on course, so he could accomplish the mission God had for his life.

Verses 26–30 show that Laban replied to Jacob's question: "why have you deceived me?" by saying, "It is not our custom here to give the younger daughter in marriage before the older one. Finish this daughter's bridal week; then we will give you the younger one also, in return for another seven years of work." And Jacob did so. He finished the week with Leah, and then Laban gave him his daughter Rachel to be his wife. Laban gave his servant Bilhah to his daughter Rachel as her attendant. Jacob made love to Rachel also, and his love for Rachel was greater than his love for Leah. And he worked for Laban another seven years.

If Laban's excuse was indeed true, he could have informed Jacob of it seven years earlier, when the request to marry Rachel was made. However, as mentioned earlier, it could be that Laban reasoned Leah would have been married before the seven years were complete. But even so, when the seven years were almost complete, and she was still not married, he could have at that time informed Jacob of the custom. Still, he never did, until after he deceived him. In essence, he made Jacob work the first seven years for Leah, rather than for Rachel.

After living 84 years without a wife, suddenly Jacob found himself with two wives. Within one week he unintentionally became a polygamist! Observe, there is no Biblical evidence to suggest a feast was given when Jacob received Rachel as his second wife. There was no wine, no after-dark merriment, because Jacob no longer trusted Laban. This time around, no doubt, he wanted to make sure he got the woman he was promised.

God knew these things would happen to Jacob, and He continued to work in his life despite his circumstances. Jacob acted honorably in accepting Leah as his wife, even though he did not love her as much as he did Rachel. As is the case with many men, his lack of love did not prevent him from continuing to have sexual relations with her. But ironically, Leah was the wife God intended for Jacob all along. This conclusion can be drawn, because she was the wife through whom the Messiah, who was promised from the beginning, came.

JACOB'S CHILDREN

Verses 31–32 indicate that when the Lord saw that Leah was not loved, He enabled her to conceive, but Rachel remained childless. Leah became pregnant and gave birth to a son. She named him Reuben (See), for she said, "It is because the Lord has seen my misery. Surely my husband will love me now."

The fact that Rachel remained childless, while Leah was able to conceive, was unspeakably important. Had she been able to conceive, Jacob would have ignored Leah, and God's plan for her would not have been realized. Namely, God's plan for the Messiah to descend from her. Jacob's lack of love for her was a source of misery to her. Therefore, she thought he would come to love her if she continued to have his children. The impact of this on their children was immeasurable. It explains why most of her sons were so filled with jealousy, and prone to violence; They knew their mother was not loved.

Leah knew she was not loved, so she used her ability to conceive as a tool to seek love. The desire for love is usually not a good reason to become pregnant, but in this case, the Lord also knew Leah was not loved, so He allowed her to conceive, in order to compel Jacob to deal with her, and to oblige him to be with her. After Reuben's birth, Leah thought, surely her husband would love her, but he did not, so her misery continued.

Verse 33 says she conceived again, and she gave birth to a son and said, "Because the Lord heard that I am not loved, He gave me this one too." She named him Simeon (Hear). Leah knew she was not loved, but she did not withhold herself from Jacob. She continued to have sexual relations with him in the hope of gaining his love, but she was also aware that the Lord knew she was not loved. She seemed to be a Godlier woman than Rachel was and may have prayed about her situation.

Verse 34 says again she conceived, and when she gave birth to a son she said, "Now at last my husband will become attached to me, because I have borne him three sons." So, he was named Levi (Attached). Yet, her husband neither loved her, nor did he become attached to her, because a man does not become attached to a woman he does not love. Hence, her misery continued.

Verse 35 shows she conceived once more, and when she gave birth to a son she said, "This time I will praise the Lord." So, she named him Judah (Praise). Then she stopped having children. Following Judah's birth, Leah's focus changed from trying to gain her husband's love, to praising the Lord, whose love she knew she had. She previously acknowledged that the Lord had seen and heard of her situation, but her focus was on gaining her husband's, rather than God's love. However, at the birth of her fourth son, her attention turned to praising the Lord, and at that point, she stopped having children.

In other words, Leah stopped using pregnancy as a tool to acquire affection. Most importantly, her fourth son Judah, became the earthly forefather of the Messiah, Jesus Christ. This offspring authenticated her marriage and affirmed her as the wife God intended for Jacob in the first place. Most importantly, it showed that imperfect situations and circumstances cannot terminate God's plans. The birth of Judah was a signal to humanity that redemption was on its way, and to Satan that his kingdom will soon end.

GENESIS CHAPTER THIRTY

Chapter twenty-nine examined events surrounding Jacob's arrival in Harran, his initial meeting with shepherds, who knew the family he was searching for, and his meeting with Rachel, who informed her father that he was in town. It was shown that Rachel's father Laban, received Jacob as one of his own, and allowed him to stay with him, and to assist in tending his flock. He offered to pay Jacob for his services, but instead of requesting a wage, Jacob indentured himself to Laban, by agreeing to work for him seven years for Rachel in return, whom he loved and wanted to make his wife. At the end of seven years, Laban deceitfully caused him to marry Leah first before he married Rachel, for whom he had to work seven additional years. So, he worked fourteen years to get both his wives.

Jacob ended up with two wives, but only Leah was initially able to conceive, and she bore him four sons. The first three were to gain his affection, but when that did not occur, by the time her fourth son Judah was born, she learned to look to the Lord for the affection she was lacking from her husband.

This chapter will examine the results of jealousy between Jacob's two wives, which caused them to commence a child-bearing competition in pursuit of his affection. It will also examine Jacob's interactions with Laban, once his fourteen years of indentured service were completed. Most importantly, it will show how Jacob gained his wealth, and that God was indeed with him as He promised to be.

RACHEL AND LEAH'S CHILD-BEARING COMPETITION

Verses 1-2 point out that when Rachel saw she was not bearing Jacob any children, she became jealous of her sister. So, she said to Jacob, "Give me children, or I'll die!" Jacob became angry with her and said, "Am I in the place of God, who has kept you from having children?"

Notice, Rachel's issue with Jacob was not only her inability to bear him any children, but her sister's ability to do so. Her jealousy toward Leah caused her to believe Jacob was doing something different with Leah to cause her to become pregnant. It should also be observed that because Leah had children (plural), Rachel was not content to have one child, but wanted children (plural) as well. As such, whereas Leah appealed to God in her efforts to bear children and to gain her husband's affection, Rachel appealed to Jacob and threatened to shorten her own life if he did not give her what she wanted.

Jacob became angry with Rachel because she attempted to put him in the place of God, and to attribute creation of life to him, rather than to God. He was compelled to remind her that children are a gift from God, rather than from men. It was God, rather than Jacob, who kept her from having children. Jacob loved Rachel and would much rather have children with her than with Leah. However, Rachel's inability to have children caused him to interact with Leah and ensured the latter was able to give birth to all her descendants, particularly Judah, the forefather of Christ in the flesh.

Because of Rachel's inability to conceive, verses 3–6 reveal that she gave her servant Bilhah to Jacob, so he could sleep with her and have children on Rachel's behalf. She thought she could build a family through Bilhah, so she gave her to Jacob, and he slept with her, and she became pregnant and bore him a son. Then Rachel felt vindicated (judged) by God, thinking He had listened to her plea (ruled in her favor) and given her a son. Because of this, she named him Dan (Judgment).

Jacob's involvement with Bilhah was not a single event, because Rachel demanded to have children (plural); therefore, verses 7–8 state that Rachel's servant Bilhah conceived again and bore Jacob a second son. Then Rachel acknowledged being in a great struggle (wrestling) with her sister, but she declared herself the winner. Hence, she named the second son to whom Bilhah gave birth, Naphtali (Wrestling).

Leah refused to be outdone by Rachel, therefore, verses 9–11 show that when she realized she had stopped having children, she also took her servant Zilpah, and gave her to Jacob as a wife. Zilpah bore Jacob a son, and Leah said, "What good fortune!" So, she named him Gad (Fortune). But she was not done, verses 12–13, indicate that Zilpah bore Jacob a second son, and Leah said, "How happy I am! The women will call me happy." So, she named him Asher (Happy).

Verses 14–15 declare that during wheat harvest, Reuben went out into the fields and found some mandrake plants, which he brought to his mother

Leah. Rachel said to Leah, "Please give me some of your son's mandrakes." But Leah said to her, "Wasn't it enough that you took away my husband? Will you take my son's mandrakes too?"

Reuben, being a young boy went out into the fields. It is not clear what the purpose was for his going into the fields, but it was likely carefree wandering, as is common among young boys. Somehow, his curiosity was aroused by mandrake plants. Speculatively, their color may have attracted him, or the fact that they were growing among the wheat, may have caused him to feel the need to uproot them. Whatever the case, Reuben knew better than to discard them; instead, he seemed to understand their value, and brought them home to his mother. Apparently, mandrakes were considered to be aphrodisiacs, and valuable for promoting pregnancy, but this plant and the exact nature of its qualities continues to be a mystery.

Somehow, Rachel discovered about the mandrake plants Reuben brought home to his mother. In so doing, she thought she had discovered Leah's secret for being able to have children. Rather than going or sending someone to the fields to get her own mandrakes, she coveted the ones Leah had. She asked Leah to give her, not all, but some of her son's mandrakes.

Notice Leah asked Rachel, "Wasn't it enough that you took away my husband?" It seems that Jacob had begun to spend more time with Rachel, and very little time with Leah. However, Leah seemed to forget that she was the one who took away Rachel's husband in the first place, by conspiring with her father to deceive him into marrying her. In any case, acquiring the mandrakes became so important to Rachel that she would have given anything to get them. Her servant Bilhah bore two sons on her behalf, but she wanted her own childbearing experience.

Therefore, she responded to her sister by saying, "Very well, he can sleep with you tonight in return for your son's mandrakes." She was willing to surrender the affection of her husband to acquire the mandrakes. This clearly showed that Rachel, the wife who knew she was loved, was in control of Jacob's conduct as it pertained to the other women in his life. While others had to compete and scheme to gain his affection, she could have him anytime she wanted.

Verse 16 reveals that when Jacob came in from the fields that evening, Leah went out to meet him. She informed him that he had to sleep with her because she had hired him with her son's mandrakes. So, he slept with her that night. Note, she hired him from Rachel who owned him, and who knew she was his number one wife.

Verses 17–18 indicate that God listened to Leah, and she became pregnant and bore Jacob a fifth son. Then Leah said, "God has rewarded me for giving my servant to my husband." So, she named him Issachar (Hire). She reasoned that God rewarded her with Issachar because she hired out her servant Zilpah to have children with Jacob. More importantly, her relationship with Jacob seemed to gain a renewed spark, as verses 19–20 show that she conceived again, and bore Jacob a sixth son.

Then she said, "God has presented me with a precious gift. This time my husband will treat me with honor because I have borne him six sons." So, she named him Zebulun (Dwelling). She reasoned that her conception of six sons for Jacob, would compel him to dwell with her out of love, if not for her, at least for his children. Verse 21 states that sometime later, she gave birth to a daughter and named her Dinah (Judged). If Jacob had other daughters their names are not mentioned in Scripture, but Dinah's name is mentioned because it will come up again in chapter 34, where she was sexually assaulted by Shechem, Prince of the Shechemites.

Verses 22–24 state that God remembered Rachel; He listened to her and enabled her to conceive. She became pregnant and gave birth to a son and said, "God has taken away my disgrace." She named him Joseph (He will Add), and said, "May the Lord add to me another son."

This passage made it clear God, rather than Jacob, or mandrakes, was the reason Rachel became pregnant and gave birth to her son Joseph. Note also, even though Rachel had given her servant Bilhah to Jacob for the purpose of having children on her behalf and building a family through her, she still felt disgraced. In other words, the children to whom Bilhah gave birth, did not satisfy Rachel's sense of disgrace. The birth of Joseph helped, but his very name (He will Add) suggested she was not satisfied.

Rather than being thankful, Rachel immediately desired God to allow her to conceive again, because her sister was able to conceive multiple times. Earlier (v 1), she demanded for Jacob to either give her children (plural), or she would die. Hence, her desire to live may have increased once she gave birth to Joseph, but it will be revealed later if her words would come to pass, and if she would indeed die at a time when her desire to have children (plural) became a reality; a time when she needed most to be alive.

JACOB'S FIRST REQUEST TO RETURN HOME

Verses 25–28 explain that after Rachel gave birth to Joseph, Jacob informed Laban of his desire to go back to his own homeland in Canaan. He demanded for Laban to give him his wives and children, for whom he had served him, and let him be on his way home. He concluded his request by saying to Laban, "You know how much work I've done for you."

Interestingly, the Bible does not say God prompted this request. But, by the time Rachel gave birth to Joseph, Jacob had ten other sons, which gave him a total of eleven, yet it was not until that time that he was willing to return home. It appears that Jacob was reluctant to return home until Rachel, the wife he loved, conceived. Incidentally, she did not conceive until the time he was supposed to work for her (fourteen years) were completed. Therefore, despite all the other sons he had with Leah and their servants, Jacob appeared to share Rachel's disgrace of being unable to conceive. Hence, once Joseph was born, he became the son Jacob loved, because he was offspring of the wife he loved, and all the other sons would come to know that Joseph was his favorite son.

Jacob's demand to return home probably coincided with his fourteenth year, when his service for both of Laban's daughters concluded. Therefore, he demanded for Laban to give him his wives and children, for whom he served him, and let him be on his way home. But God knew that Jacob was not in a financially abled position to return home. He worked fourteen years as Laban's indentured servant, and all he had were wives and children, he had no finances. He would not have been able to afford the trip to transport his family and possessions back to Canaan. His return would have revealed to everyone back home how destitute he was. This would have been unbecoming of the holder of the birthright and its associated blessings.

Verses 27–28 reveal Laban's unwillingness to let Jacob go. He said to him, "If I have found favor in your eyes, please stay. I have learned by divination that the Lord has blessed me because of you." He added, "Name your wages, and I will pay them."

Laban, like others in Harran was an idolater, which confirmed the reason God allowed Isaac and Jacob to intermarry with them, was not because they were religiously better than the people of Canaan, but as mentioned earlier, it was because He intended their descendants to inherit that land and to dispossess its people. Laban said he learned through divination that he was blessed because of Jacob, which meant he would never willingly let him go! Hence, he told Jacob to name his wages, but the last time he said that he proceeded to deceive him, so Jacob knew he could not trust him.

JACOB NEGOTIATES A NEW EMPLOYMENT DEAL

In response to Laban's offer for Jacob to name his wages, verses 29–30 show Jacob said to him, "You know how I have worked for you and how your livestock has fared under my care. The little you had before I came has increased greatly, and the Lord has blessed you wherever I have been. But now, when may I do something for my own household?"

In essence, Jacob confirmed with evidence what Laban said he learned by divination. The evidence was undeniable that his wealth increased once Jacob joined his household. And God caused it in such a way as to make it clear it was because Jacob was there. However, if Laban had granted Jacob's request to return home at that time, he would have returned more destitute than he was when he came to Harran, because while he was there, Laban's wealth increased, but Jacob had nothing, except multiple wives and children.

God still grants favor to others because of the presence and influence of his children. There may be untold numbers of employers, whose businesses are prospering because of the presence of God's people whom they employ. This may also apply to governments, and countries. What Proverbs 14:34 says is still true: righteousness exalts a nation, but sin is a reproach to any people. The presence of the righteous is salt (flavor) to the earth.

Laban knew what he would lose if Jacob left, so he entered negotiations to keep him from leaving. Verses 31–34, explain that Laban asked, "What shall I give you?" But Jacob replied, "Don't give me anything, but if you will do this one thing for me, I will go on tending your flocks and watching over them: Let me go through all your flocks today, and remove from them every speckled or spotted sheep, every dark-colored lamb, and every spotted or speckled goat. They will be my wages. And my honesty will testify for me in the future, whenever you check on the wages you have paid me. Any goat in my possession that is not speckled or spotted, or any lamb that is not dark-colored, will be considered stolen." Laban said "Agreed, let it be as you have said."

As Jacob embarked on an effort to provide for himself and his family, he refused to take anything from Laban other than what he worked for. As such, he told him, "Don't give me anything." In other words, he preferred to work for, rather than be given anything he received. His offer to continue working for Laban if he allowed him to separate for himself all spotted sheep, dark colored lambs, and spotted or speckled goats, was to carve out what he justly earned. He also asked to be given flocks, which were easy to identify because he did not trust Laban. As shrewd as Laban was, it was unlikely he would have agreed to Jacob's terms if the flocks he identified outnumber those which would remain as Laban's. And, as few as the flocks were, which Jacob would receive, Laban figured it would be a long time before they would increase enough to allow Jacob to be able to return home.

JACOB'S FLOCKS INCREASE

Verses 35–36 declare that on that very day Laban removed all the male goats that were streaked or spotted, and all the speckled or spotted female goats (all that had white on them) and all the dark-colored lambs, and he placed them in the care of his sons. Then he put a three-day journey between himself and Jacob, while Jacob continued to tend the rest of Laban's flocks.

Laban immediately applied himself to separating the flock as agreed. Notice, he placed the flock, which already met the criteria Jacob mentioned in the care of Jacob's sons. However, he kept Jacob working for him to ensure God continued to bless his flock, rather Jacob's flock, which he put in the care of Jacob's sons. He also put a three-day journey between himself and Jacob, to safeguard the flock he put in the care of Jacob's sons from interacting with those in Jacob's care.

Verses 37–39 state that Jacob, took fresh-cut branches from poplar, almond and plane trees and made white stripes on them by peeling the bark and exposing the white inner wood of the branches. Then he placed the peeled branches in all the watering troughs, so that they would be directly in front of the flocks when they came to drink. When the flocks were in heat and came to drink, they mated in front of the branches. And they bore young that were streaked or speckled or spotted.

These verses revealed how Jacob repaid Laban for his deceit. By cutting branches from poplar, almond, and plane trees, and by making white stripes by peeling barks and exposing the white inner wood, Jacob used the power of suggestion to create images of what he wanted his flocks to be. However, God's divine hand made his plan work. When Laban's flocks mated, their offspring resembled the colors that were impressed upon them by Jacob, but no such thing was possible apart from God's miraculous intervention.

Verses 40–43 show that Jacob used the streaked, speckled, or spotted lambs in the same way he used the cut branches, almond, plane trees, and peeled barks. He made Laban's flock look at them to impress upon them what he wanted their offspring to look like. It says, Jacob set apart the young of the flock by themselves, but made the rest face the streaked and dark-colored animals that belonged to Laban.

Thus, he made separate flocks for himself and did not put them with Laban's animals. Whenever the stronger females were in heat, Jacob would place the branches in the troughs in front of the animals so they would mate near the branches, but if the animals were weak, he would not place them there. So, the weak animals went to Laban and the strong ones to Jacob. In this way, Jacob grew exceedingly prosperous and came to own large flocks, and female and male servants, and camels and donkeys.

Jacob discovered a method by which he was able to siphon off some of Laban's wealth and redirect it to his own household. His flocks increased because of those which fit the criteria he and Laban agreed upon. In essence, by the time Jacob absconded from Laban's household, he had plundered him, in much the same way his descendants Israel would later plunder the people of Egypt, when they absconded from there. So, Jacob grew exceedingly prosperous, which eventually promoted jealousy and placed him on a collision course with his father-in-law.

GENESIS CHAPTER THIRTY-ONE

The previous chapter showed that Jacob's family and his wealth increased after he negotiated new terms of employment with Laban. As his desire and preparations to return home to Canaan became more urgent, God began to bless him with the wealth he needed for the trip. This chapter will examine details of Jacob's escape from Harran, Laban's pursuit of him, and their eventual parting from each other.

A HOSTILE WORK ENVIRONMENT

Verses 1-2 point out that Jacob heard Laban's sons were saying he had taken everything their father owned and had gained all his wealth from what belonged to their father. This is the first instance where it shows that Laban had sons. They may have been born after Jacob's arrival in Haran. Laban's attitude toward Jacob changed and he noticed it.

To be sure, Jacob's wealth did indeed begin from the wages upon which he and Laban agreed. However, he plundered Laban by simply finding ways to generate increase in what rightfully became his. Laban's sons possibly became jealous because their father's flocks, did not increase at the same rate as Jacob's, especially those with birth marks, which met the criteria to cause them to become Jacob's. They accused him of gaining his wealth from what belonged to their father, but this was not true. Jacob's wealth came because of terms to which their father agreed, and from God's un-seen hand on Jacob's behalf.

Verse 3 shows that the Lord said to Jacob, "Go back to the land of your fathers and to your relatives, and I will be with you." Not only did Jacob notice a change in his work environment, but God also affirmed it. In fact, He informed Jacob that it was time to make a change. When work conditions become unbearable, it may be an indication that a time for change has come. This was the case in Jacob's situation, and as such, God told him to go back home, and promised once again to be with him.

JACOB PREPARES FOR HOME

Even though God told Jacob it was time to quit his job and go back home, observe that Jacob did not abruptly leave or walk off the job; Instead, he carefully planned his exit. This is instructive for those who may be considering such a change. Verses 4–5 indicate that Jacob sent word to Rachel and Leah to come out to the fields where his flocks were. He told them he had seen that their father's attitude toward him was not what it was before, but the God of his father was with him.

Notice, Jacob asked his two wives to come out to the fields. This was a neutral location where he could converse with them privately, and where he would not have to choose one tent over another. Evidently, while Laban's sons openly expressed their jealousy and displeasure with Jacob's wealth, Laban himself said nothing. His displeasure was demonstrated in his attitude. Jacob noticed that his countenance and commitment to honoring the terms of his wages had changed. He wanted Jacob to remain in his service so he could continue to be blessed by God, but he did not want to pay him, nor for Jacob himself to also be blessed. This created a volatile situation.

Verses 6–9 reveal that Jacob said to his wives, "You know that I've worked for your father with all my strength, yet your father has cheated me by changing my wages ten times. However, God has not allowed him to harm me. If he said, 'The speckled ones will be your wages,' then all the flocks gave birth to speckled young; and if he said, 'The streaked ones will be your wages,' then all the flocks bore streaked young. So, God has taken away your father's livestock and has given them to me.

Jacob revealed details of Laban's dishonesty, which would not have been otherwise known. These details indicate why Jacob was under no obligation to continue to deal honorably with Laban, who changed the terms of their agreement multiple times. Rather than terminating Jacob's employment, he repeatedly changed his wages! Each time he changed them, he did so to maneuver them in a way that would benefit him and cheat Jacob; However, the new terms always ended up benefitting Jacob because God was the unseen arbiter.

This should have scared Laban and caused him to recognize the divine hand of God, especially since he acknowledged that God had blessed him because of Jacob. It would have been wise for him to get to know Jacob's God and beseech Him for direct blessings. Instead, he became jealous and joined his sons in envying Jacob's success. As a result, he changed Jacob's wages ten times, but each time, God protected Jacob from loss.

Jacob said in verses 10–13 that during breeding season, he once had a dream in which he looked up and saw the male goats mating with the flock which were streaked, speckled or spotted. The angel of God said to him in the dream, "Jacob, look up and see that all the male goats mating with the flock are streaked, speckled or spotted, for I have seen all that Laban has been doing to you. I am the God of Bethel, where you anointed a pillar and where you made a vow to me. Now leave this land at once and go back to your native land."

These verses provide insight into what God was doing behind the scenes to cause positive outcomes for Jacob. It was not the cut branches, almond, plane trees, or peeled barks, which Jacob prepared that made the difference in the colors of the flocks. Instead, God supernaturally changed the deoxyribonucleic acid (DNA) of the flocks, by causing the male goats to have streaked, speckled or spotted characteristics, which were not visible in the natural. Consequently, He worked things out in Jacob's favor, but He reminded him the time had come for him to return home. He identified Himself as the God of Bethel, to remind Jacob of His promise at Bethel, to be with him in Harran, and to bring him back safely to Canaan. God kept His promise, and it was time for Jacob to return home.

Verses 14–16 represent a rare occasion when Rachel and Leah agreed on anything. It says they responded by asking Jacob, "Do we still have any share in the inheritance of our father's estate? Does he not regard us as foreigners? Not only has he sold us, but he has used up what was paid for us. Surely all the wealth that God took away from our father belongs to us and our children. So, do whatever God has told you."

Apparently, Laban did not only swindle Jacob, but according to his daughters, he also dealt deceitfully with them. Apparently, his daughters became less significant to him following their marriages, and birth of his sons, to whom his estate was entrusted. So, while Jacob saw the transfer of Laban's wealth as payment for his hard work, his wives saw it as their just portion of the estate; especially since he no longer regarded them as daughters but treated them like foreigners. Hence, once Jacob informed them of what God said to him, they encouraged him to be obedient. In other words, they supported him in following his God-ordained calling. Nothing was more invigorating for Jacob than knowing he had the support of his wives. This is also true for husbands today.

JACOB FLEES FROM LABAN

Verses 17-18 show that Jacob put his children and his wives on camels, and he drove all his livestock ahead of him, along with all the goods he had accumulated in Paddan Aram, to go to his father Isaac, in the land of Canaan.

Note, Jacob spent approximately twenty years in Harran, and Isaac was still alive in Canaan. This meant that Isaac's idea of blessing his sons before he died, and his assumption that he would soon die, was premature. It would never be known how differently things might have turned out in his family, had he exercised more patience and sought God's guidance about the timing for passing on the blessing. In any case, when Jacob departed Canaan to go to Harran, he concealed his exit, for fear that Esau might try to kill him. Ironically, this passage shows that when he left Harran to return to Canaan, he also had to conceal his departure, for fear that Laban might harm him. As inheritor of the birthright and blessings, he lived a good portion of his life in fear. Despite that, when he left Canaan to flee to Haran, he was alone, and had nothing, but God allowed him to return from there with a large family and much wealth.

RACHEL STEALS LABAN'S IDOLS

Verses 19-21 show that when Laban had gone to shear his sheep, his daughter Rachel stole his gods. Moreover, Jacob deceived him, by not telling him he was running away. So, Jacob fled with all he had, crossed the Euphrates River, and headed for the hill country of Gilead.

Laban's sheep were being cared for in a location, which was three days' journey away from where he lived. Once he left on that journey, Rachel seized the opportunity to take revenge by stealing his gods (plural), which she knew he valued. Meanwhile, Jacob seized the opportunity as the perfect time to run for the hills, and head for home. Leah was the only one who did not seem to seize the moment for any parting acts of revenge.

It is not clear why Rachel stole her father's gods with the intent of taking them to Canaan. It could be, she worshipped them herself, which is another reason why Leah was considered a more ideal wife for Jacob, albeit she was not as beautiful. But it could also be, she took them, to keep him from consulting them, because she believed they might help him discover their escape route. Ultimately, there were no justifiable reasons for Rachel to steal her father's gods, or to want anything to do with them, especially since she was married to a man who knew the true God. Her father's gods paled in comparison to the God her husband knew.

LABAN PURSUES JACOB

Verses 22–24 reveal that on the third day Laban was told that Jacob had fled. Taking his relatives with him, he pursued Jacob for seven days and caught up with him in the hill country of Gilead. Then God came to Laban the Aramean in a dream at night and said to him, "Be careful not to say anything to Jacob, either good or bad."

Since Laban was told on the third day that Jacob had fled, it meant he received news just about the time when he arrived at the place where his sheep were located in the care of his sons. Therefore, his sons may have been among the relatives who accompanied him in pursuit of Jacob. This would have posed a significant threat to Jacob because of their expressed jealousy over his wealth.

It should be noted that Jacob was a free man and should not have to hide to leave Laban's service. He had completed the years of service, which he promised Laban. But the fact that he thought it best to steal away, and Laban went to such extremes to pursue him, was an indication he intended to indefinitely keep Jacob in bondage. He pursued Jacob in the same way Pharaoh of Egypt years later would pursue Jacob's descendants.

Even though Laban was an idolater, God appeared to him rather than to Jacob. He appeared to him to keep him from harming Jacob, because there was nothing Jacob could do for himself to keep Laban from harming him. The only thing Jacob tried to do was to flee, and that was the very reason Laban pursued him. However, God took control of the situation because it was He who instructed Jacob to leave Harran immediately and return to Canaan. Therefore, He intervened to stop Laban's hands from harming Jacob, and his mouth from saying anything good or bad to him. In other words, Laban was kept from speaking his mind to Jacob, and from explaining the real reason why his attitude toward him changed.

LABAN CATCHES UP WITH JACOB

Verses 25–30 show that Jacob's tent was pitched in the hill country of Gilead when Laban overtook him, and Laban and his relatives camped there too. Then Laban asked Jacob, "What have you done? You've deceived me, and you've carried off my daughters like captives in war. Why did you run off secretly and deceive me? Why didn't you tell me, so I could send you away with joy and singing to the music of timbrels and harps? You didn't even let me kiss my grandchildren and my daughters, goodbye. You have done a foolish thing. I have the power to harm you; but last night the God of your father said to me, 'Be careful not to say anything to Jacob, either good or bad.' Now you have gone off because you longed to return to your father's household. But why did you steal my gods?"

These verses reveal Laban's efforts to paint himself as the honorable person and Jacob as the scoundrel. He made it seem as if he would have gladly accepted Jacob's request to return to Canaan and would have sent him and his family away with a party! Not to mention, when Jacob made the request six years earlier, he did not let him go. His claims about all the good he would have done, were lavish pretenses to change the narrative in his favor. Therefore, he accused Jacob of having done a foolish thing by stealing away without allowing him to send him away in extravagant fashion.

He tried to exalt his supremacy by mentioning his power and right to do harm to Jacob, had God not restricted him from doing so. Hence, he was only able to mention the harm he had the power to do, but he had no right to do, because God told him not to do it, and because his reasons were unjustified. Therefore, his diatribe was characteristically deceitful and false. Notice, in his efforts to change the narrative, he attributed the reason for Jacob's departure to his longing for his father's house, rather than to the ill-treatment he received from him.

To emphasize his right to harm Jacob, he accused him of stealing his gods. It is not clear how Laban knew his gods were stolen, since he was away on a journey when they were taken from his tent. Evidently, this news was also communicated to him by the messenger who informed him that Jacob had fled. It also highlighted how important his gods were to him, and the prominent place they must have occupied in his tent.

LABAN SEARCHES FOR HIS IDOLS

Verses 31–34 provide Jacob's response to Laban's charges. He told him he fled because he was afraid of the thought of Laban taking back his daughters from him by force. As it related to his gods, he told him if he found anyone who had them, that person should not live. "In the presence of our relatives, see for yourself whether there is anything of yours here with me; and if so, take it."

Jacob did not know Rachel had stolen the gods. So, Laban went into Jacob's tent and into Leah's tent and into the tent of the two female servants, but he found nothing. After he came out of Leah's tent, he entered Rachel's tent. She had taken the household gods and put them inside her camel's saddle and was sitting on them. Laban searched everywhere in the tent but found nothing.

Notice, Jacob gave Laban a brief explanation pertaining to why he fled from him. In humility, he admitted to being afraid of losing his wives by Laban's force. This was a subtle way of admitting to Laban that he did not trust him and believed he would use his daughters as leverage to keep him from leaving. However, as it pertained to Laban's stolen gods, Jacob spoke too hastily. He did not take them himself, but at least having young children, he should have been more cautious about the sentence he so quickly pronounced on the perpetrator. He may have regretted those words later, as Rachel died soon after, while giving birth to her second son.

It was amazing that even though the true God spoke to Laban in a dream, he spent so much time and effort trying to find his false gods, rather than pursuing the true God, who spoke to him. He literally dug through the belongings of all Jacob's wives and their servants in search of his gods, and not once did it occur to him that if they were really gods, they should have the power to reveal their location. A god that can get stolen or lost is not worthy of worship!

Ironically, many try to do with the true God what Rachel did with her father's false gods; they hide Him rather than share Him with others. Hence, believers sometimes consider their relationship with God to be a private matter, and something to be hidden. This ought not be the case; A relationship with the awesome God of Heaven should be personal, but it should not be private.

Notice verse 35 indicates that Rachel said to her father, "Don't be angry, my lord, that I cannot stand up in your presence; I'm having my period." So, he searched but could not find the household gods. This must have been quite disappointing for Laban. He lost his family and his household gods at the same time. It should be noted, the excuse Rachel gave as to why she could not stand up in her father's presence was rather weak, considering her condition did not prevent her from climbing up on the camel's back in the first place. However, it is reasonable to wonder, since Laban did not find his gods, how was he ever able to replace them? And, since his gods were lost, how was he ever able to worship again? These questions cannot be answered from the text, but they are only meant to highlight the folly of idolatry.

JACOB'S RESPONSE TO LABAN'S ACCUSATIONS

Verses 36–42 say Jacob was angry and took Laban to task. He asked him, "What is my crime?" How have I wronged you that you hunt me down? Now that you have searched through all my goods, what have you found that belongs to your household? Put it here in front of your relatives and mine and let them judge between the two of us."

Jacob continued by saying:

> I have been with you for twenty years now. Your sheep and goats have not miscarried, nor have I eaten rams from your flocks. I did not bring you animals torn by wild beasts; I bore the loss myself. And you demanded payment from me for whatever was stolen by day or night. This was my situation: The heat consumed me in the daytime and the cold at night, and sleep fled from my eyes. It was like this for the twenty years I was in your household. I worked for you fourteen years for your two daughters and six years for your flocks, and you changed my wages ten times. If the God of my father, the God of Abraham and the Fear of Isaac, had not been with me, you would surely have sent me away empty-handed. But God has seen my hardship and the toil of my hands, and last night he rebuked you.[1] (NIV)

Jacob's bold response was outside his normal character. Normally, he was calm and mild-mannered, but Laban's provocations caused a more aggressive personality to emerge. He challenged Laban to prove his case by producing evidence of wrongdoing. Laban had no such evidence, therefore, Jacob proceeded to lay out his own evidence against him. He rehearsed the liability he assumed, and that which was charged to him as an employee of Laban's. He did this in the presence of their relatives, and possibly in the presence of other employees who may have had similar experiences in Laban's employ. There was no denying the case he laid out and Laban had no reasonable defense for Jacob's charges against him.

LABAN'S RESPONSE TO JACOB'S COMPLAINTS

Laban could not deny the case Jacob laid out against him. Therefore, verses 43–44 show he changed the subject. He answered Jacob by saying, "The women are my daughters, the children are my children, and the flocks are my flocks. All you see is mine. Yet what can I do today about these daughters of mine, or about the children they have borne? Come now, let's make a covenant, you and I, and let it serve as a witness between us."

Rather than addressing the injustices Jacob laid out against him, Laban basically took credit for all Jacob acquired, and sought to change the subject. He credited himself for Jacob's wives, referring to them as his, though he

---

1. Barker, et. al. *The NIV Study Bible*, Genesis 31:36–42.

treated them like foreigners. He took credit for Jacob's offspring, though he ignored them and restricted them from sharing in his estate. He also took credit for Jacob's wealth, by claiming the flocks were his, though he did everything he could to keep Jacob from acquiring them as his just wages. In essence, he viewed everything Jacob had as an extension of his. Therefore, rather than apologizing to Jacob, he proposed to make a covenant as a witness between them. Thankfully, the purpose for the covenant was to forget the past and look to the future.

COVENANT ESTABLISHED BETWEEN JACOB AND LABAN

Verses 45–50 indicate that Jacob took a stone and set it up as a pillar. He said to his relatives, "Gather some stones." So, they took stones and piled them in a heap, and they ate there by the heap. Laban called it Jegar Sahadutha, and Jacob called it Galeed (Witness). Jacob readily agreed to establishing a covenant, but he allowed Laban to establish the terms of it. Hence, Laban said, "This heap is a witness between you and me today." That is why it was called Galeed. It was also called Mizpah (Watchtower) because he said, "May the Lord keep watch between you and me when we are away from each other. If you mistreat my daughters or if you take any wives besides my daughters, even though no one is with us, remember that God is a witness between you and me."

Interestingly, Laban knew Jacob's God would be a witness between them in both places where they lived, yet he spent an exorbitant amount of time searching for his household gods, who knew nothing. He charged Jacob in the presence of God against mistreating his daughters or taking any other wives besides them. Jacob agreed to it, because he had no intention of doing such, and was actually prohibited from marrying any of the women of the land of Canaan where he was going. In fact, a peripheral charge Isaac gave him when he was fleeing to Harran was to find a wife, so that when he returned, he would not become entangled with the women of Canaan.

Verses 51–55 show that Laban also said to Jacob, "Here is this heap, and here is this pillar I have set up between you and me. This heap is a witness, and this pillar is a witness, that I will not go past this heap to your side to harm you and that you will not go past this heap and pillar to my side to harm me. May the God of Abraham and the God of Nahor, the God of their father, judge between us." So, Jacob took an oath in the name of the Fear of his father Isaac. He offered a sacrifice there in the hill country and invited his relatives to a meal. After they had eaten, they spent the night there. Early the next morning Laban kissed his grandchildren and his daughters and blessed them. Then he left and returned home.

Observe that Laban invoked the god of Abraham and Nahor. There was a period in Abraham's life, when both he and Nahor served false gods, but Jacob did not swear in the name of the god of his dead ancestors; instead, he swore in the name of the fear of his father Isaac, who never worshipped false gods. Additionally, though Jacob did not worship false gods, he was not at a place in his life where he had begun to worship the true God; hence he swore in the fear of his father. His father feared the true God.

Notice, Jacob took an oath and offered a sacrifice, but Laban did not sacrifice. He and those with him enjoyed the feast Jacob provided, slept for the night, and rose the next morning to depart in peace, after sharing farewell kisses. There is no Biblical evidence to suggest Jacob and his family ever saw Laban again. This separation essentially closed an important chapter in Jacob's life. It was a chapter in which he found himself. In other words, while in Harran he grew up because of the hardships he endured. However, as he returned home, the damage he did before leaving, which caused him to flee in the first place, had to be confronted and resolved if he were to have peace in his life moving forward.

GENESIS CHAPTER THIRTY-TWO

Chapter thirty-one discussed Jacob's escape from Harran and the early stages of his journey back home to Canaan. He was pursued and overtaken by Laban in the hill country of Gilead, where they aired grievances against each other. Ultimately, they parted company on good terms after making a covenant of peace. This chapter will summarize another stage of Jacob's journey home, particularly his incredible meeting and struggle with God and his preparations to meet his brother Esau.

JACOB PREPARES TO MEET ESAU

After parting ways with Laban and his relatives from Harran, verses 1-2 reveal that Jacob also went on his way, and the angels of God met him. When Jacob saw them, he said, "This is the camp (host) of God!" So, he named that place Mahanaim (Two Camps). It is not clear how Jacob knew those who met him were angels of God, but something about them caused him to recognize them as such. It was as though they came to welcome him back to the land of Canaan. And, the name he gave the place (Host), suggests there were quite a few of them.

Despite his encounter with the host of God, Jacob's mind was on the dreaded prospect of encountering his brother again, and somehow, he knew Esau lived in the land of Seir, and he had to pass that way on his way back to Canaan. It should be noted that Jacob did not need Esau's permission to gain passage through Seir, but since his passage was near where Esau lived, it would have garnered greater hostility had he passed by without showing brotherly love, or reaching out to him. This would have added greater offense to that which already existed between them. Most importantly, Jacob needed to initiate the process of reconciliation between them, since he deceived his brother twice. Hence, he needed to seek Esau's favor.

Notice, verses 3–6 explain that Jacob sent messengers ahead of him to his brother Esau in the land of Seir, the country of Edom. He instructed them to say to Esau, whom he referred to as his lord: "Your servant Jacob says, I have been staying with Laban and have remained there until now. I have cattle and donkeys, sheep and goats, male and female servants. Now I am sending this message to my lord, that I may find favor in your eyes." When the messengers returned to Jacob, they told him, they went to his brother Esau, and he was coming to meet him, accompanied by four hundred men.

Observe, Jacob made it clear to his servants they were to refer to Esau as his lord, and to him as Esau's servant. Having done this, and communicated everything else they were instructed to say, it appears that Esau gave them no response to take back to Jacob, other than, he was coming to meet him, with four hundred men in tow. That was an intimidating response! Indeed, it may have initially been Esau's intent to harm Jacob, otherwise there was no reason for him to bring that size of an army with him. However, God may have intervened along the way to change Esau's heart, just as He did in the previous chapter with Laban. Either this was the case, or this situation was an example of the most misunderstood assumptions of another person's motives in the entire Bible! To be sure, Jacob thought Esau was coming to harm him, and his fear was probably justified.

Verses 7–8 reveal that in great fear and distress Jacob divided the people who were with him into two groups (camps), and the flocks and herds and camels as well. He thought, "If Esau comes and attacks one group (camp), the group (camp) that is left may escape." Jacob stood no chance against Esau, so rather than dividing his company to strategize for a fight, he divided them for flight. His only hope in the face of his brother's expected aggression was for some, if not all, to escape alive.

Verses 9–12 show that Jacob's fears drove him to pray. It was the first occasion where Jacob was shown initiating a conversation with God. He had seen a host of angels, but he did not pray to them; he prayed to God. In his prayer, he rehearsed the things God said to him, and he basically reminded God that His reputation was on the line if those statements did not come to pass. Though Jacob honestly admitted his fear, he should also have been reminded from the words God spoke to him, that Esau's plans to kill him could not come to fruition. He said:

> O God of my father Abraham, God of my father Isaac, Lord, you who said to me, 'Go back to your country and your relatives, and I will make you prosper,' I am unworthy of all the kindness and faithfulness you have shown your servant. I had only my staff

when I crossed this Jordan, but now I have become two camps. Save me, I pray, from the hand of my brother Esau, for I am afraid he will come and attack me, and also the mothers with their children. But you have said, 'I will surely make you prosper and will make your descendants like the sand of the sea, which cannot be counted.[1] (NIV)

Observe that Jacob did not place any confidence in his own worthiness to call upon God; Rather he addressed Him as God of his fathers, Abraham, and Isaac. His own faith was yet in its infancy, and though his relationship with God blossomed later in life, at this point, he relied on what God said to his fathers. Thank God for faithful fathers, and mothers!

Notice also, he reminded God that he did not undertake the journey home without His counsel. He said God was the one who told him to go back to his country and his relatives, and He would make him prosper. Certainly, he could not prosper if his descendants were cut off by Esau. In repeating those statements in prayer, Jacob appealed to God's obligation to defend His word, and to his own need to have trust and confidence in what God said.

Verses 13–21 summarize Jacob's plan to appease and befriend Esau. It says he spent the night there (in Mahanaim), and from what he had with him, he selected gifts for his brother Esau. He selected two hundred female goats and twenty male goats, two hundred ewes and twenty rams, thirty female camels with their young, forty cows and ten bulls, and twenty female donkeys and ten male donkeys. He put them in the care of his servants, each herd by itself, and said to his servants, "Go ahead of me, and keep some space between the herds." He told the one in the lead that when his brother Esau meets him and asks, "Who do you belong to, and where are you going, and who owns all these animals in front of you?" Then say to him, "They belong to your servant Jacob. They are a gift sent to my lord Esau, and he is coming behind us."

He also instructed the second, the third and all the others who followed the herds to say the same thing to Esau when they met him. Also, to be sure to say, "Your servant Jacob is coming behind us." He reasoned that he would pacify Esau with his gifts, and later, by the time he got to him, perhaps he would receive him favorably. So, Jacob's gifts went on ahead of him, but he spent the night in the camp. This was an eventful night for Jacob. No doubt, it was a pivotal moment in his life, and one which became a turning point for him. Just as his deception changed his life and caused him to flee Canaan in fear of Esau, his return home had to begin with reconciliation

---

1. Barker, et. al. *The NIV Study Bible*, Genesis 32:9–12.

with his brother. His life in Canaan could not resume unless he resolved pending issues with his brother.

Therefore, Jacob's plan was to reduce Esau's anger with each wave of gifts, while concealing the fact that he was afraid. Jacob had to face his fears with humility, and yet with boldness. By sending gifts ahead of him, he allowed Esau, his twin brother, to know he desired peace with him. However, his reminders that he was coming behind the gifts, masked his fears, and were intended to make Esau feel as if, come what may, he was looking forward to seeing him. Most importantly, it gave Jacob time to receive word about whether Esau's disposition was one of friend, or foe.

JACOB WRESTLES WITH GOD

Verses 22-24 reveal that Jacob got up that night and took his two wives, his two female servants and his eleven sons and crossed the Ford of the Jabbok. After he had sent them across the stream, he sent over all his possessions. So, he was left alone, and a man wrestled with him till daybreak.

These verses describe one of the most remarkable events in Biblical history. Jacob, a man, literally appeared to engage in combat with a spiritual being. As such, it is important to carefully observe what scripture says, and what it means, so that a correct interpretation can be drawn.

Notice first, Jacob sent his family and possessions ahead and was left alone in the camp. His mind, being heavily occupied by the thought of seeing his perceived hostile brother Esau, was focused on praying to God and asking Him to save him. He was not looking to engage in a wrestling match! His sole purpose for staying behind was to spend time in solitude and prayer before God.

Secondly, notice in seeking God, it said Jacob encountered a man, who wrestled (struggled) with him till daybreak. So, the person with whom Jacob wrestled appeared in human form. Hosea 12:4 reveals the nature of this combat, it says Jacob wept and begged for his favor, as he found him at Bethel and talked with him there. Hosea reveals that what Jacob experienced was not as much a physical fight as it was a significant, all-night, prayer struggle, between Jacob and the man he encountered.

Verses 25-26 declare that when the man saw he could not overpower him, he touched the socket of Jacob's hip so that his hip was wrenched as he wrestled (struggled) with the man. Then the man said, "Let me go, for it is daybreak." But Jacob replied, "I will not let you go unless you bless me."

Jacob did not become faint or discouraged in his faith, through tears and heartfelt supplications he made his requests known to God all night long. The man with whom he struggled was not able to present anything to shake his faith, nor to cause his desires to waiver. However, the fact that he wrestled to receive a blessing from the man, showed his inferiority to the man. The man could have ended the struggle at any time, but he chose to engage with Jacob all night!

Notice, the man simply touched and disjointed Jacob's hip, rather than punching him, or applying a headlock, and ending his life! His intent was obviously not to end Jacob's life, but to provide a perpetual reminder of the struggle he had been in; that moment when he was desperate for God's intervention, and struggled all night for His blessing, refusing to allow a disjointed hip to deter him.

Also enlightening, was the fact that the man, who started the struggle with Jacob, reminded him that it was daybreak, and time for the struggle to end. It was not a curfew for the man, but a reminder that there is a time for struggle in prayer, and a time to handle the daily business of life; Jacob had important business to take care of that day.

Jacob knew the promises God already made to him; therefore, he refused to end the struggle, or to be dissuaded by daybreak. He was determined that nothing or no one in this world, including Esau, would succeed in preventing him from receiving those promises. His struggle was an example for believers, who may be facing discouragement amid trials. Jacob's case was one of perseverance, and humble persistence. He relied on God for a blessing when his situation was beginning to seem cursed. He struggled in prayer until daybreak, and bore the scares to show for it, but his scares did not deter or cause him to give up the struggle.

Verses 27–28 show that the man asked him, "What is your name?" "Jacob" (Supplanter, Follower), he answered. Then the man told him, his name would no longer be Jacob, but Israel (Wrestles with God), because he struggled with God and with humans and overcame. Notice, previous verses said Jacob wrestled with a man, but in blessing him, the man referred to himself as God. This leads to the conclusion that Jacob may have encountered the pre-incarnate Christ, the God-Man.

Observe that Jacob's name was changed to Israel because it says he also wrestled with humans; yet to this point in his life there was no evidence of him engaging in a physical struggle with any human. Evidently, his struggles with humans revolved around his skillful use of words, which he used to deceive others and to get what he wanted. Therefore, his struggle with God was most likely one of words as well, where he struggled in prayer to get the blessing he so eagerly desired.

Having told the man his name and having received a new name, verses 29–30 show that Jacob said, "Please tell me your name." But the man replied,

"Why do you ask my name?" Then he blessed him there. So, Jacob called the place Peniel (Face of God) saying, "It is because I saw God face to face, and yet my life was spared."

Jacob sought to become more familiar with the God-Man by asking Him His name, but no name was given to him. His name is too wonderful for any man to comprehend, and since names represented characteristics of those who bore them, no name in the human vernacular truly represents the characteristics of God. Therefore, no name was given to Jacob. Rather than giving His name, He gave Jacob His blessing. He gave him what he wrestled for all night long.

Therefore, Jacob did not name the man, instead he named the place where he met and struggled with the man. He called it Peniel (Face of God). He called it thus, because he saw the face of God and lived, rather than because he struggled with God and prevailed. In other words, he gave no credit to himself for making it through the struggle, but to the mercies of God, who condescended to have a face-to-face encounter with him, and allowed him to live through it.

Verses 31–32 say the sun rose above Jacob as he passed Peniel, and he was limping because of his hip. Therefore, the Israelites refused to eat the tendon attached to the socket of the hip, because the socket of Jacob's hip was touched near the tendon. Jacob bore the sign of his struggle, a limp, for the remainder of his life. But, having also received the blessing of God, a limp was a minor inconvenience. He, like the apostle Paul, saw the face of God and lived, but to keep him from becoming conceited, he was given a limp.

When Jacob reunited with his family, they probably wondered what happened to him. A limp made him far less formidable on one of the most important days in his life! When he met his twin brother Esau, his limp probably caused him to look weak, and like someone deserving pity, rather than revenge and fury. However, his descendants celebrated his injury because to them, it represented strength. It represented his struggle with God, and the fact that in his weakness, he was made strong by the blessing he received. Jacob's example is a reminder to every believer that they should never give up in prayer before God. It is the kind of combat God seems to enjoy engaging in with His people.

GENESIS CHAPTER THIRTY-THREE

The previous chapter summarized Jacob's preparations to meet Esau, and his efforts to pacify him by sending multiple waves of gifts ahead of his arrival. It also reviewed Jacob's struggle with God for a blessing. He received the blessing, but he also sustained a disjointed hip, which caused him to walk with a limp that became a perpetual mark of his struggle. His name was also changed from Jacob to Israel, because he struggled with God and humans and overcame. This chapter will examine his long-anticipated meeting with Esau and his safe arrival, and resettlement back home in the land of Canaan.

JACOB AND ESAU MEET AGAIN

Verse 1 says Jacob looked up and there was Esau, coming with his four hundred men; so, he divided the children among Leah, Rachel and the two female servants. Esau did not seem to waste any time in hurrying to meet Jacob once he was told he was coming his way. His approach was intimidating. It was swift and terrifying, with four hundred men, fit for battle. On seeing him, all Jacob could do was divide up his family, and hope some escaped alive. Based on the promises God made to him about his offspring being as numerous as sand on the seashore, he knew some would survive, but no doubt, he also expected himself, and maybe some others to die.

Jacob fully expected Esau to settle old grievances and cut him off before he made it back to his father. Therefore, verses 2-3 show that he put the female servants (Bilhah and Zilpah) and their children in front, Leah and her children next, and Rachel and Joseph in the rear. He himself went on ahead and bowed down to the ground seven times as he approached his brother.

Interestingly, as Esau approached, leading his army of four hundred men, he met Jacob, leading his family of women, children, and livestock. Esau appeared to be in a position of strength, while Jacob, inheritor of the birthright and its blessings appeared to be in a position of weakness. From Esau's perspective, having the birthright did not seem to do Jacob any good!

Notice also that Jacob went on ahead of his family, willing that if any should die, he would go first. However, he divided up his family by the order of his love for them. Those he loved most were further to the rear, which enhanced their likelihood of survival if trouble occurred. Therefore, Rachel, the wife he loved most, and her son Joseph, the son he loved most, were at the very rear of the line! Jacob's favoritism on this occasion set the tone for the dysfunction, which would be evident in his household, and among his descendants for generations to come.

In demonstrating his submission as the younger twin brother, and remorse for the things he had done, Jacob bowed to the ground seven times as he approached his elder twin brother Esau. He also did this to signal his desire for peace. His greatest fear was Esau's response to seeing him again, and though he faced this fear with boldness, he also did so with humility, having prayed and wrestled with God for assurance that everything would be well. He made all the preparations he could, but he needed God to move in Esau's heart, to cause him to forgive him.

Notice Esau's response, verses 4–5 declare that Esau ran to meet Jacob and embraced him. He threw his arms around his neck and kissed him, and they wept. Then Esau looked up and saw the women and children. "Who are these with you?" he asked. Jacob answered, "They are the children God has graciously given your servant."

Esau's forgiving and jubilant response on seeing Jacob, was more a tribute to the change God brought about in his heart, than it was the submissive manner in which Jacob approached him. Indeed, either Esau initially intended to harm Jacob when he was told he was passing his way, or Jacob totally misunderstood his intentions, and in great fear wrestled with God to find favor he did not need. Jacob was too perceptive to misunderstand his brother's intentions. No doubt, his life was in danger, had God not changed Esau's heart.

By the time of this meeting, both Esau and Jacob were well advanced in age. Yet, Esau ran to greet Jacob and embraced him; He then proceeded to shower him with kisses! This was certainly a passionate display of brotherly love. Tears were shed by both, as deep down, they knew what it was that tore them apart. And Jacob knew such a pleasant response from Esau, was due to the mercies of God. Notice, they wept, but neither said a word about their old grievances. Rather than discussing the past, Esau focused on the present and future. He asked Jacob, "Who are these with you?"

In responding, Jacob did not mention his wives, instead he referenced the children, because they were Esau's nephews and niece, Dinah. They were family, and he knew a peaceful Esau would be happy to see them. Besides, talking about the children lightened the moment even more. Recall that Jacob previously sent word to Esau telling him he had flocks and herds, but he did not mention his family, so when Esau saw them, he reasonably wanted to know who they were.

This was quite a meeting, because though Jacob appeared weak, walking with a limp, and surrounded by children, referring to them as gracious gifts from God; Esau appeared strong, flanked by four hundred men, ready for battle. It is unclear if any of his sons were among the ranks of his men, but if they were, the Bible does not show that he introduced them to Jacob.

JACOB AND ESAU RECONCILE

Once it was clear the meeting would be peaceful, the process of formal introductions began. Esau wanted to meet Jacob's family; Therefore, verses 6–7 show that Bilhah and Zilpah and their children approached and bowed down. Next, Leah and her children came and bowed down. Last of all came Rachel and Joseph, and they too bowed down. Jacob's entire family did as he did and bowed before Esau as a sign of respect for him as the elder twin brother.

Verses 8–9 reveal that once family introductions were completed, Esau asked, "What's the meaning of all these flocks and herds I met?" Jacob responded by telling him, they were to find favor in his eyes. But Esau said, "I already have plenty, my brother. Keep what you have for yourself." In refusing to take what Jacob had, Esau showed he was not covetous, but content with what he had. They both knew the reason why Jacob sought favor in Esau's eyes, but they never mentioned it.

Again, God had to be at work in this situation because Jacob's efforts to find favor in Esau's eyes were bribes, which could have easily reminded Esau of previous occasions when he bribed him. On those occasions, Jacob's schemes worked, because Esau wanted what he had to offer. This time, he exercised caution in accepting Jacob's gifts, probably remembering how he tricked him in the past. He knew Jacob did not typically give, apart from a nefarious scheme to receive.

Verses 10–11 show that Jacob said, "No, please! if I have found favor in your eyes, accept this gift from me. For to see your face is like seeing the face of God now that you have received me favorably. Please accept the present that was brought to you, for God has been gracious to me and I have all I need." And because Jacob insisted, Esau accepted it. He prevailed over Esau once again, but this time, there were no underlying motives, apart from the reasons he gave.

Jacob's gifts were sent to Esau to buy his favor, and having received the favor he sought, he urged Esau to take the gifts in thankfulness for the favor he showed him. In other words, the gifts were sent to Esau from a heart of fear, but they were eventually given to him from a heart of love and thanksgiving. Once he was received favorably, Jacob compared seeing Esau's face to seeing the face of God. In other words, he could see forgiveness, rather than bitterness in Esau's face. From the look on his face, he knew they were genuinely reconciled.

JACOB AND ESAU PART COMPANY IN PEACE

Verses 12-17 show that Esau said, "Let us be on our way; I'll accompany (guard) you." But Jacob respectfully refused by telling him, the children were tender and he had to care for the ewes and cows that were nursing their young. He said if they were driven too hard just one day, all of them would die. As such he begged Esau to go on ahead of him, while he and the children moved along slowly at the pace of the flocks and herds, until they arrived at Esau's place in Seir.

Esau then offered to leave some of his men with Jacob, but again, Jacob refused saying, "Just let me find favor in the eyes of my lord." So, Esau went back to Seir, while Jacob went on to Sukkoth, where he built a place for himself and made shelters for his livestock. That is why the place is called Sukkoth (Booth, Shelter).

The relationship between Jacob and Esau was not only reconciled, but jostling, which was evident between them before they came out of the womb ended. They displayed a friendliness to each other that was unseen before; This was all Jacob needed from Esau. He did not need his guard, as he had already met the host of God, who stood guard for him. All he needed was his favor, and forgiveness, which Esau graciously offered.

Jacob promised Esau to come to him in Seir, but the Bible does not record him going there; instead, he went to Sukkoth, where he built shelters for himself and his livestock. Interestingly, though Jacob and Esau parted company in peace, they did not sign a covenant of peace, such as was done between Jacob and Laban. Hence, a tense relationship existed between their descendants, Edom, and Israel, many years later.

JACOB SAFELY BACK IN CANAAN

Verses 18–20 reveal that after Jacob returned from Paddan Aram (NW Mesopotamia), he arrived safely at the city of Shechem in Canaan and camped within sight of the city. For a hundred pieces of silver, he bought from the sons of Hamor, the father of Shechem, the plot of ground where he pitched his tent. There he set up an altar and called it El Elohe Israel (Mighty is the God of Israel).

Interestingly, though the land of Canaan was promised to Jacob, he bought a plot of ground, where he pitched his tent. Time had not yet come for him to take possession of the land, and somehow Abraham, Isaac, and Jacob understood that. Hence, they lived as foreigners and strangers in the land, which was theirs by promise. The next chapter will explain more about Shechem.

While fleeing to Harran, when Jacob met God in a dream at Bethel, he vowed to God that if He would be with him, and watch over him on his journey, and cause him to return safely to his father's household, then the Lord would be his God. All of Jacob's requests were met. After many years in Harran, God brought him back safely to Canaan, and Jacob kept his promise. Not only did God become His God, but he declared it to everyone by the altar he set up, which declared Mighty is the God of Israel, or El (God) is the God of Israel. Jacob declared it because God had indeed proved Himself mighty in his life. Hopefully, every believer can make the same declaration today because God has indeed been mighty in their lives as well.

GENESIS CHAPTER THIRTY-FOUR

In the previous chapter it was shown that Jacob and Esau met each other again after twenty years of separation. The outcome of their meeting surpassed any expectations Jacob had, because God intervened to change Esau's heart, and to keep him from harming Jacob. Esau's old plans to kill his brother, turned into an insatiable desire to hug and kiss him! Their reunion was a beautiful display of brotherly love, which was absent in their relationship prior to that point. They parted ways peacefully, with cordial plans to see each other soon again.

In this chapter, the children, which Jacob said God had graciously given him, began to be his greatest source of grief. As his sons transitioned from boys to men, they came to prominence by an unforgettable act of revenge against the Hivites, for what Shechem, the son of their leader, did to Jacob's daughter Dinah. Most importantly, this chapter will show what the underlying impact can be for a blatant lack of parental love.

SHECHEM RAPED JACOB'S DAUGHTER

Verses 1-4 reveal that Dinah, the daughter Leah had borne to Jacob, went out to visit (see) the women of the land (in the City of Shechem). When Shechem (who bore the same name as the city), son of Hamor the Hivite, the ruler of that area, saw her, he took her and raped her. His heart was drawn to Dinah, daughter of Jacob; he loved her and spoke tenderly to her. And Shechem said to his father Hamor, "Get me this girl as my wife."

Based on what is Biblically known, Dinah was Jacob's only daughter, among eleven sons at that time. Supposedly, she was in her mid-teens when she decided to go out alone to visit the women of the land. As the only teenage female among so many males, it was likely her decision was based on her desire to bond with other females her age. The fact that Dinah went out to see the women of the land, suggest she was curious about them. She probably wanted to experience more of the city and culture around her. And since Shechem was the closest city (Gen 33:18), that was where she decided to go.

Her plan to explore the city alone, may have been an effort to exert her independence as a young woman, but it was not a good idea. Matthews noted that Dinah did not show the caution usually expected of tribal women.[1]

It is unclear how Shechem and Dinah's paths crossed. The Bible does not indicate they even had a conversation with each other prior to him raping her. She did not go to the city to see him, but somehow, he saw her. As prince of the land, he could get anything, or anyone he wanted, and it was not unusual for such men to have a harem. But interestingly, it says he raped her before his heart was drawn to her. Apparently, his heart was driven by the satisfaction his flesh received.

However, true love would have prevented him from subjecting her to the violation of rape, which has always been one of the most dehumanizing things a man can do to a woman. It remains a violation of a female's God-given right to decide whom she will share sexual intimacy with. Hence, rape may have drawn Shechem's heart to Dinah, but it was unlikely hers was drawn to him.

Despite Shechem's offense, based on the culture at that time, he attempted to do what he considered the right thing by asking to marry Dinah. By raping her, he made it unlikely any other man would want to marry her so long as he remained alive. Hence, he told his father to get her for him, which was what he should have done before raping her. His request indicated that his focus was only on himself. He gave no thought to what it would be like for Dinah to be married to the man who raped her. For her, being in such a marriage would have been consignment to life-long mental and physical torment because rape is a physically and emotionally violent act.

HAMOR AND SHECHEM'S REQUEST

Verses 5–7 point out that when Jacob heard that his daughter Dinah had been defiled, his sons were in the fields with his livestock; so, he did nothing about it until they came home. Then Shechem's father Hamor went out to talk with Jacob. Meanwhile, Jacob's sons had come in from the fields as soon as they heard what had happened. They were shocked and furious, because Shechem had done an outrageous thing against Israel by sleeping with Jacob's daughter, a thing that should not have been done.

Notice, without offering Shechem a single word of correction or rebuke for the despicable act he committed, Hamor simply honored his request by

---

1. Matthews, *Manners and Customs in the Bible, An Illustrated Guide to Daily Life in Bible Times*, 27.

going to speak to Jacob about giving his daughter in marriage to the man who raped her. Jacob, being now advanced in age, thought it best to act in consultation with his sons, who had begun to assume responsibility for his affairs. He held his peace until they came. It was not clear what he planned to do, if anything, about the situation.

No description was given about Jacob's emotional reaction to the news, but when his sons heard, it says they quit working, because they were shocked and furious. They considered Shechem's actions outrageous, and an affront to the entire family of Israel. Their disposition set the stage for revenge. In their minds, something had to be done to right this wrong.

Without a single apology, or making any mention of the offense, notice verses 8-10. Hamor came to Jacob and told him his son Shechem had his heart set on his daughter Dinah. As such, he begged Jacob to please give her to Shechem as his wife. He offered for Jacob's family to intermarry with his people, and his people to intermarry with Jacob's people. He even suggested for Jacob's family to settle wherever they pleased among them. He said they could live in the land, move about freely in it, and acquire property in it. In essence, he considered himself, lord of the land.

Though unapologetic, Hamor's proposal to Jacob was friendly and enticing, but it was contrary to the commands of God for Jacob and his descendants. They were prohibited from intermarrying with the people of the land, because in future times, God promised to disinherit the Canaanites and give their land to Jacob's descendants. Intermarrying with them would have complicated that plan. Therefore, Hamor's proposal was a non-starter for Jacob, but for the sake of peace, he may have been tempted to make a deal.

Observe that Hamor did not make the trip to speak to Jacob alone, his rapist son Shechem, also came with him. Therefore, verses 11-12 reveal that Shechem chimed in and said to Dinah's father and brothers, "Let me find favor in your eyes, and I will give you whatever you ask. Make the price for the bride and the gift I am to bring as great as you like, and I'll pay whatever you ask me. Only give me the young woman as my wife."

While Hamor made his request to Jacob alone, Shechem made his request to Jacob and his sons. Most importantly, it cannot be overemphasized that while Hamor and Shechem were negotiating with Jacob and his sons for Dinah, Shechem had not only raped her, but he had basically kidnapped her as well. She was not allowed to return home but was still being held at Shechem's house! Therefore, they were not negotiating to take Dinah, they were negotiating to keep her.

With that backdrop, it was next to impossible for him to find favor in the eyes of Jacob's sons, and nothing he offered would have been enough for them to deal with him. His offer for them to name their price, after taking

Dinah and doing as he pleased with her, sounded more like a deal for a slave, than for a dearly beloved daughter and sister. Apart from the prohibition God already gave against intermarrying with them, Jacob and his sons could not consent to giving Dinah to them because of the way Shechem went about it in the first place; He disgraced the entire family.

JACOB'S SONS' RESPONSE TO THE RAPE OF DINAH

Verses 13-17 show that because their sister Dinah had been defiled, Jacob's sons replied deceitfully as they spoke to Shechem and his father Hamor. They told them they could not do such a thing as to give their sister to a man who was not circumcised. That would be a disgrace. Instead, Jacob's sons proposed to enter an agreement on one condition only: that all their males become like Jacob and his sons and be circumcised. If they agreed to this, they promised to share daughters between each other's people and settle among each other. But, if they would not agree to be circumcised, Jacob's sons said they would take their sister and go.

This was the first recorded event where Jacob's sons were shown engaging in any kind of negotiating. Unsurprisingly, like their father, they demonstrated superior skills in deceit. The reason for their deception may be found in the words of verse 13, which said, "Because their sister Dinah had been defiled." Those words depicted the basis of their grievance. They were hurt, furious, and disgraced. Dinah had been defiled, which meant the entire family felt defiled, and for Shechem to detain her at his house while attempting to legitimize his actions, added insult to injury. Their deceitful proposal was as bad as Shechem's disgraceful conduct. And, while God was working specifically with Jacob, His special work with Jacob's sons was yet to come. Therefore, their deceitful proposal was befitting of men whose main influences were worldly.

Jacob's sons were yet worldly, but their proposal was not. Their proposal emanated from their religion. They basically required Hamor, Shechem, and all the males of the city to assume the sign of Israel's covenant with God. In other words, they used their religion for deceptive purposes, and as cover to gain advantage over others. This is a common practice to this very day, where people often use the Name of God to get over on others. However, notice neither Hamor nor Shechem asked a single question about the meaning of circumcision. They blindly went along with the plan, because to them, the benefits outweighed the risks.

Verses 18-20 indicate that Jacob's sons' proposal seemed good to Hamor and his son Shechem, who was the most honored of all his father's family. They lost no time in doing what they said, because he was (sexually) delighted with Jacob's daughter. So Hamor and his son Shechem went to the gate of their city to speak to the men of the city.

While Jacob's sons used religion to connive Hamor and Shechem, the latter basically used political persuasion to convince the men of the city. Hamor, was ruler of the region (v 2), and his son Shechem, was prince, and most honored of all his family. Therefore, when they held a meeting at the city gate to convince the men they should be circumcised, they had the political wherewithal to get what they wanted. The men of the city trusted their leaders, even though they had no clue why they were being asked to be circumcised. They were innocently drawn into Shechem's scheme to further victimize Dinah, by making her his wife.

Verses 21-24 reveal the perspectives Hamor and Shechem presented to coerce the men of the city. They told them that Jacob and his sons were friendly toward them. They said, "Let them live in our land and trade in it; the land has plenty of room for them. We can marry their daughters and they can marry ours. But the men will agree to live with us as one people only on the condition that our males be circumcised, as they themselves are. Won't their livestock, their property and all their other animals become ours? So let us agree to their terms, and they will settle among us." All the men who went out to the city gate agreed with Hamor and his son Shechem, and every male in the city was circumcised.

Hamor and Shechem gained unanimous consent from the men of the city, because they presented scenarios, which appealed to their greed. They claimed the family of Israel was friendly to them, and if they only returned the favor of appearing to be friendly, they could exploit them. They could intermarry with them and take their livestock, property, and all their animals. In other words, by making a deal, they could leave Israel with nothing!

While Shechem's only desire was to get Dinah, he and his father made their proposal appealing to the men of the city, by convincing them to agree because there was something in it for all of them as well. None of them asked any questions, because they coveted what Israel had, and this appeared to be their opportunity to take it from them.

There was only one caveat in the way of them appearing to be one people with Israel. They all had to be circumcised, just as the family of Israel were. In essence, the agreement could not be finalized unless all the men assumed the same religious sign Israel had. This required them to pretend to be people of God and to have the sign of His covenant, even though they did not.

Throughout the ages, and to this very day, there are those who did what the Hivites agreed to do, which was to pretend to be people of God, when they were not. Albeit, God chooses His people, they do not choose Him, and circumcision could not make them God's people, no more than baptism can make Church-goers today His people. Circumcision was, and now baptism is, merely a ritual, practiced by those who are God's people, but others who are not His people can practice it as well. God knows His own, therefore, today the only sign, which distinguishes the people of God is the presence of Holy Spirit living in them (Rom 8:14–17). That is the only identifying mark! If anyone does not have the Spirit of Christ, who is God, they are not His.

ISRAEL'S REVENGE ON SHECHEM

Verses 25–29 state that three days later, while all of them were still in pain, two of Jacob's sons, Simeon and Levi (Leah's sons), Dinah's brothers took their swords and attacked the unsuspecting city, killing every male. They put Hamor and his son Shechem to the sword, and took Dinah from Shechem's house and left. The sons of Jacob came upon the dead bodies and looted the city because their sister had been defiled. They seized their flocks and herds and donkeys and everything else of theirs in the city and out in the fields. They carried off all their wealth and all their women and children, taking as plunder everything in the houses.

Jacob's sons, having themselves been circumcised, knew the exact time when the effects of that procedure was most incapacitating. They attacked during that time. They killed every male to prevent them from attempting to revenge the death of their leaders, and they made sure the leaders Hamor and Shechem were among the dead. They also took their sister Dinah from Shechem's house, where she was being held while he negotiated to marry her.

Factions in Jacob's family were most evident by the fact that Leah's sons led the assault against the city. That segment of Jacob's family seemed most affected by what happened to Dinah, who was also Leah's daughter. They plundered the city and took the women and children as captives. Presumably, the children they took were females, since all the males were killed in the assault. Some of the males who were killed may have been infants, which paints a picture of the gruesome nature of the attack. It was especially egregious because those males had nothing to do with what Shechem did to Dinah. The punishment did not fit the crime. But, while Simeon and Levi appeared to be the murderers, when Jacob's other sons came upon the dead bodies, they looted the city, which made them accessories to the murders their two brothers committed.

JACOB'S RESPONSE TO HIS SONS' ACTIONS

Verses 30–31 indicate that when Jacob found out what his two sons did, he said to Simeon and Levi, "You have brought trouble on me by making me obnoxious to the Canaanites and Perizzites, the people living in this land. We are few in number, and if they join forces against me and attack me, I and my household will be destroyed." But they replied, "Should he have treated our sister like a prostitute?"

While Hamor refused to rebuke his son for what he did to Dinah, and in effect became a co-conspirator with him, Jacob wasted no time in rebuking his sons for their response to the situation. He was concerned about his reputation among the peoples of the land. He knew the punishment his sons exacted did not fit the crime, and if the entire city was destroyed because of what one of them did to his daughter, the people of the land could gang up and destroy his entire family because of the actions of his two sons.

In other words, even though Jacob knew God promised him the land as an inheritance, he did not know if the murders his sons committed, might cause God to relent in what He promised. Thus, he was not only concerned about what the people of the land might do, he was also concerned about what God would do in response to the actions of his two sons.

Interestingly, the question with which Simeon and Levi justified themselves, could also be taken as an indictment against their father. Jacob had not done or said anything about what happened to Dinah, and because he rebuked his two sons for what they did, the question they asked may suggest they believed he was fine with their sister being treated like a prostitute. However, the answer to their question was no, Shechem should not have treated their sister like a prostitute. However, they also needed to ask themselves, should they have acted like mass-murderers, and killed every male in the city in response to the actions of one man, who did not kill anyone? The reasonable answer to this question should also have been no.

Hopefully, a conversation was had with Dinah about her unwise decision to explore the city alone. The Bible does not indicate that any of the women she went to the city to see, came to see her, or attempted to help her in her time of trouble. No doubt, her decision impacted her for the remainder of her life, but it also caused many to lose their lives. Additionally, it changed the dynamics of her entire family as it related to how Jacob interacted with his sons moving forward. Dinah's decision should be instructive for those, especially Christian young people, who are tempted to throw caution to the wind to explore the "world." The repercussions can be enormous and irreparable.

GENESIS CHAPTER THIRTY-FIVE

The previous chapter examined events surrounding the rape of Jacob's only known daughter, Dinah, who decided to go out to see the women of the land where she lived. In doing so, she was raped by Shechem, the prince of that area. Jacob's sons were furious and decided to use a deceitful scheme to catch the men of the city in a vulnerable condition, so that they could take revenge on them. The scheme worked and Simeon and Levi, took revenge by killing all males in the city of Shechem. They also took the women and children (most likely girls) captive and looted the city.

Jacob was unhappy about the actions of his sons because he thought other peoples in the surrounding areas might hear about what they did and take revenge on him. Simeon and Levi showed no remorse but justified their actions. As a result, Jacob was forced to move from the area near Shechem. This chapter will examine events surrounding his return to Bethel, the place where he met the Lord. It will also review three sad events in his life, namely, the deaths of Deborah, his mother Rebekah's former nurse, Rachel, his beloved wife, and Isaac, his dear father.

JACOB'S RETURN TO BETHEL

Verse 1 declares that God told Jacob to go up to Bethel and settle there, and build an altar there to God, who appeared to him when he was fleeing from his brother Esau. God initiated this move, just as He had done on other occasions. He reminded Jacob of the occasion when He appeared to him at Bethel, while he was in great fear as he fled from his brother Esau. It was at Bethel where he set up a stone and promised God that if He would bring him back safely, that place would be established as His house, and he would give Him a tenth of everything he received (Gen 28:22). God kept His part of the promise, now it was at least seven years since Jacob returned home safely, and it was time for him to do his part.

Hence, God did as He so often does; He allowed circumstances in Jacob's life to cause him to get back on track and do the things he promised to do. He told him to go to Bethel, which meant House of God, and settle there. This admonition is instructive for believers today as well. The House of God should not be a place to simply visit on occasion but should be a permanent settlement. It should be a perpetual meeting place with God and His people, and a place where comfort for the soul can be found. This was why king David said in Psalms 23:6, he would dwell in the House of the Lord forever! He did not literally live in God's house, but God's house literally lived in him! As such, his was a life of endless thanksgiving and praise to God.

Notice the preparations Jacob made before going to Bethel. Verses 2-5 explain that he told his household and all who were with him, to get rid of the foreign gods they had with them, purify themselves, and change their clothes. Then come and go with him to Bethel, where he would build an altar to God, who answered him in the day of his distress, and who had been with him wherever he went. So, they gave Jacob all the foreign gods they had and the rings in their ears, and Jacob buried them under the oak at Shechem. Then they set out, and the terror of God fell on the towns all around them so that no one pursued them.

Questions beg to be asked as to why Jacob neglected to require members of his household to get rid of their foreign gods before? And how did they get into his household in the first place? It appears as if a few years of complacency began to set in once Jacob returned safely to Canaan. Fulfilling promises he made to God did not seem as urgent as it once was.

Undoubtedly, some of the foreign gods entered his household through his wife Rachel, who stole her father's gods and never got rid of them. Some probably also got into his household by way of the women and children, who were taken captive from the city of Shechem. And Jacob's sons themselves may have acquired foreign gods when they plundered the city. In any case, it did not matter how they got there, what mattered was, Jacob knew they were there, and finally, he determined not to take foreign gods to the house of the One, True God.

He also instructed his household to purify themselves and change their clothes. This symbolized a change of heart and behavior, and a new way of living. Simeon and Levi in particular, needed this type of refreshing. They showed themselves to be especially cruel, and revengeful men; However, the entire family could use an infusion of Godliness, and maybe Jacob should have called for it sooner.

Notice, they all complied with Jacob's requests, and not only did they give him their foreign gods, but they also gave him the rings in their ears, which they probably used to worship those gods. Jacob buried all those things as a sign of them being in the past, and so that their new focus could be on the True God and His House.

Once Jacob's household was purified, they began their sojourn to Bethel, the House of God. Interestingly, Jacob was previously afraid that the peoples of the land would attack him to take revenge for what his sons had done to the city of Shechem, but once they set out on their march to the House of God, the people of the land were afraid of him, because God put fear in them. In other words, once Jacob put away foreign gods from his household and turned his attention to going to the House of God, nothing, or no one, could stop him, because God was with him.

Verses 6-7 state that Jacob and all the people with him came to Luz (Bethel) in the land of Canaan. He built an altar there, and he called the place El Bethel (God of Bethel), because it was there that God revealed Himself to him when he was fleeing from his brother.

Notice, Bethel was not referred to as the place where Jacob found God, but it was the place where God found Jacob. In other words, God revealed Himself to Jacob, because had He not done so, Jacob could never have known Him. This is still true for anyone who comes to know God. One can only know Him if He reveals Himself. This is the reason Jesus said to His disciples in John 6:44, no one can come to Him, unless His Father draws them. Again, in John 15:16, He told His disciples, "You did not choose me, but I chose you. . ." God is far beyond human ability to independently discover. Hence, the only knowledge humans can gain about God, is that which He graciously shares about Himself. And people can only have a relationship with Him because He wants to have one with them.

DEATH OF REBEKAH'S NURSE

Jacob and his household were not insulated from grief because they were in the place where God wanted them to be and told them to go to. In fact, as soon as they arrived at Bethel, verse 8 shows that Deborah, Rebekah's nurse, died and was buried under the oak outside Bethel. So, it was named Allon Bakuth (Oak of Weeping).

This was the first of three deaths in near succession, which caused Jacob and his household to grieve. Deborah, being the nurse of his mother Rebekah, meant he would have known her from his youth. In fact, at some point in his life, she may have been his nurse as well. Though Deborah was not mentioned as a direct family member, she was treated like one, and memorialized as such in scripture. Interestingly, Deborah's death is mentioned in Scripture, but Rebekah's is not. And the fact that she was no longer serving as Rebekah's nurse, but had become a member of Jacob's household, suggest Rebekah may have preceded her in death. It also intimates that Jacob remained in contact with his father and loved ones, who still resided in Hebron, and that once he returned to Canaan, he may have brought Deborah from Hebron to join his household.

JACOB'S NAME AND GOD'S PROMISES REAFFIRMED

Verses 9-10 reiterate that after Jacob returned from Paddan Aram (NW Mesopotamia), God appeared to him again and blessed him. God said to him, "Your name is Jacob (Deceiver), but you will no longer be called Jacob; your name will be Israel (Struggles with God)." So, He named him Israel.

Apparently, God reminded Jacob of his new name, because even though his name had been changed, he continued to answer to his old name. His name was changed during a time when he struggled with God for a blessing, because he feared his brother Esau. Here, it was reaffirmed at a time when he feared the people of the land in which he lived. In essence, God was telling Israel that in times of fear and doubt, he must remember the name he was given. If he overcame in a struggle with God, by God's help, he could certainly do so in his struggles with men.

God also said to him in verses 11-13, "I am God Almighty (El-Shaddai); be fruitful and increase in number. A nation and a community of nations will come from you, and kings will be among your descendants. The land I gave to Abraham, and Isaac I also give to you, and I will give this land to your descendants after you." Then God went up from him at the place where He had talked with him.

God identified Himself to Jacob as El-Shaddai, the All-Sufficient One. He told him to be fruitful and increase in number. This command was more for his descendants than for him, as he would only have one more son. However, his descendants would increase in number, nations, and kings would emanate from them. God reminded Jacob that these very promises were made to Abraham and Isaac before him, and as they firmly believed them, so should he.

Notice, God promised to give the land to his descendants, rather than to him. Therefore, Abraham, Isaac, and Jacob, did not only believe and obey God for themselves, but also for their children, who were the beneficiaries of the promises. Note, when God was finished talking, He went up from him; His personal fellowship with Jacob (Israel), as sweet as it was, ended.

Verses 14-15 indicate that Jacob set up a stone pillar at the place where God talked with him, and he poured out a drink offering on it; he also poured oil on it. Jacob called the place where God had talked with him Bethel. This was sweet fellowship! God went up, but Jacob shared a drink with God by pouring it out on the pillar and allowing the stones to absorb it on God's behalf.

DEATHS OF RACHEL AND ISAAC

Verses 16–20 indicate that Jacob and his household moved on from Bethel. While they were still some distance from Ephrath (Bethlehem), Rachel began to give birth and had great difficulty doing so. The midwife told her not to despair, because she had given birth to another son. As she breathed her last breath, she named him Ben-Oni (Son of my Trouble). But his father named him Benjamin (Son of my right hand). So, Rachel died and was buried on the way to Ephrath (Bethlehem). Over her tomb Jacob set up a pillar, and to the day when this account was written, the pillar, which marked Rachel's tomb was still there.

Evidently, when God repeated the promise to Jacob, telling him to be fruitful and multiply, he took it to heart, and had one last son with his beloved wife Rachel. When it was almost time for her to give birth, for some reason, they departed Bethel (House of God). As they travelled, Rachel made it close to Bethlehem, but could not quite make it all the way there. She experienced great difficulty during childbirth (Gen 3:16). Her midwife informed her that she had given birth to another son, and with her last breath, she named him, "Son of My Trouble." This would have been a difficult name for her son to bear, and for Jacob to live with. Therefore, he changed the boy's name, because he preferred to remember Rachel as his right hand, rather than remember her trouble.

The fact that Rachel assigned her son the name, "Son of My Trouble," suggests she probably remembered the time when she challenged Jacob to either give her children (plural) or she would die (Gen 30:1). She previously gave birth to one child, Joseph, but as soon as she gave birth to a second (children), she died. After she died, her words probably haunted Jacob as they became a self-fulfilling prophecy.

Jacob obviously mourned for his beloved wife Rachel, and he buried her in the place where she died. He set up a pillar to mark that place, and it became a familiar marker for many years into the future. In fact, this pillar was mentioned in First Samuel 10:2. The wife Jacob loved, and worked desperately for, was the first of his wives to die, which left him with Leah, the rejected wife. As much as she had done to have Jacob to herself, the only thing that really brought it about, was the death of her sister Rachel.

REUBEN SLEEPS WITH HIS FATHER'S CONCUBINE

Verses 21-22 show that despite tragedies in his life, Israel moved on again and pitched his tent beyond Migdal Eder. While he was living in that region, Reuben went in and slept with his father's concubine Bilhah, and Israel heard of it.

It is not clear why Reuben, who was Jacob and Leah's firstborn, went in and slept with his father's concubine Bilhah, who was Rachel's servant. However, Reuben knew his mother Leah, was not his father's favorite wife. And, with the death of his favorite wife, Rachel, Reuben could have thought Bilhah, her servant, may have taken her place with his father. Hence, by sleeping with her, and by his father hearing about it, he eliminated the possibility for that to occur, and increased his mother's chances of finally being his father's favorite wife.

Note, Reuben's action was not described as a rape, Bilhah may have felt rejected by Israel, and consented to what Reuben did. However, it caused his standing as the elder son in the family to be irreparably damaged. He disqualified himself from inheriting the rights and blessings of the firstborn. His voice was essentially silenced, and Judah eventually took his place as leader. When Judah spoke, others listened. He led Israel into battle, and it was from him that Messiah descended.

JACOB'S TWELVE SONS

Verses 23-26 identify Jacob's offspring. It shows that the sons of Leah were Reuben the firstborn of Jacob, Simeon, Levi, Judah, Issachar and Zebulun. The sons of Rachel were Joseph and Benjamin. The sons of Rachel's servant Bilhah were Dan and Naphtali. The sons of Leah's servant Zilpah were Gad and Asher. These were the sons of Jacob, who were born to him in Paddan Aram. Through these sons the foundations were set for his offspring to become as innumerable as the stars of heaven, and as sand on the seashore.

ISAAC'S DEATH

Verses 27-29 indicate that Jacob came home to his father Isaac in Mamre, near Kiriath Arba (that is, Hebron), where Abraham and Isaac had stayed. Isaac lived a hundred and eighty years. Then he breathed his last and died and was gathered to his people, old and full of years. And his sons Esau and Jacob buried him.

It is important to note that when Isaac made his will (Gen 27:2), at a time which allowed Jacob and his mother to deceive him, he did so assuming the time of his death was near. However, the fact that he was still alive after twenty years while Jacob lived in Harran, and many years after he returned to Canaan, indicated that his supposition about the nearness of his death was incorrect. He lived 180 years, which covered the period when Joseph was taken captive into Egypt.

It is also important to note that after Jacob returned to Canaan, he spent many years moving about in the land, but did not take his family to live in Hebron, where his father was, until after the death of his mother, and until it was indeed near the time of his father's death. No doubt, he most likely visited his father during that time, as one of the reasons he told Laban he wanted to leave Harran and go back home, was his eagerness to see his father.

Most importantly, he probably visited his father because Scripture shows that he reconciled with God in an all-night struggle for a blessing, it also shows he reconciled with Esau as he journeyed through Seir, thus no doubt, he probably visited his father to reconcile with him as well, because his father bore the brunt of his deception.

Notice, an indication that Jacob and Esau regained a cordial relationship with each other was demonstrated by the fact that both buried their father. Esau's heart was changed, and he did not follow through with his plan to kill his brother Jacob, on the day his father died (Gen 27:41). With the death of Isaac, the covenant mantel was solely on Jacob and his twelve sons.

GENESIS CHAPTER THIRTY-SIX

The previous chapter discussed Jacob and his household's relocation from the area near Shechem, to Bethel. Before going to Bethel, Jacob cleansed his household in preparation to meet with God. During that meeting, God reminded him of his new name, Israel, and of the promises He had made to Abraham, and Isaac, and reaffirmed with him. Unfortunately, not long after meeting with God, a series of ill-fated events occurred. Firstly, the death of Deborah, who use to be his mother's nurse and may have been his as well. Secondly, the death of his beloved wife Rachel. Thirdly, his eldest son slept with his concubine. And fourthly, the death of his dear father, Isaac.

Despite these events, life continued, and this chapter will show God's promises to Abraham and Isaac, for their descendants to be like the stars of heaven, and for kings to descend from them, started to become a reality, beginning with Esau's descendants.

Verses 1-3 provide an account of the family line of Esau (Edom—Red). Esau married Canaanite women: Adah, daughter of Elon the Hittite, and Oholibamah, daughter of Anah and granddaughter of Zibeon the Hivite, also Basemath, daughter of Ishmael and sister of Nebaioth.

Esau's decision to marry Canaanite women gave reason for why he disqualified himself from inheriting the birthright and blessings as Isaac's firstborn son. Unfortunately, events did not play out in Isaac's household in a manner for God to work them out in His time and His way, since Jacob and his mother Rebekah took matters into their own hands. However, in keeping with God's promises concerning Abraham's descendants being numerous, Esau's contribution was confirmed despite his choices of wives.

Verses 4-5 point out that Esau's wife Adah, gave birth to Eliphaz, his wife Basemath gave birth to Reuel, and his wife Oholibamah gave birth to Jeush, Jalam and Korah. These were the sons of Esau, who were born to him in Canaan. It is not clear if Esau had other sons after he left Canaan, but three wives, and only five sons, seemed to be an odd calculation for his time.

In fact, his Canaanite wives, Adah, and Basemath, only bore him one son each. While his Ishmaelite wife Oholibamah, bore him three sons, suggesting he began to spend more time with her.

ESAU SETTLES IN SEIR

Verses 6-8 indicate that Esau took his wives and sons and daughters and all the members of his household, as well as his livestock and all his other animals and all the goods he had acquired in Canaan and moved to a land some distance from his brother Jacob. Their possessions were too great for them to remain together; the land where they were staying could not support them both because of their livestock. So, Esau (Edom) settled in the hill country of Seir.

While it would appear as though Esau independently decided to move to the hill country of Seir, other passages of Scripture indicate that God influenced his decision. For example, God made it clear in Deuteronomy 2:5, and Joshua 24:4, that He had given the hill country to Esau as his own. This may have been revealed to Esau through his father Isaac, who knew Canaan had become Jacob's possession, and the two brothers could not stay together. If Isaac indeed influenced Esau's decision to move, Genesis 32:3, shows that he was already living in the hill country of Seir before Jacob returned to Canaan. However, it should be noted that even though Esau had moved to Seir before Jacob returned to Canaan, he probably still maintained the portion of his inheritance from his father in Canaan. But, following the death of his father, he removed his inheritance and everything he had remaining in Canaan, to his permanent dwelling in the hill country of Seir.

ESAU'S DESCENDANTS

Verses 9-19 show Esau's descendants through his Canaanite wives. His Canaanite wife Adah bore him Eliphaz, who became father of Teman, Omar, Zepho, Gatam, and Kenaz. Eliphaz also had a concubine named Timna, with whom he had another son named Amalek. Esau's other Canaanite wife Basemath, bore him Reuel, who became father of Nahath, Zerah, Shammah and Mizzah. Esau's Ishmaelite wife Oholibama, bore him three sons, Jeush, Jalam and Korah. However, the names of their descendants were not listed. All of Esau's grandsons became chiefs (Dukes, Commanders).

DESCENDANTS OF SEIR THE HORITE

The hill country of Seir derived its name from Seir the Horite, who was also a Canaanite. He and his descendants lived in Seir before Esau arrived there. Hence, they shared that territory with Esau because he was intermarried with them (v 25). Their genealogical record was also shared with his in Scripture, as seen in verses 20–29, where the descendants of Seir the Horite is listed, along with those who were chiefs according to their divisions in the land of Seir. Their system of government appeared to be based on heredity.

In other words, Seir the Horite's sons Lotan, Shobal, Zibeon, Anah, Dishon, Ezer, and Dishan were the Horite chiefs, according to their divisions, in the land of Seir. Anah was father of Esau's wife Oholibamah. Esau was totally embedded into Canaanite culture, which nullified him and his descendants from doing what God wanted, which was to create a people for Himself, who would eventually dispossess the Canaanites.

RULERS OF EDOM

Verse 31 proves that the kings who reigned in Edom, did so before any king reigned in Israel. In other words, God's promise for kings to descend from Abraham and Isaac, became a reality through Esau, before it did through the covenant holder, Jacob. It also intimates that Edom (Esau's descendants) eventually became the most dominant people in the land of Seir.

Verses 32–43 provide a list of those who were kings in Edom. Interestingly, though Edom's system of government was like that of the Horites, succession to leadership roles seemed to be different. Leadership among the Horites was based on heredity or being the son of the current leader, but in Edom, it seemed to be based on election. Hence, kings who were not direct descendants of the previous king became leaders in Edom. However, they were all descendants of Esau, who was father of the Edomites.

Despite Esau's disdain for his birthright, due to his love of Canaanite women, God blessed him anyway. In fact, in later years, while Jacob's descendants, the nation of Israel, were enslaved in Egypt, Esau's descendants dwelt in peace in the land of Seir. In other words, Esau and his descendants received their inheritance before Jacob and his descendants received theirs. Hence, sometimes the people of God are required to wait longer than others for their blessings, but if blessings are promised, they are sure to come.

GENESIS CHAPTER THIRTY-SEVEN

The previous chapter focused on the descendants of Esau, whose legacy was connected to that of the Horites, in whose land he lived, and with whom he intermarried. He was father of the Edomites, and from him, kings of that nation descended, in keeping with God's promise. This chapter will introduce a new stage in Jacob's family and in Israel's history, where Joseph will become the main character in the family. It will show how Jacob's partiality, coupled with a series of prophetic dreams, fostered jealousy among the brothers, which almost cost Joseph his life. Instead, God used those circumstances to change his life, and to ultimately change the nation of Israel, and the world.

JEALOUSY AMONG JACOB'S SONS

As a result of Jacob's unintentional marriage to Leah, his children by her and those by his concubines suffered, because he did not show love to them in the same way he did to Rachel's children, Joseph and Benjamin. Hence, Jacob's household was one in which dysfunction seemed commonplace. Ultimately, God used this dysfunction to remove Joseph from his father's household. Albeit the means by which this was done was quite violent. However, had Joseph remained in his father's household, only God knows what would have happened to him and where he would have ended up.

Sometimes to break a cycle, God allows events such as loss of a job, loss of friends, and loss of finances to occur, so that an environmental change, more importantly, a life-change can be the result. Such changes are difficult but necessary. Therefore, verse 1 states that Jacob lived in the land where his father had stayed, the land of Canaan. However, verse 2, makes an important transition, it says it is the account of Jacob, but it proceeded to highlight Joseph, and only mentioned his brothers as they interacted with him.

It says, Joseph was a young man of seventeen years old, and after tending the flocks with his brothers the sons of Bilhah and Zilpah (Dan, Naphtali, Asher, and Gad), his father's wives he brought their father a bad report about them.

There are a few key observations from this passage, namely, it opens by showing that Joseph worked tending his father's flock, just as all his other brothers did. In this manner, Jacob did not show favoritism. He taught all his sons, without exception, the value of work, unlike some parents who insulate their children from work, claiming they do not want their children to work as hard as they did. This perspective prevents children from appreciating the value of work.

Also, notice the brothers with whom Joseph was tending the flock were Dan, Naphtali, Asher, and Gad. Those sons were Joseph's half-brothers. They were the sons of Jacob's concubines Bilhah and Zilpah, which meant they were further down the totem pole than Leah's sons. The love Jacob had for them did not come close to the love he had for Rachel's sons, Joseph, and Benjamin. The passage does not give exact details about what Joseph said to his father in the bad report he gave about his brothers. But it was quite likely his brothers found out what he said, which sowed seeds in them of both jealousy and revenge.

Notice, verse 3 points out that Jacob loved Joseph more than any of his other sons, because he was born in his old age. However, that may not have been the only reason he loved him more than his other sons, because Benjamin, was younger than Joseph, and was born when Jacob was older than he was when Joseph was born. Yet, at that time, he loved Joseph more than Benjamin. However, while he loved Joseph the most, he loved Benjamin the second most, because he loved their mother Rachel the most.

Even though Jacob was old, and presumably should have known better, observe how he chose to show his love for Joseph above all his other sons. He made a richly ornamented robe for him. In other words, he treated him as though he was prince of the family! This certainly stroked Joseph's ego, but it devastated his brothers. Verse 4 says when they saw their father loved him more than any of them, they hated him and could not speak a kind word to him.

Good parents know what Jacob did was wrong, and that it would only exacerbate the dysfunction in his family. His actions caused his other sons to feel totally unloved and unappreciated. One can only imagine them seeing what their father did, and asking the question, "what about me daddy?" For children at any age, to hear, or know their mom or dad is as proud of them, as they are of any of their siblings, is energizing and confidence-building.

It means more to them than affirmation from anyone or anywhere else in the world! Jacob withheld that affirmation from all his sons, except Joseph.

Please notice it says, Joseph's brothers saw that their father loved him more than any of them, and they hated him and could not speak a kind word to him. In other words, they saw for themselves what their father did, and how he felt about Joseph. If they merely had suspicions before, now they saw for themselves who the favorite really was, and it caused jealousy to fester in them like a cancer. From the time Jacob gave Joseph that richly ornamented robe, the only words Joseph heard from his brothers were unkind words. This meant they probably cursed him day after day.

Recall from previous chapters that Abraham and Sarah favored Isaac over Ishmael. Then Isaac and Rebekah eventually did the same, in favoring Jacob over Esau. Therefore, in the natural progression of things, Jacob followed right along by blatantly favoring Joseph over all his other sons. Truth is, parents who abuse their children, usually came from abused homes themselves; they simply continue the cycle. Therefore, when Jacob gave Joseph a highly ornamented robe, he simply perpetuated the favoritism he had seen in his own family, particularly from his mother, who loved him more than his brother Esau. As a result, Jacob was the primary reason for his sons' hatred toward their brother Joseph.

Colossians 3:21, makes it clear that parents should not provoke (exacerbate) their children to wrath, instead, bring them up in the training and admonition (teaching) of the Lord. The teachings of the Christ cause His followers to believe God loves them the most. Parents should take the same approach. No matter how many children they have, each one should be made to feel as though they are the most loved, whether it is true or not! This may be hard to do at times, but parents should try not to show blatant favoritism, even if they do indeed have a favorite. In fact, when there is a favorite the entire family usually know who it is. Parents should avoid actions to confirm their suspicions.

JOSEPH'S DREAMS

God used the pent-up anger in his brothers to bring about a change in Joseph's environment. Therefore, verse 5 says Joseph had a dream, and when he told it to his brothers, they hated him all the more. The question is, why did he tell them his dream when the only words they spoke to him were unkind words? He had to know how they felt about him; yet he told them his dream. Why did he do that?

The reasons he told them his dream could have been because of the self-assuredness his father planted in him by favoring him over his brothers. In other words, he was cocky! However, it could also have been because of the awesomeness of the dream! He was compelled to share it with others, because it was too magnificent to keep to himself; especially, since the dream seemed to confirm what his father had already done, by exalting him above his brothers. The lesson from Joseph's experience is, sharing spectacular dreams with brothers or sisters, who are consumed with jealousy, can become a recipe for disaster. They can turn dreams into nightmares.

Notice, verses 6–7, he said to them, "Listen to this dream I had: We were binding sheaves of grain out in the field, when suddenly my sheaf rose and stood upright, while your sheaves gathered around mine and bowed down to it." Observe, he said his sheaf rose suddenly! He did not plan it, he did not expect it, nor did he work for it! Apparently, God brought it about suddenly!

Attention should be given to his brothers' response to hearing his dream. Verse 8 says they asked, "Do you intend to reign over us?" They hated him all the more because of his dream, and what he had said. They began to wonder, who does this boy think he is? Does he think he is better than us? However, though Joseph at that time, had no intention of lording over them, the seeds, which were planted in him by his father, caused him to believe, somehow, he would reach greater heights than they would.

Clearly, Joseph had developed a sense of confidence about himself, which grew as his father's partiality became more evident. This caused the anger of his brothers to reach a boiling point. They could hardly listen to his dream, much less share in it. One thing kept building on the other, and eventually there had to be an eruption.

Things got worse after Joseph's second dream, as depicted in verses 9–11. It says in that dream, the sun and moon and eleven stars were bowing down to him. When he told it to his father, he rebuked (chided) him and said, "What is this dream you had? Will your mother and I, and your brothers actually come and bow down to the ground before you?" And, while his brothers were jealous of him, his father kept the matter in his mind.

The reason Joseph had dreams was because God gave them to him to show him what would happen in the future. But God was also making it clear to him that no matter how his brothers treated him, and what he would suffer at their hands, in the end, his dreams would come true. Their empty sheaves would one day bow down to his full sheaf! And God wanted him to share his dreams with his brothers to arouse their jealousy, so that their evil actions would turn out for Joseph's good, and in the future, for their good as well.

Notice again what his father asked, "Will your mother and I, and your brothers actually come and bow down to the ground before you?" In Jacob's interpretation of the dream, the sun and moon represented Joseph's mother Rachel, and his father Jacob, but his mother was dead! How was she going to bow down to him? Jacob must have thought Joseph would have some special place in the Kingdom of God. The eleven stars represented his eleven brothers. So, his father had his own ideas about what the dream meant! Joseph never mentioned any names or interpretations, but his father did! This does not sound like much of a rebuke, especially since he could not get the dream out of his mind!

BROTHERS PLOT EVIL AGAINST JOSEPH

Verses 12-17 indicate that the brothers had gone to graze their father's flocks near Shechem, and Jacob decided to send Joseph to them to see if all was well with them, and with the flocks, and bring word back to him. Joseph agreed and went, but when he got to Shechem, he could not find his brothers, and was wandering around in the fields looking for them. A man found him wandering around and asked him what he was looking for. He told the man he was looking for his brothers and asked if he knew where they were grazing. The man said he heard them say they were moving on from there to go to Dothan, so Joseph continued on and found them near Dothan.

A key observation is, on previous occasions, such as shown in verse 2, when the brothers went to graze, Joseph went with them, but on this occasion he did not go. It appears Joseph only joined his brothers in grazing the flock when the grazing was a short distance, but he did not do any long-distance grazing. He seemed to be the one who was his father's comfort while the others were gone. It also amplified his status with his father and caused his brother's jealousy to grow. They were in the fields doing difficult work with no such appreciation as a regular robe, while Joseph seemed to do much less being at home but was appreciated with an ornamented robe.

Jacob expected his sons to be grazing in Shechem, but they were in Dothan, which was approximately 13 miles north of Shechem. This was probably because Shechem may still have posed certain dangers to them, because of their history with that place. Recall in chapter 34, they wiped out all the men of the city. In any case, when Joseph went to Shechem and did not find his brothers, he could have given up and returned home. But the fact that he did not give up until he found them, showed his qualities of persistence and obedience to his father. He searched until he found them, hoping to be able to go back and report to his father about how they were doing, but he did not make it back home.

Verse 18 indicates that when they saw him in the distance, and before he reached them, they plotted to kill him. They plotted, which meant they were going to commit a premeditated murder against their brother, because: 1. their father loved him more than he loved them, 2. he showed it, and 3. they were jealous and angry about it. In essence, they plotted to kill their brother to hurt their father for showing favoritism toward him. Therefore, their grievance was more against their father than against their brother. Joseph was basically collateral damage in his brothers' efforts to acquire their father's affection.

Notice verses 19-20, they sarcastically said, "Here comes that dreamer, come now, let us kill him and throw him into one of these cisterns and say that a ferocious animal devoured him." Had they carried out the crime they were planning, they would have been acting like ferocious animals themselves, and like murderers, who were willing to lie to cover up their crime! And here lied the clincher, they said if we kill him, "Then we will see what comes of his dreams." In other words, they reasoned if they killed him, they would also kill his dreams. Hence, sharing dreams should be done with great care. Some people cannot handle the dreams and aspirations of others.

Verses 21-22 point out that when Reuben heard what they were planning, he tried to rescue Joseph from their hands. He said, "Let us not take his life, and don't shed any blood. Throw him into this cistern here in the desert, but don't lay a hand on him." Reuben said this to rescue him from them and take him back to his father.

Rueben was the first-born, which meant he should have been more jealous than any of the others. Additionally, in his father's absence, he should also have had the most influence. As the oldest, Reuben should have been able to say, 'this is wrong, and I am not allowing it to occur!' However, something happened in Reuben's life, which cause him to lose influence among his brothers, and to lose favor with his father. Back in chapter 35:22, Reuben slept with one of his father's concubines, Bilhah, and his father heard about it. After Reuben did that, his influence in the family diminished. His role of leadership among the brothers appeared to pass to Judah.

Therefore, when Reuben tried to rescue Joseph, his sphere of influence had been greatly reduced. If he still had his full influence, he could have stopped the entire event by the power of his standing in the family. Yet, if he was able to safely return Joseph to his father, it might have restored some of the favor he had lost. So, instead of killing him, Reuben suggested throwing him into a dry cistern, so that he could rescue him later. But God had another plan.

Verses 23-24 declare that when Joseph came to his brothers, they stripped off his robe, the richly ornamented robe he was wearing, and they took him and threw him in the dry, empty cistern. So, despite Reuben's diminished influence, his brothers did what he suggested, which saved Joseph's life, but God was orchestrating the entire episode.

Notice, the first thing they did to Joseph was the same thing that would later be done to Christ. They stripped him of his robe. Why did Joseph wear his robe? Did he not know it would inflame his brothers' jealousy? Didn't he know it would immediately remind them of their place in their father's heart? Was he rubbing it in a bit? It is not clear why he chose to wear the most sentimental piece of clothing he possessed, but his brothers made their feelings about it quite clear. They did not simply take it off, instead they stripped (ripped) it off.

Verses 25-27 provide insight into their frame of mind after doing what they did. It begins by saying, "As they sat down to eat their meal." This meant there was no remorse from any of them. They ate their food as if nothing happened! As they sat down to eat their meal, they looked up and saw a caravan of Ishmaelites coming from Gilead. Their camels were loaded with spices, balm and myrrh, and they were on their way to take them down to Egypt. Judah, the son who now had the most influence among the brothers said, "What will we gain if we kill our brother and cover up his blood? Come, let's sell him to the Ishmaelites and not lay our hands on him; after all, he is our brother, our own flesh and blood." His brothers agreed.

JOSEPH SOLD INTO SLAVERY

When Judah spoke, his brothers listened, but his legacy shows he seemed to have a problem doing the crime himself. For example, when his descendants turned Jesus over to the gentiles to be crucified, they tried to keep their hands clean by saying they did not have authority to put anyone to death. Here, they sold Joseph rather than killing him, even though they wanted him dead. They also wanted Jesus dead, and after Judas sold him to them, they had him killed by the Romans. By God's grace, Joseph did not suffer the same fate, but like Christ, he also became a savior of his people.

The Ishmaelites lived in the land of Midian, so they were also called Midianites. Therefore, verse 28 says when the Midianite merchants came by, his brothers pulled Joseph up out of the cistern and sold him for twenty shekels of silver to the Ishmaelites, who took him to Egypt. He was not sold for gold, but for silver. Ten pieces less than Christ would later be sold for.

The Bible does not reveal what they did with the money they received, but that is an interesting mystery.

It is not clear how many of the brothers were present when Judah conducted this transaction, but verses 29–30 reveal that Rueben was not there. Consequently, when Reuben returned to the cistern and saw that Joseph was not there, he tore his clothes. He went back to his brothers and said, "The boy isn't there! Where can I turn now?" In other words, where can I find him? Future events would reveal that they told Reuben what they did to Joseph, but he was not a part of the plot to sell him.

COVER-UP STORY AND JACOB'S GRIEF

Verses 31–33 show they got Joseph's highly ornamented robe, slaughtered a goat and dipped the robe in its blood. They took the ornamented robe back to their father and said, "We found this. Examine it to see whether it is your son's." They did not say he should examine it to see if it was their brother's, but they said, "Your son's." He recognized it and said, "It is my son's robe! Some ferocious animal has devoured him. Joseph has surely been torn to pieces."

Jacob quickly lost hope. The dreams his son told him about, which he kept in his mind, were swiftly forgotten. Before his sons got an opportunity to present the lie, they intended to tell, Jacob himself came up with a story about how Joseph died, and they did not refute it. Joseph and his dreams were replaced in Jacob's heart by guilt from regretting he sent him on such a journey by himself. But if those sons thought this was now their opportunity to get closer to their father, and to gain his affection, they made a terrible mistake.

Verse 34 shows that Jacob tore his clothes, put on sackcloth and mourned many days for his son. Notice verse 35 says that all his sons and daughters came to comfort him, but he refused to be comforted. Instead, he said, "No! I will continue to mourn until I join my son in the grave." So, he wept for Joseph.

Joseph was his father's favorite and his comfort when the brothers were away grazing the flocks. Jacob refused to allow any of his other sons to take that place. Instead, he said he would mourn for him until the day he died. Therefore, on the day when Jacob was told Joseph had died, he became a living dead man himself. All his hope was gone, and all the prophecies and dreams he heard were forgotten and replaced with grief and despair. His relationship with God was also suspended.

Verse 36 indicates that the Midianites (Ishmaelites) sold Joseph in Egypt to Potiphar, one of Pharaoh's officials, the captain of the guard. So, his brothers sold him to the Ishmaelites for twenty shekels of silver, but they resold him to the Egyptians for an unrevealed price. Assuming they made a profit, could it be they sold him for thirty shekels of silver, the price for which Jesus was betrayed? This is conjecture, but similarities between the two stories are undeniable.

During the days and years following the news of Joseph's supposed death, Jacob was obviously tormented by his decision to send him to check on his brothers. However, it is unclear what daily life was like for the brothers, knowing what they did, and how they deceived their father. The fact that none of them ever broke rank and told him the truth, suggest they all preferred to live with his grief for Joseph than his favoritism and partiality toward him. Jacob, with the help of his mother concocted a grand scheme to deceive his father Isaac, his sons did the same to deceive him. In that sense, Jacob reaped what he sowed, but God would reverse his sons' evil and work it out for their good.

GENESIS CHAPTER THIRTY-EIGHT

In the previous chapter the story was told of Jacob's love for his son Joseph above all his other sons. He chose to demonstrate his love by making Joseph a highly ornamented robe. This caused jealousy among the other sons, who nursed such a hatred that they could no longer speak a kind word to Joseph. In fact, they plotted to kill him, but after discussing it among themselves, they decided instead to put him in a dry cistern. Eventually, the opportunity presented itself for them to sell him, and that was what they did.

Joseph was sold to Ishmaelite merchants, who resold him to an Egyptian named Potiphar, one of Pharaoh's officials, captain of the guard. This chapter will take a detour from the life of Joseph to inform about an interesting incident in the life of his brother Judah. Recall from the previous chapter, it was Judah who concocted the idea to sell Joseph to the Ishmaelites.

Verse 1 declares that Judah left his brothers and went down to stay with a man named Hirah, an Adullamite. In other words, after orchestrating the sale of his brother Joseph, he also left the family and went to live with his friend Hirah. There is no indication of how Judah and Hirah met and became such close friends, but notice, it says he went down. This statement reflected the trajectory of Judah's life after he left his father's household to go live with his friend. This decision also exposed Judah to more of the Canaanite culture and lifestyle, and his behavior suggests he soon became engulfed in it. Judah's life began to resemble the life of one who abandoned, or at least, suspended their faith to live according to the ways of the world around them.

JUDAH'S FAMILY

Verses 2-5 reveal that while staying with Hirah, he met the daughter of a Canaanite man named Shua. He married her and made love to her; she became pregnant and gave birth to a son, who was named Er. Following two additional pregnancies, she gave birth to two other sons, who were named Onan, and Shelah. She gave birth to her last son, Shelah, while living in Kezib.

Judah married a Canaanite woman without seeking counsel or approval from his father Jacob. Apparently, his friend Hirah became a father-figure to him and may have been responsible for introducing him to Shua's daughter. If he had consulted his father, he may have been counseled against marrying a Canaanite woman. This marriage was quite notable because it was through Judah's line that Messiah would come. It also meant Judah's decision could have resulted in Messiah having Canaanite heritage, unless God intervened to prevent that from occurring.

DEATH OF JUDAH'S SONS

Verses 6–7 point out that Judah got a wife for his firstborn, Er, her name was Tamar; but since Er was wicked in God's sight, He put him to death. It is not clear what Er's age was when he married Tamar, or when God put him to death. Evidently, he was yet quite young. An important note here, is that Tamar's heritage was not given. The assumption is that she was Canaanite, but the Bible does not say that, she could have been Edomite.

Additionally, the nature of Er's wickedness was not revealed, but it appeared to be rather egregious and defiant, as is the case when sin is described as occurring in God's sight. Notice, God put him to death, but how He did so, was not revealed. However, Er's death ruled him out as a possible earthly forefather of the coming Messiah. And, since he was the son of a Canaanite woman, his death removed the possibility that through him, the Messiah would have Canaanite heritage.

Following Er's death, verses 8–10 show that Judah turned to his second son Onan and instructed him to sleep with his brother's wife Tamar, and fulfill his duty to her as a brother-in-law, to raise up offspring for his deceased brother. But Onan knew the offspring would not be his; so, whenever he slept with Tamar, he spilled his semen on the ground to keep from getting her pregnant. This was wicked in the sight of God; so, He also put Onan to death.

Onan's wickedness was centered around deceit. Publicly, he appeared to agree to do what his father asked of him, and what the custom of that time required him to do. But privately, he spilled his semen on the ground, so that if left to him, he would never have gotten Tamar pregnant. Meanwhile, he continued to gratify himself by having sex with her. God viewed his actions as wickedness, worthy of death. So, the Lord also put him to death. And, once again, as Judah's second son from his Canaanite wife, Onan's death removed him as a forefather of the coming Messiah, and removed the possibility that through him, Messiah would have Canaanite heritage.

Following the death of two of his most eligible sons, verse 11 indicates that Judah told his daughter-in-law Tamar to live as a widow in her father's household until his third and final son Shelah grew up. However, Judah thought his last son may die too, just like his brothers. Yet, Tamar did as she was instructed, and went back to live in her father's household. It appeared that Judah blamed Tamar for the death of his two sons. As such, he probably had no intention of keeping his promise to give his youngest son to her in marriage.

Notice verse 12 indicates that Judah eventually lost his spouse, just as Tamar had lost two of hers. It says after a while his wife, the daughter of Shua died. When he recovered from his grief, he went up to Timnah, to the men who were shearing his sheep, and his friend Hirah the Adullamite went with him.

Whereas Judah probably had no intention of ever giving his son Shelah to Tamar, once his wife died, he became eligible himself. At least this was the way Tamar saw it. And notice, in his time of grief, the Biblical narrative gives no indication that he sought comfort from his father, nor from anyone in his father's household; instead, his friend Hirah, the Adullamite continued to be his confidant.

JUDAH AND TAMAR

Verses 13–14 reveal that when Tamar was told Judah was on his way to Timnah to shear his sheep, she took off her widow's clothes, covered herself with a veil as a disguise, and sat at the entrance to Enaim, which was on the road to Timnah. The reason she did this, was because she realized that though Shelah had grown up, she had not been given to him as a wife. In other words, Tamar concluded that while she kept her end of the agreement, Judah had no intention of keeping his.

No doubt, others in her family and community probably concluded the same, which may have been the reason someone told her Judah would be passing her way. While he had forgotten about her, and the promise he made to her, she had not forgotten, and would see to it that he made good on his promise.

Verses 15–18 declare that when Judah saw her, he thought she was a prostitute, because her face was covered. Not realizing she was his daughter-in-law he went over to her by the roadside and requested for her to allow him to have sex with her. She asked him what he would give her if she allowed him to sleep with her. He promised to give her a young goat from his flock, but she asked him for a pledge until he sent the goat. Once she specified the pledge she was willing to accept, he agreed to give it to her. She asked him to give her his seal and its cord, and the staff in his hand. He gave them to her and had sex with her, and she became pregnant by him.

Judah's desire to have sex with the woman, was simply because he saw her. Lust of the eye was the basis of his desire for her. Presumably, she was beautiful, and he liked what he saw! However, he really could not have seen her in a meaningful way, because she was veiled the entire time. In that culture, prostitutes covered themselves, because it was a line of work for which they could lose their lives. It was not viewed as a respectable profession as it is in some societies today, where prostitutes are allowed to dress in the most physically salacious manner possible. Prostitution is no longer viewed with disdain, but as a valuable service. This reflects the moral decline of many of today's societies.

Most likely, the death of Judah's wife, was a contributing factor, which influenced his craving for sexual intimacy. However, his efforts to satisfy his desires by seeking a prostitute, meant he wanted to have sex with no strings attached. Yet, this woman, who pretended to be a prostitute, made sure strings were attached, because her life depended on it! She was living as a widow in her father's household; Hence, if her pretenses to being a prostitute were unsuccessful, she could have been put to death when her pregnancy was discovered. This was one reason she made sure to receive tangible pledges from Judah. She reasoned, if anything happened to her, he would be her collateral and she would take him down with her if needed.

The other reason she needed collateral, was because he had already demonstrated that his word was no good. Had she not gotten pledges, he may not have sent the goat he promised, not to mention, she would not have been able to prove he was the father of her offspring.

Verse 19 says, after she left, she took off her veil and put on her widow's clothes again. Then, Judah sent the young goat by his friend Hirah, to get his pledge back, but his friend did not find the woman. Notice, the expressed reason why he sent the young goat was to get his pledge back. Had she not gotten his pledge, it is questionable whether he would have sent the young goat! He may have had sex and forgotten about her!

Verses 20-23 show that Hirah asked the men who lived in Enaim for information to help him find the woman who was the town's shrine prostitute, but they told him no such woman lived there. So, he went back and told Judah he did not find her, and that the men who lived there said there is no shrine prostitute in that town. Hence, to keep from becoming a laughingstock, Judah decided to let her keep the pledge she had, especially since he got to keep the young goat he promised her. He expressed no remorse for sleeping with a supposed prostitute, his only concern was about the shame of others finding out about it; Consequently, he sought to keep the incident quiet by not pursuing the issue further. However, this incident would not be kept quiet.

TAMAR'S PREGNANCY AND JUDAH'S GUILT

Verses 24-26 reveal that three months later, Judah was told his daughter-in-law Tamar was guilty of prostitution and was pregnant. Without hesitation, Judah said to bring her out and let her be burned. However, as she was being brought out, she sent a message to Judah informing him she was pregnant by the man who owned the pledges he had given her. She told him to see if he recognized the seal, cord, and staff, which were in her possession. He obviously recognized them and declared that she was more righteous than he, because she realized he had no intention of keeping his promise to give her to his son Shelah. However, once he recognized her as his daughter-in-law, he did not sleep with her again.

Judah was quick to pass judgment on Tamar when he thought she had become pregnant due to prostitution, but he did not pass judgment on himself for his admitted deceit. One translation (NIV) says he judged that she be burned to death, but most others do not. Most translations agree he only said to let her be burned, which was done by branding a woman in the facial area, to identify her as a prostitute.

This story highlights the sacrifices Tamar made as a member of Judah's family. She lost two husbands, and her normal prospects for having children, since Judah refused to let his youngest son marry her. However, God blessed her unusual plan, and she became pregnant by her father-in-law, who slept with her only once, and no more. That was enough for her to become sexually tainted, such that no other man would marry her. Nevertheless, through that encounter with her father-in-law, she became a foremother in the flesh of Jesus Christ, the Messiah. Her decision to make sure she received her father-in-law's pledge, possibly saved her life.

TAMAR GIVES BIRTH TO TWIN BOYS

Verses 27-30 indicate that when the time came, twin boys were in her womb. As she was giving birth, one of the boys put out his hand; so, the midwife tagged him with a scarlet thread as the firstborn. But, when he drew back his hand, his brother came out, and the midwife said, "So this is how you have broken out!" And he was named Perez (Pharez—Broken Out). Then his brother, who was tagged with the scarlet thread, came out second. He was named Zerah (Scarlet, Brightness). Messiah, Jesus Christ, descended from the line of Perez.

Judah was willing to relinquish his pledges to keep his sexual involvement with a supposed prostitute quiet, but in reality, he did not have sex with a prostitute, he had sex with his daughter-in-law, and he could not keep that quiet, because she became pregnant and gave birth to twin boys. His actions and legacy became tied to his sexual involvement with Tamar. So, God revealed what Judah tried his best to conceal. God also used this messy situation for His own glory. He brought His son Jesus Christ in the flesh, through Judah's line, and in so doing, restored Tamar's honor, while bringing hope to Judah, and to the entire world.

GENESIS CHAPTER THIRTY-NINE

The previous chapter seemed to be a digression, in that it stepped aside from Joseph's story, to discuss Judah's family, but it was a worthwhile digression, because it provided insight into the human lineage of Jesus Christ. Judah's marriage, his offspring, the death of his sons, and his wife, and his inadvertent sexual encounter with his daughter-in-law Tamar, were valuable pieces of information for painting a complete picture about why a Messiah was needed to redeem His family, and the world. From that relationship with Tamar, Judah had twin sons, one of whom became a forefather of Jesus Christ.

This chapter will resume the discussion about Joseph's life, particularly as it related to his encounter with his master's wife. She attempted to seduce him into a sexual relationship, but when he refused, she accused him of attempted rape. This caused him to be imprisoned, but it could have been much worse, were it not for the mercies of God, who was with him and who continued to bless him in ways that were clear to him and others.

JOSEPH'S LIFE IN EGYPT

After Joseph's brothers sold him and lied to their father, claiming he had died, his father grieved bitterly for him, but there is no information about how Joseph grieved for his father. As a "daddy's boy" he most certainly grieved. It should not be forgotten that when he was sold, he was a maturing young man about 17 years old, with full awareness of what happened to him. So, not only did he grieve, but every day he probably longed for home, especially since he was taken without having a chance to say goodbye to his father.

This chapter opened by showing that God became the only father Joseph was able to rely on in Egypt. It was a tough place for him to be, and yet, because of what God was working out in his life, it was the best place to be. It was there where he matured and came to understand the peace and providence of God, and it was there where he relinquished his former arrogance and learned to give glory to God.

Notice where God placed Joseph. Verses 1–2 state that Joseph had been taken down to Egypt, and Potiphar, an Egyptian who was one of Pharoah's officials, the captain of the guard, bought him from the Ishmaelites who had brought him there. It also says, the Lord was with Joseph and he prospered as he lived in the house of his Egyptian master.

In God, Joseph found a Father. While he lived in Potiphar's house and fared better from being his slave, rather than someone else', he did not rely on his master, but on God. He had no family in Egypt, his father thought he was dead, and his brothers wished he were. Yet, the Lord was with him and he prospered.

Observe that even though God was with Joseph, and though he prospered, he was still a slave. In other words, God brought about prosperity amidst his slavery. There may be some today who are poor, and yet are prospering in their souls! They are not unlike Joseph, who lived in the house of his Egyptian master; In other words, he had no home of his own, yet he prospered!

Verse 3 declares that when Joseph's master saw the Lord was with him, and that the Lord gave him success in everything he did, Joseph found favor in his master's eyes, and became his attendant. This meant, as attendant, his master's business became his business! From this experience Joseph learned things he could never have learned grazing sheep in the land of Canaan. He was a slave, but God was training him to become a leader; God was preparing him for the future. It is not known if, or how much Joseph was paid for what he was doing, but sometimes a compromise must be made by accepting no pay, or lower pay, in exchange for training, which will pay off in the end. In such cases, God could be working out something that money cannot buy.

By placing Joseph in charge of his household Potiphar proved to be a smart man. He saw that God was with Joseph and he prospered in everything he did, so to get his household to prosper, he put it under Joseph! That meant, Joseph became more like a son to Potiphar than a slave. It is not known if Potiphar had sons, but he certainly treated Joseph like one. In fact, he gave him the treatment an eldest son would get: He entrusted to his care everything he owned.

God's hand was in this. Joseph, who was always close to his father Jacob, probably needed a father-figure, so God gave him one in Potiphar. The kind of trust afforded to him by his master, was greater than that afforded many spouses by their mates, especially in the area of finances.

Notice verse 5 points out that from the time he put Joseph in charge of his household and of all that he owned, the Lord blessed the household of the Egyptian because of Joseph. In other words, the blessings of the Lord were on everything Potiphar had, both in the house and in the field, because he placed Joseph in charge! And he did not concern himself with anything except the food he ate. Hence, with Joseph in charge, the man was prosperous and carefree!

About the time when life started to become comfortable for Joseph, trouble was around the corner. Adversity would force him out, and through strange circumstances, a greater leadership opportunity would come about. Albeit the process by which God chose to bring it about appeared undesirable, from a human perspective.

JOSEPH AND HIS MASTER'S WIFE

Verses 6–7 continued, by stating that Joseph was well-built and handsome. Hence, after a while Potiphar's wife took notice of him. She asked him to come to bed with her. When it says she took notice, it meant she lustfully took notice of every print, and imprint on Joseph's body! Mrs. Potiphar did not seem to realize, or care that as long as Joseph was in charge the blessings of the Lord were also upon her. Or maybe she realized it and wanted Joseph to bless her sexually as well! Whatever the case, the proposition she made to Joseph was a dangerous one for him to accept.

It does not say Mrs. Potiphar had a conversation with Joseph to try to get to know him. Instead, notice the shallow reasons she wanted to have an affair with him: 1. he was well built and handsome. 2. She took notice of him (because he was well-built and handsome). It doesn't say he noticed her the same way because she was married. 3. He was in a prominent position in the household. And 4. they had time on their hands while Potiphar was away from home.

None of these were good reasons for her to have an affair. Besides, not that this would be a good reason, but the passage does not even indicate any marital issues between her and her husband. Apparently, Potipher's only faults were, he was not as handsome and well-built as Joseph, and he spent too much time away from home. So, what she really wanted was Joseph's body! This was a timeless event, as it still occurs today. Notice also, she wanted Joseph to not only have sex with her in her husband's house, but also in his bed! This was wretched on Mrs. Potiphar part!

Her husband had everything, while Joseph, a slave and foreigner, had nothing, except good looks! This was an illustration of the level of immaturity usually associated with adulterous situations. People who would normally be rock-solid in most other areas of life, seem to become childish when it comes to adultery. Presidents, politicians, judges, lawyers, doctors, pastors, priest, Christians, and non-Christians alike, who become entangled in the web of adulterous relationships, often demonstrate a lack of typical prudence due to the salaciousness of adultery. It is a powerful seduction to which, without care, anyone can be susceptible.

Notice verses 8–9 say Joseph refused. Though he was yet a young man, in the prime of his sexual prowess, he could have done as many other young men might have done, but he refused. Something in his character caused him to say no! Observe his mature reasoning, he told her, with him in charge, his master did not concern himself with anything in the house; everything he owned he entrusted to him. No one was greater in the house than him. His master withheld nothing from him, except her, because she was his wife. In other words, Joseph inferred that his master did not treat him like a slave, but like a son, and a son does not sleep with his mother. His master totally trusted him!

Joseph's statement about his master withholding nothing in his household, except his wife, was not stated elsewhere by Potiphar, but if he did in fact say that to Joseph, it would be reasonable to wonder, why? Joseph should automatically know it would have been dishonorable and inappropriate to sleep with his master's wife. But, if Potiphar did indeed give him this prohibition, it would seem like an odd thing to do, unless he did not trust his wife.

Joseph continued in verse 9, by calling her proposition exactly what it was. He asked her, "How could I do such a wicked thing, and sin against God?" Joseph's approach was very mature. He did not only see her proposition as a potential sin against his master, but also against his God. This was enough to hold him back, and if many people, especially Christians, would view adultery in this way, it may also be enough to hold them back. Notice, Joseph regarded her proposition to be a wicked thing.

Verse 10 shows, she tried to wear him down. She spoke to him day after day about going to bed with her, but he refused to even be with her. Those who face this kind of pressure on the job, school, or elsewhere, should take note. He avoided being in the same area of the house where she was. Imagine, she was sleeping next to her husband at night, dreaming about Joseph, and chasing him in the day! Had God not been working it out as it pleased Himself, one might ask, since Joseph was facing this pressure day after day, why didn't he inform his master? For whatever reason, he did not do that. He probably thought he could handle it on his own, as some in similar situations often do.

Verses 11-12 declare that one day, Joseph went into the house to attend to his duties, and none of the household servants was inside. She caught him by his cloak and asked him to come to bed with her, but he left his cloak in her hand and ran out of the house. There seems to be something about Joseph and his cloaks! The highly ornamented robe his father had given him was dipped in blood by his brothers and taken back to his father claiming he was dead. Now, here it was again, Potiphar's wife would hold on to his cloak, scented with her perfume, and accuse him of attempted rape.

Verses 13-16 point out that when she saw he had left his cloak in her hand, and ran out of the house, she called her household servants. "Look," she said to them, "this Hebrew has been brought to us to make sport of us! He came in here to sleep with me, but I screamed for help, he left his cloak beside me and ran out of the house." She kept his cloak beside her until his master came home, then she told him the same deceitful story. Verses 17-18 show that she repeated the same lie to her husband, which she had told to the servants.

Joseph had done all he could to avoid this situation, yet he found himself in the midst of a scandal, because Potiphar's wife seized the opportunity to tell her husband a lie about him, before he had the opportunity to tell his master the truth about her. As such, verse 19 says when his master heard the story his wife told him, he burned with anger! In other words, he was hot! It does not tell us if he even heard Joseph's side of the story.

Verse 20 simply declares that he took Joseph and put him in prison, the place where the king's prisoners were confined. But God's hand was in it; just notice where the prison was. He could have put Joseph in a regular prison with common criminals. In fact, he could have killed Joseph! Instead, the prison in which he placed him was the place where the king's prisoners were confined. This prison was actually in Potiphar's house! In other words, even though Joseph was in prison, he really did not leave the house.

Potiphar still seemed to remember the reason his house had been blessed. More importantly, God withheld the full extent of wrath he could have exacted against Joseph. As such, verses 20-21 point out that while he was there in the prison, the Lord was with him; He showed him kindness and granted him favor in the eyes of the prison warden. So, Joseph became what might be called a prison trustee. He was without father, mother, brother, or sister in Egypt, but God was with him.

This may be instructive for Christians who may be in prison today, and those who may have been wrongfully incarcerated. It may also be helpful for those who may feel trapped by other circumstances of life. It was a demonstration that God does not abandon His children, no matter where they are in life. Just as He was with Joseph, His relentless presence is with each one of them.

JOSEPH IN PRISON

There are few things in life worse than being wrongfully imprisoned, but Joseph made the best of the situation. Verse 22 states that the warden put him in charge of all those held in the prison, and he was made responsible for all that was done there. It appeared as if Joseph was doing the warden's job for him! Not many wardens would trust a prisoner the way this warden trusted Joseph, unless of course, they knew each other. Hence, there was a reason why verse 23 says the warden paid no attention (a warden is supposed to pay attention) to anything under Joseph's care, because the Lord was with Joseph and gave him success in whatever he did. The next chapter will explain why the warden trusted Joseph, and how he knew the Lord was with him.

GENESIS CHAPTER FORTY

The previous chapter provided details about God allowing Joseph to find favor in the eyes of his master Potiphar. God's favor also extended to Potiphar's household, which was blessed because Joseph was in charge. However, trouble soon came to Joseph, because he continued to refuse his master's wife's sexual advances, which led her to wrongly accusing him of attempted rape. This accusation resulted in Joseph being thrown into prison, where the king's prisoners were confined. Again, God was with him, and he found favor with the warden, who put him (a prisoner) in charge of the prison in which he was being held.

This chapter will discuss Joseph's interactions with some of his fellow prisoners, who were former employees of the king; specifically, the king's former chief cupbearer, and his former chief baker, both of whom had dreams, to which Joseph provided interpretations.

Verses 1-4 reveal that after some time had passed, the chief cupbearer and chief baker of the king of Egypt offended him, and he was angry with them; therefore, he put them in custody in the house of the captain of the guard, which was the same prison where Joseph was confined. The captain of the guard assigned them to Joseph, and he attended to them.

Notice, these verses confirmed that the prison where Joseph was confined was in the house of the captain of the guard, who was his master Potiphar (Gen 39:1). Therefore, Joseph was basically under home-confinement. The prison in which he was confined was in the same house where he worked as a slave, and as head of his master's household. Observe also, the captain of the guard, who was Potiphar, assigned the king's prisoners to Joseph, who was supposed to be their fellow prisoner.

Apparently, after Potiphar's wife accused Joseph of attempted rape, his master removed him from being head of his house but kept him working in his prison. This was also how the warden knew Joseph and knew the Lord had given him success in whatever he did (Gen 39:23).

PHARAOH'S TWO PRISONERS HAVE DREAMS

Continuing in verses 4–8, it is stated that after Pharaoh's officials had been in custody for some time, each of the two men had a dream on the same night, but each dream had a different meaning. When Joseph came to them the next morning, he saw that they were dejected. So, he asked them why they looked so sad. They told him they both had dreams, but there was no one to interpret them. Then Joseph informed them that interpretations belong to God, and he invited them to tell him their dreams.

It is important to note that Pharaoh's officials were in prison for a while before they had dreams, which troubled them deeply. In other words, God allowed them to settle into the prison, and to develop a trusting relationship with Joseph before He allowed them to be troubled by their dreams. Interestingly, being in prison was no longer a source of sadness for them, but their dreams were. This was how Joseph knew something in their countenances was different. Just as they were imprisoned at the same time, they both had dreams on the same night. They were both saddened by their dreams on the same morning, but that was where the similarities ended.

Notice, by the time they told Joseph their dreams, they may have told them to each other, and to other prisoners. Hence, they concluded, there was no one who could interpret them because the people they normally relied on to interpret dreams were not available in prison where they were. However, Joseph informed them that interpretation of dreams comes from God, and he invited them to share their dreams with him, because he trusted God to give him the interpretation. Most likely, by then they knew he was a worshipper of the Hebrew God.

It should be noted here that not all dreams come from God. Some occur because during sleep, the mind may still be preoccupied with activities of life. In fact, a majority of dreams may be attributed to this reason. However, God can, and does use moments of sleep to reveal things, which the dreamer may not hear otherwise, or may pay little attention to, if they were spoken during the busyness of daily life. Hence, sometimes God speaks to His people, as well as those who are not His people, by way of dreams. In this case, He did so to Pharaoh's two officials, and it will be shown that He did the same to Pharaoh himself, to Nebuchadnezzar, to the apostles Peter, Paul, and John, and numerous others. And, when God speaks through dreams, He gives the interpretation by allowing the dreamer to experience the fulfillment of the dream in real life.

JOSEPH PROVIDES INTERPRETATION TO EACH PRISONER'S DREAM

Verses 9-11 show the chief cupbearer told Joseph his dream. He revealed that in his dream he saw a vine in front of him, and on the vine were three branches, which budded and blossomed, and then ripened into grapes. He saw Pharaoh's cup in his hand, and he took the grapes, squeezed them into Pharaoh's cup, and put the cup in his hand. So, he basically saw himself serving Pharaoh again.

Joseph confirmed this in verses 12-13, by explaining, the three branches meant three days. He told him within three days, Pharaoh would lift up his head again, and restore him to his position, and he would put the cup in Pharaoh's hand, just as he did in former days, when he was his cupbearer.

This news obviously pleased the cupbearer, but in verse 14 Joseph added a personal request. He admonished the cupbearer, when all goes well for him, to remember him and show kindness to him by mentioning him to Pharaoh to get him out of prison. In other words, God showed Joseph the cupbearer's deliverance, but He did not show him his own. Hence, Joseph sought the cupbearer's assistance in bringing it about.

It is not clear if the cupbearer and baker were Hebrews like Joseph, but verse 15 shows that Joseph proceeded to share his personal story with them. He told them about how he was forcibly carried off from the land of the Hebrews, and how he had done nothing to deserve being put in a dungeon. He did not reveal all the details of his circumstances, but what he said showed he was well aware of the injustices, which has occurred in his life.

It was interesting that even though he found favor in the eyes of the warden, and was placed in charge of the prison, he described it as a dungeon. This meant his living conditions were deplorable! Hence, he did not ask for assistance in getting into the palace, he simply wanted to get out of the dungeon. Yet, God was with him, and was working out a greater purpose for his life, which he was unable to see at that time.

Verses 16-19 indicate that when the chief baker saw that Joseph had given a favorable interpretation to the chief cupbearer, he told him that he too had a dream. He shared that in his dream he had three baskets of bread on his head. In the top basket were all kinds of baked goods for Pharaoh, but the birds, rather than Pharaoh, ate them out of the basket. There was no need for him to mention what happened to the other two baskets he saw in the dream, because Joseph interrupted to explain that the three baskets were three days. Within three days, Pharaoh would have him beheaded, and have his beheaded body impaled on a pole, where the birds would eat away his flesh.

This was a horrific interpretation, which probably increased the chief baker's agony before he died. It is not clear what his offense was, and why his punishment was so much more severe than the cupbearer's. He was probably encouraged to share his dream after hearing the positive interpretation the chief cupbearer received, but he may have kept it to himself if he knew the interpretation for him would be so gruesome. Verses 20–22 show, the outcome occurred just as Joseph said they would.

DREAMS COME TRUE

The third day was Pharaoh's birthday, and he gave a feast for all his officials. He lifted up the heads of both the chief cupbearer, and the chief baker in the presence of his officials, which probably meant he put them on trial. The outcome was, rather than beheading the chief cupbearer, he restored him to his position, but he beheaded the chief baker and impaled his body on a pole, just as Joseph said in his interpretations. Neither should have been surprised by their fate, but the chief baker's fate was no less horrifying.

Verse 23 shows that when the cupbearer got his job back, he did not remember Joseph. In fact, it clearly says he forgot him! The cupbearer did not remember Joseph because the time had not yet come for him to do so. He was not the one orchestrating Joseph's situation, God was! Had the cupbearer remembered Joseph, and prematurely gotten him released from prison, what was he going to do with his life? Where would he find a job? His only skills so far were in management, and as a foreigner, with a criminal record, who was going to trust and hire him to manage anything?

For Joseph to have gotten out of prison when he wanted, meant he would have ended up in a dead-end situation. Besides, he was still Potiphar's slave, and since he was profitable to his master, only someone higher in rank than his master could change his situation. Joseph needed to hang on a little longer to see how God would bring to fruition the dreams He had given him before he was uprooted from his father's household in the land of Canaan.

GENESIS CHAPTER FORTY-ONE

The previous chapter highlighted Joseph's time in prison, where he found favor in the eyes of the warden, and enjoyed continued favor with his master, the captain of the guard. Details were given about his interactions with two of his fellow prisoners, who were former employees of the king; specifically, the king's chief cupbearer, and his chief baker, who both had dreams, to which Joseph provided interpretations. His interpretations came to pass, and the chief cupbearer was restored to his former position, while the chief baker was put to death.

Joseph made a request to the chief cupbearer, asking him to remember him, when he was restored to his position, but he soon forgot him. This chapter will examine circumstances, which eventually caused the chief cupbearer to remember Joseph, and which resulted in Joseph's sudden move from the prison to the palace, and ultimately to becoming second in charge of the entire country of Egypt. It will present a contrast between wisdom, which comes from God, and counterfeits, which surrounded Pharoah.

PHARAOH'S DREAMS

Verses 1-8 indicate that when two full years had passed, Pharaoh had a dream. In this dream, he saw himself standing by the Nile, when seven cows came up out of the river, sleek and fat, and they grazed among the reeds. After them, seven other cows, ugly and gaunt, came up out of the Nile, and stood next to those on the riverbank. The cows that were ugly and gaunt ate up the seven sleek, fat cows. Then Pharaoh woke up!

He fell asleep again and had a second dream. This time, he saw seven heads of grain, that were healthy and good, growing on a single stalk. After them, seven other heads of grain sprouted, which were thin and scorched by the east wind. The thin heads of grain swallowed up the seven healthy, full heads. Then Pharaoh woke up and was glad it was only a dream.

Notice, Pharaoh's dreams occurred when two full years had passed. During that time Joseph remained in prison, longing for his freedom, and probably wondering if God had forgotten him. Now, Pharaoh was not a worshipper of the Most-High God, and yet, God spoke to him by way of dreams and showed him the future before He showed it to Joseph. In his dreams, Pharaoh saw unusual things, such as cows, which are herbivores, behaving like carnivores, and devouring their own kind. Then he saw heads of grain, which have no capacity to eat, devouring other heads of grain. These images were so strange that they deeply troubled Pharaoh and caused him to become aware that a divine hand was behind them. It was these dreams, and the inability of anyone else in Egypt to interpret them, which caused the cupbearer to remember Joseph.

PHARAOH SUMMONED JOSEPH

Notice, verse 9 shows, the cupbearer said to Pharaoh, "Today I am reminded of my shortcomings." Those were beautiful words of repentance! It would be easy to criticize this man for forgetting about Joseph's request. But once again, it would have been premature for Joseph to have been released from the dungeon earlier, and God saw to it that he wasn't, until the right time. However, this man should be applauded for acknowledging his shortcomings, and addressing them as soon as he recognized them.

Continuing in verses 10–14, the chief cupbearer reminded Pharaoh about when he was angry with his servants, and when he imprisoned him, along with the chief baker, in the house of the captain of the guard. He told him, while in prison, both of them had a dream on the same night, and each dream had a meaning of its own. There was a young Hebrew there, in prison with them, a servant of the captain of the guard, they told him their dreams, and he interpreted them, giving each man the interpretation of his dream. He said things turned out exactly as the Hebrew said they would. He was restored to his position, while the chief baker was impaled. Having heard this, Pharaoh sent for Joseph, and he was quickly brought from the dungeon.

Notice where the chief cupbearer said he was imprisoned: in the house of the captain of the guard. Who was the captain of the guard? Potiphar! Therefore, since Joseph was also imprisoned there, it meant he really did not leave home when his master became angry with him. However, his living conditions most likely changed, such that he considered himself to have been consigned to a dungeon. This also explains why the warden trusted Joseph and showed favor to him. He knew him! In fact, as head of Potiphar's house, it is likely Joseph used to be his boss.

When the time came for Pharaoh to send for Joseph, it was the opportunity of a lifetime for him, and he needed to capitalize during the lifetime of the opportunity. He had been thoroughly trained in managing Potiphar's house and personal affairs. He had also been trained in running Potiphar's prison; albeit he was an inmate there, but it prepared him for the massive promotion of running a country. What an awesome promotion it was! He literally moved from the prison to the palace! He was about to become a Prince of Egypt! As a slave of the captain of the guard, only someone with Pharaoh's rank could change his circumstances. Therefore, he needed to make the best of the opportunity before him.

JOSEPH PREPARES TO MEET PHARAOH

As Joseph prepared to make the best of the opportunity before him, observe what verse 14 says: Pharaoh sent for him, and he was quickly brought from the dungeon. However, he did not go before the king looking like someone who had just ascended from a dungeon; Instead, it says he shaved and changed his clothes, before going to Pharaoh. In other words, he cleaned himself up and took off his prison clothes, before going into the palace and presence of the king. Joseph, who was handsome and well-built, understood even then that people are judged by their appearance.

PHARAOH REHEARSED DETAILS OF HIS DREAMS

Verse 15 shows Pharaoh began his discourse with Joseph by cutting straight to the purpose for which he summoned him. There were no introductory niceties, or inquiries about Joseph's plight; instead, Pharaoh began by telling him, "I had a dream, and no one can interpret it. But I heard it said of you that when you hear a dream you can interpret it." On hearing this from the king, Joseph could have gotten a big head and said, "Yeah, I have been known to interpret a few dreams in my time!" But notice in verse 16 he said, "I cannot do it, but God will give Pharaoh the answer he desires." In essence, he deflected the glory from himself, and directed it to God, where it rightfully belonged.

Verses 17–21 show that Pharaoh proceeded to rehearse to Joseph the details of his dreams. He told him in his first dream, he was standing on the bank of the Nile, when out of the river came seven cows, fat and sleek, and they grazed among the reeds. After them, seven other cows came up—scrawny and very ugly and lean. He said he had never seen such ugly cows in all the land of Egypt. The lean, ugly cows ate up the seven fat cows, which came up first. After they ate them, no one could tell they had done so; they looked just as lean and ugly as before! Then he woke up.

In verses 22–24, he proceeded to inform Joseph about his second dream, once he was able to go back to sleep. He said he dreamt he saw seven heads of grain, full and good, growing on a single stalk. After them, seven other heads sprouted, withered and thin and scorched by the east wind. The thin heads of grain swallowed up the seven good heads. He told his dreams to the magicians, but none of them could explain them to him.

JOSEPH PROVIDES INTERPRETATIONS TO PHARAOH'S DREAMS

After patiently listening to the details of Pharaoh's dreams, verses 25–32 show Joseph's response. He informed Pharaoh that the two dreams were one and the same. He told him God had revealed to him what he was about to do. The seven good cows were seven years, and the seven good heads of grain were seven years; it was one and the same dream. The seven lean, ugly cows. which came up afterward, were seven years, and so were the seven worthless heads of grain scorched by the east wind: They were seven years of famine.

He reiterated that it was just as he said before: God was showing Pharaoh what He was about to do. Seven years of great abundance were coming throughout the land of Egypt, but seven years of famine would follow. All the abundance in Egypt would be forgotten, and the famine would ravage the land. The abundance in the land would not be remembered, because the famine would be so severe. Joseph closed his interpretations by telling Pharaoh, the reason the dream was given to him in two forms, was because the matter had been firmly decided by God, and God would soon do it.

If God had given those dreams to anyone else in Egypt other than Pharaoh, he probably would not have believed them if they were told to him. However, God gave them directly to him in two forms, because as Joseph said, the matter was firmly decided by God, and it was imminent. Therefore, Pharaoh should have considered it an honor that God of the universe spoke directly to him and gave him forewarning of what He was about to do.

Once again, it was interesting that God did not forewarn Jacob, a righteous man, who lived in the Promised Land, about the famine, which would affect that land also; instead, he informed Pharaoh, a pagan king. Yet, the outcome was more for Jacob's benefit than for Pharaoh's. God would use this famine to deliver Jacob and reunite him with all his sons. Most importantly,

Joseph's childhood dreams would come true, his sheaf would rise, and his family's sheaves would bow before his (Gen 37:7–11).

JOSEPH'S COUNSEL TO PHARAOH

Joseph did not only provide Pharaoh with Godly interpretations of his dreams, but he also provided him with Godly counsel about how to prepare for the disaster God forewarned him about. Verses 33–36 reveal that he advised Pharaoh to look for a discerning and wise man and put him in charge of the land of Egypt. He also encouraged him to appoint commissioners over the land, to take a fifth of the harvest of Egypt during the seven years of abundance. He said they should collect all the food from the seven good years that were coming and store up the grain under the authority of Pharaoh, to be kept in the cities for food. This food should be held in reserve for the country, to be used during the seven years of famine, which would soon come upon Egypt, so that the country would not be ruined.

If Joseph had not advised Pharaoh about how to prepare for the disaster ahead, it was doubtful Pharaoh, or anyone else in his kingdom, would have known how to prepare for it. His magicians were certainly no help to him at that time. Therefore, Joseph displayed wisdom, which Pharaoh recognized was lacking in those who were leaders in his kingdom. In other words, Pharaoh immediately became aware of what the captain of his guard already knew, that God was with Joseph.

PHARAOH'S RESPONSE TO JOSEPH'S COUNSEL

Verses 37–40 indicate that the counsel Joseph proposed seemed good to Pharaoh and to all his officials. He asked his officials, "Can we find anyone like this man, one in whom is the Spirit of God (the gods)?" Pharaoh told Joseph, since God made all he spoke of known to him, there was no one so discerning and wise as him. Therefore, he declared that Joseph should be in charge of his palace, and all his people were to submit to his orders. Only with respect to the throne was he greater than Joseph. This was quite a promotion!

Joseph's proposal for Pharaoh to select a discerning and wise man and put him in charge of the land of Egypt, initially met the approval of Pharaoh's officials, because each of them may have hoped to be the one selected. However, their approval may have waned once Pharaoh revealed the person, whom he would select, would be Joseph. Not only did he put him over the rest of Egypt (the land), but he also put him in charge of the palace.

Potiphar, Joseph's former slave master may have been among those officials who were present at that occasion. One of two conclusions can be drawn if this was the case: it was either a source of pride that someone from his household reached such a level of prominence; Or it was more likely Joseph's promotion sent a fearful shockwave through him and his household, considering the treatment he received after being wrongfully accused of attempted rape. Thankfully, Joseph saw it as God's way of getting him out of the dungeon and placing him where he needed to be to become a savior for Israel.

Despite all Joseph had done as a slave in Potiphar's house, and an inmate in his prison, he was not promoted because of a recommendation from his master, or anyone in his master's household. Instead, his opportunity came because of a recommendation from someone who was with him in the dungeon. Most importantly, he was promoted because of his relationship with the true God, who gave him insight to interpret dreams. Pharaoh was a heathen, but when he promoted Joseph, he also promoted Joseph's God over other gods in his kingdom, as he recognized the Spirit of God operating in Joseph's life.

PHARAOH'S EFFORTS TO TRANSFORM JOSEPH

Verses 41–45 reveal that Pharaoh put Joseph in charge of the whole land of Egypt. Then he took his signet ring from his finger and put it on Joseph's finger. He dressed him in robes of fine linen and put a gold chain around his neck. He had him ride in a chariot as his second-in-command, and people shouted before him, "Make way (Bow down)!" Thus, he put him in charge of the whole land of Egypt. Then Pharaoh said to Joseph, "I am Pharaoh, but without your word no one will lift hand or foot in all Egypt." He gave Joseph the name Zaphenath-Paneah (Revealer of Secrets) and gave him Asenath, daughter of Potiphera, priest of On (Heliopolis), to be his wife. And Joseph went throughout the land of Egypt.

In his efforts to transform Joseph, Pharaoh gave him a new name to signify his authority over him. The Bible does not reveal how others in Pharaoh's kingdom responded to Joseph's promotion, but it was quite likely some, if not many, were jealous and did not like it. Certainly, the magicians, who were unable to interpret Pharaoh's dreams, were likely objectors, because Joseph showed up their craft for the counterfeit it was, and always will be.

Notice, Pharaoh also gave Asenath to Joseph to be his wife. She was not given by her father, but by the king, so Joseph could not refuse her.

The Bible is silent about their marriage, but conceivably, being married to a woman who, as daughter of the priest of On (Heliopolis), was immersed in idolatry from her youth, would have presented challenges for Joseph, a man who worshipped the true God. Additionally, this marriage would have been unusually interesting because Genesis 43:32, indicates that Egyptians did not even eat with Hebrews. Thankfully, their sons identified with their Israelite, rather than their Egyptian heritage.

The king's declaration: "I am Pharaoh, but without your word, no one will lift a hand or foot in all Egypt," seemed to be affirmation of Joseph in the face of opposition from others. It seemed to be the king's way of telling Joseph and others, the only person in the kingdom he needed to answer to was Pharaoh. He placed his entire kingdom in Joseph's hands. However, in all of this, Joseph was a perfect example of what it meant to be in the world, but not of the world (John 17:15-16). He was in Egypt, but he was not of Egypt. In fact, he insisted that after his death, not even his bones be allowed to remain buried there (Gen 50:25).

JOSEPH IN PHARAOH'S SERVICE

Verse 46 says Joseph was thirty years old when he entered the service of Pharaoh, king of Egypt. This meant it took Joseph approximately thirteen years to rise from the dysfunctional home of his father Jacob, and from a life of slavery, which included a few years of imprisonment, to becoming second-in-command in Egypt. God truly changed his environment. No longer was he a dreamer, hated by his jealous brothers and struggling to survive in the bottom of a pit, no longer was he a slave in Potiphar's house being seduced by his wife, no longer was he a prisoner waiting for the day his innocence would be proven, now he was second in authority in all of Egypt, and now he was also Potiphar's boss. Joseph had come a mighty long way!

It is reasonable to wonder if Joseph and Potiphar ever had a conversation about Mrs. Potiphar. She was not able to get Joseph to go to bed with her, but she may have been able to get some other handsome, well-built man to do it. It is also reasonable to wonder if the Potiphars stayed together, or if their marriage ended due to her passion for an extramarital affair. These concerns have not been Biblically addressed, but as for Joseph, his example showed that honesty and integrity triumphs in the end.

Verses 47-49 state that during the seven years of abundance, the land produced plentifully. Therefore, Joseph collected all the food produced in those seven years of abundance, and stored it in the cities. In each city he put the food grown in the fields surrounding it. He stored up huge quantities of grain, like the sand of the sea; it was so much that he stopped keeping records because it was beyond measure. Joseph had explained to Pharaoh that it would take someone with wisdom to store up during the years of plenty, for the lean years, which were ahead. He displayed that wisdom by storing up beyond measure. His example is still relevant, as lean years are always a threat to every family, community, and nation.

JOSEPH'S FAMILY

Having been given an Egyptian wife by Pharaoh, Joseph knew years of famine would not be a good time for babies to be born. Hence, verses 50–52 reveal that before the years of famine came, two sons were born to Joseph by his Egyptian wife, Asenath daughter of Potiphera, priest of On. Joseph named his firstborn Manasseh to signify that God had made him forget all his trouble, and all his father's household. The second son he named Ephraim because God had made him fruitful in the land of his suffering.

With approximately twenty years having passed, life in Canaan for Jacob and his family may have returned to as normal as possible without Joseph around. There was no evidence to suggest his brothers thought much about him, and it is not clear how much Joseph thought about them, and about his father. He was compelled to carry on life in Egypt, though his heart was broken and could not be mended by anything Egypt had to offer. He made it to the top, but the people who mattered most were not there to see it or share in it; at least not yet. In other words, though he had become successful, life in Egypt was probably full of emptiness for Joseph. There are many successful people today who can identify with this. They are empty because those who matter most to them are not there to share their success. Victory is very unfulfilling to those who are lonely.

It is reasonable to wonder why Joseph did not take a trip back home to Canaan after he became so powerful in Egypt. It is possible he may not have been able to go back because he did not have time to do so. His promotion was specifically to prepare Egypt for the years of famine that were shortly ahead. As such, he was a busy man, not to mention, God was in charge, and He would choose the right time for Joseph to reunite with his family. In any case, the names he gave his sons revealed that he had not gotten over what his brothers did to him, even though he could also see God's hand in it.

THE FAMINE

Verses 53–57 indicate that the seven years of abundance in Egypt came to an end, and the seven years of famine began, just as Joseph predicted. There was famine in all the other lands, but in the whole land of Egypt there was food. When all Egypt began to feel the impact of the famine, the people cried to Pharaoh for food. Then Pharaoh told them to go to Joseph and do whatever he told them. When the famine spread over the whole country, Joseph opened all the storehouses and sold grain to the Egyptians, because the famine was severe throughout Egypt. All the world came to Egypt to buy grain from Joseph, because the famine was severe everywhere.

It is interesting that even though Pharaoh made Joseph second-in-charge, and had him traveling throughout Egypt for seven years, leading the famine relief effort, once the famine began, the people did not cry out to Joseph, instead, they cried out to Pharaoh. He was their leader and his reputation depended on Joseph doing his job the way he was supposed and trusted to. Therefore, as the famine started, the wisdom of Joseph's counsel began to pay off for Pharaoh. He understood exactly what was going on and he expected it. Consequently, when his people began to cry out to him, he gave them one answer, "Go to Joseph (Zaphenath-Paneah) and do what he tells you." In other words, Joseph made Pharaoh appear to be the wisest leader in the world, because he and his country were prepared for the famine, while others were not. In fact, other countries had to depend on Egypt for their survival.

Those who despised Joseph because of the promotion he received, were finally able to see the wisdom in it. He made Pharaoh a profit on his investment in storing up all the grain he could during the years of plenty. Most importantly, he saved Egypt and those who depended on it, from the ravages of famine. He would soon learn that his family in Canaan would be among those whom he would save. This would also help him understand more clearly God's purpose for his life all along.

GENESIS CHAPTER FORTY-TWO

In the previous chapter it was shown that Pharaoh's dreams, and the inability of anyone in his kingdom to interpret them, caused his chief cupbearer to remember his old friend Joseph. He recommended Joseph to the king, because he remembered he interpreted his dream, and that of the chief baker, while they were imprisoned together. Their dreams unfolded just as Joseph said they would. On hearing this, Pharaoh summoned Joseph, told him his dreams, and God gave him the interpretation. His dreams were forewarnings about a dreadful famine in the near future, which required immediate action to reduce its impact upon Egypt.

Joseph was chosen to lead the famine-relief effort, and his situation drastically changed, as he was suddenly promoted from the prison to the palace. No longer was he a slave in Egypt, instead he became a savior of it. Once the famine finally started, he skillfully implemented and managed relief efforts, which saved Egypt, and surrounding countries.

This chapter will examine events surrounding Joseph's first encounter with his brothers, who came to Egypt to buy food. They did not recognize him as the one from whom they were buying it, but he recognized them, and used the encounter with them to learn firsthand details about how the plan to sell him into slavery was conceived. Finally, this chapter will describe the plan Joseph used to draw other members of his family to Egypt.

JACOB SENDS HIS SONS TO EGYPT TO BUY FOOD

Verses 1–2 begin with an interesting introduction. It says Jacob saw there was grain in Egypt and asked his sons why they were simply staring at each other. He told them he had heard there was grain in Egypt, and he commanded them to go there and buy some so they may live and not die. The remarkable paradox here was, Jacob and his sons were living in the Promised Land, yet they were not sheltered from the problems of the world. They experienced famine just as others did, and their main source of food was to be found in Egypt.

Jacob scolded his sons for simply staring at each other and doing nothing to address the situation at hand. It was as if each of them was waiting on the other to make a move! Obviously, the reason Jacob heard there was grain in Egypt was because others had gone there, seen there was grain, bought some, and came back and shared the good news! However, it appears as if his sons simply did not want to go to Egypt. They may have either been too proud to do so, hoping the situation in Canaan might change, or they may have been waiting on him to tell them what to do.

Recall, it was mentioned back in chapter thirty-seven, that Jacob's love for his sons (Joseph and Benjamin) from his wife Rachel, was by far stronger than his love for his sons from the three other women with whom he had offspring. This fact will be highlighted in the following verses, which will show the family dynamics after Joseph was taken from them. The only son who came close to being the new favorite was Benjamin.

Notice verses 3-4, which show that while the other ten sons went to Egypt to buy grain, Benjamin stayed at home with his father. In other words, Benjamin did what Joseph use to do! Jacob did not allow him to go because he was afraid harm might befall him. He did not seem to have such fear for his other sons. Benjamin became a sheltered kid and there was nothing the other sons could do to acquire the love their father had for Rachel's sons. This meant the jealousy they had for Joseph, which caused them to sell him, did not change the fundamental problem, which was really with their father. He was the one who showed favoritism.

Verse 5 notes that the sons of Israel went to buy grain along with others, because the famine was also in the land of Canaan. This may indicate how Jacob heard there was grain in Egypt. Other residents of the land of Canaan routinely went to Egypt, purchased food, and came back and told him. His sons seemed to be among the only holdouts who were reluctant to go.

JOSEPH RECOGNIZED HIS BROTHERS

Verse 6 indicates that Joseph was ruler over the land and was the one who sold grain to all the people. Therefore, the messengers who told Jacob about the abundance of grain in Egypt, should have encountered Joseph, but they either did not know him, or did not recognize him. The fact that they did not recognize him was interesting. It is not clear if any of them would have known him as a young boy, but for whatever reason, they did not recognize him! This could have been because he was not supposed to be alive, in which case, if they knew him from his youth, they were not expecting to see him again, and would not have believed their eyes if they did.

It is uncertain if Joseph expected his brothers or someone from his family to come to Egypt, due to the severity of the famine. If he expected them, he may have been eagerly anticipating the moment he would lay eyes on them. However, little did he or they know, the very moment he encountered them, the dream he had (Gen 37:7) as a young boy would begin to become reality. Recall, in his dream, he and his brothers were in the field binding sheaves, when his sheaf rose up and stood erect, while his brothers' sheaves came and bowed down to his. This dream touched off hatred, which was already in them from seeing overt expressions of their father's love for him more than them. As such, notice in verse 6, when they arrived in Egypt and encountered him, they came and bowed down to him with their faces to the ground. Albeit they did not yet recognize who he was, but the symbolism of the dream was still there.

They did not recognize who he was, but he immediately recognized who they were. They did not recognize him, because it says he disguised himself and spoke harshly to them. It would be interesting to learn what physical methods Joseph used to disguise himself. However, the idea of disguising is common in today's society as well. People have become experts at hiding who they really are! This occurs in all walks of life, and the Church is no exception.

Most importantly, Joseph's disguise was symbolic of Jesus', whose Jewish brothers did not recognize him at his first coming. Therefore, the apostle Paul said (1 Cor 2:7–8), he spoke the wisdom of God in a mystery. . . which none of the rulers of his age knew, because had they known, they would not have crucified the Lord of glory. Hence, God hid the mystery of Christ so His redemptive work could be accomplished. They would not have crucified Him if they knew who He was. In a similar fashion, if Joseph's brothers had believed his dreams when he shared them as a young boy, they would not have sold him into slavery and the redemptive work he was positioned to do would not have occurred. In essence, God also hid who Joseph really was, his purpose in life, from his brothers.

Being in the presence of his brothers again for the first time in at least 20 years, Joseph's questions helped form the basis of his disguise. Observe verse 7, he asked them, "Where have you come from?" And they said, "From the land of Canaan, to buy food." This answer confirmed his first suspicion about their identity. Yet, again in verse 8, it says he recognized them, but they did not recognize him. The fact that they did not recognize him was necessary for Joseph to be in the position he was in, but it was also sad because biological, or spiritual brothers are supposed to be able to recognize each other. Hence, either Joseph pulled off the perfect disguise, or his brothers thought he was dead and did not expect him to be in the position in which he was, a ruler in Egypt.

Many things can change in twenty years. After such a long time, the sons of Israel may have been showing signs of aging. Some may have been losing their hair, or even their teeth. Those who still had hair may have been graying, but the one thing that remained unchanged, was Joseph's dreams, they would come to pass, and no efforts to sabotage them could change that! As such, verse 9 points out that after remembering his dream from 20 years earlier, to add to the mystery about his identity, Joseph accused them of being spies, who had come to see where the land of Egypt was unprotected.

This was a bold and scary accusation by such a high-ranking Egyptian official! If other Egyptians were present, from that moment on they kept a close eye on these men. Verses 10–11 show, the brothers denied the charge by saying, "No, my lord, your servants have come to buy food. We are all the sons of one man. Your servants are honest men, not spies."

Once again, much can change in 20 years, and Joseph would have known that most of the information in the brothers' responses was true. Having recognized them, he knew they had come to buy food, and were all sons of one man, but he needed to test their claim to be honest men. Those were the same men who threw him into a pit with the intention of killing him! Then they thought better of it, sold him, and lied about it to their father, claiming a wild animal had killed him! If they had become honest men, it would have been a miracle, which happened over time. It would have been interesting to learn what Joseph's thoughts were, on hearing such a claim.

To reinforce his disguise, Joseph insisted in verse 12 that indeed they were spies, who had come to see where the land was unprotected. They gave a heart-wrenching response to his assertion. They said in verse 13, "Your servants were twelve brothers, the sons of one man, who lives in the land of Canaan. The youngest is now with our father, and one is no more."

These men did not know whether Joseph was dead or alive, but to describe him in past tense, as one who once made up twelve sons, and then in the present tense, as being "no more," must have been difficult. What did they mean by "no more?" Did this mean he was no more a brother, or did it mean he was no more alive? Looking ahead to verse 22, it seems clear they thought Joseph was dead, which meant none of them remembered his dreams, and were unlikely to recognize him.

JOSEPH TEST HIS BROTHERS

Beginning in verses 15-17, clearer insight began to emerge about whether Joseph believed his brothers' assertion that they were honest men. He made a proposal to them: He said, "Send one of your number to get your brother; the rest of you will be kept in prison, so that your words may be tested to see if you are telling the truth. If you are not, then as surely as Pharaoh lives, you are spies!" Then he put them in custody for three days.

This was not the way you treated men whom you believe to be honest! Based on his own past, Joseph had reasons to be suspicious about the well-being of his younger brother Benjamin, and about whether these men would ever come back to Egypt if he let all of them go, especially, since they did not seem to want to go there in the first place, but were coerced by their father, and by circumstances.

In verses 18-20, after remanding them to custody for three days, Joseph slightly softened his proposal. He said to them, "Do this and you will live, for I fear God: If you are honest men, let one of your brothers stay here in prison, while the rest of you go and take grain back for your starving households. But you must bring your youngest brother to me, so that your words may be verified, and you may not die."

Notice, he began with a statement of his own honesty by letting them know he feared God. A person who truly fears God should be honest, because such a person is aware of God's unfavorable disposition toward dishonesty. Joseph's brothers claimed they were honest men, but they never gave him any reason to believe it. He gave them reason to believe his honesty by telling them of his fear of God. Since they did not give him any reason to believe they were honest men, he began his proposal with the words, "If you are honest men. . ."

When Joseph saw that his brothers had come to Egypt to buy grain, his immediate recollection was about the dream he had over 20 years earlier. However, the first hint of any sign that their sin against him was never far from their minds, was given in verse 21, where they said, "Surely, we are being punished because of our brother. We saw how distressed he was when he pleaded with us for his life, but we would not listen; that's why this distress has come upon us." They were convinced God was repaying them for what they had done to their brother, who they thought was "no more."

Verse 22 shows Reuben, the oldest brother, the one who wanted to rescue Joseph, and the one to whom they also lied about his whereabouts, said, "Didn't I tell you not to sin against the boy? But you wouldn't listen! Now we must give an accounting for his blood." This statement was a reference to the command God gave Noah and his sons (Gen 9:5-6). It is not clear if any of the other brothers honestly believed Joseph was dead, but Reuben may have honestly believed it, because they told him so, and he was not present when they sold him to the Ishmaelites. Obviously, Joseph was not dead, he was right there listening to them! He overheard first-hand details about what transpired when their vicious jealousy erupted against him. Verse 23, says they did not realize he could understand them, since he used an interpreter. This means Joseph also hid his Hebrew accent.

JOSEPH'S RESPONSE TO HIS BROTHER'S CONFESSIONS

On hearing his brothers discuss how the plan against him unfolded, the information weighed so heavy that verse 24 indicates, Joseph turned away from them and began to weep, then he came back and spoke to them again. It must have been difficult listening to such a devious plot, which was executed by his "brothers." Notice, after this he had Simeon bound before their eyes and taken from them.

Truly, Joseph had to fear God to hear such details and not react vengefully. Instead, he had Simeon bound before their eyes and taken from them. Maybe, he did this as a reminder to them of how he was bound. All of them deserved to be bound, but only Simeon was. Revenge would have been a reasonable human response from Joseph, but the evidence shows his response was Godlier than it was human.

It is not clear why Joseph chose to bind Simeon, rather than anyone else. Judah would have been a good choice since he devised the scheme to sell him. However, Genesis 34 shows Simeon was an especially fierce man. He and his brother Levi led the assault against Shechem and killed all the men of the city. Yet, in this case his power was muted in light of Joseph's power. As mighty as he thought he was, he was bound in the presence of his brothers, and there was nothing he or they could do about it. This obviously broke their spirits when they saw Simeon, the fierce one, bound and rendered helpless, which meant, the same could have been done to anyone of them.

JOSEPH'S PLAN TERRIFIED HIS FATHER AND BROTHERS

Verses 25–26 reveal Joseph gave orders to fill their bags with grain, put each man's silver back in his sack, and give them provisions for their journey.

After this was done for them, they loaded their grain on their donkeys and left; probably thinking their encounter with Joseph was over, because he terrified them! But verses 27–28 show that on their journey back to Canaan, they stopped for the night, and one of them opened his sack to get feed for his donkey. He saw his silver in the mouth of his sack and declared to his brothers, "My silver has been returned, here it is in my sack." Their hearts sank and they turned to each other trembling and said, "What is this that God has done to us?"

Joseph's kind gestures would normally have been viewed as underserved generosity, but his brothers did not view it that way, because their consciences bothered them. Hence, when they realized their silver had been returned, their hearts sank, they trembled, and blamed God for orchestrating a nefarious plan against them. They demonstrated unreasonable paranoia, which emanates from a guilty conscience.

Verses 30–35 show that once they made it back to Canaan, Jacob's sons rehearsed to him all the details of their trip, and their encounter with Joseph. They told him the man who was lord over the land spoke harshly to them and treated them as though they were spies. They said they told the man they were not spies, but honest men. They told him they were twelve brothers, sons of one father, one was no more, and the youngest was with their father in Canaan.

On hearing the youngest was with their father, they said the man told them, he would test their honesty by having one of them left in prison in Egypt, while the others took food for their starving households. Most importantly, they said the man insisted they bring their youngest brother to him, so he would know they were not spies, but honest men. The man told them if they followed his instructions, he would give their brother back to them, and they could trade in the land.

They also told their father that as they were emptying their sacks, in each man's sack was his pouch of silver. When they and their father saw the money pouches, he and they were frightened! They communicated everything to their father, except one important thing. They did not tell him the man said, he feared God. That was the only thing he said, which should have assured them he was also an honest man, and one who would keep his word, if they did all he told them to do.

While Joseph's acts of kindness were viewed by his brothers as part of a nefarious plan, because they had guilty consciences, it was viewed that way by his father as well, because he had an inconsolable heart of grief. Notice, his response in verses 36–37: he accused them of trying to deprive him of his children. He said Joseph was no more, and Simeon was no more, and he loathed the fact that they wanted to take Benjamin from him. He concluded that everything was against him! In that moment, he seemed to forget every promise God made concerning his offspring. He saw them decreasing, rather than increasing as God promised.

His thoughts that life was against him, was far from the truth! The fact was everything was for him! God was working out everything for his good, and for the good of his family, but he was not yet able to see it, because the plan of God was still unfolding. Jacob's misconception is a common human thought to this day. When adversity comes, it is still common for people to think everything is against them, especially when God's divine hand is unseen.

Continuing in verse 37, Reuben tried to reassure his father by offering him permission to put both of his own sons to death, if he did not bring Benjamin back. In other words, he swore on the life of his sons! But verse 38 shows Jacob refused and said, "My son will not go down there with you; his brother is dead, and he is the only one left. If harm comes to him on the journey you are taking, you will bring my gray head down to the grave in sorrow." Besides, Jacob was probably hesitant to trust Reuben with Benjamin's safety, because when Reuben slept with his father's concubine (Gen 35:22), he proved he could not be trusted. Therefore, he lost favor with his father.

Once again, Jacob showed his partiality toward Rachel's two sons. He thought one (Joseph) was dead, and he was vehement about preserving the life of the other (Benjamin). Not to mention, he seemed to be intimating that if he had to lose another son, he would rather it be Simeon than his baby boy Benjamin. His sons said they were honest men, but their father's conduct showed he did not view them as such. He did not trust them! In fact, it would take an escalation in the severity of the famine in Canaan, before Jacob would change his mind. His sons swore on their own lives, and the lives of their children, yet to Jacob, none of them was worth as much to him as Benjamin.

Despite all his sons and grandsons, which he still had with him, Jacob considered Benjamin the only one left, because he was the only one of Rachel's sons left. This added insult to injury, because the situation the brothers were hoping to solve by ridding the family of Joseph, was not solved. Instead, Benjamin took Joseph's place as their father's favorite son and they all knew it.

GENESIS CHAPTER FORTY-THREE

In the previous chapter, it was shown that Joseph's brothers, like other inhabitants of countries affected by the famine, came to Egypt to buy grain. Joseph immediately recognized them, but they did not recognize him because he disguised himself from them. Part of his disguise was the harsh way he spoke to them, accusing them of being spies. In so doing, he lured them into revealing more about the family they came from, and about a younger brother they had, who was at home with their father. On hearing this, Joseph imprisoned Simeon, asserting that he would test their honesty until they returned with their youngest brother.

He also sent them on their way with grain, while returning to them the money they thought they had paid for it. This chapter will examine details of their second trip to Egypt, this time bringing Benjamin along with them. A review will be made of their efforts to convince their father to send Benjamin on the journey. Finally, Simeon's release from prison, and the brothers' reunion will be discussed.

JUDAH REPLACES REUBEN AS LEADER OF THE BROTHERS

Verses 1–2 point out that the famine was still severe in the land. When they had eaten all the grain they had brought from Egypt, their father asked them to go back and buy a little more food. Observe, the famine was so severe that Jacob did not ask his sons to go buy a lot more food, but under the circumstances, he was content to make do with just a little more. He realized if he could get a little more, he would still have more than many others. Rather than trying to hoard plenty for himself and his family, he was probably trying to get by with as little as possible in the hope that better days were soon coming. Indeed, famines of any kind are difficult while they last, but they do not last forever.

Recall, in the previous chapter, Reuben tried unsuccessfully to convince his father to entrust Benjamin to his care in order to return to Egypt and secure Simeon's release. He even told his father if he did not bring Benjamin back safely, he could put his two sons to death. Yet, that was not enough to convince his father to entrust Benjamin to his care.

However, verses 3–5 indicate Judah, rather than Reuben, spoke up this time, and told his father, the man had solemnly warned them they would not see his face again, unless their brother was with them. As such, he told his father if he would send Benjamin along with them, they would go down and buy food for him. But, if he would not send him, they would not go, because of what the man said.

Judah was the one who orchestrated the sale of his brother Joseph to the Ishmaelites (Gen 37:26). After he did this, Genesis 38:1 shows he left his father's household and went to live in Adullam with a friend named Hirah. He married a Canaanite woman, and together they had three sons. Two of his sons died, then his wife later died. He subsequently slept with his daughter-in-law, Tamar, assuming she was a prostitute, and together they had twin sons, Perez and Zerah. Obviously, by the time the famine occurred he had returned to the area where his father and brothers lived.

Jacob was undoubtedly still torn by what happened to Joseph many years earlier and was concerned the same could happen to Benjamin. He did not want to lose both of Rachel's sons. However, the way Judah presented his case, Jacob was left with few reasonable options. He asserted that the only way he and his brothers would risk their safety, was if Jacob was willing to risk Benjamin's safety, and the entire family's survival rested on his decision.

Verse 6 shows that Jacob tried to resist the inevitable, by asking his sons why they brought trouble on him by telling the man they had another brother. He simply did not want Benjamin to go, and tried to reason, after the fact, about alternatives, which may have allowed him to avoid sending him with them. However, no such alternatives made sense, because God was working it out for his good, even though he could not yet see it.

In verse 7, they explained to their father that they did not have the benefit of hindsight, as he did. They told him, the man questioned them closely about themselves and their family. They said, he asked them if their father was still alive. He asked if they had another brother. They simply answered his questions, not knowing he would tell them to bring their brother to him.

Judah then pressed his case to convince his father to send Benjamin along with him, by saying if he would do so, they would leave at once, so they and he, and their children may live and not die. He said he would guarantee Benjamin's safety. He told his father he could hold him personally responsible for him. He promised that if he did not bring him back, he would bear the blame before him all his life. These claims showed how much Jacob valued Benjamin above his other sons, and sadly, it also shows, his sons knew it. In other words, they were clear about who the favorites were.

Despite the dysfunctional circumstances of Jacob's household, his sons were determined to get on with the business at hand since it was a matter of life or death for the family. Hence, in verse 10, they told their father, if they had not delayed spending so much time trying to convince him to send Benjamin along with them, they could have gone to Egypt and returned twice! They were obviously being sarcastic, but the seriousness of the situation was, their father cared little about their safety, or if they had indeed gone to Egypt and returned twice, he only cared about the safety of Benjamin, and about his return, if he allowed him to go there once.

Ultimately, he seemed more willing to entrust Benjamin to Judah's care than to the care of Reuben, who seemed incapable of repairing their broken relationship, which occurred when he slept with his father's concubine (Gen 35:22).

JACOB'S INSTRUCTIONS

After concluding there was no other way out of his predicament, verses 11–14 show Jacob agreed to allow Benjamin to go to Egypt with his brothers. He told them, if it must be, then do it. He prepared them for the journey by telling them to put some of the best products of the land in their bags, and take them to the man as a gift, a little balm and a little honey, some spices and myrrh, some pistachio nuts and almonds.

He also instructed them to take double the amount of silver with them, and to return the silver that was put back into the mouths of their sacks, assuming it was a mistake. Most importantly, he told them to take their brother also and go back to the man at once. He prayed that God Almighty (El-Shaddai) would grant them mercy before the man, so that he will let their other brother and Benjamin come back with them. Pertaining to himself, he resolved, if it meant he would be bereaved, then he would be bereaved.

Jacob was previously vehement in his determination to refrain from allowing Benjamin to go down to Egypt with his brothers (Gen 42:38). However, after further consideration, he probably concluded that Benjamin's chances of survival were better in Egypt, where at least there was food, than they were in Canaan, where there was very little. The gifts Jacob instructed his sons to take along with them, indicated they still had a few things on hand in Canaan. Balm, honey, spices, and myrrh, were valuable, and may not have been readily available in Egypt. Pistachios, and almonds, were also important, but by themselves were not enough to make up a balanced meal, and, due to the famine, it would not be long before they too would become scarce; they needed grain.

Notice, Jacob instructed his sons to return the money, which was put back in the mouths of their sacks and take double the amount as a gesture of their honesty and willingness to compensate for any mistakes, which may have occurred. His instructions were wise, as they showed he placed greater value on food than on money. Having done all of this, he prayed for the mercies of God, because he knew this was what his sons would need, to be successful in dealing with a man they said dealt harshly with them (Gen 42:30).

Verse 15 indicates that his sons followed his instructions. They took the gifts and double the amount of silver, and they took Benjamin also. Then, they hurried down to Egypt and presented themselves to Joseph.

PREPARING FOR A MEAL AT JOSEPH'S HOUSE

When they arrived in Egypt with all the gifts their father had them take back with them to appease the ruler they encountered, not knowing it was their brother, and their father's beloved son Joseph, verse 16 says when Joseph saw Benjamin with them, he told his steward to take them to his house, slaughter an animal and prepare a meal so they could eat with him at noon. They would get to meet and have lunch with the second highest official in Egypt, and little did they know, he was the brother, whom they hated, intended to kill, but thought better of it, and sold into slavery. What an incredible lunch meeting this would be!

Verses 17-18 indicate the absolute terror Joseph's brothers experienced at hearing they were to eat with him at noon. It says Joseph's steward did as his master instructed him and took the men to his house. However, the men were frightened when they were taken to his house. They thought they were taken there because of the silver, which was put back into their sacks after the first trip. They concluded that Joseph wanted to attack them, overpower them, seize them as slaves, and take their donkeys. How ridiculous!

Their guilty consciences caused them to suspect Joseph's intentions in a negative way. They were sure he would harm them, but none seemed to wonder why he would bring them to his house and feed them before doing so! They thought this meeting had to do with the silver, which was returned to them, and as recompense, they expected to be attacked, overpowered, enslaved, and dispossessed. In other words, they saw no hope for themselves! Benjamin was with them, and he had not done any of those things! They were totally irrational, as they charged themselves with crimes Joseph had no intentions of bringing against them.

Verses 19–22, show they went to Joseph's steward and spoke to him at the entrance to the house, hoping he could mediate their case for them. They introduced themselves politely and proceeded to rehearse to him their coming to Egypt the first time to buy food, but on their return home, at the place where they stopped for the night, they opened their sacks and each of them found his silver, the exact weight, in the mouth of his sack. They brought it back with them along with additional silver to buy food. They said they didn't know who put the silver back in their sacks.

Verse 23 shows the steward's response, and his kind words to them. He said, "It's alright, don't be afraid." He also hinted Joseph's spiritual influence on his life. He told them, their God, the God of their father, had given them treasure in their sacks, and that he (the steward) had received their silver. Notice, this Egyptian steward said their God, rather than gods, and the God of their father, rather than the gods of Pharaoh gave them treasure. He spoke of God in singular terms, rather than plural, as most Egyptians would have. How did he know about their God? It was quite likely Joseph told him about Him.

He also informed them that the grain they thought they received free of charge, was paid for by someone other than them. He said he received their silver, because the God of their father had given them treasure in their sacks. In other words, the God of their father may have used Joseph to pay the price on their behalf, without their knowledge. Clearly, Joseph had given orders to put the silver back in their sacks (Gen 42:25), but the steward's words infer that God used him to do it. This should have perplexed the brothers further, especially since following this startling pronouncement, the steward brought Simeon out to them. He was kept as collateral, until they returned with Benjamin.

THE SECOND ENCOUNTER

Anticipation was probably running high for Joseph and his brothers. While they were eager to find out why they were being treated differently and afforded such attention, Joseph probably could not wait to get home to spend time with them, and to see them again. As such, verses 24–26 reveal that the steward took them all into the house, gave them water to wash their feet, and provided straw for their animals to eat. Meanwhile, they prepared their gifts for Joseph and waited for his arrival, because they were told they were to eat with him at noon.

When he came home, they presented him the gifts they had brought into the house, and they bowed down before him to the ground. Here was another incident of the fulfillment of Joseph's dream, as recorded in Genesis 37:7. That was the very dream, which exacerbated their hate and anger against him. Notice verse 27, his first question to them was, "How are you?" Maybe, he asked this question because he knew they were scared.

There is no record of their response to that question, but no doubt, if a response was given, it may have been as superficial as a response would be today. Today, when a stranger asks, "how are you doing?" whether or not this is true, the trivial response is usually, "fine!" Joseph also asked them how was their aged father they told him about, and was he still alive? In verse 28, they responded to this question and assured him their father was still alive and well, and again they bowed down, prostrating themselves before him, and fulfilling the dream he had in Genesis 37:7.

It should be noted that Joseph did not have dreams because he found pleasure in them and longed for them to come true. Instead, he had dreams because God gave them to him, and they were certainly going to be fulfilled. They were also meant to provide Joseph the comfort he needed amid trials, and assurance for a brighter future. Incidentally, it would have been an unimaginable blow to him if they had responded and told him his father was no longer alive. This would have been devastating! But the dream revealed he would yet be alive, and he was.

Verse 29, indicates that when Joseph saw his brother Benjamin, he asked them, "Is this your youngest brother, the one you told me about?" And he said to Benjamin, "God be gracious to you, my son." Notice, in his inquiries about his father and then about his brother, to keep up his disguise, he reminded them that they had told him about them. The question begs to be asked, did they not see any resemblances between him and them? Their minds were obviously blinded until the appropriate time! No doubt, to this point Joseph probably continued to speak to them through an interpreter, so they could not recognize him.

This is what happens to believers before spiritual transformation occurs. Prior to that time, their minds are blinded, but after their eyes are opened, they look back and can easily identify events which brought them to that moment. However, it should be noted that believers are sometimes unable to recognize each other, which causes them to become as suspicious about each other's motives as Joseph's brothers were about his.

Joseph pronounced a powerful blessing on Benjamin because he was the only one of the brothers who was totally innocent, and who had no involvement or knowledge of what the others had done. He had no part in it whatsoever! In fact, as the only remaining son of Rachel, and because of Jacob's love for him as it was for Joseph, Benjamin may have been hated like Joseph was, and may have endured a lonely life, even though he was a member of a large family. Clearly, his father saw the need to protect him from them, as he may have become suspicious over the years about whether they did indeed have something to do with Joseph's disappearance.

In any case, Joseph was very encouraged to see Benjamin, who was his only brother from his mother Rachel. All the other brothers had a different mother, as Jacob had a truly blended and fragmented family. Having the same father and mother, Benjamin probably looked more like Joseph than his other brothers did. In him, Joseph probably saw resemblances of his father, mother, and himself. This would also have caused memories of his ordeal to flood his mind like a torrent!

In fact, verses 30–31 reveal that Joseph was deeply moved when he saw Benjamin, such that he had to hurry out of the room and find a private place to weep. After that, he washed his face, came out, gained control of himself, and gave orders to serve the food. This was a very emotional lunch meeting for Joseph. In fact, it is not clear if he was able to eat. Verse 32 shows he was served alone, his brothers were served by themselves, and his Egyptian servants were served by themselves, because Egyptians could not eat with Hebrews. It is not clear why Joseph chose to eat lunch by himself, since by that time he had a wife and two sons (Gen 41:45; 51–52).

EGYPTIAN SEGREGATION

The seating arrangements at Joseph's house revealed a sad reality about the workings of various kinds of segregation, and its universal history. Even though Joseph was the second highest official in Egypt, and was financially better off than all his servants, they were considered socially better off than he was, because they were Egyptians. This meant, despite his position, there were social circles they could operate in that he could not, because he was a Hebrew.

This scenario still plays out in many societies today. It certainly plays out in the United States, where racial tensions are so high, and where no matter how much African American and other minority citizens accomplish, they are still treated as inferior, because of the color of their skin. Racial and ethnic dispositions can become such powerful social maladies, that generally speaking, if it were possible for the poorest members of the dominant race to change places (culture, ethnicity, religion, etc.) with the richest members of the minority race, they would not do it, because of the privileges afforded them simply from being in the majority, and the feeling of superiority that goes along with it.

However, Acts 10:34-36, shows this was never God's plan for the human race. Every human was created in the image of God and has equal racial and ethnic value to Him. As for religious value, all religions have exclusive biases, which means while they can all be respected, they cannot all be equally accepted, but this does not mean people cannot work together in peace. Pharaoh demonstrated this by making Joseph second in command, despite their racial, ethnic, and religious differences.

Verse 33 shows the brothers were seated by the order of their ages, from the firstborn to the youngest, and they looked at each other in astonishment. They were probably astonished because the seating order was correct, and they did not tell the stewards nor Joseph what their ages were. They were probably wondering how did they know? This should have been another hint to them about Joseph's identity, but because their eyes were not yet opened, it may have done more to convince them he was an Egyptian diviner, than a Hebrew who feared the true God.

Being seated from oldest to youngest may have also suggested to them that the oldest (Reuben) would receive the most honor and food, but once again, they were astonished to notice that Benjamin's portion was five times as much as anyone else'. Back home this may have caused a fight! It may have caused them to envy Benjamin the way they use to envy Joseph. However, the abundance of food for Benjamin was more a message of Joseph's abundant love for him, than it was a message of his hatred for his other brothers.

Notice, Benjamin shared his meal with them, as it says they ate and drank freely with him. In other words, Benjamin hosted the meal in the room where the brothers were eating by themselves, and all the while, none of them knew why they were afforded such special treatment. Joseph showered his brothers with the kind of grace with which Christ showers His brothers. They did not deserve Joseph's kindness no more than the Church deserves Jesus'. The apostle Paul stated (Rom 8:32) that He who did not spare His own Son, but delivered Him up for us all, how shall He not with Him also freely give His people all things? Yes, Christ gives freely, but a gift is not a gift unless it has been received. Therefore, the gift Christ gives means nothing to those who have not received it.

GENESIS CHAPTER FORTY-FOUR

In the previous chapter, Joseph's brothers' second journey to Egypt to buy food was discussed. After much persuasiveness, they were able to convince their father to allow Benjamin to travel with them. Their father instructed them to take the best of the land of Canaan as gifts to appease the ruler in Egypt, and he prayed for God's mercies upon them. On arrival in Egypt, they were taken to the ruler's house to eat lunch with him, but they thought it was for some evil reason. Simeon was released to them, and they eventually ate with joy, not knowing the real identity of the ruler.

This chapter will represent conflicting events for the brothers. After eating and enjoying themselves at the home of the Egyptian official, as they set out on their journey back home, he orchestrated a plan to accuse Benjamin of stealing his silver cup. He threatened to enslave Benjamin for this crime, which the brothers explained would be a death-sentence for their father. Judah, who was responsible for Benjamin's safety, would have to make a passionate plea to convince the official to relent from his plan to imprison Benjamin.

CONTROVERSY OVER JOSEPH'S CUP

After the feast at Joseph's house, the brothers prepared for their journey home. No doubt, they were still perplexed about the special treatment they received on this trip as compared to the previous one. They had no answers for why the ruler was so concerned about them and showed such good favor to them, after the way he treated them on their first visit. It was as though the man's personality had taken a complete turn! Hence, as they packed their bags for home, despite nagging unanswered questions, conceivably, they felt good about their mission so far.

Verses 1–2 reveal that Joseph gave his steward instructions to fill their sacks with as much food as they could carry and put each man's payment of silver back in his sack. However, he also instructed that not only should

Benjamin's payment be returned to him, but his silver cup should also be placed in Benjamin's sack. This was a set-up! It is not clear where in Egypt the brothers spent the night before heading off for home, whether at Joseph's house, at an inn, or out in the open country, but verse 3 says as morning dawned, they were sent on their way with their donkeys. And notice, once again they left without checking their bags to see what was in them.

After what happened on the first trip, when they left Egypt and later discovered the silver they thought they paid for the food was still in their sacks, it would seem reasonable for them to check to make sure such a thing did not happen again, but they did not do that. Again, they left without verifying the contents of their sacks. Under normal circumstances this would be a foolish mistake; However, in this case, it was God-ordained.

Observe verses 4–6, where it points out that they had not gone far from the city when Joseph said to his steward, "Go after those men at once, and when you catch up with them, say to them, 'why have you repaid good with evil? Isn't this the cup my master drinks from and also uses for divination? This is a wicked thing you have done.'" When the steward caught up with the men, he repeated the words Joseph told him. Now, unless the steward was aware of what Joseph was doing, he must have been confused about why he had been given conflicting instructions. He was caught in the middle of a family feud and presumably did not know the reason why.

Verses 7–9 indicate that the accusation caught Joseph's brothers by surprise! They tried to justify themselves and give reasons why they were innocent of the charges against them. They even proposed the drastic resolution that if any of them was found in possession of the cup, that person should be put to death, and the rest of them should be made to become slaves. The steward agreed but knowing he would find the cup, for their own good, he reduced the terms of their proposal. Verse 10 shows he proposed, "Very well, then, let it be as you say. Whoever is found to have it will become my slave; the rest of you will be free from blame." Notice, he did not propose that anyone should die, nor that anyone other than the one who was found with the cup should pay for the crime. What a relief!

Verses 11–12 shows that each man lowered his sack to the ground and opened it. The sacks were searched, beginning with the oldest to the youngest. Finally, when Benjamin's bags were searched, the cup was found. Oh, no! Not Benjamin! They were probably thinking, 'why did it have to be Benjamin?' They would have been willing for anyone else who was found with the cup to pay with their life, except Benjamin, because if Benjamin died, Jacob their father would also die. This meant, their original proposal to the steward, was one which would not only have caused Benjamin to lose his life but would have also caused their father to die from the grief associated with it.

Verse 13 indicates that after discovering the cup in Benjamin's sack, they all loaded their donkeys and returned to the city. This was probably a silent, dejected, and humiliating journey back into the city. The noise from their donkeys' hoofs may have been the only noises to be heard among them on the dusty road back to Egypt.

Verse 14 says, when they arrived at Joseph's house he was still at home and no doubt was expecting them. Notice, Judah who had become leader among them led the way. In fact, he may have been the one to propose that whoever was found with the silver cup should die. Observe also, this time, when they saw Joseph, they did not simply bow, it says they threw themselves to the ground before him. They were desperate for his mercy, and in that moment, life came full circle once again. The very things he prophesied to them were occurring before their eyes; yet they could not see it, yet. His sheaf had risen, and they were bowing down before him.

JOSEPH TEST HIS BROTHERS

As his brothers threw themselves down before him, Joseph knew they were innocent of what they were being accused. He knew it because he was the one who orchestrated the set-up against them. Their distress under the circumstances was obvious, but it was no different from what he experienced when they orchestrated the set-up to sell him into slavery. Recall, on their first trip they discussed among themselves, in his hearing, the extent of his distress (Gen 42:21); Yet they showed him no mercy. In the case at hand, he would get to witness their distress, but he would show them mercy.

Verse 15 shows, as they threw themselves down before him, he asked them, "What is this you have done? Don't you know that a man like me can find things out by divination?" It was true a man in Joseph's position in Egypt could use divination to get information, but Joseph himself did not do that. The reason Joseph was promoted to his position was because he exposed the magicians and diviners as the counterfeits they were. As such, they were unable to interpret Pharaoh's dreams. Therefore, he did not use their services, because he gained a reputation of his own. He was Zaphenath-Paneah (Revealer of Secrets), and his revelations were sure, because they came from the One and Only True God, and not through divination. However, the way he spoke to his brothers was to test them and was part of his disguise.

JUDAH'S DEFENSE

Verse 16 shows that Judah spoke up for the group and said, "What can we say to my lord, what can we say? How can we prove our innocence? God has uncovered your servants' guilt. We are now my lord's slaves, we ourselves, and the one who was found to have the cup."

Every time Judah spoke so far, he proved he was not a very good negotiator. Here he was, proposing to Joseph that they would all become his slaves, which would mean Jacob would have lost all eleven of his remaining sons at once. Judah's proposal reflected his and his brothers' preference for all of them to become slaves in Egypt, than for any of them to return to their father without Benjamin, the son he loved.

Verse 17 shows Joseph's response to Judah and his brothers, which was a pivotal test. He tested whether their love for Benjamin, his only brother from his mother Rachel, was greater than it was for him when he was with them. Therefore, he responded to Judah's proposal by telling them, far be it from him to do such a thing as to enslave all of them for the apparent crime of one. Instead, he demanded, only the one who was found to have his cup would become his slave, while the rest of them were free to go back to their father in peace.

Joseph's verdict forced Judah to change his negotiating strategy. While he initially proposed that the man found with the cup should die, once the one found with it turned out to be Benjamin, he tried to step back from that proposal by suggesting all of them should become Joseph's slaves. He did this, because he believed his father would die if Benjamin did not return from Egypt with them. However, Joseph's response ruled out the option of Benjamin returning with them, since he was the only man who appeared to be guilty of taking the cup. Therefore, the situation became more desperate and Judah, who orchestrated the sale of Joseph into slavery, seemed under heavier distress than all his brothers. As such, he was forced to present his case from a different angle.

Verses 18-25 show that Judah spoke again, and to make his case this time, he came physically closer to Joseph. His presentation was a heartfelt rehearsal of how they got to that point. It also provided greater transparency into the dynamics of Jacob's family. He rehearsed the events, which occurred on their first trip to Egypt, and how it came about that Benjamin was brought with them on their second trip. He basically stated their honesty in answering the questions Joseph asked, which in their minds caused him to know they had a younger brother.

He informed Joseph about the difficulty they had in convincing their father to allow Benjamin to come with them to Egypt. In essence, Judah's presentation this time, was more convincing than all the previous proposals he made. Joseph also learned some of the missing details about what happened in the family after he was sold into slavery.

If over the years Joseph wondered why his father never came looking for him, Judah's statements filled in some of those details. As Judah talked about details of the conversation with their father, in verse 27, he told Joseph his father said ". . . my wife bore me two sons. One of them went away from me, and I said, 'He has surely been torn to pieces. And I have not seen him since.'"

This statement demonstrated the premium at which Jacob valued his sons from Rachel, compared to his sons from his other women. Most importantly, it also informed Joseph that his father did not come after him, because he never knew the truth about what happened to him (v 28). He learned for the first time that his father thought he was dead (torn to pieces), because this was exactly what he was told, probably by Judah, who orchestrated the sale, and became the brothers' chief spokesman. Reuben could not have told his father that because he was not present when Joseph was sold to the Ishmaelites.

Judah's presentation also raised the possibility that over the years, there may have been remorse over what they had done, because of the grief it brought to their father; Apparently, Jacob was never the same again. This was deduced from verse 29, where Jacob responded to his sons' request to take Benjamin with them to Egypt. He told them, "If you take this one from me too and harm comes to him, you will bring my gray head down to the grave in misery."

As a result of this, Judah pleaded with Joseph about his unwillingness to see the grief his father would have if Benjamin did not return with them. He remembered what it was like when Joseph did not return, and he did not want to see his father grieve like that again. Verses 30–34 shows a summary of his presentation with the following heartfelt words:

> So now, if the boy is not with us when I go back to your servant my father, and if my father, whose life is closely bound up with the boy's life, sees that the boy isn't there, he will die. Your servants will bring the gray head of our father down to the grave in sorrow. Your servant guaranteed the boy's safety to my father. I said, 'If I do not bring him back to you, I will bear the blame before you, my father, all my life!' Now then, please let your servant remain here as my lord's slave in place of the boy, and let the boy return with his brothers. How can I go back to my father

if the boy is not with me? No! Do not let me see the misery that would come on my father.[1] (NIV)

Judah was probably in tears by the time he concluded his speech and would rather have been a substitute for Benjamin than return to his father without him. His words, "Do not let me see the misery that would come upon my father," struck at Joseph's heart, because Jacob was his father too, and he would never willingly cause him such grief. Judah demonstrated he was not only concerned about Benjamin's safety, but he was also more madly in love with his dad, than his dad showed he was with him.

Life came full circle as the mercy Judah was asking for was greater than that which they showed Joseph when they threatened to kill him but decided instead to sell him into slavery. Most importantly, it is similar to human requests to God for mercy, while ignoring the fact that His Son Jesus Christ, did not receive such mercy when He was nailed to a cross and crucified. Still, Joseph extended mercy in the same way Christ did, who said in Luke 23:34, "Father, forgive them, because they do not know what they are doing." In like manner, Joseph's brothers did not know what they were doing when they sold him into slavery.

---

1. Barker, et. al. *The NIV Study Bible,* Genesis 44:30–34.

GENESIS CHAPTER FORTY-FIVE

The previous chapter provided a summary of Joseph's brothers' second trip to Egypt. While there, he saw to it that they received special treatment. They ate lunch at his house, after which, they were sent on their way home with all the food they could carry. But, as they set out on their journey home, they did not realize he had arranged a criminal set-up against Benjamin, which caused all of them to be brought back to the city to stand trial. Joseph's proposed verdict was to set all of them free, except Benjamin, because he appeared to be the only one who was guilty.

Judah was forced to defend the case, and to provide heartfelt evidence about why they could not go back home without Benjamin. He literally explained that such a scenario would result in the death of their father, which would also bring more guilt on him, and be more than he could bear for the remainder of his life. This chapter represents a significant change in events, as Joseph would reveal his identity to them. His revelation would compel them to deal with a difficult past, and to surrender to the fact that God's hand was at work in Joseph's life all along, despite all they had done to destroy him. Ultimately, Joseph's kindness, words of forgiveness, and direct actions to let them know he meant them no harm, would give them hope, and result in reconciliation and reunification of the family of Israel.

JOSEPH REVEALS HIMSELF

Verse 1 shows Judah's appeal was so strong, that Joseph could no longer control himself before all his attendants, and he cried out, "Have everyone leave my presence!" That was, everyone except his brothers. This must have been a scary moment for the brothers. Imagine during a major court appeal, suddenly the judge explodes with a loud cry! The court would immediately be seized with deafening silence! The defendant would probably consider their fate to be one of doom! This was probably what happened at Joseph's house. No doubt, the attendants, as well as the brothers were probably dumbfounded!

Verse 2 says he wept so loudly that the Egyptians heard him, and Pharaoh's household heard about it. News traveled quickly! To this point Joseph had portrayed himself in the presence of his brothers and attendants as cold and callous, but nothing was further from the truth! This was a powerful moment! It was an important crossroad, which intersected his past, present, and future. Anyone who has ever been at such a crossroad knows the decisions and moves made at such a point, can either make, or break their own future, or that of others. The wrong move can cost years of recovery if recovery is at all possible. Joseph made all the right moves at this crossroad.

Notice verse 3, amid his tears he uttered words, which rendered Judah speechless. Other than Benjamin, who may have been confused by the entire event, when the brothers heard what Joseph said, his words paralyzed them with fear. The words Joseph uttered during his tears were, "I am Joseph! Is my father still alive?" They may not have known what his Egyptian name, Zaphenath-Paneah (Revealer of Secrets) meant, but they certainly knew what Joseph (He will Add) meant. And it is highly likely that this time when Joseph spoke to them, he did not use an interpreter. He probably spoke those words in their Hebrew tongue.

Recall, it was mentioned in chapter 42 that Joseph's disguise was similar to that of Jesus', whose Jewish brothers did not recognize Him at his first coming. The apostle Paul makes it clear, had they recognized Him, they would not have crucified Him (1 Cor 2:7–8). However, just as Joseph revealed himself to his brothers, on their second visit to Egypt, so too will Christ reveal Himself to His brothers at His second coming to earth. The prophet Zechariah says they will look on Him whom they pierced and will mourn for Him as one mourns for an only son and grieve as one grieves for a firstborn (Zech 12:10).

During Joseph's discourse with his brothers, they had told him on numerous occasions that his father was still alive, so it was not clear why he asked that again. Maybe, he did so to lighten the moment, and to get the conversation started. However, his pronouncement that they were literally standing in Joseph's presence, was, to say the least, absolutely shocking! It rendered them speechless! They were not able to answer him, because they were terrified at his presence. They thought they were in big trouble! They expected retribution but would receive forgiveness.

JOSEPH'S WORDS OF FORGIVENESS AND COMFORT

Amidst their fear, the brothers seemed immobilized, and in disbelief. Therefore, verse 4 shows that Joseph said to them, "Come close to me." When they came close and could get a better look at him, he repeated the words, "I am your brother Joseph, the one you sold into Egypt!" Those words must have cut deeper to the core of every emotion in their being. They were disgraced, ashamed, humiliated, and afraid; Yet, with many years having passed, they were probably also glad, and relieved to discover he was still alive.

Quite often, people would rather forget the past than deal with it. Religious people are especially prone to be this way because they reason, the past is over, or some would say, has been covered under the blood of Christ, and should be remembered no more. While this is true, and while God does not keep a record of repented sins, the fact remains, others who were offended still do, and life also has a way of counting people's sins against them. In other words, there is much truth to the Biblical axiom which says, "you reap what you sow" (Gal 6:7).

If serious unresolved issues from the past persist, they will assuredly come back at some time in the future. In fact, unresolved issues from the past are often un-forgiven issues. They are usually issues, for which people have not forgiven themselves and others, or others have not forgiven them. Joseph and his brothers came to that moment. While it brought relief to Joseph, it brought fear to his brothers.

Knowing this, verse 5 indicates that Joseph dealt with his past and theirs by encouraging them, and telling them not to be distressed, or angry with themselves for selling him there, because it was to save lives that God sent him ahead of them. Joseph's counsel may have been easier for him to say than it was for them to accept. How could they help but be angry with themselves? They knew when they sold him, they were not trying to do the will of God!

The fact that they sold him, was the better of two evils, since they were really planning to kill him! They were eager to get him out of the way, because they thought he was an obstacle between them and their father's love. So, how could they help but be angry with themselves? A mature perspective, such as what Joseph counseled, would take time, and that was exactly what was needed for them to leave the past behind.

In verse 6, Joseph informed them of the seriousness of the situation. He told them that for two years there had been famine in the land, and for the next five years there would be no plowing or reaping. In other words, it was not a time for looking back. Things were already bad after two years of famine, but they would get worse over the next five. What is not known from Scripture, is how many people died because of the famine. Conceivably, there were already many deaths due to starvation.

Verse 7 shows that Joseph again offered them soothing words of comfort, by telling them it was God who sent him ahead of them, to preserve them and to save their lives by a great deliverance. Little did they know, the great deliverance about which he spoke, had present, as well as future implications. Notice, he presented a concluding resolution in verse 8, by saying, "So then, it was not you who sent me here, but God. He made me a father to Pharaoh, lord of his entire household, and ruler of all Egypt."

What an awesome thing God did in Joseph's life! Most importantly, it was great that Joseph never lost sight of who did it. He did not laud any honors upon himself but gave God all the glory for what he was able to accomplish, seemingly against the odds. Most importantly, he gave them a reason to view themselves as instruments in, rather than enemies of, God's hand. It is worth pondering if at this point any of them remembered his dreams.

God had a plan for Israel and for Joseph. Although He allowed them to play a role, His plan was different from the plan Joseph's brothers had for him. Few people would want to be used by God the way Joseph's brothers were, or the way Judas Iscariot was, but it demonstrated that God can take evil desires of the human heart, and turn them around to fit His preordained plan. That said, it is still always better when the desires of human hearts are meant for good and not for evil, in which case, the results are, less pain and suffering.

JOSEPH'S MESSAGE TO HIS FATHER

Joseph was approximately 39 years old, when he revealed his identity to his brothers. After calming their anxieties from fear of discovering who he was, he told them in verses 9-11, to hurry back to his father and share the good news! He wanted them to go tell his father that God had made him lord of all Egypt and to come down to him without delay! He instructed them to tell his father that he would live in the region of Goshen, where he would be near him. Not only him, his children, and grandchildren, his flocks and herds, and all he had, would be relocated to that area.

Most importantly, he told him he would provide for him there, because five more years of famine were still to come. If his father did not do as instructed, he and his household, and all who belonged to him would become destitute. In other words, God's plan for Israel would not come to fruition. The message Joseph sent to his father was not only for him, but for his brothers as well.

Joseph proposed for them to leave the land of Canaan, the Promised Land, and move to Egypt, where they had no inheritance. This was not an easy decision! Had there not been a severe famine, they would not have taken Joseph's advice to move. There was also another factor worth considering. Pause for a moment to consider how such a message affected Jacob, who thought Joseph was dead, and who had been grieving for years based on that assumption!

Consider what it must have been like receiving such a message and being asked by a son, who had not been seen in over twenty years, to make such a big move; A son who was now supposed to be alive! Imagine the emotions associated with discovering, rather than being dead, his son was the one proposing to save the entire family from death!

Notice Joseph said to them, five more years of famine remained! So, if they were desperate for food after two years, think about how much worse it would get with five more years to go! For a moment, they might have wondered, how did he know five more years of famine remained? Then, they should have remembered, he knew it the same way he knew that one day his sheaf would rise and their sheaves would bow down before his. It was all part of God's plan.

In verse 12, he said, "You can see for yourselves, and so can my brother Benjamin, that it is really I who am speaking to you." How did they and Benjamin come to see what they were unable to see before? God finally opened their eyes to see the family resemblances. In other words, after they sold Joseph, they were never again able to recognize him as their brother, until he revealed himself to them as such. They lost their ability to recognize him, but he never lost his to recognize them. They would never have regained their ability to recognize him if he had not helped them do so. They would have continued to view him as a stranger and enemy, rather than the brother he was. This is instructive even today, where brothers and sisters are at war with each other because they refuse to pause, and recognize each other's resemblances, and realize that at the end of the day, they are alike in many ways as children of God.

In verse 13, Joseph reiterated the message he wanted his father to hear. He again insisted they tell him about all the honor he was being afforded in Egypt. He did not want his father to be afraid to come to him, but to be proud that his son was not dead, but very much alive and doing well! He said, "Bring my father down here quickly!" Then, verse 14 indicates that Joseph finally did what he had been longing to do, he threw his arms around Benjamin and wept, and Benjamin embraced him weeping also. What a touching scene this was! Brothers, Rachel's sons, weeping as they embraced each other! Who said men are not supposed to cry?

Notice verse 15, as a parting gesture of forgiveness, after embracing and weeping on Benjamin, the next thing Joseph did was to kiss all his brothers. It does not say he embraced them as he did Benjamin, but he kissed each of them as a gesture of love and forgiveness, rather than a kiss of betrayal. Next, it says his brothers talked with him. This was significant, because they had not talked with him in over twenty years, and in fact, they may have ceased talking with him long before they sold him (Gen 37:4). However, in this conversation, they probably begged for his forgiveness, and tried to fill him in on some of the family details he missed over the years.

PHARAOH HEARS AND WELCOMES THE GOOD NEWS

Joseph had given instructions to tell his father Jacob that God had made him a father to Pharaoh (v 8). Verses 16-23 show the truthfulness of that statement. Pharaoh responded to Joseph's family as if they were his own. It says, when the news reached Pharaoh's palace that Joseph's brothers had come, Pharaoh and all his officials were pleased. He told Joseph to tell his brothers, load their animals and return to the land of Canaan, and bring their father, and their families back to him! Notice he did not say, bring them to Joseph, but to him! In other words, the relationship between Pharaoh and Joseph was so close, that he considered Joseph's family to be his own.

He said he would give them the best of the land of Egypt, and they could enjoy the fat of the land. He also directed to tell them, take some carts from Egypt for their children, and their wives, and get their father and come. He told them not to worry about their belongings, because the best of all Egypt would be theirs. Having heard this, Joseph's brothers did as they were instructed.

Joseph gave them carts, as Pharaoh had commanded, and he also gave them provisions for their journey. To each of them he gave new clothing, but to Benjamin he gave three hundred shekels of silver and five sets of clothes. He sent his father ten donkeys, loaded with the best things of Egypt, and ten female donkeys loaded with grain, bread and other provisions for his journey.

Pharaoh was extremely generous to Joseph and his family, and in a real sense he treated them like his own. His benevolence to Israel gave them the head-start they needed to establish themselves in a new location, but it also became a source of jealousy in future years when he and Joseph were no longer on the scene (Exod 1:6-11). The prominence he afforded Israel, as a separate nation in the land of Egypt, created tensions, which would ultimately lead to Israel's enslavement.

Notice, verse 24 says Joseph sent his brothers away, and as they were leaving, he said to them, "Don't quarrel on the way!" This was an important directive, because it was likely they would have argued about who was responsible for what happened to Joseph. Rueben, who tried to rescue him may have been infuriated at the others, particularly Judah, who orchestrated the scheme to sell him. Benjamin may have been the most offended, since he had no clue what happened to his older brother, the only one from his mother Rachel.

Most importantly, Joseph probably warned them not to quarrel, because he knew if they did, they would focus more on the past, than the present, and future. Their minds would have been clouded with regret for what they had done to take Joseph's life, rather than thankfulness for how God had preserved his life to save theirs.

JOSEPH'S MESSAGE CONVINCES JACOB

Joseph gave his brothers a great send-off from Egypt, with a caravan of goods to take back to their families. By then, Jacob must have been wondering what was taking his sons so long in Egypt, especially in light of his anxiety pertaining to Benjamin's safety. Verses 25–26 indicate that they went up out of Egypt and came to Jacob in Canaan. When they arrived, they told him, "Joseph is still alive! In fact, he is ruler of all of Egypt." Those words sent Jacob into shock! It says he was stunned and did not believe them. This was the reason why Joseph gave his brothers specific words to speak to his father, and why he did specific things to help them convince him that what he would hear was indeed true! He knew his father would need convincing proof!

Verses 27–28 reveal that when they told Jacob everything Joseph had said, and when he saw the carts, Joseph had sent to carry him back to Egypt, his spirit revived, and he said, "I am convinced! My son Joseph is still alive. I will go and see him before I die." He was convinced once he heard what was said in the messages, and once he could clearly see that his son had become the ruler he was foretold to be. In other words, in that moment, Jacob probably remembered Joseph's dreams.

Jacob's spirit was in the dumps from the day he was told Joseph was dead. Benjamin was the only one who came close to taking Joseph's place in his father's heart, but none of the other brothers even came close. Jacob showed deliberate partiality in his parenting, and it ripped his family apart. Thankfully, God brought them back together as part of His divine plan. It all worked out for good, and it showed that God's plan will always be accomplished, even though along the way, it reveals the fallen nature, and flaws of His people.

GENESIS CHAPTER FORTY-SIX

In the previous chapter Joseph revealed his identity to his brothers, then he gave them specific messages to communicate to his father to convince him to relocate to Egypt. He also encouraged his brothers by telling them, what they meant for evil, God meant for good, and it was He who brought him to Egypt ahead of them, in order to save their families from death.

This chapter will provide details about what God said to Jacob to convince him to go to Egypt. It will provide a list of Jacob's family, who moved with him to Egypt. The reunion between Joseph and his father will be discussed, as well as his instructions to his family about what they should say to Pharaoh, when the opportunity came for them to meet with him.

GOD CONVINCES JACOB TO GO TO EGYPT

Verses 1-4 state that Israel (Jacob) set out with all he owned, and when he reached Beersheba, he offered sacrifices to the God of his father Isaac. During the night God spoke to him in a vision, called him by his old name, Jacob, and identified Himself to him as the God of his father. Then He told him, "Do not be afraid to go down to Egypt, for I will make you into a great nation there. I will go down to Egypt with you, and I will surely bring you back again. And Joseph's own hand will close your eyes."

God called Jacob by his old name, rather than his new name, Israel, because apparently, he had returned to his old ways. There is no Biblical record of Jacob sacrificing to God or seeking Him during the entire time while Joseph went missing and was thought to have died. Nor is there any Biblical record of God speaking to Jacob during that time to tell him Joseph was still alive. That period of Jacob's life was full of grief and seemed to be one of silence between him and God.

As he set out to go to Egypt, his spirit was alive again, and he sought God once more. Notice, he called on God at Beersheba. That was the place where Abraham called on God, (Gen 21:33), and where Isaac also called on Him (Gen 26:25). Since it was conveniently located on the way to Egypt, and since Jacob was facing a colossal decision, it was an ideal place for him to also call on God. Notice, God identified Himself to Jacob as the God of his father, Isaac. This was important, because when his father faced a famine (Gen 26:1–3), he thought about moving to Egypt, but God instructed him not to do so. Instead, He told him to stay in the land of Canaan, and promised to bless him there.

In Jacob's case, God instructed him to go to Egypt, where He would be with him, and make him into a great nation. He also promised to bring him back to the land of Canaan, even though Joseph's own hand would close his eyes. This was God's way of telling Jacob he would not return from Egypt alive, but his body would be returned to the land of Canaan for burial (Gen 50:12–13). It was also God's way of confirming to Jacob that his son Joseph was indeed still alive.

Having been convinced by God that he should go to Egypt, verses 5–7 reveal that Jacob left Beersheba, and his sons took him, their children, and their wives in the carts Pharaoh had sent to transport them. So, they all went to Egypt, and they took with them their livestock and possessions they had acquired in Canaan. Jacob brought with him to Egypt his sons, grandsons, daughters, granddaughters, and all his offspring. This move established the foundation for the Nation of Israel to be formed as a sub-nation within the Nation of Egypt. They grew and developed within Egypt but remained distinct from it. This eventually became a problem, which led to the Egyptians enslaving them due to fear of their population size and strength.

JACOB'S DESCENDANTS WHO MOVED TO EGYPT

Verses 8–25, provide a list of all Jacob's direct descendants who went to live in Egypt. Verse 26 mentioned that the list does not include his sons' wives, but only his direct descendants, which in all numbered sixty-six. However, with Joseph, his two sons, and himself, the number of Jacob's family in Egypt were listed at seventy. This was quite a colony with which to get started!

Verse 28 indicates that Jacob sent Judah ahead of him to Joseph to get directions to Goshen. Again, Judah, rather than Reuben emerged as leader of the brothers. Therefore, his father sent him to Joseph to get directions to Goshen. Jacob wanted to make sure they went to the right place, since it would have been a major offense if they settled in an unauthorized location. Notice, because they were reconciled, this time Judah had no fear about seeing Joseph again.

JOSEPH SEES HIS FATHER AGAIN

Verse 29 shows Joseph's eagerness to see his father again. It says, as soon as they arrived in Goshen, Joseph had his chariot made ready and went there to meet his father, Israel. There is no evidence he took either his wife or two sons with him. As soon as he appeared before him, he threw his arms around his father and wept for a long time. One can only wonder what the other brothers thought as they observed that scene, and as they recalled their role in causing the separation of Jacob and Joseph. Quite possibly, they also wept.

It had been over twenty years since the last time Joseph had seen his father. He was seventeen years old when he was taken from him, but at the time of this reunion he was approximately forty years old. No doubt, he looked different, spoke different, probably acted different, and indeed was different. He was no longer just a dreamer but had become ruler of all of Egypt. His sheaf had indeed risen suddenly, and theirs were compelled to bow down to it! However, this meeting was highly emotional for both Joseph and his father. As far as Jacob was concerned, God had in essence brought his son back from the dead! After all those years of thinking he was dead, then to see him alive again, what a moment!

Following a long embrace, where no spoken words were recorded, other than those communicated through the language of tears, finally, Jacob spoke. He said to Joseph, "Now I am ready to die, since I have seen for myself that you are still alive." That meant, Jacob finally came to a place of contentment, knowing his son Joseph was still alive. By that time he was approximate 130 years old (Gen 47:9), before then, he was not ready to die because the nagging question in his mind was yet unanswered; what really happened to his dear son Joseph. He needed an answer to that question before he died.

Jacob's ordeal speaks to the unimaginable torment experienced by those whose loved ones go missing. Not a day goes by without thinking about them, wondering what happened to them, and pondering if by some chance they may show up again. Grief is a tough human emotion, but grief without closure is tougher. It can feel like daily torment, which momentarily gets better, but can be easily triggered, and reoccur during odd moments.

It was quite likely that since Judah emerged as leader among the brothers, the responsibility became his to finally tell their father the truth about what really happened to Joseph over twenty years earlier. More importantly, after learning that his sons had lied to him for all those years, it was possible Jacob's trust in them diminished further. Hence, even though the family was together again in Egypt, it was probably still a fragmented family. The main issues, which caused division in the first place, were still present. Jacob still loved his sons Joseph and Benjamin the most because they were from the wife he loved the most. And, when they were all reunited, the others had to accept their role as second-class sons. In fact, the outcome seemed to justify Jacob's love for Rachel's sons, particularly Joseph, since he was the one God used to save them and preserve them for generations into the future.

JOSEPH PREPARES HIS FAMILY TO MEET PHARAOH

Verses 31–34 state that Joseph told his brothers and his father's household he would go up and speak to Pharaoh and inform him that his family, who were living in the land of Canaan, had come to him. He said he would tell him they were shepherds, who tend livestock, and they brought along their flocks and herds and everything they owned. He then instructed his family that when Pharaoh called them in and asked what their occupation was, they should tell him they have tended livestock from their youth, just as their fathers did. Then they would be allowed to settle in the region of Goshen, because all shepherds were detestable to the Egyptians.

Bibleatlas.org represents that Goshen was an irrigated plain, which is still considered to be some of the best land in Egypt. It was a secluded area located in the eastern part of the Nile Delta. When Israel moved there it was not heavily populated.[1] This allowed Israel to exist without imposing too heavily on the Egyptians by competing with them for the same space. The fact that Israel brought their flocks and herds, and everything they owned, communicated their reluctance to become a burden, or liability to the Egyptians. For the most part, they had all they needed, and were assigned to occupy an area, which had good pastureland and was of little use or interest to the Egyptians, who detested shepherds and their line of work. So, Goshen, a wasted pastureland, seemed to be an ideal place to which such detestable people could be relegated.

Joseph was obviously in a position where, if he so desired, he could have acquired other types of work for his brothers and family, so that they would no longer have to be shepherds. However, if he had done so, it would certainly have made them more acceptable to the Egyptians. Such work would also have made it easier for them to integrate into the culture of their new homeland. But Joseph wanted the Egyptians to know what his brothers' profession was, because he wanted his brothers to be proud of who they were. He also knew from the outset, it would make them detestable to the Egyptians, and keep them separated from them.

1. Unknown Author, *Goshen*, https://bibleatlas.org/goshen.htm:Bibleatlas.

By presenting themselves as shepherds, Joseph wanted to make sure his family did not easily lose their identity, and religious distinctiveness while living in Egypt. In other words, while in Egypt, Israel was not to become part of Egypt, just as the Church is in the world, but is not of the world (John 17:16). For this reason, as prominent as Joseph was, his two sons Manasseh and Ephraim most likely became shepherds as well, so that they were also detestable to their own Egyptian people and compelled to remain separated from them.

Ultimately, Joseph's story and that of his father's family was a tragedy, and yet a triumph. On the one hand, God chose that family as His own, yet on the other hand, it was a fragmented and dysfunctional family. When it came to parenting, Jacob and his forefathers fell short, or at least displayed poor skills. It was only by the grace of God, that Jacob's family was reunited, and that Joseph did not indeed die. This example should give hope to families today, which are experiencing various levels of dysfunction. Since God reconciled Jacob's family, despite its dysfunctions, He proved He can certainly reconcile brokenness in any family that is responsive to Him and to His Word. Most importantly, because of Christ and His sacrifice, while some human differences may remain irreconcilable, there is no reason for this to be the case between God and anyone who desires to have a relationship with Him.

GENESIS CHAPTER FORTY-SEVEN

The previous chapter provided details about Israel's reunion in Egypt. It began by highlighting Jacob's meeting with God at Beersheba, after many years of silence between him and God. It showed that God affirmed Jacob's move to Egypt, where he would see Joseph again. It provided a list of those who moved and lived in Egypt with Jacob, seventy in all. It revealed instructions Joseph gave his father and brothers about what to say to Pharaoh, when the opportunity came for them to meet with him. This chapter will review details of the family's meeting with Pharaoh. It will also disclose additional details about what commercial activities in Egypt were like during the famine, when Joseph led the food distribution and relief effort.

JACOB AND HIS SONS MEET PHARAOH

Verse 1 indicates that Joseph went and told Pharaoh his father and brothers, with their flocks and herds and everything they owned, had come from the land of Canaan and were in Goshen. Even though Pharaoh had agreed that Joseph should relocate his family to that area, once it was done, Joseph extended the courtesy of informing him they were there. This spoke to Joseph's character and magnitude of respect for, and relationship with Pharaoh.

Verse 2 indicates that Joseph chose five of his brothers and presented them before Pharaoh. It is unclear which five he chose, but it is almost certain Benjamin, his only brother from his mother Rachel, was among the five. It was a tremendous honor for Joseph's brothers to meet Pharaoh because this was an honor many Egyptians never had, and one his brothers did not deserve. Joseph had every right to disown them, as they disowned him; Instead, he honored them by presenting them to the king.

Ironically, their meeting might also have been a testimony to Pharaoh, as it was quite likely by then he knew the circumstances, which caused Joseph's separation from his family, and which caused him to become a slave in Egypt. Hence, Pharaoh witnessed Joseph's spirit of mercy and forgiveness, which he showed toward his family.

Joseph had already told his father and brothers what questions Pharaoh would ask them (Gen 46:33), and what they should say when they answered him. As predicted, verses 3–4 state that Pharaoh asked them what their occupation was, and they answered him as Joseph instructed, by informing him they were shepherds as their fathers before them were. They also told him, they had come to live in Egypt for a while, because the famine was severe in Canaan and their flocks had no pasture, so they requested his permission to let them settle in Goshen.

Notice, Pharaoh did not ask the brothers if they had an occupation, instead he assumed they did, and inquired about what it was. They were able-bodied men, and thus expected to have a job to feed themselves and their families. Besides, Pharaoh would have been less accommodating if they did not have an occupation but were expecting to be taken care of by the State, especially during a famine. They also reduced his anxiety by telling him they were not planning to stay in Egypt forever, but only for a while, until the famine subsided in Canaan. History shows they remained there for over four hundred years (Exod 12:40–41; Gal 3:17).

Having heard their plea, Pharaoh put their request, as he did all others, back in Joseph's hands. However, he also showed kindness to them for Joseph's sake. Verses 5–6 shows he told Joseph, his father and brothers had come to him, and the land of Egypt was before him; therefore, settle them in the best part of the land; he granted permission for them to live in Goshen. He also told him, if he discovered any among them with special ability, put them in charge of his own livestock.

By telling Joseph his father and brothers had come to him, Pharaoh was in essence asserting that they were Joseph's responsibility. Therefore, he needed to make sure they were settled in Goshen, which he agreed was the best part of the land. The question begs to be asked, why did Pharaoh give Israel the best part of the land of Egypt? The answer to this question may be summed up in one word, Joseph. He did it because of Joseph. This was his way of thanking Joseph for all he had done for Egypt.

When Pharaoh restored his chief cupbearer to his position (Gen 40:21), he proved his ability to be forgiving. When he beheaded his chief baker (Gen 40:22), he proved his propensity to be ruthless if necessary. When he declared that Israel should be located in the best part of the land of Egypt, he proved his supreme generosity, and as an instrument in God's hand, he evidenced the fact that God can use anyone He chooses to accomplish His will.

Verses 7–10 indicate that after presenting his brothers to Pharaoh, Joseph brought in his father Jacob and presented him. Jacob introduced himself by blessing Pharaoh. Then Pharaoh asked him, "How old are you?" And Jacob told him, the years of his pilgrimage were one hundred and thirty. He also told Pharaoh that his years had been few and difficult, and that they did not equal the years of the pilgrimage of his fathers. Then he blessed Pharaoh and went out from his presence.

Observe that as the highlight of his introductions, Joseph brought (or helped) his father in, to present him to Pharaoh. The first thing Jacob did on entering the room, was to bless Pharaoh, and the king showed his respect by allowing him to do so. It was Pharaoh's court, but he did not speak until Jacob was finished blessing him. His first and only recorded question to Jacob was, "how old are you?" Presumably, one of the reasons Pharaoh was so respectful to Jacob, was because he immediately recognized he was an old man. The time and culture they lived in was one in which old age was respected (Lev 19:32).

Jacob gave Pharaoh an interesting response, which should have been instructive. He described his life as a pilgrimage. To the king, and everyone else, it was a reminder that no matter what accomplishments are achieved, life is just a pilgrimage. Every human being is simply passing through this world on a journey to another. To be sure, this world as it is currently constituted, is not mankind's permanent dwelling. Yet, Jacob was one hundred and thirty years old when he made that statement! Having lived so long, he could have easily forgotten that life was just a pilgrimage, or temporary journey, but he did not forget that, and no one else should.

Notice also, as old as he was, he still regarded his years to have been relatively few, compared to those of his fathers, and certainly compared to eternity, where one day is as a thousand years (Ps 90:4; 2 Pet 3:8). His father Isaac lived 180 years (Gen 35:28), and his grandfather Abraham lived 175 years (Gen 25:7). Compared to his forefathers, Jacob did not only regard his 130 years of life to have been few, but he also regarded them to have been difficult. His difficulties undoubtedly stemmed from his early years of deception and his time living in Haran.

Recall, he started off early in life using deception to trick his brother Esau into selling him his birthright. Then, he used deception to trick his father into giving him the blessing of the first-born. These actions caused him to spend many years living in Haran with his uncle Laban, who in turn tricked him into marrying both of his daughters, when he only intending to marry one. As a result, he spent approximately twenty years in Haran living and working for his uncle as an indentured servant.

Finally, as he was able to leave his uncle, Rachel, the wife he truly loved died on the journey, which caused him to become stuck with women and children he did not truly love. Then, one of the two sons he loved, Joseph, was taken from him, which caused him to live in grief for a significant portion of his life. Therefore, Jacob's life was indeed difficult, but as he got closer to the end of it, it was clear those difficulties resulted in the healthy perspective he gained and was able to share with Pharaoh. Life in this world is indeed only a pilgrimage, rather than a permanent dwelling.

Notice once again, as Jacob entered Pharaoh's court, he blessed him (v 7), and he did the same as he exited (v 10). Not much else is given about the conversation, but since Pharaoh was intrigued by Jacob's age, and since Jacob told him his fathers lived longer than he did, it seems reasonable to assume Pharaoh might have inquired about their ages as well, and about events he would have witnessed during his 130 years of life. On the other hand, the meeting could have been quickly expedited, because the underlying reality was, shepherds were detestable to the Egyptians, and Jacob and his sons were shepherds.

Verses 11-12 declare that Joseph settled his father and brothers in Egypt and gave them property in the best part of the land, the district of Rameses, as Pharaoh directed. Joseph also provided his father and brothers and all his father's household, food according to the number of their children.

In essence, Joseph became provider for his father's family, and through him God preserved Israel through the famine, which ravaged the entire region at that time. His brothers once thought about killing him, but sold him instead; Yet, figuratively, God raised him from the dead and caused him to become a savior to Egypt and surrounding countries. God also placed him in a position of authority and influence, "for such a time as this" (Esth 4:14).

FAMINE HIGHLIGHTS JOSEPH'S GIFTS OF ADMINISTRATION

Verse 13 points out that there was no food, in the entire region, because of the severity of the famine; both Egypt and Canaan wasted away. Thankfully, God gave Joseph foresight and wisdom for their time of crisis. Again, He placed him in a position to not only save his family, and Egypt, but to also save the entire region.

Verses 14-26 provide details about how Joseph used his God-given administrative skills to lead the food relief effort. Specifically, verse 14 indicates that Joseph collected all the money in Egypt and Canaan as payment for grain the people were buying, and brought it to Pharaoh's palace. He did not keep the money for himself, but as a faithful and trustworthy servant, he brought it into Pharaoh's palace. The people's money was no help to them without food. They could not eat their money, so they were willing to spend it all to buy food.

Notice verses 15–17, that when their money was all gone, all the people of Egypt came to Joseph and begged him to give them food. They asked, "Why should we die before your eyes? Our money is all gone." He responded by telling them to bring their livestock and he would sell them food in exchange for their livestock, since their money was gone. So, they brought their livestock to him, and he gave them food in exchange for their horses, their sheep and goats, their cattle and donkeys. He brought them through that year with food in exchange for all their livestock.

Everything the people of Egypt and Canaan worked to accomplish was slowly depleted by the famine. One might wonder why they were willing to sell their sheep, goats, and cattle, in exchange for grain, when they could have used them for food. In times of famine, as was pictured in Pharaoh's dream (Gen 41:1–7), the famine had probably ravaged the livestock to the point where they were becoming gaunt and sick. Therefore, it was better to trade them to buy grain, than to keep them and let them die due to lack of pastureland on which to feed. So, Joseph brought them through an entire year by trading their livestock in exchange for grain.

After using up all their money and all their livestock, when more grain was needed, verses 18–19 declare the people came to Joseph the following year and told him they could not hide from him the fact that since their money was gone, and their livestock belonged to him, there was nothing left for them to trade, except their bodies and their land. They asked, "Why should we perish before your eyes, we and our land as well?" Then, they implored him to buy them, and their land in exchange for food, promising that they and their land would be in bondage to Pharaoh. They said, "Give us seed so that we may live and not die, and that the land may not become desolate."

Verses 20–21 indicate that Joseph bought all the land in Egypt for Pharaoh. The Egyptians, one and all, sold their fields, because the famine was too severe for them. The land became Pharaoh's, and Joseph reduced the people to servitude, from one end of Egypt to the other. In essence, the people of Egypt hit rock-bottom. They had nothing else to sell but themselves to maintain their basic survival.

Joseph, who rose from slavery to a position of power, instituted slavery in Egypt as a means by which people could stay alive through the famine, and Pharaoh could receive his just due in helping them do so. The servitude he instituted was not like that which he experienced. Besides, both he and Pharaoh knew exactly how long the famine would last, and that it was only temporary. So, their main objective was to get the people and country through it from year to year, without losing all of them, and without the nation being ruined in its entirety.

Notice verse 22 points out that Joseph astutely did not buy the land of the priests, because they received a regular allotment from Pharaoh and had food enough from the allotment Pharaoh gave them. That is why they did not sell their land. In other words, he did not attempt to buy land, which was not for sale. The priest did not need to sell their land, because they received, and had enough food to sustain them. Regular citizens did not have that luxury, which made selling their land in exchange for food, a necessity. The fact that priests were well supplied by Pharaoh, showed the value he attributed to them, and to his religion, and Joseph's wisdom in avoiding conflicts in that area.

The people of Egypt proposed to Joseph that they and their properties should become Pharaoh's in exchange for food, but the system Joseph proposed in verses 23–26, illustrated the strength of his administrative prowess. He told the people, since on that day he had bought them and their land for Pharaoh, he gave them seed to plant the ground. But, when the crop comes in, a fifth of it must be given to Pharaoh. The other four-fifths, they may keep as seed for the fields, and as food for themselves and their households and children.

The people responded by saying, "You have saved our lives, may we find favor in the eyes of our lord; we will be in bondage to Pharaoh." Hence, Joseph established it as a law concerning land in Egypt, that a fifth of the produce belonged to Pharaoh. The only exception was the land of the priests, which did not become Pharaoh's. In other words, Joseph respected separation between religion and State.

Observe that Joseph's proposal lightened the impact of the people's servitude. Technically, once they sold their property to Pharaoh, he was under no obligation to return it to them. Yet, this was exactly what he did! He allowed them to keep their properties, and he even gave them seed to plant. Their only obligation was to return to Pharaoh one-fifth of the land's produce. This was an extremely generous offer! It showed that servitude in Egypt was not as egregious as it otherwise could have been. In fact, the people's response was one of gratitude, and willingness to be in bondage to Pharaoh under such menial terms. He basically implemented a taxation system.

JACOB GIVES BURIAL INSTRUCTIONS TO JOSEPH

Verse 27 declares that the Israelites settled in Egypt in the region of Goshen. They acquired property there and were fruitful and increased greatly in number. In essence, they became a sub-nation within a nation. History shows this eventually became a problem for them, which resulted in their subjugation by later generations of Egyptians.

Verses 28–31 reveal that Jacob lived in Egypt seventeen years, and the years of his life were a hundred and forty-seven. When the time drew near for him to die, he called for his son Joseph and told him, "If I have found favor in your eyes, put your hand under my thigh and promise that you will show me kindness and faithfulness. Do not bury me in Egypt, but when I rest with my fathers, carry me out of Egypt and bury me where they are buried." Joseph responded by promising to do as his father requested. However, his father insisted that he swear to him. Then Joseph swore to him, and Jacob worshipped as he leaned on the top of his staff.

Joseph was taken from Jacob as a young man and sold into slavery when he was seventeen years of age. God gave them seventeen more years together following their reunion in Egypt. It was also interesting that as Jacob contemplated his death and burial, he did not call for Reuben, Judah, Benjamin, or any of his other sons. Instead, he summoned Joseph and gave him instructions about his final wishes to be buried in Canaan. None of his sons, other than Joseph had the wherewithal to carry out his final wishes.

Jacob's request was exactly what God told him at Beersheba would happen to his dead body following his stay in Egypt (Gen 46:4). Once Joseph swore to carry out his wishes, Jacob accepted the approaching finality of his demise, as he worshipped God. With all final matters settled, Jacob resorted to worship, rather than worry, and not even the prospect of death changed his perspective or demeanor. This was a great attitude by one who lived 147 years, yet one who characterized his time on earth as merely a pilgrimage, rather than a permanent dwelling.

GENESIS CHAPTER FORTY-EIGHT

In the previous chapter, Joseph presented his father and brothers to Pharaoh, who agreed to allow them to settle in Goshen. Details were also provided about the severity of the famine, and Joseph's leadership in guiding Egypt and surrounding countries through that seven-year crisis. Once Israel was settled in Goshen, the chapter concluded with Joseph being summoned by his father, who gave him his final burial wishes. He made him swear to take his body back to Canaan, and bury him where his fathers were buried. Following Joseph's oath to do as he was instructed, Jacob worshipped the Lord as he leaned on his staff. This chapter will examine details of Jacob's incredible blessings on Joseph and his two sons, Manasseh and Ephraim.

GOD'S PROMISE CONCERNING JACOB AND HIS DESCENDANTS

Verses 1-4 declare that sometime later, Joseph was informed his father was ill. So, he took his two sons Manasseh and Ephraim with him and went to see his father. When they arrived, and Jacob was told they were there, he rallied his strength, and sat up on the bed. He said to Joseph, "God Almighty (El Shaddai) appeared to me at Luz in the land of Canaan, and there he blessed me, and said to me, 'I am going to make you fruitful and increase your numbers. I will make you a community of peoples, and I will give this land as an everlasting possession to your descendants after you.'"

This passage painted an interesting scene, which can be easily missed by the casual reader. It said Jacob was ill, so Joseph went to see him and took his two sons along with him. The Bible at no other time, indicated that Joseph had previously introduced his sons to his father. Nor does it show he ever introduced his wife Asenath, daughter of Potiphera, priest of On (Heliopolis), to him. Yet he introduced his father to Pharaoh and finally to his two sons. The mention of his sons being with him on this occasion, when he went to see his sick father, was to emphasize the fact that it was not only an introduction, but also a farewell visit.

Recall, God had told Jacob (Gen 46:4) that Joseph's own hand would close his eyes when he died. Therefore, when Joseph arrived with his two sons, and Jacob was told they were there, he mustered his strength one last time, because he knew this was their final meeting. He knew the moment of his eternal transition was at hand. Therefore, he mustered his strength as he pronounced final words to his sons. He did so by first recalling what God said to him at Luz (Bethel—Gen 28:19), where God blessed him and made a promise to him and his descendants after him.

It was important for Joseph's sons to hear what Jacob had to say, because they needed to know that their heritage was not from their Egyptian, but from their Israelite lineage. As such, their inheritance was not in the land of Egypt, but in the land of Canaan. This reality would change, or establish their associations and conduct moving forward; specifically, it meant they could not worship the gods of Egypt, but rather, the God of Israel.

Jacob said that God told him He would make him fruitful and increase his numbers and would give him the land of Canaan as an everlasting possession to his descendants after him. He knew the fullness of the promise was not for him, but for his descendants after him. Having come to the end of his days, the promise was no longer his, but theirs. They needed to know what God said, so they could place their hope in His word. It was especially important for Manasseh and Ephraim to learn about the promises directly from their grandfather, who heard them directly from God. After his death they probably never forgot what he said to them from the pulpit of his dying bed.

JACOB ADOPTS MANASSEH AND EPHRAIM AS SONS

Verses 5–6 declare that Jacob told Joseph, considering what God said to him at Luz about making him fruitful, and increasing his descendants, Manasseh and Ephraim, who were born to Joseph in Egypt before he came to him there would be reckoned as sons of Israel. He said, "Ephraim and Manasseh will be mine, just as Reuben and Simeon are mine." He told Joseph any other children born to him after those two would be his; but in the territory those two sons would inherit, they would be reckoned as part of Israel, and under the names of their brothers.

Joseph did not object to his two sons being reckoned as his father's, and as part of the nation of Israel. Despite his success in Egypt, and the likelihood that his sons would also have been successful there, he was willing to allow them to be counted as Hebrews. This was no small sacrifice for Joseph, especially since there is no record of him having any other offspring. He was willing to allow his sons to be counted among his brothers who mistreated him and attempted to cut him off from being counted among them.

JACOB REMEMBERS RACHEL

As Jacob neared his own death and was making final provisions for his offspring through Rachel, he reminisced about her and the way she died. In verse 7, he recalled that as he was returning from Paddan, to his sorrow, Rachel died in the land of Canaan, while they were still on the way back home, a short distance from Ephrath. He buried her there beside the road to Ephrath (Bethlehem).

It was not clear if Joseph had ever spoken to his sons about their grandmother Rachel, and about where and how she died, but Jacob found it necessary to rehearse those events in their hearing. He was obviously grieved by her death, and his mention of her again highlighted his love for her beyond any of the other women he had. It also gave him comfort as he faced his own death, knowing there were others, particularly his beloved wife, who preceded him, and whom he expected to join in that eternal realm. As death closed in, he mentioned none of his other loved ones who preceded him, other than Rachel. He was never able to let go of his love for her.

JACOB'S BLESSING UPON JOSEPH AND HIS SONS

Verses 8–9 indicate that when Jacob saw Joseph's sons, he asked, "Who are these?" Joseph told him they were the sons God had given him there in Egypt. Then Jacob told him to bring them closer to him so he may bless them. The writer of the Book of Hebrews refers to this as a blessing by faith (Heb 11:21). In other words, the blessing Jacob pronounced on them was based on things he had not seen himself, but only had evidence of because of what God told him. Therefore, he blessed them with the confidence of knowing what he said would come true simply because God said it.

Notice verse 10 says Jacob's eyes were failing because of old age, and he could hardly see. This meant while his physical eyesight was failing, his spiritual sight was sharper than it had ever been! He was nearing death and had reached a point where he could no longer rely on what he could see on his own but had to rely on what God was showing him. Hence, the blessing he pronounced was not from him, but from God. Observe, verse 10 continued by saying Joseph brought his sons close to his father, who kissed them and embraced them.

Verses 11–14 indicate that Jacob told Joseph, he never expected to see his face again, and yet God had not only allowed him to see his face, but to see his children also. Having heard this, Joseph removed them from his father's knees, and bowed down with his face to the ground. Then Joseph took both his sons, Ephraim on his right toward Israel's left hand, and Manasseh on his left toward Israel's right hand and brought them close to him. But Jacob reached out his right hand and put it on Ephraim's head, though he was the younger, and crossing his arms, he put his left hand on Manasseh's head, even though Manasseh was the firstborn.

Notice, when Jacob told Joseph, he never expected to see his face again, Joseph's only response was to bow with his face to the ground. He never recalled the evil, which his brothers did to separated them. Instead, both considered it a blessing that God brought them back together, and even blessed him with two sons. Joseph's response was as if to get the focus off himself and to say, "to God be the glory!" He presented his two sons to his father in a manner that would allow his first-born son to receive the blessing of the first-born, and his younger son to receive the blessing that was due him.

Verses 15–17 show that Jacob literally crossed his hands on the heads of Joseph's two sons and blessed them by saying, "May the God before whom my fathers, Abraham and Isaac walked faithfully, the God who has been my Shepherd all my life to this day, the Angel who has delivered me from all harm, may He bless these boys. May they be called by my name and the names of my fathers, Abraham, and Isaac, and may they increase greatly on the earth." When Joseph saw his father placing his right hand on Ephraim's head he was displeased; He took hold of his father's hand to move it from Ephraim's head to Manasseh's head.

Joseph was displeased and tried to move his father's hands as he crossed them on the heads of his sons to bless them, thereby giving the younger the blessing of the first-born, and the older the blessing of the younger. He thought since his father could no longer see, he was making a mistake. He also knew his father was prone to showing favoritism, and as such, he tried to advocate for the rights of his first-born son Manasseh.

Additionally, Joseph knew his father had deceitfully received the blessing of the first-born, though he was not the first-born. So, he was displeased and wanted to make sure such an unfortunate situation was not repeated. Notice in verse 18, he said to Jacob, "No, my father, this one is the firstborn; put your right hand on his head." However, verse 19 shows that Jacob refused to change the way his hands were arranged, but said, "I know, my son, I know. He too will become a people, and he too will become great.

Nevertheless, his younger brother will be greater than he, and his descendants will become a group of nations."

Jacob set the record straight with Joseph by informing him that what he had done in crossing his hands to bless the two boys, was not a mistake. His physical sight was failing, but his spiritual sight was as clear as could be. He blessed them through the eyes of faith (Heb 11:21). Though speculations may abound, the identity of Manasseh's and Ephraim's descendants today, continues to be an enduring mystery, just as it is with descendants of most of Jacob's other sons, except Judah.

Verse 20 shows Jacob blessed them that day and said, "In your name will Israel pronounce this blessing: 'May God make you like Ephraim and Manasseh.' He elevated Ephraim ahead of Manasseh." In other words, Ephraim, who was the younger, was put before Manasseh, who was the older. It was like Jacob being put before Esau; however, the reason for the latter was clearly because of Esau's evil ways. But it was not clear why Ephraim was put ahead of Manasseh in this case, except it was God's will to do so. Interestingly, when Jacob adopted them as his own, they became more than sons to their biological father Joseph, they also became his brothers. This may explain his final instructions later as seen in Genesis 50:24-25.

Having blessed his two grandsons, whom he counted as his own sons, verses 21-22 indicate that Jacob told Joseph, he was about to die, but he prophesied that God would be with Joseph, and would take him back to the land of his fathers. And to him Jacob said he gave one more ridge of land than to his brothers, the ridge he took from the Amorites with his sword and his bow. It is not clear when Jacob engaged the Amorites in battle during his lifetime, or if he was speaking prophetically about when Israel as a nation would take and settled in the land of Canaan. The tract of land to which Jacob was referring was purchased from Hamor, the father of Shechem, when Jacob returned to Canaan from Harran (Gen 33:19; Josh 24:32). Evidently, the land may have been occupied by the Amorites while Israel was in Egypt, but Israel recaptured it under the leadership of Moses and Joshua.

Interestingly, this additional ridge of land bequeathed to Joseph, became the final resting place for his bones when they were eventually taken up out of Egypt (Josh 24:32; John 4:5). Despite all his successes in this world, ultimately, the only assured property allotted to him was that which served as his grave. This is true for all of mankind; Therefore, it makes more sense for people to build their hopes on things eternal, than on things temporal. Joseph became highly successful in Egypt, but his resting place in this world was the same as that of any other human, a grave, albeit, in the Promised Land.

GENESIS CHAPTER FORTY-NINE

In the previous chapter, it was pointed out that Joseph and his two sons Manasseh and Ephraim went to see Jacob, because he was ill. When they arrived, Jacob mustered his strength and sat up on his bed to talk with them. He blessed Joseph's two sons by crossing his arms to place the blessing of the first-born on the younger son Ephraim, while Manasseh, the older son, received the blessing of a younger son. He also adopted Joseph's two sons as his own and declared they would be reckoned among the tribes of Israel. This chapter will examine the prophetic pronouncements Jacob made over all his sons immediately before he died.

JACOB'S PROPHETIC PRONOUNCEMENTS OVER HIS SONS

After meeting with and blessing Joseph and his two sons, verses 1-2, declare that Jacob, who was on his dying bed, called together all his other sons for a family meeting. He asked them to gather around him, so he could tell them what would happen to them in days to come.

Jacob summoned his sons to do two things: 1. assemble, and 2. listen. He assembled them to listen to their father Israel. Interestingly, Jacob's final words to each of his sons, were spoken in the hearing of each other, so they all heard what he said, and would be able to hold each other accountable for living up to what was expected of them. Sadly, his final words to some of them were difficult words for sons to hear in their father's final moments. Hid daughter Dinah was not addressed at all.

Notice verses 3-4, he told Reuben, who was he and Leah's first son, that he was his firstborn, his might, the first sign of his strength, excelling in honor, excelling in power, but turbulent as the waters, he would no longer excel, because he went up onto his father's bed, and onto his couch and defiled it. This was a reference to the occasion when Reuben slept with his father's concubine, Bilhah (Gen 35:22). As a result, Reuben's influence diminished to the point where his brothers stopped listening to him (Gen 42:22). His tribe also lost its honor and influence. No king, prince, judge, or prophet is known to have descended from the tribe of Reuben. Forty years had passed, since Reuben committed that terrible sin against his father, but for it to be remembered among the last words he spoke before he died, was like a wound, which never healed.

In verses 5–7, Jacob addressed Simeon and Levi, who were brothers, his second and third sons by the same mother, Leah. He said their swords were weapons of violence, and he prayed never to enter their council, or join their assembly, because they killed men in their anger and hamstrung oxen as they pleased. He cursed their anger for being fierce, and their fury for being cruel. He said they would be scattered in Jacob and dispersed in Israel.

Simeon and Levi were particularly angry and fierce in their dealings with the Shechemites (Gen 34:30). In that incident, they killed all the men of the city, because the prince raped their sister Dinah. Jacob regarded Simeon's and Levi's swords as weapons of violence, which were used to perpetrate aggression, rather than to defend against it. Their eagerness to shed blood caused him to refrain from entering their council or joining their assembly. In other words, these sons were not the type to be listened to or associated with. While he did not curse them, he cursed their anger, and their fury. Levi's case became an interesting irony, because his descendants were indeed scattered among the tribes and eventually served as priests before God. What a testimony of change!

In verses 8–12, Jacob turned his attention to Judah, his fourth son with Leah. He told him his brothers would praise him, and his hand would be on the neck of his enemies. He foretold that his father's sons would bow down to him. He said:

> You are a lion's cub, Judah; you return from the prey, my son. Like a lion he crouches and lies down, like a lioness—who dares to rouse him? The scepter will not depart from Judah, nor the ruler's staff from between his feet, until he to whom it belongs shall come and the obedience of the nations shall be his. He will tether his donkey to a vine, his colt to the choicest branch; he will wash his garments in wine, his robes in the blood of grapes. His eyes will be darker than wine, his teeth whiter than milk.[1] (NIV)

Notice, the blessings, which should have been Reuben's, the firstborn, were pronounced on Judah. He would be a successful warrior, and

---

1. Barker, et. al. *The NIV Study Bible*, Genesis 49:8–12.

his brothers would praise him and bow down to him. In other words, they would follow his leadership. Judah was compared to a lion, because he would be strong, and others would know it, but his strength would be used as a deterrent, rather than a source of unwarranted terror. As such, Judah was depicted as a lion who crouches, rather than one who attacks and makes war for the sake of it, and simply because he could.

Most importantly, Judah was told the scepter (royal and legal authority) would be his, which began with king David, and would remain with his tribe, until He to whom it belonged came, which was a prophetic reference to Jesus Christ, who is a descendant of the tribe of Judah. The scepter is His, and so shall it be forevermore. It will not pass from Him to anyone else. He is King and Lawgiver forever.

In verse 13, Jacob revealed that Zebulun, Leah's fifth son, would live by the seashore, and become a haven for ships; his border would be extended toward Sidon. Joshua 19:10–16 show this was accomplished when their territory was apportioned by lot, rather than human decree. It says (Josh 19:11, KJV) Zebulun's territory went up toward the sea and Maralah, and reached to Dabbasheth, and to the river that is before Jokneam. In essence, Zebulun's descendants were predicted to be a sea-fearing people.

In verses 14–15, Jacob turned his attention to Issachar, his sixth and final son with his wife Leah. He said Issachar was like a rawboned donkey, lying down among the sheep pens. When he sees how good his resting place is and how pleasant his land is, he will bend his shoulder to the burden and submit to forced labor. This meant, Issachar would be a hardworking and industrious people. His descendants were later described as people who understood the times, to know what Israel ought to do (1 Chron 12:32).

Verses 16–18 declare Jacob's prophetic pronouncements on his son Dan, who was his first son with Rachel's servant Bilhah. He said Dan would provide justice for his people as one of the tribes of Israel. However, Dan would be like a snake by the roadside, a viper along the path, that bites the horse' heels so that its rider tumbles backward. Jacob concluded his statements about Dan with this plea: "I look for your deliverance, Lord."

The prediction that Dan would judge or provide justice for his people was accomplished in the days of his descendant Samson, who judged the tribe for twenty years (Judg 13:2). However, Dan was compared to a serpent, like the one in the Garden of Eden. This meant he would not remain faithful to God and would lead others into unfaithfulness. In this regard, the tribe of Dan became the first to institutionalize idolatry in their worship (Judg 18). First Kings 12:28–30, and Second Kings 10:29, show they continued in idolatry for most of their existence as a people, and contributed to leading Israel into idolatry. Jacob's plea for their deliverance, was very appropriate considering their idolatrous path. Thankfully, he prophesied that they would be delivered.

In verse 19, Jacob predicted that Gad, his first son with Leah's servant Zilpah, would be attacked by a band of raiders, but he would in turn attack them at their heels. First Chronicles 12:8, indicates that Gad's descendants were brave warriors, ready for battle, and able to handle the shield and spear. Their faces were like faces of lions, and they were swift like gazelles. They were successful in subduing their Canaanite neighbors during the times of Saul and David.

In verse 20, Jacob's only prediction concerning Asher, his second son with Leah's servant Zilpah, was his food would be rich, and he would provide delicacies fit for a king. Asher's history was not as illustrious as that of his brothers, but as his name suggests, his descendants appeared to live happy and prosperous lives.

Verse 21 presents Jacob's prediction concerning Naphtali, his second son with Rachel's servant Bilhah. He said Naphtali was like a doe set free that bears beautiful fawns. This pronouncement seemed to infer that Naphtali, whose name signified struggle, would struggle as a people, but would eventually be free, and would be a pleasant and sociable people.

Rachel's sons were the last to receive prophetic pronouncements from their father Jacob. In verses 22–26 he said Joseph would be a fruitful vine near a spring, whose branches climb over a wall. With bitterness archers would attack him, and they would shoot at him with hostility. But his bow would remain steady, his strong arms would stay limber, because of the hand of the Mighty One of Jacob, because of the Shepherd, the Rock of Israel, because of his father's God, who would help him; because of the Almighty, who blesses him with blessings of the skies above, blessings of the deep springs below, blessings of the breast and womb. His father's blessings are greater than the blessings of the ancient mountains, and greater than the bounty of the age-old hills. Jacob said, let all these blessings rest on the head of Joseph, on the brow of the prince among his brothers.

Joseph had endured many attacks from his own brothers, who hated him and sold him into slavery after contemplating about killing him. While in Egypt he was attacked by his master's wife and accused of attempted rape, because he refused to sleep with her. Having been chosen by Pharaoh to be second in charge in his kingdom, meant he probably endured opposition from those who thought such a lofty role should not be afforded to a foreigner with a criminal record. Yet, in all of this, he prevailed because the hand of the Almighty was with him. In other words, God was credited for his success. It should be noted, his father's pronouncements were not only pertaining to his past, but also his future. The tribes of Ephraim and

Manasseh, which formed the House of Joseph, became two of the strongest, and most prominent tribes in Israel.

Jacob's final pronouncement was reserved for his beloved son Benjamin. The words he spoke proved he was speaking under divine, rather than human influence, because if they were Jacob's own words, he would have been far more complimentary to his dear son Benjamin. Instead, verse 27 points out that Jacob described Benjamin as a ravenous wolf, who in the morning devours the prey, and in the evening divides the plunder. The ravenousness of Benjamin's descendants was highlighted in Judges 20, where a man's wife was raped and murdered in the Benjamite city of Gibeah. Rather than judging and punishing the men who committed the evil act, they gathered from all their cities to defend them, and to fight a war against the other tribes of Israel. They lost the war, and by the end of it, Judges 21 reveals the tribe had been cut off from Israel, and its numbers were significantly reduced.

Saul, the first king of Israel was of the tribe of Benjamin (1 Sam 9:1–2). Queen Esther and her uncle Mordecai were also descendants of that tribe (Esth 2:5). The apostle Paul was a notable descendant of Benjamin (Rom 11:1; Phil 3:5). He fulfilled Jacob's prophecy more than any other known descendant of Benjamin. As a young Pharisee, he ravaged the Church and was responsible for the deaths of numerous Christians (Acts 7:58–59; Acts 22:4; 1 Cor 15:9; Gal 1:13). However, after his conversion he did more than any other, as a preacher of the gospel, to share the spoils of his ministry, which continues to this very day.

Verse 28 provided an interesting summation by stating that all of them formed the twelve tribes of Israel, and those pronouncements were what their father said to them when he blessed them, giving each the blessing appropriate to him. Some of what he said were very unflattering, and difficult last words, but his statements were appropriate for each son, because he was not only speaking directly to them, but also to their descendants after them, and they had no way of controlling the conduct of their descendants in the future.

JACOB'S DEATH

Jacob had already given instructions to Joseph about his burial wishes (Gen 47:29–30). However, in verses 29–32, he repeated his final wishes in the hearing of all his sons. He told them he was about to be gathered to his people and he expressed his desire to be buried with his fathers in the cave in the field of Ephron the Hittite, the cave in the field of Machpelah, near

Mamre in Canaan, which Abraham bought along with the field as a burial place from Ephron the Hittite. He said Abraham and his wife Sarah were buried there, Isaac and his wife Rebekah were buried there, and he had buried Leah there. The field and the cave in it were bought from the Hittites.

Jacob knew where he wanted to be buried, and he wanted to make sure his sons knew as well. It was the only piece of property the patriarchs owned on this earth. It was their grave, and interestingly, while Rachel, the wife he dearly loved was buried alongside the road to Ephrath (Gen 48:7), Leah was buried with the patriarchs and in the same place where he would be buried. In essence, she was the wife who received the highest honor by resting beside him in his earthly grave, and symbolically resting beside him in eternity, as mother of Jesus Christ, the Messiah.

Verse 33 shows when Jacob had finished giving instructions to his sons, he drew his feet up into the bed, breathed his last and was gathered to his people. Observe that he drew his own feet up into the bed as he prepared to die. God gave him the strength he needed to assume an appropriate posture for peaceful rest. The strength he mustered to sit up on his bed and bless Joseph and his two sons (Gen 48:2), then to make prophetic pronouncements over all his other sons (Gen 49:1), was depleted the moment he drew his feet up into the bed. When he died, he was gathered to his people, the patriarchs about whom he so fondly reminisced, who were also God's people. He did all he needed to do, and said all he needed to say, then he drew his feet up into the bed and died. What a way to go!

GENESIS CHAPTER FIFTY

The previous chapter examined Jacob's prophetic pronouncements over each of his sons, after which he drew his feet up into the bed and died. This chapter will assess details surrounding his burial back in the land of Canaan, as he requested in his final wishes. It will also review Joseph's words of comfort and assurance to his brothers, and finally his own death.

MOURNING FOR JACOB

Verse 1 points out that when Joseph saw his father Jacob was dead, he threw himself on him and wept over him and kissed him. It would also have been at that point when the words God foretold (Gen 46:4) occurred, when Joseph's hand closed his father's eyes. His grief was distinctly described, but no doubt, his brothers probably grieved and wept profusely as well. Despite Jacob's partiality toward Rachel's sons, his other sons demonstrated their love, and utmost respect for him.

Verses 2–3 indicate that Joseph directed the physicians in his service to embalm his father. So, they embalmed him, taking a full forty days, because that was the time it took for embalming. And the Egyptians mourned for him seventy days. Notice, Joseph called on the resources of Egypt to take care of his father's dead body, and to preserve it for burial back in Canaan. Jacob's wishes to be buried with his fathers, back in Canaan, could not have been honored if Joseph did not have access to the embalming resources of Egypt. Without such resources a dead body would not have lasted, for obvious reasons, or endured the long funeral procession back to Canaan.

Notice, the Egyptians also mourned for Jacob, though he was old when he moved there, did not really interact with them, and few, if any of them probably knew him. Obviously, their mourning was for Joseph's sake, whom they respected because of all he had done for their country and people. Therefore, they mourned for seventy days (ten weeks) because they knew Joseph, a great leader among them, was in mourning. That was quite a sacrifice on their part, and Pharaoh allowed it.

JOSEPH REQUEST PHARAOH'S PERMISSION TO LEAVE EGYPT

Verses 4-5 reveal that when the days of mourning had passed, Joseph asked members of Pharaoh's court to speak to Pharaoh on his behalf and tell him, his father made him swear an oath to bury him in the tomb he dug for himself in the land of Canaan. Therefore, he asked to be allowed to go up and bury his father; then he would return. Joseph may have asked others to intervene on his behalf, because being in a state of mourning, it would not have been appropriate for him to enter the presence of the king with a sad countenance. He was also careful to inform Pharaoh that after discharging the duty of burying his father, as he promised to do, he would return. In other words, that obligation would be behind him, and he would be able to regain his focus on his work.

Verses 6-7 show that Pharaoh not only agreed to allow Joseph to go, but he also allowed others who loved and respected Joseph to go with him to the land of Canaan. He told him to go up and bury his father, as he swore to him to do. So, Joseph went up to bury his father, and all of Pharaoh's officials accompanied him, the dignitaries of his court and all the dignitaries of Egypt, besides all the members of Joseph's household, his brothers and those belonging to his father's household.

In other words, Jacob received a royal farewell and a stately funeral. Though Egyptians did not normally associate with Hebrews (Gen 43:32), they were willing to do so out of respect for Joseph. As an interesting side note, the Pharaoh for whom Joseph worked was willing to allow him to go to Canaan to bury his father Israel, but history shows, years later, Moses would ask another Pharaoh to let Israel go, so they may worship their God and return, but he would refuse.

JACOB'S FUNERAL PROCESSION FROM EGYPT TO CANAAN

Verses 8-11 reveal that only the Israelite children, their flocks, and herds were left in Goshen, while chariots and horsemen accompanied Jacob's body to Canaan. It was a very large company of people, such that when they reached the threshing floor of Atad, near the Jordan, they lamented loudly and bitterly; and there, Joseph observed a seven-day period of mourning for his father. It says when the Canaanites who lived there saw mourning at the threshing floor of Atad, they said, "The Egyptians are holding a solemn ceremony of mourning." That is why that place near the Jordan was called Abel Mizraim (mourning of the Egyptians).

Note that Atad, located near the Jordan river was renamed because of the solemnity and compassion with which the Egyptians mourned for Israel. However, years later, history shows the Egyptians would no longer mourn with compassion for Israel but would hate and enslave them. It would take God's intervention to bring deliverance at the waters of the Red Sea, where Israel once again cross back over into the land of Canaan. Meanwhile, the Egyptians who accompanied Joseph and his family, on their mission to funeralize Jacob, showed extraordinary sympathy toward them during their season of grief.

JACOB'S BURIAL

Verses 12–14 affirm that Jacob's sons did as he commanded them. They carried him to the land of Canaan and buried him in the cave in the field of Machpelah, near Mamre, which Abraham bought along with the field as a burial place from Ephron the Hittite. After burying his father, Joseph returned to Egypt, together with his brothers and all the others who had gone with him.

The Bible gives more information about events leading up to Jacob's burial, than about the burial itself. Once the burial occurred, Joseph and his brothers returned to Egypt to resume life as normal. However, with their forefathers buried in the land of Canaan, and with the looming promise that Canaan would one day be theirs, it was likely they always looked forward to returning, yet, none of them did at that time; They all returned to Egypt.

JOSEPH CALMS HIS BROTHERS' FEARS

Verse 16 indicates that after their father's death, Joseph's brothers wondered, "What if he holds a grudge against us and pays us back for all the wrongs we did to him?" Their guilty consciences got the best of them, and they began to doubt the authenticity of Joseph's forgiveness. But his forgiveness was real, because he never harbored the kind of resentment toward them, which they did toward him. Besides, he attributed the apparent unfortunate events in his life to the divine hand of God working things out for their good.

Most importantly, as far as he was concerned, those things were in the past, but his brothers kept bringing them up because of their guilt, and because the forgiveness Joseph offered was unconditional and new to them; It was Christlike, and worth emulating by those today who may have been mistreated and who harbor malice in their heart. Notice, because of their overwhelming guilt, verses 16–17 declare they sent word to Joseph, telling him his father left instructions before he died, asking him to forgive them for the sins and wrongs they committed in treating him so badly. Therefore, they asked him to please forgive their sins, as they referred to themselves as the servants of the God of his father. But when their message reached Joseph, he wept.

It is not clear if their father Jacob, really instructed them to ask for Joseph's forgiveness after his death. If he did, it would seem to imply that Jacob believed Joseph's forgiveness was conditional, and like that of Esau's, who swore to kill Jacob as soon as his father Isaac died (Gen 27:41). In any case, their consciences bothered them to the extent that they sent word to appeal to Joseph. They also described themselves as servants of the God of his father. In other words, they represented themselves to be changed men of God!

Observe Joseph's response on receiving their message. It says he wept. He was grieved to learn they were still stuck in the past. He had moved on, and the thought of revenge against them was the farthest thing from his mind! However, to them the past remained the present because they knew they had sinned against him, and he, being in a position of power could take revenge if he wanted. But he did not want to, and their inability to see that, grieved him to tears.

Verse 18 shows they did not only send a message, but they also came to make a personal appeal to Joseph. It says they came and threw themselves down before him, declaring themselves to be his slaves! Interestingly, their bowing down before him, was another fulfillment of what was prophesied in his dream (Gen 37:7, 9), which was the reason they hated him in the first place!

Notice Joseph's mature and Godly response to their appeals. Verses 19–21 reveal Joseph said to them, "Don't be afraid. Am I in the place of God? You intended to harm me, but God intended it for good to accomplish what is now being done, the saving of many lives. So then, don't be afraid. I will provide for you and your children."

Joseph reassured them of his forgiveness, his unwillingness to take revenge, or to harm them, and he spoke kindly to them. He did not establish any conditions or set expectations of future behaviors for them to continue to earn his favor. Instead, he promised to provide for them, and for their children as well! In other words, they were totally and unconditionally forgiven!

JOSEPH'S DEATH

Verses 22–23 state that Joseph stayed in Egypt, along with all his father's family. He lived a hundred and ten years and saw the third generation of Ephraim's children. Joseph also saw the children of Makir, son of Manasseh, who were placed on his knees at birth. This meant Joseph continued for many years to be protector and provider for his and his father's family. As noted, he lived to see his great, great, great grandchildren through his younger son Ephraim, and his great grandson through his older son Manasseh.

Having lived to such a ripe old age, verses 24–26 indicate that Joseph told his brothers, he was about to die, but God would surely come to their aid and take them up out of Egypt to the land He promised on oath to their fathers. Joseph also made them swear an oath that they would carry his bones up from that place with them. After that, he died at the age of a hundred and ten, they embalmed him, and placed his body in a coffin in Egypt.

As Israel's protector and provider in Egypt, Joseph informed his brothers that he was about to die. This obviously caused trepidation, and concern about their survival in his absence. But he assured them, though he would be gone, God would still be there, and He would come to their aid. This was also an admission that conditions in Egypt would change for them after his death, and they would indeed need aid from God. Notice, the aid God would render would be to take them out of Egypt, to the land He promised on oath to Abraham, Isaac, and Jacob. Hence, there was no need for them to become integrated into Egypt because God's aid was not to destroy the idolatrous Egyptians and give their land to Israel. Instead, He would take them out from there, back to Canaan, where He would destroy its idolatrous inhabitants and establish Israel as His people.

Joseph made his brothers promise to take his bones with them back to the Promised Land, where his forefathers were buried. Which of his brothers did he make swear to do this? More than likely this is a reference to Ephraim and Manasseh, who were not only his sons but were adopted by his father, which also made them his brothers. This conjecture is reasonable, because Joseph was Jacob's eleventh son, and most of his brothers, who were older than he, may have already been dead and buried. It is not clear if their bodies were buried in Egypt, or returned to Canaan, but Joseph made it clear, he did not want to be buried in Egypt. As such, his body was embalmed and kept in a coffin, but never buried, until three hundred years later, when Israel was delivered from slavery in Egypt.

CONCLUSION

The book of Genesis commenced with creation of new life, and with God giving authority to mankind to rule over everything, except each other. However, because mankind, as represented by Adam and Eve, abdicated their authority by listening to Satan, sin entered the world, and death became its justified penalty. By the end of the Book of Genesis, the need for a Savior, as predicted (Gen 3:15) was clear. Joseph became a savior for Israel, but the world still needed one. That need is more evident today. Hence, God sent His Son at His first appearing, to save the world through His sacrifice for sin, but He will send Him again, so that the prophecy revealed in Genesis 3:15, about Eve's descendant who will crush the serpent's head, will be completely fulfilled. Until then, with eager anticipation, mankind should enthusiastically shout the declaration found in Revelation 22:20, which says, "...even so, come Lord Jesus!"

BIBLIOGRAPHY

Archer, Gleason. *A Survey of Old Testament Introduction*. Chicago, IL: Moody, 1981.

Barker, Kenneth, et al. *The NIV Study Bible*. Grand Rapids, MI: Zondervan, 1995.

Bible Atlas. *Goshen*. Accessed April 10, 2021 from https://bibleatlas.org/goshen.htm: Bibleatlas.

Braterman, Paul. *How Science Figured Out the Age of Earth*. https://www.scientificamerican.com/article/how-science-figured-out-the-age-of-the-earth/.

Erickson, Millard. *Christian Theology, Second Edition*. Grand Rapids, MI: Baker, 2001.

Geisler, Norman, and Frank Turek. *I Don't Have Enough Faith to be an Atheist*. Wheaton, IL: Crossway, 2004.

Henry, Matthew. *Matthew Henry Commentary On the Whole Bible Complete and Unabridged*. Peabody, MA: Hendrickson, 1998.

MacArthur, John. *The Battle for the Beginning*. Nashville, TN: Thomas Nelson, 2001.

Marshall, Taylor. *Testimony and Testicles, the Oath of Abraham's Servant,* Accessed March 3, 2021, https://taylormarshall.com/2008/10/testimony-and-testicles-oath-of.html.

Matthews, Victor. *Manners and Customs In the Bible: An Illustrated Guide to Daily Life in Bible Times*. Peabody, MA: Hendrickson, 2000.

Ryrie, Charles. *Basic Theology*. Chicago, IL: Moody, 1999.

Tillman, Nola. *How Old is the Earth?* https://www.spave.com/24854-how-old-is-earth.html.

Tillman, Nola. *How Old is the Universe?* https://www.space.com/24054-how-old-is-unverse.html.

Webster, Miriam. *Synonyms for Eternity*. https://www.merriam-webster.com/dictionary/eternity?src=search-dict-box2021.

Wright, William. *Beginning with Genesis: A Journey from Knowledge to Wisdom*. Eugene, OR: Wipf and Stock, 2022.

Youngman, Bernard. *The Lands and Peoples of the Living Bible*. New York, NY: Bell, 1982.

SUBJECT INDEX

Abel, 39, 40, 41, 42, 43, 44, 46, 48, 49, 349
Abida, 177
Abimael, 78
Abimelech, 114, 144, 145, 146, 147, 148, 149, 150, 156, 157, 185, 186, 187, 188, 189, 190
Abraham, 77, 79, 81, 82, 83, 85, 94, 111, 114, 119, 120, 121, 122, 123, 124, 125, 126, 127, 128, 129, 130, 131, 132, 133, 134, 139, 140, 141, 143, 144, 145, 146, 147, 148, 149, 150, 151, 152, 153, 154, 155, 156, 157, 158, 159, 160, 161, 162, 163, 164, 165, 166, 167, 168, 169, 170, 171, 172, 173, 174, 175, 176, 177, 178, 179, 180, 181, 182, 183, 185, 186, 187, 188, 189, 191, 193, 201, 203, 204, 205, 206, 207, 209, 230, 231, 232, 234, 235, 243, 254, 256, 258, 260, 263, 325, 331, 339, 346, 349, 351, 353
Abram, 82, 83, 85, 86, 87, 88, 89, 90, 91, 92, 93, 94, 95, 96, 98, 99, 100, 101, 102, 103, 104, 105, 106, 107, 108, 109, 110, 112, 113, 114, 115, 116, 117, 118, 119, 125
Accad, 76
Adah, 46, 258, 259
Adam, 14, 19, 22, 23, 27, 30, 34, 35, 36, 37, 39, 40, 42, 43, 45, 46, 47, 48, 49, 50, 52, 66, 71, 72, 73, 75, 143, 352
Adbeel, 180

Admah, 77, 96, 97
Adultery, 88, 107, 145, 186, 279
Ahuzzath, 189
Ai, 86, 92
Alcoholic, 142
Almodad, 78
Almond, 221, 225
Almonds, 305
Altar, 66, 69, 86, 88, 92, 95, 161, 189, 206, 207, 243, 251, 252, 253
Amalek, 259
Amalekites, 97
Ammonites, 143
Amorite, 77, 98
Amorites, 97, 105, 106, 107, 130, 340
Amraphel, 96, 97
Anah, 258, 260
Anamim, 76
Ancestors, 105, 106, 232
Aner, 98, 99, 100, 101
Angel, 37, 115, 116, 139, 141, 154, 161, 162, 169, 225
Angels, 34, 37, 50, 52, 53, 133, 134, 137, 204, 205, 233, 234
Angry, 40, 41, 132, 200, 216, 229, 266, 282, 287, 319, 342
Animals, 12, 13, 14, 19, 20, 23, 24, 26, 33, 40, 42, 57, 59, 60, 61, 65, 66, 69, 76, 195, 221, 230, 235, 248, 259, 266, 307, 322
Anthropomorphic, 31, 54, 63, 80, 107, 130
Aram, 77, 78, 81, 163, 170, 181, 202, 203, 226, 243, 254, 256

355

SUBJECT INDEX

Arioch, 96, 97
Ark, 56, 57, 58, 59, 60, 61, 62, 63, 64, 65, 66, 68, 69, 70, 71, 75
Arkite, 77
Armenian, 21
Arphaxad, 77, 78, 79, 82
Arvadite, 77
Asenath, 291, 293, 336
Asher, 216, 256, 262, 344
Ashkenaz, 75
Ashteroth, 97
Ashur, 21, 77, 180
Ashurites, 177
Asia Minor, 21
Asshur, 76
Assyria, 21
Atad, 348, 349
Atonement, 35, 40, 69

Babel, 76, 79, 81
Babylon, 76, 79, 80, 96
Baker, 282, 284, 285, 286, 287, 295, 330
Balm, 267, 305
Baptism, 120, 121, 249
Basemath, 191, 258, 259
Bed, 134, 145, 205, 278, 279, 280, 292, 336, 337, 341, 346, 347
Beer Lahai Roi, 116, 176, 179
Beeri, 191
Beersheba, 153, 157, 162, 165, 189, 190, 192, 204, 324, 325, 329, 335
Beka, 172
Bela, 96, 97
Belly, 33
Ben-Ammi, 143
Benjamin, 255, 256, 261, 262, 296, 299, 301, 302, 303, 304, 305, 306, 307, 308, 309, 310, 311, 312, 313, 314, 315, 316, 317, 318, 321, 322, 323, 327, 329, 335, 345
Ben-Oni, 255
Bera, 96, 102
Bethel, 86, 88, 92, 204, 205, 206, 225, 236, 243, 251, 252, 253, 255, 258, 337
Bethuel, 163, 171, 172, 173, 174, 181, 202, 203

Bible, 1, 5, 6, 13, 27, 39, 40, 45, 46, 81, 83, 87, 99, 106, 111, 116, 129, 130, 133, 135, 142, 143, 144, 149, 155, 159, 160, 162, 175, 180, 197, 199, 201, 204, 219, 230, 234, 235, 241, 242, 245, 250, 268, 271, 291, 292, 316, 336, 342, 349, 353
Big Bang theory, 2
Bilhah, 212, 216, 217, 218, 239, 241, 256, 262, 266, 342, 343, 344
Billion Years, 3, 7, 11
Billions, 5, 18, 19
Bird, 11, 23, 56, 58, 107
Birds, 12, 105
Birsha, 96
Birthday, 65, 285
Birthright, 177, 182, 183, 184, 185, 191, 192, 193, 194, 196, 198, 200, 201, 202, 204, 207, 210, 219, 226, 240, 258, 260, 331
Bitterness, 41, 42, 242, 344
Blood, 24, 43, 44, 69, 103, 104, 108, 110, 121, 209, 266, 267, 268, 280, 299, 319, 342
Bonded Atoms, 4
Bone, 24
Bread, 100, 126, 134, 183, 195, 284, 322
Brother, 39, 40, 41, 42, 43, 44, 46, 48, 49, 69, 74, 78, 82, 83, 86, 98, 146, 148, 150, 163, 171, 172, 173, 174, 175, 177, 182, 185, 191, 193, 194, 195, 196, 197, 198, 199, 200, 202, 203, 211, 212, 233, 234, 235, 236, 238, 239, 240, 241, 244, 251, 253, 254, 257, 259, 263, 265, 266, 267, 268, 270, 271, 274, 275, 298, 299, 300, 301, 302, 303, 304, 305, 306, 308, 309, 314, 319, 321, 323, 329, 331, 340
Buz, 163

Cain, 39, 40, 41, 42, 43, 44, 45, 46, 47, 48, 49, 53, 69, 72, 75, 76
Calah, 76
Calneh, 76
Calvary, 160
Camels, 88, 170, 171, 172, 173, 175, 176, 221, 226, 234, 235, 267

Canaan, 71, 73, 74, 75, 76, 77, 83, 85, 86, 91, 92, 94, 96, 100, 107, 108, 109, 112, 119, 120, 129, 164, 165, 166, 169, 177, 178, 180, 186, 192, 194, 200, 203, 204, 205, 207, 210, 218, 219, 223, 225, 226, 228, 231, 233, 235, 236, 239, 243, 252, 253, 254, 257, 258, 259, 261, 277, 285, 293, 294, 296, 297, 298, 301, 302, 305, 311, 321, 322, 323, 325, 327, 329, 330, 332, 333, 335, 336, 337, 338, 340, 346, 347, 348, 349, 351
Canaanites, 86, 92, 107, 119, 144, 162, 168, 169, 191, 201, 202, 203, 204, 246, 250, 260, 349
Carbon Dating, 7
Carnivores, 287
Casluhim, 76
Cattle, 88, 134, 141, 148, 157, 234, 333
Cave, 141, 144, 165, 166, 179, 345, 346, 349
Chaldeans, 104, 168, 175
Chaldees, 82, 83, 85, 86, 92, 96, 104, 106, 163
Cherubim, 36
Childbearing, 34, 109, 110, 217
Christ, 36, 48, 51, 52, 53, 61, 62, 75, 114, 121, 127, 150, 152, 160, 161, 162, 179, 195, 214, 216, 237, 249, 263, 267, 274, 275, 276, 297, 310, 316, 318, 319, 328, 343, 346
Christians, 4, 6, 9, 18, 195, 279, 280, 345
Chromosome, 25
Church, 173, 208, 249, 297, 310, 328, 345
Circumcised, 120, 122, 123, 124, 126, 151, 180, 247, 248, 249
Circumcision, 118, 120, 121, 123, 124, 126, 170, 247, 249
Cistern, 266, 267, 268, 270
City, 45, 46, 79, 80, 81, 85, 111, 131, 132, 133, 134, 135, 136, 137, 138, 140, 141, 142, 166, 167, 179, 206, 243, 244, 245, 247, 248, 249, 250, 251, 252, 253, 265, 292, 300, 312, 313, 317, 342, 345
Cloud, 9, 70
Concubine, 163, 256, 258, 259, 302, 342
Cord, 273, 274

Covenant, 49, 51, 55, 56, 64, 70, 71, 74, 78, 82, 107, 111, 112, 113, 114, 115, 118, 119, 120, 121, 122, 123, 124, 125, 151, 158, 169, 170, 177, 178, 179, 181, 183, 186, 190, 191, 193, 194, 201, 202, 204, 210, 230, 231, 233, 242, 247, 248, 257, 260
Cows, 235, 242, 286, 287, 288, 289
Creation, 1, 2, 3, 5, 6, 7, 8, 10, 12, 14, 15, 16, 17, 18, 19, 20, 22, 25, 31, 35, 43, 54, 56, 59, 60, 69, 74, 75, 216, 352
Creator, 20, 100
Creatures, 6, 8, 11, 12, 13, 14, 24, 26, 54, 56, 57, 58, 59, 60, 61, 63, 65, 66, 68, 70
Cupbearer, 282, 284, 285, 286, 287, 295, 330
Cush, 21, 76

Dabbasheth, 343
Damascus, 99, 102, 168
Dan, 98, 216, 256, 262, 343
David, 11, 252, 343, 344
Death, 21, 23, 27, 29, 36, 42, 44, 49, 50, 51, 52, 71, 72, 74, 86, 106, 107, 138, 147, 158, 164, 165, 168, 176, 177, 178, 179, 180, 185, 187, 188, 192, 200, 249, 253, 254, 255, 256, 257, 258, 259, 267, 269, 271, 272, 273, 274, 276, 286, 292, 302, 304, 305, 311, 312, 317, 321, 324, 335, 337, 338, 347, 349, 350, 351, 352
Dedan, 76, 177
Demons, 35, 37
Deoxyribonucleic acid (DNA), 225
Descendants, 22, 23, 28, 29, 30, 34, 35, 36, 37, 39, 46, 47, 48, 49, 53, 64, 70, 71, 72, 74, 75, 76, 77, 78, 79, 81, 82, 85, 96, 104, 105, 106, 107, 109, 116, 118, 119, 120, 122, 124, 151, 156, 157, 162, 163, 169, 170, 175, 177, 178, 180, 181, 182, 185, 186, 189, 191, 194, 199, 200, 201, 202, 203, 204, 207, 216, 219, 222, 227, 235, 238, 240, 242, 246, 254, 258, 259, 260, 261, 267, 325, 336, 337, 340, 342, 343, 344, 345

358 SUBJECT INDEX

Desert, 153, 155
Diklah, 78
Dinah, 218, 240, 244, 245, 246, 247, 248, 249, 250, 251, 341, 342
Dishan, 260
Dishon, 260
Divination, 219, 220, 312, 313
Divine, 3, 4, 13, 56, 121, 132, 174, 205, 221, 224, 287, 302, 323, 345, 349
Divorce, 25, 94, 153, 212
Donkey, 116, 159, 160, 301, 342, 343
Dove, 64, 65, 104, 105
Dream, 18, 145, 148, 156, 204, 207, 225, 227, 229, 243, 263, 264, 265, 283, 284, 285, 286, 287, 288, 289, 295, 297, 298, 299, 308, 333, 350
Drunk, 72, 73, 128, 142, 143, 211
Dumah, 180
Dungeon, 284
Dust, 20, 21, 33, 34, 35, 36, 94, 95, 103, 131, 204

Earth, 1, 2, 3, 5, 6, 7, 8, 9, 10, 11, 12, 13, 14, 16, 17, 18, 19, 20, 31, 39, 44, 45, 46, 51, 52, 53, 54, 55, 56, 58, 59, 60, 61, 62, 63, 64, 65, 66, 67, 68, 70, 71, 74, 75, 76, 78, 79, 80, 81, 85, 86, 94, 95, 100, 103, 108, 129, 130, 131, 142, 162, 164, 168, 172, 180, 185, 187, 197, 199, 204, 205, 220, 318, 335, 339, 346, 353
Eber, 77, 78
Eden, 19, 21, 36, 45, 72, 74, 93, 141, 343
Edom, 183, 234, 242, 258, 259, 260
Egypt, 10, 76, 77, 85, 87, 88, 91, 92, 93, 94, 96, 107, 109, 119, 140, 141, 155, 180, 185, 222, 227, 257, 260, 267, 269, 276, 277, 280, 282, 286, 287, 288, 289, 290, 291, 292, 293, 294, 295, 296, 297, 298, 299, 301, 303, 304, 305, 306, 307, 309, 311, 312, 313, 314, 315, 317, 318, 319, 320, 321, 322, 323, 324, 325, 326, 327, 328, 329, 330, 332, 333, 334, 335, 336, 337, 338, 340, 344, 347, 348, 349, 351

Egyptians, 87, 88, 186, 269, 292, 294, 298, 307, 309, 318, 325, 327, 329, 332, 333, 335, 347, 348, 349, 351
El Bethel, 253
El Paran, 97
Elam, 77, 96, 97
Eldaah, 177
Eliezer, 102, 103, 110, 168
Eliphaz, 258, 259
Elishah, 75
Ellasar, 96, 97
Elohim, 1, 4, 5, 13, 20, 21, 27, 28
Elon, 191, 258
El-Shaddai, 118, 121, 125, 128, 254, 305
Embalm, 347
Emites, 97
En Mishpat, 97
Enaim, 272, 273
Enoch, 45, 49, 50, 51, 52, 54, 178
Enosh, 46, 47, 48, 49
Environment, 13, 94, 98, 107, 115, 147, 155, 223, 263, 292
Ephah, 177
Epher, 177
Ephraim, 293, 328, 336, 337, 339, 340, 341, 344, 351
Ephrath, 255, 338, 346
Ephron, 165, 166, 179, 345, 346, 349
Er, 270, 271
Erech, 76
Esau, 177, 178, 182, 183, 184, 185, 190, 191, 192, 193, 194, 195, 196, 197, 198, 199, 200, 201, 202, 203, 204, 205, 207, 209, 211, 226, 233, 234, 235, 236, 237, 238, 239, 240, 241, 242, 244, 251, 254, 256, 257, 258, 259, 260, 261, 263, 331, 340, 350
Esek, 188
Eshkol, 98, 99, 100, 101
Eternity, 8, 34, 36, 37, 38, 67, 178, 179, 331, 346, 353
Euphrates, 21, 107, 226
Eve, 19, 22, 30, 35, 36, 37, 39, 40, 42, 45, 46, 47, 48, 71, 72, 73, 75, 352
Evening, 8, 9, 10, 11, 12, 14, 16, 17, 19, 64, 133, 170, 176, 211, 217, 345
Evil, 8, 21, 22, 23, 26, 27, 28, 30, 31, 33, 35, 36, 37, 39, 42, 43, 49, 54, 56,

66, 137, 201, 264, 269, 311, 312, 320, 324, 339, 340, 345
Evolution, 12
Ex nihilo, 2
Ezer, 260

Faith, 1, 2, 353
Famine, 87, 91, 92, 93, 185, 186, 187, 188, 190, 192, 289, 290, 293, 294, 295, 296, 297, 302, 303, 304, 306, 319, 320, 321, 325, 330, 332, 333, 334, 336
Farmer, 39, 40, 43, 44, 45
Father, 24, 25, 40, 42, 46, 49, 50, 51, 52, 61, 71, 72, 73, 74, 76, 77, 78, 82, 83, 85, 86, 88, 119, 122, 142, 143, 144, 147, 148, 155, 160, 161, 162, 163, 169, 172, 173, 174, 175, 176, 178, 179, 180, 181, 182, 183, 184, 185, 186, 187, 188, 189, 191, 192, 193, 194, 195, 196, 197, 198, 199, 200, 202, 203, 204, 205, 206, 207, 208, 209, 210, 211, 212, 215, 217, 222, 223, 224, 225, 226, 228, 229, 230, 231, 232, 234, 239, 243, 244, 245, 246, 247, 248, 250, 251, 252, 254, 255, 256, 257, 258, 259, 260, 261, 262, 263, 264, 265, 266, 267, 268, 269, 270, 271, 272, 273, 274, 276, 277, 280, 285, 291, 292, 293, 296, 297, 298, 299, 301, 302, 303, 304, 305, 306, 307, 308, 309, 311, 312, 314, 315, 316, 317, 318, 319, 320, 321, 322, 323, 324, 325, 326, 327, 328, 329, 330, 331, 332, 335, 336, 337, 338, 339, 340, 341, 342, 344, 345, 347, 348, 349, 350, 351
Fellowship, 31, 32, 254, 255
female, 13, 18, 19, 25, 48, 56, 60, 88, 123, 148, 221, 228, 234, 235, 236, 239, 244, 245, 322
Female, 58
Field, 34, 42, 165, 166, 167, 176, 179, 197, 264, 278, 297, 345, 346, 349

Fire, 4, 34, 72, 140, 159, 160, 161
Firmament, 8, 9, 10, 11, 12, 13
Firstborn, 40, 43, 77, 163, 180, 195, 197, 200, 202, 256, 258, 271, 274, 293, 310, 318, 339, 341
Fish, 12, 13, 14, 23, 60, 68
Flesh, 13, 24, 25, 30, 35, 46, 52, 53, 103, 104, 108, 110, 119, 120, 121, 124, 159, 160, 209, 216, 245, 267, 274, 275, 284
Flock, 40, 157, 193, 208, 209, 210, 215, 221, 225, 262, 265, 273
Flood, 9, 44, 47, 49, 51, 53, 56, 58, 59, 60, 61, 62, 63, 64, 66, 68, 70, 71, 72, 74, 75, 76, 78, 80, 81, 82, 131, 309
Food, 13, 14, 21, 29, 34, 35, 57, 68, 98, 153, 154, 158, 173, 192, 193, 194, 195, 196, 197, 206, 267, 278, 290, 292, 294, 295, 296, 297, 298, 301, 303, 304, 305, 306, 307, 309, 310, 311, 312, 317, 321, 329, 332, 333, 334, 344
Fossil, 7
Fruit, 10, 14, 19, 22, 27, 29, 30, 32, 33, 34, 68, 119

Gad, 216, 256, 262, 344
Gaham, 163
Galeed, 231
Gap Theory, 5, 6, 8
Garden, 19, 21, 22, 23, 26, 27, 31, 32, 36, 37, 72, 74, 93, 141, 143, 343
Garments, 35, 195, 342
Gatam, 259
Gaza, 77
Gentile, 69
Geological, 9
Gerar, 77, 144, 145, 150, 156, 185, 186, 187, 188, 189, 192
Gihon, 21
Gilead, 226, 227, 233, 267
Girgashites, 107
Girgasite, 77
Goat, 104, 196, 198, 220, 268, 273, 274
Goats, 193, 220, 221, 225, 230, 234, 235, 333
Godhead, 4, 5, 20, 33, 35

Gold, 21, 91, 172, 174, 267, 291
Gomer, 75
Gomorrah, 67, 77, 96, 97, 98, 114, 125, 129, 130, 131, 132, 133, 136, 139, 140, 144
Goshen, 320, 325, 326, 327, 329, 330, 336, 348, 353
Goyim, 96, 97
Grace, 35, 36, 38, 39, 44, 106, 132, 143, 267, 310, 328
Grain, 197, 199, 264, 286, 287, 289, 290, 293, 294, 295, 296, 299, 300, 301, 303, 306, 307, 322, 333
Grapes, 284, 342
Grave, 160, 165, 179, 268, 302, 315, 340, 346
Gulf of Mexico, 7

Hadad, 180
Hadoram, 78
Hagar, 83, 89, 109, 110, 111, 112, 113, 114, 115, 116, 117, 118, 119, 122, 126, 145, 148, 151, 152, 153, 154, 155, 157, 158, 159, 178, 180
Ham, 51, 55, 70, 71, 73, 74, 75, 76, 77, 79, 85, 97
Hamathite, 77
Hammurabi, 83
Hamor, 243, 244, 245, 246, 247, 248, 249, 250, 340
Hanok, 177
Haran, 82, 83, 85, 86, 92, 175, 177, 223, 226, 331
Harran, 200, 202, 203, 204, 205, 207, 208, 209, 210, 215, 219, 220, 223, 225, 226, 227, 231, 232, 233, 243, 257, 340
Havilah, 21, 76, 78, 180
Hazarmaveth, 78
Hazezon, 97
Hazo, 163
Heart, 43, 54, 66, 114, 115, 124, 126, 131, 147, 165, 174, 191, 234, 240, 242, 244, 245, 246, 252, 255, 257, 267, 268, 293, 298, 301, 316, 320, 323, 350
Heaven, 11, 13, 22, 37, 60, 74, 81, 85, 100, 140, 147, 154, 161, 162, 168, 169, 172, 197, 199, 204, 205, 256, 258
Heavens, 1, 2, 3, 5, 6, 9, 10, 11, 13, 16, 17, 20, 56, 60, 61, 63, 80, 139
Hebrew, 4, 5, 16, 18, 22, 98, 143, 280, 283, 287, 300, 309, 310, 318
Hebron, 95, 96, 164, 165, 166, 254, 256, 257
Heifer, 104
Hell, 38
Herbivores, 287
Heth, 77
Hip, 236, 237, 238, 239
Hirah, 270, 271, 272, 273, 304
Hittites, 77, 107, 165, 166, 168, 179, 346
Hivite, 77, 244, 258
Ho- rites, 97
Hobah, 99
Holy, 16, 17, 49, 50, 152
Homosexual, 134, 135
Honey, 305
Horite, 260
Horses, 333
House, 41, 42, 89, 113, 114, 127, 134, 135, 136, 145, 150, 172, 173, 193, 195, 202, 206, 228, 246, 247, 249, 251, 252, 277, 278, 279, 280, 282, 287, 288, 291, 292, 306, 307, 308, 309, 311, 312, 313, 317, 318
House of Joys, 83
House of the Great Light, 82
Human, 9, 14, 22, 23, 25, 26, 27, 29, 30, 31, 32, 42, 43, 44, 46, 48, 49, 51, 52, 54, 55, 65, 66, 69, 71, 73, 83, 105, 106, 107, 121, 141, 149, 150, 151, 159, 187, 236, 237, 238, 253, 276, 278, 300, 302, 310, 316, 320, 326, 328, 331, 340, 343, 345
Humans, 3, 6, 7, 11, 12, 13, 14, 17, 28, 30, 32, 35, 36, 37, 46, 51, 52, 53, 54, 59, 60, 62, 66, 69, 71, 72, 74, 76, 93, 171, 178, 237, 239, 253
Husband, 26, 27, 29, 30, 33, 34, 87, 88, 110, 111, 112, 113, 121, 128, 148, 164, 171, 174, 176, 194, 210, 213, 214, 215, 216, 217, 218, 226, 278, 279, 280
Hydrogen Atoms, 4

SUBJECT INDEX   361

Image, 13, 14, 19, 42, 48, 49, 69, 127, 195, 310
Immortal, 23
Incest, 142, 144
Instinct, 20, 37
In-Vitriol Fertilization (IVF), 103
Iraq, 21, 93
Isaac, 77, 83, 119, 122, 123, 150, 151, 152, 156, 157, 158, 159, 160, 161, 162, 164, 168, 169, 170, 171, 172, 173, 175, 176, 177, 178, 179, 180, 181, 182, 183, 184, 185, 186, 187, 188, 189, 190, 191, 192, 193, 194, 195, 196, 197, 198, 199, 200, 201, 202, 203, 204, 205, 206, 207, 209, 211, 219, 226, 230, 231, 232, 234, 235, 243, 251, 254, 256, 257, 258, 259, 260, 263, 269, 324, 325, 331, 339, 346, 350, 351
Iscah, 83
Ishbak, 177
Ishmael, 116, 117, 118, 119, 122, 123, 125, 128, 145, 148, 150, 152, 153, 154, 155, 158, 159, 178, 179, 180, 181, 191, 203, 204, 258, 263
Israel, 10, 11, 69, 74, 77, 87, 182, 197, 222, 237, 239, 242, 243, 245, 246, 247, 248, 254, 256, 258, 260, 261, 291, 296, 298, 317, 320, 322, 324, 325, 326, 327, 328, 329, 330, 332, 336, 337, 339, 340, 341, 342, 343, 344, 345, 348, 349, 351, 352
Issachar, 217, 218, 256, 343

Jabal, 46
Jacob, 77, 170, 177, 178, 182, 183, 184, 185, 191, 192, 193, 194, 195, 196, 197, 198, 199, 200, 201, 202, 203, 204, 205, 206, 207, 208, 209, 210, 211, 212, 213, 214, 215, 216, 217, 218, 219, 220, 221, 222, 223, 224, 225, 226, 227, 228, 229, 230, 231, 232, 233, 234, 235, 236, 237, 238, 239, 240, 241, 242, 243, 244, 245, 246, 247, 248, 249, 250, 251, 252, 253, 254, 255, 256, 257, 258, 259, 260, 261, 262, 263, 265, 268, 269, 270, 271, 289, 292, 293, 295, 296, 301, 302, 303, 304, 305, 306, 309, 312, 314, 315, 316, 321, 322, 323, 324, 325, 326, 327, 328, 329, 331, 332, 335, 336, 337, 338, 339, 340, 341, 342, 343, 344, 345, 346, 347, 348, 349, 350, 351
Jalam, 258, 259
Japheth, 51, 55, 70, 71, 73, 74, 75, 77, 79
Jared, 49
Javan, 75
Jebusite, 77
Jebusites, 107
Jehovah, 5, 20, 21, 39, 104, 118
Jerah, 78
Jerusalem, 21, 111, 160
Jesus, 5, 17, 29, 34, 36, 37, 48, 51, 53, 95, 112, 114, 140, 160, 161, 179, 214, 253, 267, 269, 274, 275, 276, 297, 310, 316, 318, 343, 346, 352
Jetur, 180
Jeush, 258, 259
Jew, 69, 297
Jidlaph, 163
Jobab, 78
John, 5, 8, 17, 29, 43, 49, 95, 162, 253, 283, 292, 328, 340, 353
Jokshan, 177
Joktan, 78
Jordan, 93, 94, 141, 235, 348, 349
Joseph, 170, 218, 219, 239, 240, 241, 255, 256, 257, 261, 262, 263, 264, 265, 266, 267, 268, 269, 270, 276, 277, 278, 279, 280, 281, 282, 283, 284, 285, 286, 287, 288, 289, 290, 291, 292, 293, 294, 295, 296, 297, 298, 299, 300, 301, 302, 303, 304, 306, 307, 308, 309, 310, 311, 312, 313, 314, 315, 316, 317, 318, 319, 320, 321, 322, 323, 324, 325, 326, 327, 328, 329, 330, 331, 332, 333, 334, 335, 336, 337, 338, 339, 340, 341, 344, 345, 347, 348, 349, 350, 351, 352
Jubal, 46
Judah, 182, 214, 215, 216, 256, 266, 267, 268, 270, 271, 272, 273, 274, 275, 276, 300, 304, 305, 311, 313, 314,

Judah (continued), 315, 316, 317, 318, 323, 325, 326, 335, 340, 342, 343
Judge, 50, 107, 113, 136, 230, 231, 317, 342, 343
Judgement, 59, 81, 113
Judith, 191

Kadmonites, 107
Kedar, 180
Kedemah, 180
Kedorlaomer, 96, 97, 99
Kemuel, 163
Kenan, 49
Kenaz, 259
Kenites, 107
Kenizzites, 107
Kesed, 163
Keturah, 119, 177, 178, 179
Kezib, 271
Kiriath Arba, 164, 256
Kittites, 75
Knife, 36, 159, 160, 161
Knowledge, 7, 21, 22, 23, 26, 27, 28, 30, 31, 33, 35, 36, 42, 146, 157, 196, 253, 307, 308
Korah, 258, 259

Laban, 172, 173, 174, 175, 181, 200, 202, 203, 208, 209, 210, 211, 212, 213, 215, 218, 219, 220, 221, 222, 223, 224, 225, 226, 227, 228, 229, 230, 231, 232, 233, 234, 242, 257, 331
Lamb, 160, 161, 220
Lamech, 46, 51, 61
Language, 24, 31, 54, 63, 79, 80, 81, 85, 130, 154, 326
Lasha, 77
Law, 44, 46, 69, 83, 100, 111, 120, 137, 138, 145, 211, 222, 271, 272, 274, 275, 276, 304, 334
Leah, 210, 211, 212, 213, 214, 215, 216, 217, 219, 224, 225, 226, 228, 239, 241, 244, 249, 255, 256, 261, 262, 341, 342, 343, 344, 346
Lehabim, 76
Letushites, 177
Leummites, 177

Levi, 214, 249, 250, 251, 252, 256, 300, 342
Light, 4, 7, 8, 9, 10, 11, 29, 43, 119, 122, 176, 200, 212, 300, 323
Likeness, 13, 14, 48, 49
Livestock, 12, 13, 14, 20, 23, 33, 46, 61, 63, 91, 224, 226, 239, 242, 245, 248, 259, 325, 327, 330, 333
Lord, 19, 20, 21, 23, 24, 26, 28, 31, 33, 35, 36, 39, 40, 41, 42, 43, 45, 46, 48, 49, 50, 51, 54, 58, 59, 60, 66, 73, 74, 76, 80, 81, 85, 86, 87, 88, 89, 92, 93, 94, 95, 100, 102, 104, 105, 107, 109, 113, 115, 116, 118, 125, 127, 128, 129, 130, 131, 132, 133, 137, 138, 139, 140, 141, 146, 148, 150, 157, 161, 162, 168, 169, 170, 171, 172, 173, 174, 175, 181, 185, 187, 188, 189, 190, 193, 195, 196, 197, 204, 205, 206, 207, 213, 214, 215, 218, 219, 220, 223, 231, 234, 243, 251, 252, 263, 271, 277, 278, 280, 281, 282, 297, 336, 343, 352
Lot, 82, 83, 85, 86, 88, 89, 91, 92, 93, 94, 95, 96, 97, 98, 99, 100, 102, 103, 113, 114, 125, 132, 133, 134, 135, 136, 137, 138, 139, 140, 141, 142, 143, 144, 147, 175
Lotan, 260
Lud, 77
Ludim, 76
Lust, 29, 30, 53
Luz, 206, 253, 336, 337

Maakah, 163
Machpelah, 165, 166, 179, 345, 349
Madai, 75
Magicians, 289, 290, 313
Magog, 75
Mahalalel, 49
Mahalath, 203
Mahanaim, 233, 235
Male, 13, 18, 19, 25, 48, 56, 58, 60, 82, 88, 118, 120, 122, 123, 125, 135, 148, 151, 221, 225, 234, 235, 248, 249, 250
Mamre, 95, 96, 98, 99, 100, 101, 125, 144, 156, 166, 179, 256, 346, 349

Man, 6, 13, 14, 17, 18, 19, 20, 21, 22, 23, 24, 25, 26, 27, 28, 29, 30, 31, 32, 33, 34, 35, 36, 37, 39, 42, 44, 45, 46, 50, 54, 55, 58, 59, 61, 62, 64, 66, 72, 80, 82, 83, 98, 99, 104, 111, 113, 116, 118, 119, 121, 123, 133, 135, 136, 137, 141, 142, 143, 145, 146, 147, 153, 164, 165, 168, 171, 172, 174, 175, 176, 178, 179, 181, 182, 192, 194, 203, 210, 212, 214, 226, 227, 236, 237, 238, 245, 246, 247, 250, 262, 265, 268, 270, 274, 276, 277, 278, 279, 287, 289, 290, 292, 293, 298, 300, 301, 304, 305, 306, 310, 311, 312, 313, 314, 331, 335, 345
Manasseh, 293, 328, 336, 337, 339, 340, 341, 345, 351
Mandrake, 216, 217
Mankind, 13, 14, 16, 19, 20, 26, 28, 29, 34, 38, 46, 48, 52, 54, 56, 57, 58, 59, 61, 66, 69, 70, 71, 72, 74, 79, 136, 331, 340, 352
Maralah, 343
Marriage, 23, 25, 30, 34, 46, 73, 88, 114, 140, 175, 176, 177, 178, 181, 186, 191, 202, 204, 210, 211, 212, 214, 245, 246, 261, 271, 272, 276, 292
Mary, 52, 53
Massa, 180
Meat, 40, 69, 107, 151, 158
Medan, 177
Melchizedek, 99, 100, 102
Mesha, 78
Meshek, 75, 78
Mesopotamia, 170, 202, 254
Messiah, 49, 55, 130, 152, 213, 214, 256, 271, 272, 274, 275, 276, 346
Meteorites, 6
Methuselah, 50, 51, 52
Mibsam, 180
Midian, 177, 267
Migdal Eder, 256
Milcah, 83
Milk, 126, 151, 158, 342
Milkah, 163, 171, 172
Mishma, 180
Mizpah, 231

Mizraim, 76, 349
Mizzah, 259
Moab, 143
Moabites, 143
Money, 30, 120, 122, 268, 277, 301, 303, 306, 332, 333
Monotheism, 4
Moon, 6, 7, 11, 82, 83, 85, 264, 265
Moreh, 86
Moriah, 158, 159, 160
Morning, 8, 9, 10, 11, 12, 14, 16, 17, 19, 134, 140, 147, 153, 159, 174, 190, 206, 211, 212, 232, 283, 312, 345
Moses, 5, 18, 145, 340, 348
Mother, 24, 25, 35, 43, 88, 110, 111, 116, 121, 147, 151, 152, 155, 158, 163, 168, 172, 173, 174, 175, 176, 178, 180, 182, 184, 191, 194, 195, 196, 197, 200, 201, 202, 203, 204, 213, 216, 217, 251, 253, 256, 257, 258, 262, 263, 264, 265, 269, 279, 280, 309, 314, 323, 329, 338, 342, 346
Murder, 39, 44, 49, 69, 87, 88, 107, 186, 266
Myrrh, 267, 305

Naharaim, 170
Nahath, 259
Nahor, 82, 83, 85, 163, 170, 171, 172, 174, 208, 231, 232
Naked, 25, 30, 31, 32, 33, 35, 75
Naphish, 180
Naphtali, 216, 256, 262, 344
Naphtuhim, 76
Nation, 86, 96, 97, 105, 122, 129, 130, 146, 153, 154, 155, 158, 180, 197, 220, 254, 260, 261, 293, 322, 324, 325, 334, 335, 337, 340
Naturalist, 2
Neandertal, 20
Nebaioth, 180, 203, 258
Nebuchadnezzar, 283
Negev, 91, 92, 144, 176, 186
Nephilim, 53
Nile, 286, 288, 327
Nimrod, 67, 76, 79, 80
Nineveh, 76

Noah, 9, 47, 49, 51, 52, 54, 55, 56, 57, 58, 59, 60, 61, 62, 63, 64, 65, 66, 68, 69, 70, 71, 72, 73, 74, 75, 77, 78, 79, 106, 130, 131, 143, 178, 299
Nod, 45
Nostrils, 20, 61

Oath, 100, 101, 107, 157, 169, 170, 183, 185, 190, 231, 232, 336, 348, 351, 353
Obal, 78
Oholibamah, 258, 259, 260
Old Testament, 5, 7, 18, 353
Omar, 259
On, 291
Onan, 271
Ophir, 78

Paganism, 82, 104
Palace, 88, 89, 284, 286, 288, 290, 295, 322, 333
Paradise, 37
Paran, 155
Pathrusim, 76
Patriarchs, 51, 60, 63, 346
Paul, 30, 33, 34, 111, 112, 115, 123, 238, 283, 297, 310, 318, 345, 353
Peniel, 238
Pentateuch, 5
Perez, 275, 304
Perizzites, 92, 107, 250
Persian Gulf, 21
Peter, 283
Pharaoh, 88, 89, 90, 91, 101, 109, 111, 119, 145, 148, 155, 186, 227, 269, 270, 283, 284, 285, 286, 287, 288, 289, 290, 291, 292, 293, 294, 295, 299, 307, 310, 313, 318, 320, 322, 324, 325, 327, 329, 330, 331, 332, 333, 334, 336, 344, 348
Phicol, 156, 157, 189
Philistine, 144, 150, 156, 187
Philistines, 76, 157, 185, 186, 187, 188, 189, 190, 192
Pigeon, 104, 105
Pildash, 163
Pishon, 21
Pistachio Nuts, 305

Plane, 221, 225
Planet, 6, 9, 16, 19
Planets, 6, 17, 20
Polygamist, 83, 213
Polygamy, 46, 83
Poplar, 221
Potiphar, 269, 270, 277, 278, 279, 280, 282, 285, 287, 288, 291, 292
Potiphera, 291, 293, 336
Pregnant, 112
Pride, 29, 30, 80, 291
Prison, 280, 281, 282, 283, 284, 285, 286, 287, 288, 291, 295, 299, 301, 303
Promised Land, 77, 95, 164, 289, 321, 340, 351
Prophecy, 27, 116, 127, 128, 130, 255, 345, 352
Prophet, 146, 147, 156, 318, 342
Prostitute, 250, 272, 273, 274, 275, 304

Raamah, 76
Rachel, 208, 209, 210, 211, 212, 213, 214, 215, 216, 217, 218, 219, 224, 225, 226, 228, 229, 239, 240, 241, 251, 252, 255, 256, 258, 261, 262, 265, 296, 302, 304, 308, 309, 314, 315, 321, 323, 327, 329, 332, 338, 343, 344, 346, 347
Radioactive Mineral Decay Rates, 7
Rain, 20, 21, 58, 59, 63
Rainbow, 70, 71
Ram, 104, 162, 164
Rameses, 332
Rape, 134, 135, 245, 251, 256, 276, 280, 282, 291, 344
Raven, 64, 65
Rebekah, 163, 171, 172, 173, 174, 175, 176, 177, 178, 181, 182, 185, 186, 187, 189, 191, 192, 193, 194, 195, 196, 198, 199, 200, 201, 202, 203, 208, 211, 251, 253, 254, 258, 263, 346
Rebellion, 34, 44, 79, 80, 81, 85, 97
Red Sea, 10, 180, 349
Rehoboth, 76, 188, 189
Rephaites, 97, 107
Resen, 76

Reuben, 213, 216, 217, 256, 266, 267, 268, 299, 300, 302, 304, 305, 310, 315, 325, 335, 337, 341, 342
Reuel, 258, 259
Reumah, 163
Ribs, 24
Rings, 252
Riphath, 75
Rivers, 20, 21, 64
Robe, 262, 263, 265, 267, 268, 270, 280
Rodanites, 75

Sabbath, 16, 17, 22
Sabtah, 76
Sabteka, 76
Sacrifice, 40, 66, 68, 82, 83, 87, 88, 92, 107, 158, 159, 160, 161, 162, 164, 179, 231, 232, 328, 337, 348, 352
Salem, 99, 102, 160
Salt, 139, 140, 220
Salvation, 56, 57, 59, 61, 62, 72, 130, 137, 152
Same-Sex, 23
Samson, 343
Sarah, 83, 121, 122, 123, 125, 126, 127, 128, 129, 130, 133, 144, 145, 146, 147, 148, 149, 150, 151, 152, 153, 155, 156, 157, 159, 163, 164, 165, 166, 168, 176, 177, 178, 179, 180, 181, 186, 263, 346
Sarai, 83, 86, 87, 88, 89, 90, 91, 92, 95, 103, 104, 108, 109, 110, 111, 112, 113, 114, 115, 116, 117, 118, 119, 121, 125
Satan, 22, 26, 28, 33, 34, 35, 36, 37, 43, 48, 66, 73, 81, 152, 214, 352
Saul, 344, 345
Savior, 26, 30, 37, 38, 74, 352
Scepter, 342, 343
Scientist, 7, 12, 20
Sea, 10, 11, 12, 13, 14, 60, 68, 235, 293, 343
Seal, 193, 273, 274
Seba, 76
Seir, 97, 233, 234, 242, 257, 259, 260
Semen, 271
Sephar, 78

Serpent, 26, 27, 28, 29, 30, 33, 34, 35, 37, 39, 72, 143, 343, 352
Servant, 52, 102, 103, 109, 110, 111, 113, 114, 115, 126, 134, 138, 168, 169, 170, 171, 172, 173, 174, 175, 176, 177, 189, 191, 203, 209, 211, 212, 216, 217, 218, 219, 234, 235, 240, 256, 287, 315, 331, 333, 343, 344
Seth, 46, 47, 48, 49, 52, 53, 54
Sex, 25, 52, 134, 137, 143, 271, 272, 273, 275, 278
Shame, 25, 30, 31, 35, 143, 274
Shammah, 259
Shaveh, 97, 99
Shaveh Kiriathaim, 97
Sheaf, 264, 290, 297, 313, 321, 326
Sheba, 76, 78, 177
Shechem, 86, 218, 243, 244, 245, 246, 247, 248, 249, 250, 251, 252, 253, 258, 265, 300, 340
Sheep, 88, 148, 157, 207, 208, 220, 226, 227, 230, 234, 272, 277, 333, 343
Shekels, 148, 166, 172, 267, 269, 322
Shelah, 78, 271, 272, 274
Sheleph, 78
Shem, 51, 55, 70, 71, 73, 74, 75, 77, 78, 79, 81, 82, 85, 178
Shemeber, 96
Shepherd, 39, 182
Shepherds, 182, 207, 208, 211, 215, 327, 328, 330, 332
Shibah, 190
Shinab, 96
Shinar, 76, 79, 96
Shobal, 260
Shua, 270, 271, 272
Shuah, 177
Shur, 115, 144, 180
Siddim, 96, 97, 99
Sidon, 77, 343
Silver, 91, 148, 166, 174, 243, 267, 269, 300, 301, 305, 306, 307, 311, 312, 313, 322
Simeon, 214, 249, 250, 251, 252, 256, 300, 301, 302, 303, 304, 307, 311, 337, 342
Sin, 23, 29, 30, 31, 32, 33, 34, 35, 36, 37, 38, 39, 40, 41, 42, 54, 62, 66, 70,

71, 72, 73, 81, 88, 105, 106, 116, 130, 135, 140, 145, 146, 162, 179, 220, 271, 279, 299, 342, 352
Sinite, 77
Sister, 83, 88, 89, 91, 109, 110, 144, 145, 146, 147, 155, 156, 172, 173, 175, 181, 186, 187, 189, 203, 209, 210, 211, 215, 216, 217, 218, 247, 249, 250, 255, 258, 280, 342
Sitnah, 188
Sky, 9, 10, 11, 12, 13, 14, 23, 24, 63, 68, 70, 103, 162, 163, 185
Slave, 73, 74, 77, 111, 112, 113, 115, 118, 151, 152, 153, 155, 157, 159, 178, 180, 247, 277, 278, 279, 282, 285, 288, 291, 292, 295, 312, 314, 315, 329
Slaves, 73, 74, 105, 111, 148, 306, 312, 314, 350
Sleep, 24, 105, 106, 109, 111, 112, 139, 142, 143, 204, 205, 216, 217, 230, 271, 273, 274, 279, 280, 283, 289, 344
Sodom, 67, 77, 94, 96, 97, 98, 100, 101, 102, 114, 125, 129, 130, 131, 132, 133, 134, 135, 136, 137, 138, 139, 140, 141, 142, 143, 144
Solomon, 11, 21
Son, 32, 39, 42, 43, 45, 46, 47, 48, 49, 50, 51, 52, 54, 55, 60, 73, 74, 75, 76, 79, 82, 83, 86, 89, 98, 103, 111, 116, 117, 118, 121, 122, 123, 125, 127, 128, 133, 143, 145, 148, 150, 151, 152, 153, 154, 157, 158, 159, 160, 161, 162, 164, 165, 168, 169, 170, 171, 172, 173, 174, 175, 177, 178, 179, 182, 183, 185, 191, 192, 193, 194, 195, 196, 197, 198, 199, 200, 202, 203, 204, 208, 209, 213, 214, 215, 216, 217, 218, 219, 229, 240, 244, 246, 247, 248, 249, 250, 254, 255, 256, 258, 259, 260, 267, 268, 270, 271, 272, 274, 275, 277, 279, 293, 296, 302, 306, 308, 314, 318, 321, 323, 325, 326, 335, 339, 341, 342, 343, 344, 345, 351
Soul, 20, 106, 133, 164, 252
Spices, 267, 305

Spies, 298, 299, 301, 303
Spirit, 5, 6, 27, 53, 54, 61, 121, 124, 249, 290, 291
Staff, 234, 273, 274, 335, 336, 342
Streams, 20
Suicide, 69
Sukkoth, 242
Sulfur, 139, 140
Summer, 67
Sun, 7, 9, 11, 83, 85, 105, 107, 139, 140, 204, 208, 211, 238, 264, 265
Sword, 36, 199, 249, 340

Tahash, 163
Tamar, 97, 271, 272, 274, 275, 276, 304
Tarshish, 75
Tebah, 163
Tema, 180
Teman, 259
Tent, 72, 75, 86, 92, 112, 125, 126, 127, 128, 129, 130, 133, 134, 176, 189, 199, 224, 227, 228, 243, 256
Terah, 82, 83, 85, 86
Testicles, 169, 353
Theophany, 127, 130, 131
Thigh, 168, 169, 170, 335
Thunder, 70
Tidal, 96, 97
Tigris, 21
Time, 2, 3, 6, 7, 8, 10, 11, 16, 19, 24, 26, 28, 30, 33, 34, 35, 36, 37, 38, 40, 42, 44, 45, 48, 49, 50, 51, 52, 53, 54, 55, 57, 58, 59, 61, 62, 64, 65, 66, 67, 72, 73, 74, 76, 77, 78, 80, 83, 86, 87, 88, 91, 92, 94, 96, 99, 103, 104, 105, 106, 107, 109, 110, 111, 112, 113, 115, 118, 121, 122, 123, 125, 126, 127, 128, 129, 133, 134, 137, 138, 139, 144, 145, 146, 148, 150, 151, 152, 153, 156, 157, 159, 160, 161, 162, 166, 168, 170, 174, 175, 177, 178, 179, 182, 184, 185, 186, 187, 188, 189, 190, 191, 193, 194, 197, 198, 199, 205, 206, 207, 208, 209, 210, 211, 212, 213, 214, 215, 217, 218, 219, 220, 222, 223, 224, 225, 226, 227, 229, 231, 235, 236, 237, 239, 240, 241, 242,

244, 245, 248, 249, 250, 251, 254, 255, 257, 258, 259, 262, 263, 264, 271, 272, 273, 274, 278, 282, 283, 284, 285, 286, 287, 288, 290, 293, 297, 298, 303, 304, 305, 307, 308, 309, 313, 314, 315, 316, 318, 319, 324, 325, 326, 331, 332, 335, 336, 337, 347, 349
Timna, 259
Timnah, 272
Tiras, 75
Tithing, 100
Togarmah, 75
Tomb, 165, 255, 348
Tower, 80, 81, 85
Tower of Babel, 67, 78, 79
Tree, 10, 14, 21, 22, 23, 26, 27, 28, 30, 32, 33, 34, 35, 36, 37, 126, 127, 157
Trinity, 4
Tubal, 46, 75

Universe, 2, 3, 4, 9, 17, 31, 289
Ur, 82, 83, 85, 86, 92, 93, 96, 104, 106, 163, 168, 175, 178
Uz, 78, 163
Uzal, 78

Vault, 8, 9, 10, 11
Visitors, 125, 126, 127, 128, 129, 131, 133, 134, 135, 136, 137, 138

Wadi, 107
Warden, 280, 281, 282, 284, 286, 287
Water, 4, 5, 6, 8, 9, 10, 11, 12, 13, 21, 55, 61, 63, 64, 65, 126, 153, 154, 156, 170, 171, 173, 175, 188, 190, 207, 208, 307
Wheat, 216, 217
Wife, 19, 24, 25, 26, 30, 31, 32, 33, 34, 35, 37, 39, 45, 46, 49, 56, 60, 65, 66, 73, 83, 85, 86, 87, 88, 89, 90, 91, 92, 103, 104, 109, 110, 112, 115, 119, 121, 122, 125, 127, 129, 137, 138, 139, 140, 142, 144, 145, 146, 147, 148, 149, 150, 155, 156, 164, 165, 166, 168, 169, 170, 171, 173, 174, 175, 176, 177, 178, 179, 181, 185, 186, 187, 189, 191, 200,
202, 203, 204, 207, 209, 210, 211, 212, 213, 214, 215, 216, 217, 219, 226, 231, 240, 244, 246, 248, 251, 252, 255, 256, 258, 259, 260, 271, 272, 273, 276, 278, 279, 280, 282, 291, 292, 293, 296, 304, 309, 315, 326, 327, 332, 336, 338, 343, 344, 345, 346
Wind, 13, 63, 64, 250, 286, 289
Wine, 72, 73, 75, 100, 142, 143, 197, 199, 211, 213, 342
Winter, 67
Wisdom, 25, 29, 286, 290, 293, 294, 297, 332, 334
Woman, 19, 21, 22, 23, 24, 25, 26, 27, 28, 29, 30, 31, 32, 33, 34, 87, 88, 110, 111, 112, 114, 121, 143, 145, 148, 151, 152, 153, 157, 159, 169, 170, 171, 172, 177, 178, 202, 203, 204, 210, 212, 213, 214, 245, 246, 271, 273, 274, 292, 304
Wood, 56, 159, 160, 161, 221
world, 3, 7, 22, 27, 28, 31, 40, 49, 55, 56, 66, 72, 79, 81, 83, 106, 130, 137, 138, 142, 154, 162, 165, 166, 167, 179, 237, 250, 261, 263, 270, 275, 276, 292, 294, 295, 328, 331, 332, 340, 352
Worship, 17, 22, 40, 43, 49, 53, 55, 62, 80, 82, 83, 85, 95, 104, 160, 206, 229, 232, 252, 335, 337, 343, 348

Yahweh, 159
Yaweh" (YHVH), 5
Yemen, 21
Yom, 18, 19, 22

Zaphenath-Paneah, 291, 294, 313, 318
Zeboyim, 77, 96, 97
Zebulun, 218, 256, 343
Zemarite, 77
Zepho, 259
Zerah, 259, 275, 304
Zibeon, 258, 260
Ziggurat, 82, 83
Zillah, 46
Zilpah, 211, 216, 218, 239, 241, 256, 262, 344

Zimran, 177
Zoar, 93, 94, 96, 97, 139, 141, 142

Zohar, 165, 179
Zuzites, 97

SCRIPTURE INDEX

Genesis

1:1–31	1–15	33:1–20	239–243
2:1–25	16–25	34:1–31	244–250
3:1–24	26–38	35:1–29	251–257
4:1–26	39–47	36:1–43	258–260
5:1–32	48–51	37:1–36	261–269
6:1–22	52–57	38:1–30	270–275
7:1–24	58–62	39:1–23	276–281
8:1–22	63–67	40:1–23	281–285
9:1–29	68–74	41:1–57	286–294
10:1–32	75–78	42:1–38	295–302
11:1–32	79–84	43:1–34	303–310
12:1–20	85–90	44:1–34	311–316
13:1–18	91–95	45:1–28	317–323
14:1–24	96–101	46:1–34	324–328
15:1–21	102–108	47:1–31	329–335
16:1–16	109–117	48:1–22	336–340
17:1–27	118–124	49:1–33	341–346
18:1–33	125–132	50:1–26	347–351
19:1–38	133–143		
20:1–18	144–149	**Exodus**	
21:1–34	150–157	1:6–11	322
22:1:24	158–163	12:40–41	330
23:1–20	164–167	17:14	5
24:1–67	168–176	24:4, 7	5
25:1–34	177–184	34:27	5
26:1–35	185–191		
27:1–46	192–201	**Leviticus**	
28:1–22	202–206	19:32	331
29:1–35	207–214		
30:1–43	215–222	**Numbers**	
31:1–55	223–232	23:19	13
32:1–32	233–238		

Deuteronomy
2:5	259
31:9	5

Joshua
19:10–16	343
24:2	82, 106
24:4	259
24:32	340

Judges
13:2	343
18:28–30	343
20:1–48	345

1 Samuel
10:2	255
9:1–2	345

1 Kings
12:28–30	343

2 Kings
10:29	343

1 Chronicles
12:8	344
12:32	343

2 Chronicles
21:8–10	199

Esther
2:5	345
4:14	332

Psalms
19:1	11
23:6	252
90:4	331

Proverbs
14:34	130, 220

Ecclesiastes
3:1	11

Isiah
14:12–15	37

Ezekiel
27:20	76
38:13	76

Hosea
11:9	13
12:4	236

Zechariah
12:10	318

Malachi
3:6	38

Matthew
5:9	189
6:24	112
19:8	5
24:37	62
25:31–46	178

Mark
12:25	53
12:26	5

Luke
16:13	112
16:19–31	179
16:26	179
17:26	62
17:29–33	140
18:19	38
23:34	316

John

1:29	162
5:17	17
5:46–47	5
6:44	253
7:19	5
14:2	95
15:16	253

Acts

3:22	5
7:8	120
7:58–59	345
10:34–36	310
22:4	345

Romans

2:28–29	123
4:11	82
4:11–13	120
4:13	119
8:9	120
8:16	121
8:32	310
11:1	345

1 Corinthians

2:7–8	297, 318
7:19	123
15:9	345

Galatians

1:13	345
3:17	330
3:29	119
4:21–26	111
4:21–31	152
4:29	152
5:3	120
6:7	319

Ephesians

2:14–16	114
4:26	41

5:22–25	34

Philippians

3:5	345

Colossians

2:8–15	120
3:21	263

1 Timothy

2:13	33

2 Timothy

2:14	30
3:16	27

Hebrews

4:1–7	17
5:12	151
6:1	151
7:1–10	99
7:18, 22	152
11:3	3
11:4	104
11:10	167, 179
11:19	160
11:21	338, 340
12:16–17	191, 199, 202
13:8	38

James

1:17	11
2:1–4	173

2 Peter

1:21	27
2:5	55
2:7	141
3:8	331

1 John

2:16	29
3:12	43

Jude
14 ... 50

Revelation
22:20 ... 352